Date: 2/18/21

LOST IN A GALLUP

ALSO BY W. JOSEPH CAMPBELL

Getting It Wrong: Debunking the Greatest Myths in American Journalism

1995: The Year the Future Began

The Year That Defined American Journalism: 1897 and the Clash of Paradigms

Yellow Journalism: Puncturing the Myths, Defining the Legacies

The Spanish-American War: American Wars and Media in Primary Documents

The Emergent Independent Press in Benin and Côte d'Ivoire: From Voice of the State to Advocate of Democracy

LOST IN A GALLUP

POLLING FAILURE IN U.S. PRESIDENTIAL ELECTIONS

W. Joseph Campbell

 UNIVERSITY OF CALIFORNIA PRESS

University of California Press
Oakland, California

© 2020 by W. Joseph Campbell

Cataloging-in-Publication Data is on file at the Library of
Congress.

ISBN 978-0-520-30096-5 (cloth : alk. paper)
ISBN 978-0-520-97213-1 (ebook)

Manufactured in the United States of America

28   27   26   25   24   23   22   21   20
10   9   8   7   6   5   4   3   2   1

To Ann-Marie

The publisher and the University of California Press Foundation gratefully acknowledge the generous support of the Barbara S. Isgur Endowment Fund in Public Affairs.

"To start with, political polling is inherently imperfect."

—Michael Barone in *Wall Street Journal* ("Are the polls accurate?"),
   October 22, 2008

"The only crime in this business is to be on the wrong side" of a
prediction.

—George H. Gallup, quoted in *New York Herald-Tribune*, November 9, 1952

"The interaction between journalists and polls is a troubled union."

—Karlyn Keene, managing editor, *Public Opinion Magazine*, quoted in
   New York Times, November 10, 1988

"Polls get plenty of respect. But they get very little affection."

—Andrew Kohut, presidential address, American Association for Public
   Opinion Research, 1995

"Polls go wrong, and that's all there is to it."

—James Farley, Democratic National Committee chair, in *Behind the
   Ballots* (1938), 323

CONTENTS

FIGURES, TABLES, AND BOXES

TABLES

BOXES

ACKNOWLEDGMENTS

Researching this book took me to archival collections in quite a few places and brought me in touch with many generous people. Notable among them was the staff at the Thomas J. Dodd Research Center at the University of Connecticut at Storrs, home to important collections of papers of the pollsters Archibald M. Crossley, Warren J. Mitofsky, and Elmo Roper. I am grateful for the courtesy and assistance of personnel there, including Nicholas Hurley, Matthew Slowik, and Trisha Sundman, and the university archivist, Betty Pittman.

My research into polls, pollsters, and journalists took me to presidential libraries as well. Paul Sparrow, Virginia Lewick, and their colleagues at the Franklin D. Roosevelt library were welcoming and most helpful. So, too, were Randy Sowell and his colleagues at the Harry S. Truman library, and Kevin Bailey at the Dwight D. Eisenhower library.

The Library of Congress in Washington, DC, is an exceptional research institution and on this and other book projects I benefited from the insights, expertise, and courtesy of Georgia M. Higley, Arlene Balkansky, Jeff Flannery, and their colleagues. Rick Mastroianni of the now-closed Newseum in Washington was welcoming and generous with his time in early phases of my research. Matthew Turi of the special collections staff at the University of North Carolina at Chapel Hill was helpful as I worked through the Louis Harris papers. Lin Fredericksen and her colleagues were accommodating during my review of the Alf Landon papers at the Kansas Historical Society in Topeka.

My research trips were supported by the generosity of the Association for Education in Journalism and Mass Communication (which also considers polling issues from time to time at its annual conferences) and my academic home, the School of Communication at American University. I am most grateful to Jennifer McGill, the executive director of AEJMC, and to her gracious colleague, Lillian Coleman, for the research grant that helped enable my travels. Jeff Rutenbeck, the former dean of the university's School of Communication, was unstinting in supporting my research, for which I am deeply grateful. My colleagues at American, including Laura DeNardis and Amy Eisman, were also very supportive, and I enjoyed and benefited from conversations with them.

Graduate assistants made important contributions to the research. Special thanks goes to Kip Dooley for his diligence, suggestions, and the hours he spent at the Library of Congress. Kurt Wirth, another graduate assistant, was quite helpful in latter stages of the project. Ruxandra Giura, a talented data journalist, made important contributions—as she has on several of my book projects. Her willingness to field my inquiries patiently and with courtesy was much appreciated.

Shane Hickey of American University's interlibrary loan staff did outstanding work in locating obscure and elusive material important to this project. Chris Lewis at the university's Bender Library provided important guidance in my tracking down decades-old audio files of programs such as those of George Gallup's appearance on *Meet the Press*. Gallup's papers are housed at the University of Iowa's special collections, where I spent a number of productive days.

The support and suggestions of Reed Malcolm, a senior editor at University of California Press, were vital to this book's coming together. It was a pleasure to collaborate with Reed on this, my fourth book project with the press. His colleagues Dore Brown, Peter Perez, and Archna Patel were wonderful to work with.

The press arranged for Madeleine Adams to copyedit the book and her efforts were outstanding. I am grateful for her scrutiny, patience, talents, and good cheer.

Dominic Lusinchi, who has done outstanding work on the sociology and history of election polling, offered valuable observations on early versions of the manuscript. Joel Best read the near-final manuscript closely and provided important suggestions.

I enjoyed my talks with pollsters and polling experts, especially those conversations with Charles Franklin, director of the Marquette University Law School poll; Spencer Kimball, director of the Emerson College poll; Samuel Wang of the Princeton Election Consortium; and Tim Johnson, a past president of the American Association for Public Opinion Research, or AAPOR. Survey research is a notably innovative field that also is wrestling with profound challenges, including the steep decline in participation by would-be poll respondents. AAPOR conferences offered important insights into the state of contemporary opinion polling and, to be sure, into the performance of polls in the 2016 presidential election.

My wife, Ann-Marie Regan, was patient and supportive as I researched and wrote this book. She is a Connecticut native and especially enjoyed joining me on research trips to Storrs. It is to Ann-Marie this book is dedicated.

Introduction

Of Pollsters, Journalists, and Presidential Elections

It was the eve of the 2016 presidential election, and Natalie Jackson, senior polling editor for the *Huffington Post*, seemed supremely confident. She pegged Hillary Clinton as the near-certain winner. So did many pollsters, analysts, pundits, and journalists. But Jackson had ample data to support her confidence. Or so she thought.

Jackson coordinated the *Huffington Post*'s polls-based statistical model that was designed to forecast the election's outcome. She did not equivocate in her final analysis. "The HuffPost presidential forecast model," she wrote, "gives Democrat Hillary Clinton a 98.2 percent chance of winning the presidency. Republican Donald Trump has essentially no path to an Electoral College victory. Clinton's win will be substantial, but not overwhelming. The model projects that she'll garner 323 electoral votes to Trump's 215." Clinton, she added, "should fairly easily hold onto Michigan, Wisconsin and Pennsylvania" and stood better than an 80 percent chance of carrying Florida and North Carolina.[1]

A 98.2 percent probability of winning seemed unassailable. And yet, Jackson's polls-based forecast wasn't even the most adamant. Samuel Wang, a neuroscientist who forecasts election outcomes using his Princeton Election Consortium model, set Clinton's win probability slightly higher, at 99 percent. Both models were derived from pre-election polls, including surveys conducted in key states.

Both were dramatically wrong. Trump did find a "path to an Electoral College victory," an unlikely path in which he carried Michigan, Wisconsin,

FIGURE 1. "The problem was that I placed way too much faith in polls," Natalie Jackson said of the 2016 election forecast she prepared for the *Huffington Post*. Her polls-based model said Hillary Clinton had a 98.2 percent chance of winning the presidency. (Courtesy Natalie Jackson)

Pennsylvania, and Florida, as well as North Carolina. Jackson returned to her forecast two days after the election and wrote, "It gutted me to realize I had been wrong." No one, she added, "wants to feel like this—to be so utterly and publicly mistaken. People on Twitter have been calling for me to be fired. But what happened is done."[2] Within six months, she had left the *Huffington Post*.

"The problem," Jackson wrote in her after-election assessment, "was that I placed way too much faith in polls. I assumed they would be right. . . . I kept looking at the consistency of the polls. They wavered in the exact margins, sure, but always showed Clinton winning in the key states that she needed to win. I saw no reason to question that the polls would be accurate overall. So I defended and stood by the numbers—as anyone who trusts their work does. That's left me eating some crow."[3]

Jackson's embarrassment was acute but hardly exceptional or without precedent in U.S. presidential elections. The 2016 election cycle abounded

FIGURE 2. "There is no horse race here," Jamelle Bouie said of the 2016 campaign in an essay for Slate.com. His was among many confident predictions about the election that proved erroneous. (Credit: Wikimedia Commons, https://www .flickr.com/photos/jbouie/with /17020553422/)

with overoptimistic predictions that were buoyed by pre-election polls and proved embarrassingly wrong. They included a bold assertion by the chief political correspondent for *Slate*, Jamelle Bouie, whom the Poynter Institute for journalism studies proclaimed a "breakout star" of the campaign.[4] "There is no horse race here," Bouie wrote in late summer 2016. "Clinton is far enough ahead, at a late enough stage in the election, that what we have is a horse running by itself, unperturbed but for the faint possibility of a comet hitting the track. Place your bets accordingly."[5]

Over the past eighty years or so, polls and poll-based forecasts have misfired in many ways in U.S. presidential elections, leaving pollsters, journalists, and pundits baffled or humiliated, and often without immediate explanation as to what went wrong. Polls in presidential elections do not always go wrong. Or dramatically wrong. But they have been wrong often enough to invite skepticism and wariness. Indeed, it is a rare election that does not produce polling controversies of some sort. As Mack C. Shelley and Hwarng-Du Hwang wrote nearly thirty years ago, "The accuracy of presidential election polls has been argued in every presidential election year since polls first gained wide recognition" in the 1930s.[6] Their observation is relevant still.

Just as no two presidential elections are quite alike, no two polling failures are precisely analogous. Not all polling failures are akin to the shock result of 2016. Their distinctiveness notwithstanding, polling failures tend to produce broadly similar effects—surprise, anger, bewilderment, and frustration at their failing to provide the American public with accurate clues about the most consequential of all U.S. elections.

Such reactions are hardly surprising, given that polls drive, color, and help fix news media narratives of presidential elections in the United States. They set expectations. They are central to how journalists, and Americans at large, understand the dynamics of presidential campaigns. Polls are critical to shaping conventional wisdom about the competitiveness of those races. And they have long been recognized as such. Years ago, in a series of articles about polling, the *New York Post* recalled that in "the fall of 1948, the press of the nation, acting on the advisory of the political pollsters, in effect recorded an event that never took place—the election of Thomas E. Dewey as President of the United States."[7] Or as George H. Gallup, opinion polling's tireless evangelist, said about that polling failure, "We gave birth to a monster in 1948, the year when all of us pollsters elected Tom Dewey," who lost to President Harry Truman.[8]

This is not to say that polling failures are typically on the order of the epic fiasco of 1948 or the shock of 2016. In fact, some political scientists have argued that the record of election polling has been admirable in the United States and elsewhere.[9] But polls have been in error often enough, and are beset by so many variables and potential contaminants (which pollsters don't always discuss), that treating them cautiously is sensible. Election polls are not always accurate prophesies, and they certainly are not beyond challenge.

This book addresses in detail polling's checkered record in U.S. presidential elections since 1936—a record that rarely has been considered in depth and never collectively. It is a history that is not especially well known. American journalists and, indeed, the American public are largely oblivious to the catalog of polling flubs and miscalls. They may be faintly familiar with the "Dewey defeats Truman" polling debacle of 1948.[10] They may have a nebulous sense that election polls were in error in 2016. But little else. This unfamiliarity— along with the certitude that can attach to polls and poll-based forecasts— surely contributed to the immense surprise that greeted Trump's split-decision victory over Clinton. He handily won the Electoral College; she clearly won the popular vote, and yet lost the election.

This book does not dwell on trivial shortcomings. The polling failures considered here—whether spectacular or somewhat more modest—were all surprising and controversial when they occurred. They were much commented on at the time. The book also addresses, and offers a fresh assessment about, the intriguing, intricate, and sometimes exasperating interplay between pollsters and journalists, a complex relationship that over the years has given rise both to sustained collaboration and to expressions of bitter disdain. The virus of poll-hatred is not especially potent in the news media nowadays, but for decades many prominent journalists reveled in their contempt for opinion polling and poll-takers. And yet, paradoxically, there has never been a time when polling was not of some fascination to journalists[11]—a fascination that persists, even if journalists are not entirely at ease with the intricacies or dynamics of survey research.

This book revisits prominent cases of polling failure while illuminating and presenting fresh insight into some of the characters, colorful and otherwise, who have shaped election polling and how it has been covered. Among these figures are George Gallup, the prickly founding father of public opinion research, who did much to promote and solidify expectations about the accuracy of election polling; Elmo Roper, a one-time retail jeweler and contemporary of Gallup, who by 1948 thought that election polling had little left to prove; and Warren J. Mitofsky, a brash yet brilliant innovator whose admonition to pollsters rings true across generations: "There's a lot of room for humility in polling. Every time you get cocky, you lose."[12] Once-prominent journalists also enter the narrative; they include David Lawrence, Haynes Johnson, and Jimmy Breslin—all of whom were practitioners of "shoe-leather" journalism, an intensive and revered kind of out-of-the-newsroom reporting that frequently has been considered a response or alternative to indulgence in election polls.

The book does not consider at length the well-documented troubles afflicting contemporary survey research—notably, the sharp and sustained declines in would-be respondents' willingness to answer polls conducted by telephone, which once was the industry's "gold standard" methodology. Since 1999 at least, pollsters have been experimenting with and incorporating internet-based approaches, generally with mixed results.[13] Nor is the book steeped in the jargon and the opaque methodological arcana that pollsters and polling experts are keen to invoke, and for which they occasionally have been rebuked. Gallup, for example, once was taken to task for promoting impenetrable terms like "quindimensional analysis."[14]

This study is not one of methodologies, of the mechanics and different ways of conducting election polls. As such, only occasional attention will be devoted to topics such as "mode effects" or "differential nonresponse" or "nonprobability internet panels." Or "multilevel regression and post-stratification"— a statistical technique that pollsters know as "MRP" and refer to as "Mister P." This is not to say such matters are trifling. They are not. But they are not central to this narrative study of the interplay of pollsters, journalists, and polling failure in modern U.S. presidential elections.

Polling failures and controversies arise from no singular template. Pollsters have forecast tight elections when landslides have occurred. They have pointed to the wrong winner in closer elections. The work of venerable pollsters has been singularly and memorably in error. Exit polling has thrown Election Day into confusion. Failed state-level polls have upended widely anticipated national outcomes. Poll-based data aggregators have miscalled elections. Narratives like these make for compelling accounts of expectations dashed and hubris exposed; they are centerpieces of the chapters of this book that address polling failure in the elections of:

> **1936:** It was the dawn of modern election polling, and it was a year of "polls gone wild," as one newspaper described it. Polls seemed everywhere as the election drew near in 1936, and their conflicting findings fortified a sense that the race between President Franklin D. Roosevelt and Alf Landon was to be the closest in twenty years. The venerable *Literary Digest* magazine, whose mass mail-in survey never had been wrong, forecast a comfortable victory for Landon. Roosevelt swept to victory in one of the most lopsided elections in presidential history. Gallup, Roper, and Archibald Crossley debuted their quasi-scientific election polls that year, and all of them outperformed the *Digest*.

> **1948:** The "Dewey defeats Truman" election humiliated Gallup, Roper, and Crossley, whose respective polls failed dramatically. Roper called the election for Dewey in early September, pledging to publish no further poll results unless a political catastrophe intervened. In late October, Roper quietly took another survey, but did not publicize the results because they showed Dewey still far ahead. President Harry S. Truman, who denounced the "sleeping polls" during the campaign, won narrowly but clearly. Journalists flayed themselves afterward for having leaned so heavily on the findings of the polls—and for having effectively delegated their legwork to pollsters.

> **1952:** Mindful of their excruciating failure four years earlier, pollsters turned exceedingly cautious in interpreting the first Dwight Eisenhower–Adlai Stevenson election. At the end, they said the race was close, but Eisenhower was slightly ahead. They also said Stevenson, who seemed to be surging as the campaign closed, could win. He didn't. Eisenhower swept to the presidency in a thirty-nine-state landslide that no pollster saw coming. As an editorial writer in Massachusetts observed, the pollsters in 1952 were "unable to tell a tidal wave from a photo finish."[15]

> **1980:** Large news organizations had conspicuously entered pre-election surveying by 1980, and polls were more numerous than ever. The incumbent, Jimmy Carter, seemed locked in a tight race with Republican Ronald Reagan and the election may have turned on a late in the campaign surge of support for Reagan. Pollsters couldn't agree. Reagan won handily—by

near-landslide proportions that no poll had anticipated. To some pollsters, the miscall evoked a lesson they presumably had learned in 1948: do not stop polling too soon.

2000: The closest presidential race in American history was decided by the U.S. Supreme Court, thirty-seven days after the election, in favor of George W. Bush. The delayed result revolved around the ambiguous outcome in Florida, a dispute that capped a trifecta of polling errors in 2000: the pre-election polls mostly signaled a tight race, but mostly pointed to the wrong popular vote winner; the Gallup organization's daily tracking polls swung wildly, even implausibly, during the campaign; and exit polls in Florida erroneously indicated Al Gore was headed to victory in that pivotal state.

2004: Exit polls figured prominently in the 2004 election, erroneously indicating that Democrat John Kerry was destined to win the presidency. Exit-poll results seemed so certain that they inspired a top adviser to Kerry to refer to him as "Mr. President." They also prompted George Bush to mope around the White House for a while, thinking he had been turned out of office after a single term, much as his father had. And exit-poll results touched off fierce but never-substantiated charges that the election had been stolen in Ohio, the state pivotal to the outcome.

2012: In a faint echo of the 1936 election, the most venerable election pollster—the Gallup Organization—miscalled the outcome, and was chastised and outperformed by a sports-loving data journalist named Nate Silver. He became Gallup's bête noire. Silver's poll-based statistical model correctly forecast the outcomes in all fifty states in 2012; Gallup picked the wrong winner. It estimated that Mitt Romney held a one-point advantage over the incumbent, Barack Obama. Romney lost by nearly four points. Gallup thereafter left election polling.

2016: Trump upset Clinton in an outcome that wasn't supposed to happen. The statistical forecast models of Jackson, Wang, Silver, and others veered off target, largely because they relied on state polls that misfired in key places such as Michigan, Pennsylvania, and Wisconsin. Pollsters and journalists learned anew that election results can be correlated—that if a candidate does poorly in one state, she may do poorly in other states having similar demographic characteristics.

To be sure, the universe of polling failure in U.S. presidential elections is not confined to those eight episodes. Although the book's principal focus is on prominent polling missteps and errors, less flagrant miscalls, such as those of 1968, 1976, and 1996, won't be ignored. They will be addressed, though not at chapter length: they will be incorporated into the narrative as relevant.[16]

This book argues that polling's uneven, messy, and controversial past merits being addressed collectively and in its sweep. It proceeds in the recognition that polling failure often is correlated with journalistic failure. The correlation was pronounced in 2016, when poll-based prediction models and key state polls anticipated victory by Hillary Clinton. The correlation was likewise strong in 1948, 1952, and 1980.

So why write a narrative and interpretative study of prominent polling failure? Why focus on the interplay of journalists, pollsters, and failed polls in presidential elections? The motives are several. Presidential elections are the most consequential of campaigns, the most closely followed and most anticipated of all American elections. They represent the country's only nationwide political race. No other campaigns are as intensely covered and analyzed by the news media. And polls are never more conspicuous—or commented on—than in presidential campaigns. Polling failures are most magnified in such races, and the stakes for pollsters and poll-based statistical analysts are seldom higher.

Polling, moreover, occupies an intriguing niche in American popular culture. Opinion polls exert an undeniable allure, even if their workings seem mysterious. Gimmick polls dreamed up in presidential elections—in the "Pullet Poll" of 1948, for example, farmers buying chicken feed preferred sacks stamped "a vote for the Democratic candidate" over the Republican option[17]— are hardly sophisticated or meant to be taken seriously. But they are expressions of popular interest in election polls and what they presume to foretell. That presumption can also invite sarcasm and satire—and occasionally the graphic wit of the cartoonist's pen.

Examining the interplay of journalists, pollsters, and failed polls serves to highlight the priorities they share of accuracy and timeliness. Polls have long been integral to American journalism's election coverage in part because they lend an impression of assurance amid the confusion and rhetorical conflict of political campaigns. As Irving Crespi, a former senior official for the Gallup Organization, once noted, "Interest in pre-election polls has always been based on the expectation that they can provide accurate advance indications of election outcomes."[18]

Addressing the interplay also highlights recurring or unresolved phenomena in election polling. Opinion polling is a dynamic field given to experimentation, especially so in recent years as once-controversial methodologies like internet-based polling have edged into mainstream practice. Still, the field is

WHEN GOOD POLLSTERS GO BAD

RICE

"WHO CARES WHAT YOU THINK!"

FIGURE 3. Cartoonists occasionally have lampooned pollsters and their methods, as Richard Rice did here in imagining a survey-taker gone rogue. (Credit: Richard Rice)

troubled by infirmities that seem chronic and can affect polling accuracy. "Pollster cockiness" is one of the infirmities.

It is a recurrent ailment that predates the first known use of "pollster"; the term appeared in *Time* magazine in 1939.[19] Cockiness certainly afflicted the *Literary Digest*, which declared in touting the launch of its ill-fated mail-in poll in 1936: "Who will win—Roosevelt or Landon? Will the country repudiate the New Deal or give its leader a new, four-year mandate? To-day, nobody knows. But the Digest is seeking the answer—in the same way that has enabled it, time after time, to tell the country exactly what was going to happen when the voters went to the polls."[20]

The polling debacle of 1948 was another high moment in pollster cockiness. Elmo Roper was conspicuously adamant in predicting Dewey's victory, delivering repeated assurances of the accuracy of his forecast in speeches, in newspaper columns, on radio programs. "In so far as the Presidential contest goes," he told an audience at the Waldorf Astoria Hotel twelve days before the election, "the outcome is settled and has been settled for at least six or eight weeks. Mr. Dewey will be the next president, barring any error of catastrophic dimensions which he might make between now and election day. . . . Mr. Dewey is in, and we have found the campaigning to be so much Sound and Fury signifying little in the way of change of sentiment on the part of the voters."[21] Campaigning, Roper figured, didn't alter election trajectories much at all. After the election, Roper conceded that pollsters "had gotten pretty smug, and I was one of the smuggest of the lot." He chided the public, though, for having "put too much dependence in the accuracy of the polls."[22]

The shock of 1948 left pollsters gun shy for years. In an unpublished memoir written in the late 1960s, Arch Crossley declared that the "polls were given a black eye in 1948 from which they have never fully recovered."[23] But the metaphoric black eye certainly didn't prevent pollster cockiness from reemerging from time to time after 1948. In the afternoon on Election Day in 2004, exit-poll data pointing to John Kerry's victory circulated among journalists and analysts. John Zogby, a pollster who was hailed for his accurate estimates in elections in 1996 and 2000, issued an updated prediction late in the day, as votes were still being cast. Kerry, he said, would win handily, carrying at least 311 electoral votes. Kerry won 251 electoral votes, and lost the election.

Zogby was nonchalant about his unconventional forecast. "I don't know that anyone was hospitalized over my prediction," he told the *New York Times*. "If there are any orphans that are out there, from the bottom of my heart, I apologize. We'll try to start up a fund."[24]

The 2016 election also gave rise to misplaced cockiness. Samuel Wang, a poll-based forecaster at Princeton University, vowed to eat a bug on live television should Donald Trump win more than 240 electoral votes. Afterward, Wang conceded to having been "excessively certain" in forecasting Clinton's victory[25] and went on CNN to fulfill his pledge. With a hint of reluctance stealing across his face, Wang dipped a spoon into a can of gourmet crickets, dug out a sample, and redeemed his promise.[26]

Late in the 2016 campaign, Ryan Grim, then the Washington bureau chief for the *Huffington Post*, declared that Clinton's prospects of winning the election were unshakable. His assertion followed a widely noticed, late-campaign dustup on Twitter with Nate Silver, the data journalist who runs the FiveThirty-Eight.com predictions and analysis site. Grim accused Silver of interpreting polling data so that Trump's prospects appeared stronger than they deserved to be.[27] "If you want to put your faith in the numbers," Grim wrote, alluding to the *Huffington Post* forecast model that showed Clinton almost certain of victory, "you can relax. She's got this."[28]

Another recurring feature of election polling is vulnerability to surprise, which can be tied to developments late in presidential campaigns—the gaffes, dramatic gestures, and eleventh-hour disclosures that can confound poll estimates and expectations. These episodes materialize unpredictably, but with some frequency. Political history, as *Politico* has noted, "is littered with the charred remains of . . . late-in-the-election bombshells that scramble political calculus just as the stakes are at their highest."[29]

Some analysts, for example, have argued that Clinton lost the 2016 election when FBI director James Comey announced in late October that the FBI had reopened its inquiry into the private email server she had used while secretary of state.[30] Barack Obama may have ensured his reelection in 2012 in a high-profile response to the devastation of Superstorm Sandy, which battered New Jersey days before the election. George W. Bush may have lost the popular vote to Al Gore in 2000 when a television reporter in Maine disclosed shortly before the election that Bush had been arrested for drunk driving in 1976—an episode Bush had never disclosed. President Jimmy Carter probably ensured defeat in 1980 by interrupting his campaign days before the election to return to the White House and focus on the prospective release of American diplomatic personnel taken hostage in Iran a year earlier. Carter's move was futile, and had the effect of redirecting public attention to his administration's most conspicuous foreign policy failure.

Dwight Eisenhower's dramatic pledge late in the 1952 campaign to "go to Korea" in seeking an end to the war there may have altered the trajectory of what was mistakenly thought to be a close race. Thomas Dewey let the mask slip one afternoon in October 1948 when he berated as a "lunatic" the engineer of his "Victory Special" campaign train after it backed toward a crowd surging to see him. The outburst did not cost Dewey the election, but the flash of temper offered insights into a buttoned-up candidate who ran a tightly controlled campaign that emphasized few specifics and abided no surprises.[31]

In a way, polling failure in presidential elections is not especially surprising. Indeed, it is almost extraordinary that election polls do not flop more often than they do, given the many and intangible ways that error can creep into surveys. And these variables may be difficult or impossible to measure or quantify.[32] Unintended bias in wording the questions is an example. "Nothing matters if you've got a bad question," Stephanie Marken, a survey methodologist for the Gallup Organization, has noted.[33] "You can ask a question in such a way as to get any answer you want," Elmo Roper said in an oral history interview more than fifty years ago.[34] More subtly, there is some evidence that including, or excluding, a candidate's job title can shape an election poll's results.[35]

The order in which candidate-preference questions are posed, the day of the week interviews are conducted, and the gender of the interviewer can inject distortion into poll results. The way the survey is conducted—whether by telephone, internet, or mail, or in person—also can give rise to differing results. These are "mode effects," as pollsters call them. Survey respondents can be a source of distortion, too. Pollsters have long recognized that respondents sometimes give answers that may be socially desirable or acceptable— while keeping their true feelings or unpopular opinions to themselves. This phenomenon was suspected as a factor in Trump's unexpected victory in 2016. But pollsters and public opinion researchers report having found little evidence that a "shy Trump" effect was extensive, let alone decisive.[36]

Opinion polls can never flawlessly reflect the views of the entire population. It's a statistical fact of life that some amount of error resides in every poll taken of some portion of a target group. This is true even when rigorous and reliable polling techniques are applied, such as taking pains to ensure that everyone in the target population has theoretically an equal chance of being interviewed, a key element in what is called probability sampling. The inevitable distortion in sample surveys is called the margin of error (or, more precisely, the margin of sampling error). A description of the margin of error often can be found in the small type accompanying newspaper reporting about election polls. Usually this caveat is described in phrases such as, "This poll's margin of error is plus or minus three or four percentage points." Such a notice is an expression of the precision and reliability of the poll result.

But the challenges facing election pollsters are more extensive than question wording, socially palatable responses, or unavoidable sampling error. Pollsters essentially attempt to estimate the decision-making behavior of the electorate—a self-selecting, ephemeral population that takes shape only when time comes to vote. Afterward, the electorate dissolves itself.[37] Attempting to assess the behavior of such an evanescent population—the characteristics of which cannot be fully known beforehand—"presents a rather unique set of challenges to election pollsters, with an impact on reliability that is both potentially large and impossible to measure in advance," as researchers Joel David Bloom and Jennie Elizabeth Pearson have pointed out.[38]

In addressing the phenomenon of the electorate, pollsters have developed various ways of estimating who among the respondents to pre-election polls are most likely to vote. Weeding out nonvoters is essential because many poll respondents fail to follow through on assurances that they will vote. But screening too rigorously for nonvoters can produce significant differences in pollsters' estimates about who is in the lead. So can screening too loosely.

Some weeding-out techniques are more elaborate than others; Gallup's multistep method, for example, was developed and refined over several decades and included questions about whether respondents knew the location of their polling place and whether they had voted in past elections. But no screening technique is foolproof. As we'll see, Gallup's technique sometimes led to puzzling swings in poll results in the weeks before the 2000 election. It is no exaggeration to say, as a writer for the *Atlantic* observed in 2016, that screening for likely voters is "a vexing bit of psychological prediction pollsters have never gotten quite right."[39] Or as Arch Crossley observed more than fifty years ago, figuring out who will vote "is the great question we have not answered."[40]

Crossley's "great question" has nagged at pollsters for decades. Elmo Roper's son, Burns (who was known as "Bud" and was something of a contrarian character in survey research),[41] said in 1984: "One of the trickiest parts of an election poll is to determine who is likely to vote and who is not. I can assure you that this determination is largely art."[42] A generation later, Jon Cohen, then the *Washington Post*'s polling director, similarly noted, "One of the trickiest parts of political polling is determining which of the people interviewed in pre-election surveys will really vote."[43] Even now, after many years of testing, pollsters do not agree on the best method for deciding who will vote. "There are as many 'likely voter' models as there are pollsters," Kyley

McGeeney, a polling expert in Washington, DC, noted at a conference of public opinion researchers in 2018.[44]

The distorting effects of screening for likely voters were strikingly demonstrated in 2016, when Nate Cohn of the *New York Times* arranged for four well-regarded pollsters to calculate the results of a pre-election poll in Florida in which voters pronounced themselves in favor of Trump or Clinton for president. The pollsters were given the same raw data to analyze, and their results differed markedly, ranging from a four-point advantage for Clinton to a one-point lead for Trump.[45]

The discrepancies resulted from the divergent ways in which the respective pollsters assessed who among the respondents was most likely to vote, and in how the pollsters statistically adjusted the sample to align it to Florida's demographic makeup, a modification known as "weighting." None of their decisions about screening for likely voters or weighting the sample were extraordinary or indefensible, as Cohn pointed out in describing the experiment. "I have seen polls that make truly outlandish decisions with the potential to produce even greater variance than this," he wrote.

The five-point difference in the results, Cohn said, illustrated "just a few of the different ways that pollsters can handle the same data" and how personal judgments can influence results. Cohn added: "You can see why 'herding,' the phenomenon in which pollsters make decisions that bring them close to expectations, can be such a problem. There really is a lot of flexibility for pollsters to make choices that generate a fundamentally different result."[46] Or, as William Saletan of Slate.com once wrote, "Every pollster has fudge factors he can apply to massage his numbers at the last moment."[47]

Another potential source of polling error, one long known to pollsters, rests with respondents who declare themselves "undecided," or say they favor no candidate.[48] Trying to determine what the "undecided" will do—for whom they will vote, if they vote at all—has confounded more than a few election forecasts over the decades. "Historically," as Nate Silver has noted, "the more undecided and third-party voters there are the more volatile and less accurate the polling has tended to be." After all, Silver added, "There's not much a pollster can do when a voter hasn't yet made up her mind."[49]

What to do about them poses another tricky circumstance for pollsters, especially in elections when "undecided" respondents are numerous. "The public and pollsters judge polls by how closely they reflect the outcome of the election," Robert Daves and Sharon Warden noted years ago, "and polls with high numbers of undecided or 'no opinion' responses simply cannot accurately reflect election day results."[50] Eliminating "undecided" respondents altogether from polling results is a tempting option, but risky—as Gallup learned in the 1948 presidential election. Reckoning that the "undecided" respondents would not vote, Gallup mostly ignored them that year, a decision he regretted. Based on post-election polling, Gallup figured that the undecided voters, rather than staying home, went for Truman over Dewey by a margin of about 3 to 1.

Allocating the "undecided" voters proportionally among the candidates is another option, as is dividing those voters between the leading candidates. Another approach is to assign them all to the challenger. None of these techniques is foolproof. As Gallup pointed out in 1952: "No scientific method is known today which can accurately predetermine the voting intentions of people who are either undecided or unwilling to reveal their preference."[51] In his final pre-election poll in 1952, Gallup reported that Eisenhower led Stevenson by 47 percent to 40 percent, with 13 percent undecided, most of whom, he figured, were Democrats. By allocating the undecided voters on a 3-to-1 basis to Stevenson, the Democratic candidate—the ratio by which Gallup estimated that undecided voters had favored Truman—produced a 50–50 tie. A tossup. Gallup concluded the 1952 election would be very close and that Stevenson could win a popular vote majority.[52] Eisenhower swept to victory in a landslide.

More recently, "undecided" voters in key states who made up their minds late in the 2016 campaign help deliver the presidency to Trump. Late-deciders in Florida, Michigan, Pennsylvania, and Wisconsin voted heavily for Trump, according to exit polling, and the 75 combined electoral votes of those states were decisive to his victory.[53]

Pollsters' decisions can give rise to predictive error in other ways. They might, for example, underestimate the size of voter turnout in a presidential election—yet another way in which polling can be more practitioner's art than science. Wrapping up fieldwork prematurely has been another recurring problem, remarkable as that may seem. It's almost as if pollsters have never fully absorbed the lesson, which has presented itself periodically since 1936. That was the first time Gallup polled a presidential election and he underestimated Franklin Roosevelt's popular vote by six percentage points. The miscalculation, Gallup said, was due to disregarding "the key importance of the time factor" by ending fieldwork prematurely.[54] "Many voters," he figured, "changed sides in the final weeks of the campaign" in 1936.[55]

The election of 1948 stands as a classic and often-cited example of the hazards of poll-taking completed too soon. Elmo Roper released his final published polling results in early September 1948, declaring, "Thomas E. Dewey is almost as good as elected to the presidency of the United States." Roper likened the campaign to "a very ordinary horse race—a race in which one horse already has a commanding lead over the other horse."[56] Archibald Crossley likewise rued wrapping up his pre-election polling weeks before the election in 1948. He figured "there was no need for late polling" because "there had been little late shift" in polls he conducted during Franklin Roosevelt's campaigns in 1936, 1940, and 1944.[57]

Crossley's decision to end polling prematurely in 1948 also was driven by the expense of conducting late-in-the-campaign surveys. "We most certainly should have carried on later polls," Crossley said in a letter in January 1949 to the sociologist Alfred McClung Lee. "We stopped our fiedl [sic] interviewing three weeks before the election because while Truman was rising we didn't see he could rise enough to win, and the cost of additional polls would have had to come out of our own pockets."[58] Separately, Crossley acknowledged, "We were dead wrong not to carry on polls much later than we did, but the fact is that money would have had to come out of our own pockets and, as you know, they are expensive."[59] And they still are. A telephone poll using random-digit dialing procedures and conducted by professional interviewers during the 2016 campaign cost close to one hundred thousand dollars, according to a report for the American Association for Public Opinion Research (AAPOR).[60]

Wrapping up too soon may have explained why Gallup missed the Reagan landslide in 1980. His final pre-election poll, taken three days before the election, gave Reagan a lead of 3 percentage points.[61] Gallup—who had speculated that the 1980 election "could very well be a cliff-hanger, just like 1948"[62]—said polling ended when it did because of the time required to compile results from its "secret ballot technique, which has the effect of simulating the actual election and reducing the undecided vote."[63]

Warren Mitofsky of CBS News said after the 1980 election that he was angry with himself because his polling unit had ended its fieldwork on the Saturday before the election. Had polling continued through the weekend, Mitofsky claimed, CBS News would have detected what he said was the closing trend to Reagan. The final CBS News/*New York Times* poll in 1980 showed Reagan ahead by just one percentage point.

Irony lurked in that failed forecast, given that Mitofsky had emphasized months before the election how vital the final pre-election poll would be. "That's the one poll everyone will remember and [use to] evaluate how well we did," he wrote in an internal memorandum."[64]

In 2016, polling in key states such as Wisconsin was wrapped up too soon to detect late swings to Trump. The Marquette University Law School poll, regarded as Wisconsin's most prestigious, completed fieldwork nine days before the election—and its final poll showed Clinton ahead by 6 percentage points. Her aggregate lead in Wisconsin, compiled by the Real Clear Politics website, was 6.5 percentage points. Trump won Wisconsin by less than a point.

Yet another recurring feature of election surveying are complaints that the public—and journalists—do not adequately understand polling and probabilities, and that pollsters are obliged to improve their explanations about the workings of their craft. It's an objective that's gone largely unfulfilled.

In 2018, for example, Kyley McGeeney of the Penn Schoen Berland research firm told a conference of journalism educators that "people don't understand" polls, their methodologies, and sampling procedures. "As an industry," McGeeney said, "we have to do better" and explain "polling in general."[65] Her remarks were an echo of a lament that has been raised across the decades. "The polls have never done a good job of telling the public how they operate," George Gallup complained in 1960 in a letter to David Lawrence, the political columnist. "Somehow we have never found a way of doing this in our news releases. Consequently, we find that no one outside of this field has any knowledge about the way a poll operates. I say this . . . to point [out] our own failings."[66] Gallup had expressed similar sentiments at the 1953 meeting of AAPOR. "We as a group, and as individuals, have done a poor job in explaining how polls are conducted and what their limitations are," he said. "People in government and in journalism still haven't the faintest idea what polling is all about. We face a longtime job of educating them."[67]

In late December 1948, Gallup complained in a speech: "Most laymen see no difference between forecasting an election and picking the winner of a horse race. In due time these people will be educated to the difference, I hope."[68] Gallup's reference to the "horse race" evoked another timeless feature—and a never-ending complaint: election polls reduce political campaigns to the unedifying spectacle of a game or a horse race, an emphasis that produces a distorted and superficial focus on the question of "who's ahead?" Only in America, wrote Thomas E. Patterson, a Harvard University professor, "have polls elevated the horse race to the point where it overshadows all else." Journalists' "game-centered angle on campaigns inclines them to direct their gaze at the horse race," he wrote. "Polls serve to keep it there."[69]

The horse-race complaint has a long pedigree: It has been invoked almost predictably for years. In the midst of the 1948 campaign, for example, Arch Crossley wrote to George Gallup, saying, "I have a distinct impression that polls are still thought of as horse-race predictions, and it seems to me we might do something jointly to prevent such a reputation."[70]

Although they are many and persistent, critics of the horse-race treatment of campaigns tend to overlook that such poll-based reporting can stimulate interest in the campaign and its dominant issues.[71] As the media critic Jack Shafer observed: "Horse-race stories help focus reader attention on the races. Without the work of election handicappers, coverage would come to resemble an endless series of policy white papers that nobody reads."[72] Popular interest inevitably swings toward the horse race and not to policy positions. David Yepsen, formerly of the *Des Moines Register*, who has called himself "a great practitioner of horse race journalism," once noted he had covered politics in Iowa for many years and "every four years all sorts of people come up to me with the question: 'Who's going to win?' That's understandable. They want to know who their President is going to be." But never, Yepsen added, has anyone "ever come up to me and asked: 'What's Howard Dean's infrastructure policy?'"[73] (Dean ran a short-lived campaign for the Democratic nomination for president in 2004.)

Elections inescapably are akin to horse races: voters choose the winners by expressing their preferences. Patrick Caddell, who was the private pollster for Carter's campaigns in 1976 and 1980, accurately observed: "Everyone follows polls because everything in American life is geared to the question of who's going to win—whether it's sports or politics or whatever. There's a natural curiosity."[74] Similarly, Thomas Littlewood, in his 1998 book *Calling Elections*, noted: "The origins of horse-race journalism are buried in the American past and in the human psyche. To deplore the status of the contest as interesting news is to ignore the reality of human nature."[75]

And Gallup wrote in the early days of modern election polling, "Imagine how meaningless and uninteresting a football game would be for the spectator if he could not learn how the teams stood at half time, or if the question 'Who is leading?' were left solely to the guesswork or imagination of players and parti-sans."[76] Philip Meyer, author of the influential book *Precision Journalism*, which encouraged journalists to adopt the techniques of survey and social science research, once said: "Why journalists should feel so guilty about their obsessive concern with who is ahead is hard to fathom. The most interesting fact about an election is who wins. The most interesting thing about a campaign at any given moment is who is ahead."[77] On another occasion, Meyer declared, "Information on who is ahead [in an election campaign] has value in the marketplace of ideas, and participants in democracy are entitled to have that knowledge and make what use of it they choose."[78]

One attempt in 1976 to deemphasize horse-race reporting about election polls ended in keen embarrassment. That year, the CBS News/*New York Times* poll refrained from reporting figures that showed who was leading and who was trailing, to avoid calling attention to the horse-race component of the campaign. It was described as an experiment "in enlightened news reporting,"[79] and the objective, Mitofsky said a few years later, "was to keep the focus of our reporting away from the horserace and on those subjects that we thought would provide more insight and substantitive [sic] dialogue about the campaign."

The experiment did not turn out well. "The outcry was overwhelming," Mitofsky said. "Not only did we get criticized by the public, we were also taken to task by a number of the pollsters" for not releasing numerical results.[80] The experiment was abandoned in 1980, after Mitofsky privately told a senior CBS executive, "I have no desire to go through this sham" again.[81]

With their message about who's ahead or who's likely to win, election polls lend themselves readily to "horse-race" news coverage. They are, after all, "manifestations of political developments that can be readily reported," as Charles Atkin and James Gaudino once observed.[82] Indeed, polling has long intrigued journalists. They have been enamored with the outcomes of pre-election surveys long before polling was ever remotely thought of as embody-ing "scientific" research principles. Reports of crude pre-election polls were published in U.S. newspapers as long ago as 1824, in the run-up to the country's first vigorously contested presidential election after 1800.[83]

By the mid-twentieth century, polls were recognized as representing "a logical extension of 'the inquiring reporter' carried to a new technology."[84] Likewise, polls can allow journalists insights into what their audiences have on their minds. "One of a newspaper's functions is to determine as well as it can what people are thinking," the *Los Angeles Times* noted in 1952, "and a well-conducted poll is a very useful tool in the exercise of this function."[85] And that is just one of several ways in which journalism and opinion polling intersect. Both fields operate in the public eye. Both have grand pretenses about promoting the public good, be it the journalist's cry of championing the public's right to know or the pollster's cause of capturing public opinion in a democratic republic.

More specifically, polls correspond to long-standing normative values of American journalism of timeliness, relevance, significance, and authority. They project the sense, or illusion, of certainty and confidence, which has been irresistible to generations of journalists. Given that precision is highly valued in a profession that constantly deals with ambiguity, it is little surprise that journalists, routinely and predictably, have taken a lead from poll results. As Richard Morin, the former polling director of the *Washington Post*, once observed, "There's something addictive about polls and poll numbers."[86] Polls help shape and hone the media's messaging about election campaigns. And yet, the relationship between journalists and pollsters has seldom been smooth. As we'll see, pollster-bashing used to be fairly common among prominent journalists.

CHAPTER I

Of Poll-Bashing Journalists and the "Babe Ruth" of Survey Research

Newspapers were vital to the rise and prominence of modern opinion polls. Beginning in the mid-1930s, George H. Gallup syndicated polling reports to daily newspapers, an early step in establishing his assessments of public opinion as a staple of U.S. news coverage.[1] Aligning his polls with journalism helped make Gallup a familiar name. Along with the lucrative market research conducted for commercial clients,[2] polling helped make him rich. At the time of his death in 1984, Gallup had a farm near Princeton, a summer retreat in central Switzerland, and a winter home in the Bahamas.[3]

Frank Newport, a former editor-in-chief of the Gallup Organization and admirer of the company's founder, once said it was a "combination of journalism and polling that made Dr. Gallup so successful."[4] At least in his early years, Gallup emphasized polling's parallels to journalism. He said on the *Meet the Press* interview program shortly after the polling debacle of 1948 that poll-taking was "a new branch of journalism, and I think you gentlemen of the press would agree that it's just as important to report what people think as it is what they do. This, I think, is a new, legitimate, and important field of journalism."[5]

And yet, despite shared interests and commonalities, the relationship between election pollsters and prominent journalists has been often stormy, tainted by hostility and mutual suspicion. Poll-bashing among journalists arose from the resentment and distrust of the methods, presumptions, and intrusiveness of election pollsters. Poll-bashing may have eased in American newsrooms in recent years, but its pedigree is extensive. It afflicted such prominent journalists as broadcast legend Edward R. Murrow, former CBS

News anchor Dan Rather,[6] New York City writer Jimmy Breslin, Chicago columnist Mike Royko, and social commentator Christopher Hitchens.[7]

Skeptics in journalism doubted whether opinion polling could accurately divine the opinions or inclinations of millions of people—and doubted whether trying to do so was even a good idea. Such reservations date to 1936 and the dawn of polling's modern era. The *New York Herald Tribune* said after the election that year it doubted whether "there is any scientifically reliable

---

BOX 1. JOURNALISTS ON POLLS AND POLLSTERS

Although their hostility has receded in recent years, journalists prominent and otherwise have delighted in skewering polls and pollsters, as this selection makes clear:

- "I should be very happy if all the polls turned out to be wrong."—Walter Lippmann, syndicated columnist, *Salt Lake Tribune*, November 1, 1936

- "To a vast number, these polls have been an irritation and annoyance."—Frank R. Kent, columnist, *Baltimore Sun*, November 24, 1936

- "Defending pollsters these days is a dirty, rotten, thankless job, but somebody has to do it."—Theo Lippman Jr., columnist, *Baltimore Sun*, November 10, 1980

- "Without these polls, we would never know what cattle feel like."—Russell Baker, *New York Times* humor columnist, November 9, 1988

- "If you lied to a pollster, then voted the way you intended, elections would still come out the way they would have if you told the truth. The only difference would be that the pollsters would have nervous breakdowns and be institutionalized, and we wouldn't be assaulted by their silly numbers every election year."—Mike Royko, columnist, *Chicago Tribune*, October 28, 1992

- "The political polls are everywhere—but do they really mean anything?"—Susan Aschoff, *St. Petersburg Times*, October 10, 2000

- "Being a clever pollster means never having to say you're sorry."—William Saletan, *Slate*, October 27, 2000

- "What is going to happen on Election Day? It depends on which pollster you ask." —Jim Rutenberg, *New York Times*, October 19, 2004

- "Polls are as accurate and precise as human nature, which is to say they are not accurate and they are not precise. This is witchcraft."—Jim Pinkerton, on *Fox News Watch* program, October 30, 2004

- "If you think about it, talking to a polling company is an odd way to behave. Strangers ask you to give them time and personal information for nothing so that they can profit from it."—Nick Cohen, columnist, London *Observer*, October 31, 2004

method of telling what 120,000,000 people are thinking."[8] Edward Murrow expressed similar misgivings. On the day after Dwight Eisenhower won the presidency in 1952, Murrow said on CBS Radio:

> Yesterday, the people surprised the pollsters, the prophets, and many politicians. They demonstrated, as they did in 1948, that they are mysterious and their motives are not to be measured by mechanical means. The result contributed something to the demechanization of our society. It restored to the individual, I suspect, some sense of his own sovereignty. Those who believe that we are predictable . . . who believe that sampling depth, interviewing, allocating the undecided vote, and then reducing the whole thing to a simple graph or chart, have been undone again. (They were as wrong as they were four years ago.) And we are in a measure released from the petty tyranny of those who assert that they can tell us what we think, what we believe, what we will do, what we hope and what we fear, without consulting us—all of us.[9]

Such thinking resonated in American journalism for years, driven by uneasiness about polling's presumptions rather than by evaluations of its techniques. "I hope profoundly," Murrow said after the 1948 election, "that they never succeed in making the measuring of public opinion into an exact science."[10] Other critics like Eric Sevareid, a commentator for CBS News, were uncomfortable with polling's audacity in challenging the mystique of the American voter. Sevareid wrote in 1964 of "a secret glee and relief when the polls go wrong" and said the reasons for feeling that way "were obvious: We hate to have the mystery and suspense of human behavior eliminated by clinical dissection."[11] James Reston of the *New York Times* argued that "the more the pollsters fail, the more the democratic process is likely to succeed." If pre-election polls "were a sure bet," he reasoned, "who would vote?"[12]

The ornery Mike Royko, who was perhaps Chicago's most engaging and entertaining newspaper columnist, delighted in his contempt for polls. The pollster, he wrote, was "a hired brain-picker trying to figure out what your personal fears, hopes or prejudices are, so that he can advise a politician how to more skillfully lie to you."[13] In the mid-1980s, Royko waged a noisy campaign urging readers to lie to the interviewers conducting exit polls. He said he wanted to confound the projections that television stations relied on. Besides, Royko wrote, exit polling was draining the fun from Election Night. "Do they care," he wrote, "that their exit polling is completely ruining what used to be the most entertaining and exciting part of an election—the suspense of watching the results trickle in?"[14]

"The election is a few days off," Royko wrote in early November 1984, "but it's never too early to begin planning to tell a lie to a TV exit pollster. As some readers might recall, urging people to lie to exit pollsters has long been one of my few constructive civic endeavors. The idea is to mess up their polling results and cause them to go on TV and project the wrong candidate as the winner. And that could cause them to swallow their tongues, which would be fun to see."[15]

It was a perversely amusing and, of course, an ineffective campaign. Royko's tongue-in-cheek advocacy troubled the likes of the *Washington Post*. Lying to pollsters, the *Post* declared, was neither wise nor prudent advice, warning that it could even lead to a debacle akin to the "Dewey defeats Truman" miscall of 1948.[16] Royko's campaign resonated for years after his death in 1997. It was recalled in 2018 at the conference of the American Association for Public Opinion Research, when the organization's genial then-president, Tim Johnson, complained about efforts he said were intended to delegitimize opinion polling. He cited Royko's lie-to-a-pollster advocacy and asked, "How can we expect the public to take our surveys seriously when some of our opinion leaders make a mockery of them?"[17]

Johnson also recalled the snarling, poll-bashing crusade waged by Arianna Huffington, a syndicated columnist who founded the popular online news and commentary site *Huffington Post*. Hers was an aggressive campaign called the "Partnership for a Poll-Free America." Huffington encouraged people "to take the no-poll pledge and hang up on pollsters" should they call. "If they can't hang up, if they don't have the strength yet to do that," she advised, "at least lie to them—anything to contaminate the sample and demonstrate how unreliable polls are."[18] She said her crusade was intended "to get the dominance of polling out of our political life."[19] She lamented that polling results had come to be regarded "with the kind of reverence that ancient Romans gave to chicken entrails"[20] and said they were treated by "media mavens . . . as if Moses just brought them down from the mountaintop."[21]

A high moment in Huffington's campaign came in 2003, when AAPOR invited her to address the organization's annual conference. She opened her remarks by saying that friends had asked her who was crazier—she, for accepting the invitation, or AAPOR, for offering it. Huffington demonstrated on that occasion that she was more inclined to offer insouciant and humorous asides than a serious or sophisticated critique of polling, its methodologies, and its failures. The speech was less a confrontation than a theater for witty exchanges and sly repartee. Richard Morin, the polling director at the *Washington Post*, was one of the designated respondents to Huffington's speech. Morin said drolly that the talk revealed there "are actually two Arianna Huffingtons. There's the one who just spoke to us: What a charming woman— intelligent, witty. She's critical but insightful about polls." Morin turned to Huffington and added, "But then there's the shrieking pundit from hell who writes about polls in a syndicated newspaper column under your name. Have you ever met this dreadful woman?" Laughter swept the room. The evening closed with Huffington's being asked to place her hand on the convention program and vow never again to try to kill off survey research.

A hint of naïveté characterized Huffington's campaign. And Royko's. Not many people ever are called or interviewed by a pollster, and a few deceptive responses would not significantly distort a poll's results. In time, Huffington's poll-bashing campaign faded away. Its end effectively came in 2010 when the *Huffington Post* acquired Pollster.com, an aggregator and interpreter of polling data that was renamed HuffPost Pollster. "Polling, whether we like it or not, is a big part of how we communicate about politics," Huffington said then. "And with this [acquisition], we'll be able to do it in a deeper way. We'll be able to both aggregate polls, point out the limitations of them and demand more transparency."[22] Huffington left *Huffington Post* in 2016, after Verizon acquired AOL, which owned the site.

Poll-bashing also arose from a tension between anecdote-based reporting and data-based methods of information-gathering, a tension between qualitative and quantitative methods of assessing public opinion. While election polls were valuable in addressing the inevitable questions about elections— who's ahead, who's likely to win—they posed a challenge to the celebrated news-gathering technique of "shoe-leather" reporting, which obliged journalists to leave the newsroom and rely on direct observation and in-person interviews. "Some newspaper folk are antagonistic to opinion polls, chiefly because they are skeptical of the methods employed," the director of the Philadelphia *Evening Bulletin* poll wrote in 1949. "They doubt that the cross-section is an accurate portrayal of the community at large, and feel that for their purposes they can obtain results as conclusive by a much more limited number of spot interviews."[23]

Generations of American journalists have assigned outsize value to "shoe-leather" reporting, a practice steeped in presumptive virtue and sometimes identified as an antidote to the failures of election polling. Jay Rosen, a journalism educator, has observed—with, perhaps, only faint exaggeration—that "in the U.S. press there is thought to be a single source of virtue. The mythical term for it is 'shoe leather reporting.' There can never be enough of it. Only good derives from it. Anything that eclipses it is bad. Anything that eludes it is suspect. Anything that permits more of it is holy." It is, Rosen added, "the one god an American journalist can officially pray to. Fine writing, great storytelling, aggressive questioning, toughness in the face of attacks: these are universally admired. Amusing and inventive word play, quick and biting sarcasm, superior crap detection: these will win you points in any newsroom or press bus. But godliness is reserved for shoe leather reporting."[24]

Such sentiment can be traced to the presumed high moments of "shoe-leather" journalism, such as the dogged reporting of the early Watergate scandal by Bob Woodward and Carl Bernstein for the *Washington Post*. Their work—which often and wrongly has been credited with bringing down Richard M. Nixon's corrupt presidency[25]—was memorialized in *All the President's Men*, a best-selling book and an eponymous, much-acclaimed motion picture. "The scenes in *All the President's Men* that show Woodward and Bernstein crisscrossing Washington on foot or ringing doorbells at night" represent "shoe leather mythology in its most concentrated form," Rosen wrote. This determined quest for vital truths makes poll-taking seem like an unglamorous slog.

Another enormously influential example of "shoe-leather" journalism was *The Making of the President, 1960*, Theodore White's deeply reported, behind-the-scenes narrative of John F. Kennedy's presidential campaign and election victory over Nixon. *Making of the President* spawned great interest and imitation in political journalism, and confirmed the appeal if not the soundness of detail-driven "shoe-leather" journalism. White's approach inspired numerous book-length imitations, many of which borrowed his formula of describing politics in novelistic fashion, as a struggle of great personalities, as Timothy Crouse noted in his equally famous campaign book, *The Boys on the Bus*.[26] Eventually, the appeal of White's "dramatic, inside style swept over into daily journalism," James David Barber wrote in *The Pulse of Politics*. He noted that scores of reporters "muscled their way into the campaigns of 1972, frantically jotting down what the candidates had for breakfast, how he did his hair, what his children thought of him."[27]

Crouse's *Boys on the Bus* turned the lens from the candidates to the journalists who covered the 1972 presidential campaign. It was "shoe-leather" reporting about the reporters, and Crouse presented a humorous but unsettling account of the frenetic yet collaborative packlike behavior of supposed rivals in the traveling campaign press corps. "Campaign journalism," Crouse wrote, "is, by definition, pack journalism: to follow a candidate, you must join a pack of other reporters; even the most independent journalist cannot completely escape the pressures of the pack."[28] "Pack journalism" was both a reality and a failing. Crouse pressed the term into the argot of American journalism as a defect or distortion of "shoe-leather" reporting.

The pedigree of "shoe-leather" reporting of political campaigns is rich. Years before White's book, or Crouse's, or *All the President's Men*, syndicated columnist David Lawrence crisscrossed the country in quadrennial efforts to detect and assess voters' moods in the weeks before presidential elections. His analyses sought to combine direct observation with judgment born of extensive experience. Lawrence's analyses were not always on target, but they were invariably detailed. They were sometimes celebrated as responses or alternatives to pre-election polling.

Extensive travel likewise characterized the "shoe-leather" reporting of Haynes Johnson, who wrote long, long, interview-based reports about the moods of Americans for the *Washington Post* in the runup to presidential elections in the 1970s and '80s. Johnson derided opinion polls, saying they could never match the texture and detail produced by rigorous shoe-leather reporting. "I wish we would disband all polls," he once said in an interview on the C-SPAN cable network. "I hate the polls. We rely on them, I use them, I've cited them, and I've even gone out, God help me, and done polling myself and knocked on doors and so forth. But I think we make too much of polls. . . . They give you a little fragmentary snapshot of a moment in time."[29]

Johnson also inveighed against the perceived intrusiveness of polls, long an indictment by critics in the news media. "People resent them," Johnson said of polls in 1980. "They are tired of being told how they think, according to the polls; how they will vote, according to the polls; and why they didn't think the way they were supposed to think or vote the way they were supposed to vote, according to the polls." He added that when people "say that they resent the polls, they invariably go on to criticize the press for relying on them so heavily." Never, he wrote, have polls been so numerous. Never, he said, "have they been so widely cited as ultimate wisdom."[30]

Years ago, the journalism magazine *Nieman Reports* published a collection of tips and suggestions for covering political campaigns, a lengthy compilation that had been prepared by the now-defunct Committee of Concerned

Journalists. The suggestions touted "shoe-leather" reporting while advising reporters not to rely too much on polling: "Cover voters, not polls. It is voters—what they think, how they live, what they are worried about—that are important (and also more interesting). Polls turn the public into an abstraction, reacting to questions and constructs of the pollster/journalist. . . . Polls are only a tool to get at voters and only one tool. Relying on that one tool too much will bias your coverage. Other tools include focus groups, or panels (a recurring group of voters you visit), knocking on doors, talking to people in malls, talking to people at rallies."[31]

"Shoe-leather" reporting was identified as a response and prospective remedy following the polling embarrassment of the 2016 election—embarrassment in which the news media shared deeply. "If I have a mea culpa for journalists and journalism," Dean Baquet, executive editor of the *New York Times*, said soon after the election, "it's that we've got to do a much better job of being on the road, out in the country, talking to different kinds of people than the people we talk to—especially if you happen to be a New York–based news organization—and remind ourselves that New York is not the real world."[32] In an essay in the *Columbia Journalism Review* that addressed how the news media botched their coverage in the 2016 election, Neal Gabler, a journalist and historian, suggested doing away with "media-financed, pre-election polling altogether. This would leave a lot of reporters twiddling their thumbs, thinking of something to write about—which would, frankly, not be a bad thing—forcing them out from behind their desks or their seats on the campaign planes to tour the country and listen to citizens and interpret their grievances."[33]

Left unsaid was that "knocking on doors," "talking to people in malls," and interpreting "their grievances" are techniques that are prone to producing hazy and misleading impressions, which undercut the value of "shoe-leather" reporting. Impressions gathered that way can easily be misinterpreted. That is a serious shortcoming, and perhaps an explanation as to why "shoe-leather" reporting has never fully been embraced as an adequate substitute for election polling. It can be an impressionistic, nonsystematic method of information-gathering. As Nate Silver has noted, it can be "easy to misread the vibrations on the ground" during a campaign[34]—easy to misinterpret the size and enthusiasm of crowds or the prevalence of such totems as campaign yard signs. The *New York Times* cited impressionistic indicators in 2012, for example, suggesting the presidential race in Pennsylvania was tilting toward Mitt

Romney, the Republican nominee.[35] Romney lost Pennsylvania by five percentage points.

This is not to scoff at "shoe-leather" journalism: it can be an important prod to journalists, a supplement to office-bound "screenwork" reporting, which has become common in the digital age. "Shoe-leather" reporting is probably best understood as a supplemental technique that can be oversold as a useful and effective response to flawed polling. Without reliable polling, as the *Columbia Journalism Review* once observed, campaign coverage would be "governed by instinct, hunch, and whispered plane conversations."[36]

Election polling has grown enormously since the mid-1930s, when it was mostly a profile-raising pursuit of marketing researchers like Archibald Crossley, Elmo Roper, and George Gallup. Pollsters these days number in the hundreds and include news organizations, colleges and universities, and private research firms. Even then, they represent a modest portion of the much larger market and research services industry, which is estimated to generate annual revenues in the United States of $18 billion.[37]

The vernacular of survey research is imposing and seemingly intent on excluding. A frequent complaint among pollsters is that journalists just don't grasp, or convey very well, the intricacies of polling, that they lack an essential command of probabilities and rudimentary aspects of survey research. Amy Walter, national editor of the *Cook Political Report*, has said that journalists talking about polls are akin to pre-teens discussing sex. "They know all the words," Walter said. "They talk about it a lot. But they have no idea what they're talking about."[38] Charles Franklin of the Marquette Poll said at an AAPOR conference a few years ago that pollsters should expect frustration in trying to explain concepts such as the margin of sampling error to reporters "and people who talk about these things on TV."[39]

Such complaints are of long standing. One of the lessons of the 1952 election, according to Elmo Roper, was "that the press is not ready to handle the survey tool properly." Newspaper editors, he complained, were too eager to turn to polls for predictive purposes while failing to recognize their analytical value. Roper argued that "it is not the function of public opinion polls to predict elections .... I think what we lose in the plaudits of newspaper editors we more than make up in the approval of the many social scientists who find something really constructive to work with in the information we produce."[40]

Gallup, too, sometimes spoke resentfully of pre-election polls, especially after their frailty became clear in the 1948 election. He referred to pre-election polls as "this Frankenstein" that he, Roper, and Crossley had created.[41] For pollsters, Gallup said on another occasion, pre-election surveys were akin to "having another baby. One hopes that it will not be two-headed and that it will have the proper number of fingers and toes. You will recall we gave birth to a monster in 1948, the year when all of us pollsters elected Tom Dewey President of the United States."[42]

Gallup also became inclined to describe election forecasts as "the least socially useful function that polls perform."[43] Even so, it was Gallup, more than anyone else, who went to lengths to proclaim the accuracy of pre-election polls. After the presidential election in 1940, for example, Gallup bought advertising space in *Editor and Publisher*, a journalism trade journal, to proclaim: "The Gallup Poll Sets a New Record for Election ACCURACY!" The advertisement declared that Gallup's poll, which had been launched just five years earlier, had set "a new all-time record in polling history with its forty-eight-state pre-election survey" that estimated results with an average error of 2.5 percentage points.

Four years later, Gallup placed a similar self-congratulatory ad in *Editor and Publisher*, this one carrying the headline: "Gallup Poll Sets Another Record for Election ACCURACY." The ad copy described a "virtual bullseye's prediction"[44] of the 1944 presidential election, in which Franklin D. Roosevelt defeated Thomas Dewey by 53 percent to 46 percent. Gallup's final poll in 1944 showed a closer race, with Roosevelt leading by 51 percent to 48 percent. During much of the campaign, in fact, Gallup's figures "indicated a very close race and played up factors favorable to Dewey," a post-election analysis noted.[45] And in 1948, as we will see, Gallup brushed aside late-in-the-campaign doubts about his poll showing Dewey with a comfortable lead and declared that on Election Day "the whole world will be able to see down to the last percentage point how good we are."[46]

Gallup apparently was interested in devising some sort of polling "championship," an idea he raised in a letter to Roper after the 1940 election. "Frankly," Gallup wrote, "I think it would be a good idea sometime during the next year for the [journal] Public Opinion Quarterly, or those of us who are interested in this job of measuring public opinion, to set up the rules by which we could stake our claims for the championship" of, presumably, the most accurate pre-election poll.[47] Roper wasn't much interested and said so in a letter that he drafted but apparently never sent.[48]

Gallup's interest in asserting the accuracy of election polling was clear enough: by insisting on and demonstrating the accuracy of pre-election polling, he could stake a claim to the trustworthiness of *all* opinion polling,[49] including the far more numerous surveys on public policy issues and consumer-product preferences. Accuracy in forecasting elections, in other words, would translate to confidence in polling techniques generally.[50]

Gallup sometimes characterized election polling as "an acid test"[51] of polling techniques—even though pre-election polls, especially those taken near the end of campaigns, tend to be quite atypical. Sample sizes are usually larger in the final polls of presidential campaigns, as pollsters seek results with smaller margins of sampling error. As such, they "bear very little resemblance to the vast majority of polls," as J. Michael Hogan noted in a detailed and critical assessment of Gallup and his techniques. Hogan wrote that "final election forecasts are not so much a 'test' of their general procedures, but instead unique, special events," methodologically "different from all other polls."[52] They are in a sense uncharacteristic beauty contests of opinion polling.

From the beginning, Gallup's polling on policy issues was prodigious. His frequent reports were syndicated to a few dozen client newspapers including major dailies such as the *Washington Post* and *Boston Globe*. The *Post's* publisher, Eugene Meyer, was an early and unabashed cheerleader for Gallup and his work.[53] Meyer wrote in 1940 that the *Post* "was one of the first to publish the results of Dr. Gallup's work . . . and deems itself fortunate in having this interesting information to present to its readers." Meyer declared that the "accuracy and quality" of Gallup's reports "have met my highest expectations."[54] Gallup's output, his ties to newspapers, his frequent speeches to clubs and organizations, and his willingness to appear on radio and television interview programs heightened his profile and eventually made his the most recognizable name in opinion polling.[55]

Gallup was outwardly cordial to his rivals, Elmo Roper and Arch Crossley. They were a fascinating trio, collectively credited with having "transformed polling from alchemy to home-brewed chemistry."[56] They were men of ego, varied backgrounds, and differing political views. Gallup was the best educated of the three, having earned a doctorate in psychology at the University of Iowa in 1928. He taught journalism at Northwestern and Drake universities before accepting a research position at Young & Rubicam in New York City. He ran his Princeton-based polling company, the American Institute of Public Opinion, while holding an executive position at Young & Rubicam until 1947.

Privately, Gallup and Roper entertained suspicions about each other. According to interview notes of Phyllis L. Gillis, his would-be biographer, Gallup disliked Roper because Roper had been a failed retailer jeweler in Iowa and possessed no scientific credentials.[57] That could be a sore subject for Roper who, according to Jean Converse's history of survey research, "bristled at negative comments beamed from the ivory tower."[58] Gallup also complained to Gillis that Roper had not presented the polling business very favorably in television interviews.[59]

Roper's papers at the University of Connecticut include an unflattering letter he apparently solicited in 1947 from William J. Gaskill, a former associate of Gallup who discussed what he said were Gallup's insecurities and his private "lack of faith" in opinion polling. Gaskill, who had worked with Gallup for six years and knew him by his nickname "Ted," told Roper in a brief but remarkable letter:

> We shouldn't be human, no matter how great, without some weaknesses. Ted's has always been a lack of faith in the great instrument which you fellows developed. He has always had the notion for some reason or other he has to deny man's intellectual and developmental shortcomings, instead of recognizing them as a challenge for tomorrow. He can't help but feel personal assault every time the public doesn't say what he wants it to say and every time someone mentions the shortcomings of research in the public opinion field. Ted's great curse is too great a love—and too great a fear—for a thing, which God knows, is one of the most beautiful devices of the 20th Century, a device which will only grow as the people leading the field can recognize its shortcomings as challenges for further development.[60]

In reply Roper thanked Gaskill for his insights and said: "I think your explanation of George's sensitivity about what seemed to be attacks on him is a sound one, and I shall remember it the next time he gets unusually annoyed at me over something which was not intended to reflect on him personally."[61] Roper showed Gaskill's correspondence to Frank Stanton, the president of CBS, who wrote in a brief reply, "This is quite a letter. Thanks for letting me see it."[62]

It is not known what Gallup may have said or done to disturb Roper. Gallup cultivated an engaging, aw-shucks demeanor, but he could be prickly and intemperate, and acutely sensitive to criticism.[63] He was known to be openly contemptuous of his detractors. In a speech in Cleveland at the end of 1948, for example, Gallup publicly thrashed Rensis Likert, the director of the Survey Research Center at the University of Michigan, who had written a critical article for *Scientific American* about the Dewey-Truman polling debacle. Likert pointedly questioned whether the election outcome meant that polls weren't to be trusted on other topics. "If the polls could be so inaccurate in predicting an election, what of their activities in sampling public opinion on complex social, economic and international issues? In that field there has been skepticism for some time," he wrote.[64]

Likert impugned the quota-control sampling methods then used by Gallup and other election pollsters, in which interviewers were instructed to seek out respondents who appeared to correspond to specific attributes of age, gender, race, and income levels. "A major source of bias in quota samples is the fact that interviewers, in perfectly human fashion, endeavor to fill their quotas in the easiest manner possible," Likert noted. "They go to places where people are readily available and seek any who will fill the age, sex and socio-economic specifications of their quotas." The result, he wrote, were polling samples that included "more people who are easily contacted than a truly representative sample should include." Likert advocated random-sampling techniques, saying they would produce more reliable results—and less discretion "in selection of the persons to be interviewed."[65]

Likert's criticism about flaws and shortcomings in opinion research were piercing but they were not new.[66] But coming soon after the election debacle, they aggravated Gallup, who replied angrily—much in the fashion that Gaskill had observed in his letter to Roper. Gallup treated Likert's observations as a personal assault and prepared a mocking response. "I regard him as an honest researcher who is such a good salesman that he has oversold himself on his own remedies" for opinion polling, Gallup said, sneeringly, of Likert.[67]

Gallup turned to what was then, and is now, an unresolved conundrum of election surveys—that of discerning which poll respondents are most likely to vote. He said that "if Mr. Likert can tell us just how to identify in advance those who will vote and those who will stay at home, he can be sure of a niche in the Researchers' Hall of Fame." He suggested that Likert subscribe to *Public Opinion Quarterly*, where Gallup had published articles about polling's intricacies, and urged him to "catch up with his reading before he undertakes to write his next article on the matter."

He also challenged Likert to try his hand at election polling, at the local level. "If Mr. Likert, or anyone else, wants to prove to the world that he can do a better job than the rest of us, then he has his chance . . . and the cost, at least in a local election, should be a minor consideration." Gallup said he would "be the first to cheer if Mr. Likert does have all the right answers. It will save me many a headache in years to come and many an hour explaining away my own shortcomings."[68]

It was a harsh and petty attack. But it was hardly the only occasion when Gallup publicly assailed an outspoken critic. In 1949, Lindsay Rogers of Columbia University published *The Pollsters*, a thin book that criticized polling as a practice that did little to promote representative democracy. The argument was a thrust at the heart of one of Gallup's central tenets—that polling was a continual sampling referendum, an effective and expansive town meeting through which the public regularly informs elected representatives of its collective will, judgments, and preferences. Rogers scoffed at such sentiments. "Dr. Gallup does not make the public more articulate," he argued, not without justification. "He only estimates how in replying to certain questions, it would say 'yes' or 'no' or 'don't know.' Instead of feeling the pulse of democracy, Dr. Gallup listens to its baby talk." He also wrote that "Dr. Gallup is on the side of angels and relegates critics to the camp of devils who distrust democracy."[69]

Gallup bristled at such observations and, as if to prove Rogers's point, excoriated *The Pollsters* in a letter to *Public Opinion Quarterly*. "This book," Gallup wrote, "draws upon all the literature or material derogatory to polls that has ever been published, without regard to whether the statements have been proved erroneous or not." He likened Rogers to "perhaps the last of the arm-chair philosophers in this field. I, for one, do not begrudge this last— albeit futile—charge by an arm-chair warrior, even if the weapons he chooses are tomahawks and poisoned arrows."[70] In his feud with Rogers, Gallup showed he could also nurse a grudge. Several years later, Gallup renewed his attack, declaring that Rogers had contradicted himself "in almost every chapter, if not every paragraph," of *The Pollsters*.[71]

Mean-spirited outbursts are decidedly at odds with what has been the conventional, popular view of Gallup as the kindly patriarch—big, likable, and well-meaning, the "Babe Ruth of the polling profession," as *Time* magazine described him in a cover story in May 1948.[72] Gallup, the magazine said, "is still the rumpled, well-fed Iowa boy who first came east to make his fortune. Tweedy, balding, good-humored, unhurried, he talks earnestly in a deep, Midwestern voice, addresses everyone indiscriminately as 'my friend.' . . . Gallup loves children and animals, hates cities and crowds."[73]

David Ogilvy, the legendary advertising executive, offered a somewhat more nuanced assessment of Gallup, for whom he worked at the Audience Research Institute. Gallup set up the institute in New Jersey in 1939 to survey moviegoers about what they liked in motion pictures. He later opened an office in Hollywood, where Ogilvy worked early in his career. "Gallup was a man of remarkable humility," Ogilvy recalled in his autobiography. "When a magazine published an article attacking his methods on thirty-eight accounts, he summoned his lieutenants and told us that he agreed with thirty-six of them."[74] Gallup "had one curious quirk: he paid [paltry] wages," Ogilvy wrote. "I got $40 a week, which was less than the gardeners of the Hollywood moguls I was advising. Saul Rae, who later became Canadian ambassador to the United Nation, was employed to help Gallup write a book—for $50 a week."[75]

Ogilvy's other recollections were like stealthy insults. He wrote, for example: "I would have been happy to pay Gallup for the education he gave me. Apart from polling he taught me three things of consummate value: 1. 'Grant graciously what you dare not refuse.' 2. 'When you don't know the answer, confuse the issue.' 3. 'When you foul the air in somebody else's bathroom, burn a match and the smell will vanish.'"[76]

Survey research has had few more dependable, media-wise, and high-profile advocates than Gallup, who once declared that "polls constitute the most useful instrument of democracy every devised."[77] But Gallup's vision of polls as a continual referendum assumed a public both attentive and well-informed, which even he, on occasion, conceded it was not.[78] Usually Gallup praised the wisdom of the masses,[79] saying they tended to be savvier and more in front on issues than their leaders.[80] But sometimes he let the mask slip. In an appearance in 1956 on Edward R. Murrow's televised *Person to Person* interview program, Gallup said:

> It is always shocking to me when we interview people who have the advantage of an education . . . to find that these people are very ill-informed about the world. . . . I remember one study in which we found that only a third of all adults of the country knew where the Suez Canal is. A good many people do not know that we have two senators from each state. They know very little about the Electoral College. They know very little about geography generally and particularly the geography of Asia and the sad part is that these are people who have had the advantage of an education.[81]

In time, Gallup came to be regarded as "the elder statesman" of survey research,[82] and his memory was celebrated for years after his death in Switzerland in 1984. A few months before the 2016 election, for example, the *New York Times* recalled Gallup and his legacy, describing him as "an Iowan with a commanding presence and a bone-crushing grip." Gallup, said the

FIGURE 4. Iowa-born George H. Gallup, shown here in 1948, was the prickly evangelist of survey research. He could be openly contemptuous of critics. (Credit: W. Eugene Smith/ Getty Images)

Times, "could not, and probably would not, tell you who he thought would win in November. But he could tell you what forces were driving public opinion, from fear of crime and terrorism to a widespread unease about rapid cultural and demographic changes. And he most certainly would have pointed out the flaws in a presidential primary system that produced two candidates with such high negative ratings and so many voters in despair."[83]

There always was a fair amount of hagiography in the media's profiles of Gallup.[84] Ogilvy and another former employee, Phyllis L. Gillis, both described Gallup as detached, professionally. "I could not have had a better boss than Dr. Gallup," Ogilvy wrote, offering perhaps another backhanded compliment. "His confidence in me was such that I do not recall his ever reading any of the reports I wrote in his name."[85] Gillis, a former research assistant for Gallup, set to work in 1979 on an authorized biography about the pollster and explained to one of her sources that she was "doing my best to avoid a white-wash." She noted that it was "part of Gallup's personality to let his seconds take over the reins of a particular project after he lost interest (which was usually immediately after the original idea had been conceived.) That benefited all of us who worked for him—and he was delighted to have someone else do the details and dirtywork."[86]

Gillis drafted project proposals and a sample chapter, which she shared with a New York literary agent,[87] but the book was never completed. Gallup, despite his standing in survey research, has never been the subject of a full-fledged biography.[88] The nearest such work was Susan Ohmer's *George Gallup in Hollywood*, which focused on Gallup's audience research in cinema while commending his contributions to opinion research. "Gallup probably did more than any other figure . . . to disseminate the idea that polls are accurate, reliable indicators of public opinion," she wrote.[89] Jean Converse also offered a highly favorable assessment of Gallup in her influential study about the emergence of public opinion research. "Gallup," she wrote, "had daring."[90]

Neither Ohmer nor Converse identified or addressed Gallup's inclination to spin, to interpret favorably and generously those election outcomes that contradicted his polling results. Gallup could be downright brazen in doing so. He thoroughly missed Eisenhower's landslide in 1952, saying in his final pre-election poll that the race was very close. Afterward, Gallup declared the outcome an occasion for him to dine on pheasant instead of crow. That's because his final poll showed Eisenhower narrowly in the lead—a lead that, according to Gallup, Stevenson had been positioned to overtake.[91] Even in the weeks after the fiasco of 1948, Gallup insisted that election polling was sound. "Probably in no other field has human behavior been predicted with such a high degree of accuracy," he said at a conference in Iowa in early 1949. "The mistakes made by polling organizations in the 1948 presidential election were," he said, "largely mistakes in judgment—and not in basic procedures. They were mistakes which can be laid, in part at least, to lack of experience in this new field."[92] In reality, the "basic procedures" that Gallup and other pollsters used in the 1948 election—their quota-sampling methods, notably—were deeply flawed, as a panel of the Social Sciences Research Council indicated in its far-reaching review of the polling debacle.[93]

Gallup often made it known he refrained from voting in presidential elections after 1928. Nonetheless, he held strong if private views about politicians. He deeply admired Thomas Dewey, describing the twice-failed presidential candidate as "the ablest man I've ever known in public life." He was an honorary pallbearer at Dewey's funeral in New York City in 1971.[94] Gallup was suspicious of Ronald Reagan and described the 1980 campaign in which Jimmy Carter sought reelection as a race between a second-rate politician and a third-rate actor, according to interview notes made by Gillis.[95] Her notes indicate that Gallup felt Abraham Lincoln would have been a better president had "he kept us out of war" in 1861. Gallup found Lyndon B. Johnson "so non-intellectual, non-mental that it affected my respect for him."[96]

It was the election of 1936 that helped make Gallup's reputation as a pollster. His final pre-election poll pointed to Roosevelt's victory, but the forecast fell well short of anticipating the landslide that carried the president to a second term. Gallup claimed success nonetheless. Doing so, as we shall see, went beyond merely spinning the outcome. Accuracy in forecasting was essential to his supplanting the leading pollster of the day, the *Literary Digest*. After the 1936 election, Gallup basked in what he declared was a triumph for his polling methods. "Scientific sampling of public opinion came of age this week," he wrote, adding that his polls had "become a dependable instrument for reporting public opinion as news."[97]

Gallup was eager then for endorsements of his polling success. The *Washington Post* sought to oblige and published lavish praise for Gallup's election surveys in an article headlined, "Leaders in many walks of life here congratulate Post on poll results."[98] On the day after the 1936 election, Gallup was in Florida and feeling unwell. It may have been a case of nerves.[99] He instructed an associate, Jack Tibby, to send the White House two copies of the final Gallup poll of the campaign, asking that Roosevelt keep one copy, and sign and return the other, presumably as a keepsake.[100] Roosevelt complied, signing Gallup's polling report and sending it back.[101] Gallup's request of the president was a little-known tale from modern opinion polling's first national election, to which we turn next.

CHAPTER 2

"A Time of Polls Gone Mad"

The Literary Digest *Debacle of 1936*

Alf Landon was a mild-mannered, middle-of-the-road governor of Kansas who lived to be one hundred. In 1936, he suffered one of the most crushing defeats in U.S. presidential history, losing to President Franklin D. Roosevelt in what the *Literary Digest* magazine called a "superlandslide."[1] Landon won only two states: Maine, then considered a presidential election bellwether, and Vermont, for a total of 8 electoral votes. Roosevelt swept the rest of the country, rolling up 523 electoral votes in what was a referendum on his Depression-era New Deal policies that expanded government spending, increased taxes on the rich, and set up work-relief programs.

Not even Roosevelt, a shrewd and crafty liberal politician who won four terms as president, anticipated the magnitude of his victory in 1936. On the eve of the election, he reckoned he would win 360 electoral votes.[2] Asked later why he wasn't more generous in his prediction, Roosevelt replied with a grin, saying his comparatively modest forecast was attributable to "my well-known conservative tendencies."[3]

Nearly as humiliating as Alf Landon's defeat was the abject polling failure of the *Literary Digest*, the undisputed oracle of American presidential elections. The *Digest*'s massive mail-in straw poll tallied the voting preferences of more than 2.3 million Americans, returns that indicated the election would be a landslide—for Landon. The *Digest* estimated the Republican would carry 33 states and 370 electoral votes to Roosevelt's 15 states and 161 electoral votes.[4] The *Digest* poll pegged Roosevelt to win 41 percent of the popular vote. It missed by nearly 20 percentage points.

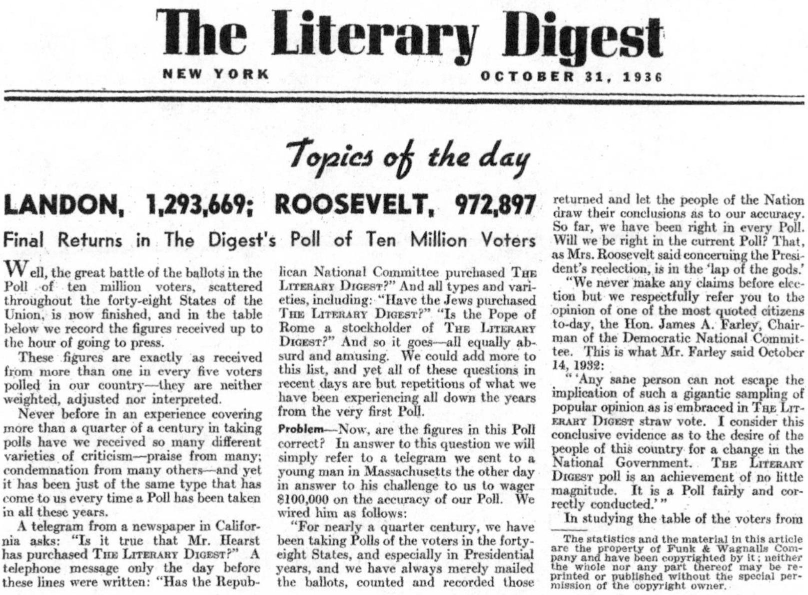

The Literary Digest

NEW YORK   OCTOBER 31, 1936

Topics of the day

LANDON, 1,293,669; ROOSEVELT, 972,897

Final Returns in The Digest's Poll of Ten Million Voters

Well, the great battle of the ballots in the Poll of ten million voters, scattered throughout the forty-eight States of the Union, is now finished, and in the table below we record the figures received up to the hour of going to press.

These figures are exactly as received from more than one in every five voters polled in our country—they are neither weighted, adjusted nor interpreted.

Never before in an experience covering more than a quarter of a century in taking polls have we received so many different varieties of criticism—praise from many; condemnation from many others—and yet it has been just of the same type that has come to us every time a Poll has been taken in all these years.

A telegram from a newspaper in California asks: "Is it true that Mr. Hearst has purchased THE LITERARY DIGEST?" A telephone message only the day before these lines were written: "Has the Repub-

lican National Committee purchased THE LITERARY DIGEST?" And all types and varieties, including: "Have the Jews purchased THE LITERARY DIGEST?" "Is the Pope of Rome a stockholder of THE LITERARY DIGEST?" And so it goes—all equally absurd and amusing. We could add more to this list, and yet all of these questions in recent days are but repetitions of what we have been experiencing all down the years from the very first Poll.

Problem—Now, are the figures in this Poll correct? In answer to this question we will simply refer to a telegram we sent to a young man in Massachusetts the other day in answer to his challenge to us to wager $100,000 on the accuracy of our Poll. We wired him as follows:

"For nearly a quarter century, we have been taking Polls of the voters in the forty-eight States, and especially in Presidential years, and we have always merely mailed the ballots, counted and recorded those

returned and let the people of the Nation draw their conclusions as to our accuracy. So far, we have been right in every Poll. Will we be right in the current Poll? That, as Mrs. Roosevelt said concerning the President's reelection, is in the 'lap of the gods.'

"We never make any claims before election but we respectfully refer you to the opinion of one of the most quoted citizens to-day, the Hon. James A. Farley, Chairman of the Democratic National Committee. This is what Mr. Farley said October 14, 1932:

"'Any sane person can not escape the implication of such a gigantic sampling of popular opinion as is embraced in THE LITERARY DIGEST straw vote. I consider this conclusive evidence as to the desire of the people of this country for a change in the National Government. THE LITERARY DIGEST poll is an achievement of no little magnitude. It is a Poll fairly and correctly conducted.'"

In studying the table of the voters from

The statistics and the material in this article are the property of Funk & Wagnalls Company and have been copyrighted by it; neither the whole nor any part thereof may be reprinted or published without the special permission of the copyright owner.

FIGURE 5. Returns in the *Literary Digest*'s mass mail-in poll of 1936 suggested Alf Landon was headed for an easy victory over President Franklin D. Roosevelt. The poll missed the outcome by almost twenty percentage points. (Credit: *Literary Digest*)

"I'm simply astounded," Wilfred Funk, the *Digest*'s editor-in-chief, told the Associated Press news agency as the dimensions of Roosevelt's landslide became clear. Funk confided that he had not been entirely sure about his magazine's poll, saying his "personal belief was that Roosevelt would win. I thought it would be close. But I can't explain that apparent landslide." Figuring out how the *Digest*'s poll went wrong, Funk said, "will take time—and a lot of pencils and paper and figuring."[5]

It was a shattering outcome for a venerable magazine. Its nationwide straw polls had identified the winning candidate in every presidential election since 1920. In 1932, the poll estimated Roosevelt's winning vote total to within 1.5 percentage points. The *Digest*'s forecasting record was so impressive and seemingly sound that many newspapers hailed the "uncanny accuracy" of its poll.[6] After miscalling the election for Alf Landon, the *Digest* never conducted another poll. It went out of business less than two years later, absorbed by an upstart rival, *Time* magazine.

TABLE I   "UNCANNY," UNTIL IT WASN'T

Here are the *Literary Digest*'s forecasts in the four presidential elections to 1936, when the magazine's mass mail-in poll failed dramatically to anticipate Franklin D. Roosevelt's landslide reelection. Before that debacle, many newspapers had praised the *Digest*'s polls for "uncanny accuracy."

Year	Vote		Winner		Prediction error
	Digest	*Actual*	*Digest*	*Actual*	
1924	56.5%	54.0	Coolidge	Coolidge	2.5 points
1928	63.3	58.2	Hoover	Hoover	5.1 points
1932	56.0	57.4	Roosevelt	Roosevelt	1.4 points
1936	40.9	60.8	Landon	Roosevelt	19.9 points

SOURCES: *Literary Digest* polls; Dominic Lusinchi.

The wrong-way landslide projection undeniably qualifies the *Digest* for a singular place in the pantheon of polling failure. It lives on as "one of history's finest examples of how not to conduct a survey," as one statistician observed.[7] But the 1936 election was a pivotal moment in polling history for reasons that go beyond the *Digest*'s jaw-dropping miscall. The election that year brought the emergence of three *arrivistes* who helped transform survey research, three rivals with roots and experience in marketing research who brought novel if imperfect sampling techniques to election polling. They were Archibald Crossley, an avuncular figure who used to work for the *Digest* and was well-known for his ratings service for radio shows; Elmo Roper, a failed retail jeweler in Creston, Iowa, whose connections brought him to New York City, where he established a market research company;[8] and George Gallup, a former journalism instructor known invariably by the honorific "Dr.," as if to project an aura of authority and erudition.

Gallup earned a doctorate at the University of Iowa's psychology program and taught journalism before becoming director of research for Young & Rubicam in New York City.[9] He kept his position there while launching a modest polling operation from the Young & Rubicam address on Madison Avenue. He grandly called his operation the American Institute of Public Opinion and likened it to a news service for reporting public opinion.[10]

Gallup publicized the results of his first opinion poll in October 1935, a few months after Roper's first survey had appeared in *Fortune* magazine. Roper said years later, "There was never any thought in my mind that he was in any sense copying us or that we inspired him, because it takes long enough to get ready. He had to be thinking about the [polling] thing before he ever saw the Fortune Survey in order to be in shape to publish. And, of course, that helped the whole field because we were sort of regarded as curiosities."[11]

Seldom has election polling been the theater of a clash such as that of 1936, an encounter that pitted against each other the starkly divergent techniques of the *Digest* and of the newcomers. Never before had the *Digest*, "the flagship of straw polling,"[12] been confronted by such aggressive contrarians, each of whom pointed in the fall of 1936 to an outcome that diverged from the *Digest*'s findings. If hesitantly and, in Roper's case, belatedly, the polls of the newcomers each anticipated Roosevelt's victory.

It was a very public clash that took shape in the summer and intensified as Election Day approached; some newspaper columnists found it more captivating than the race between Roosevelt and Landon. It was, moreover, a clash that ushered in a new era in survey research, a clash that highlighted, in embryonic form, some of the controversies and challenges that have dogged election polling for more than eighty years. The significance of the clash of 1936 was not lost on Gallup, who wrote a few years later that "the modern methods" that he, Crossley, and Roper had developed "represented a new epoch in the history of public-opinion measurement."[13]

A single purpose "characterized the modern polls" of Gallup, Roper, and Crossley, Gallup claimed. "They had but one concern: to get a true picture of public opinion,"[14] whereas the *Digest*, he pointed out, used polling as a tactic to boost circulation. With the millions of postcard-ballots it sent out, the *Digest* included an invitation to subscribe to the magazine.

Still, Gallup, Roper, and Crossley were neophytes in 1936, untested in national elections. They could claim nothing akin to the *Digest*'s standing or prestige in soothsaying. The upstarts, as Arch Crossley acknowledged, "had not made reputations" as pollsters.[15] The newcomers used variations of quota-control sampling, a technique now out of fashion, in which survey respondents were selected according to attributes such as age, occupation, gender, race, geographic distribution, and economic standing.[16]

The presumed predictive power of the *Digest*'s poll was widely thought to rest on the magnitude of its sample, on what the magazine once called a "great monument of freshly gathered statistics."[17] Millions of postcard-ballots were sent to automobile owners, telephone subscribers, and many others on a mailing list drawn from city directories, rosters of clubs and organizations, and mail-order records. Ballots were sent to would-be respondents in forty-eight states, to people of "every vocation, every voting age, every religion and every nationality extraction in the country," the *Digest* claimed, adding, "Thus an amazing machine goes into action."[18] The *Digest* delighted in emphasizing the pains it took in preparing and tabulating a nationwide survey.[19]

The newcomers of 1936 were each aligned with U.S. print media, associations that granted them a degree of national standing. Gallup syndicated his polling reports to seventy-eight newspapers, including the *Boston Globe* and *Washington Post.* Roper's surveys were reported quarterly in *Fortune* magazine, which called its collaboration with the pollster "a new technique in American journalism."[20]

Crossley's media affiliation was the most delicate. His pre-election polls in 1936 were distributed by King Features Syndicate, which was owned by William Randolph Hearst, a seventy-three-year-old media tycoon. Hearst was a lifelong Democrat who had turned vehemently against Roosevelt and the New Deal. Hearst condemned Roosevelt as a "dictator" who was "intoxicated with popular applause." By returning Roosevelt to the presidency, Hearst declared, Americans "will have established despotism as a government system." Democracy, he claimed, "will be ended as an American institution."[21]

Hearst's holdings included seventy-seven titles in America's largest cities, including the flagship *New York American,* which presented Crossley's poll results in such a way as to suggest the Roosevelt-Landon race was very close. Three weeks before the election, for example, the *American* published Crossley's report on its front page beneath a huge black headline that read, "Landon needs only Michigan to win election, poll shows." The accompanying article, though, made clear that Roosevelt was in the lead.[22] A week later, Crossley's updated findings were reported on the *American's* front page beneath the headline, "Presidential race tightens as Election Day draws near," suggesting Landon was gaining relentlessly in key states.[23]

The *American* reported Crossley's final poll as if to suggest the outcome was going to be close, even though Crossley's results indicated that Roosevelt was assured of 247 electoral votes, or 19 votes short of victory, and that he was leading in states with a total of 159 votes. Winning all those states would give the president 406 electoral votes. Even so, Crossley concluded his analysis by stating, "The election is close enough to make Landon's victory possible by a concentrated effort to get his supporters to the polls."[24]

Years later, Crossley recalled the dissonance between the newspaper's headlines and the details of his polling reports, but said Hearst's editors had "in general . . . lived up" to contractual obligations "insofar as space permitted. They were, of course, strongly [in favor of the] Republican and made use of headlines in a way which sometimes might have given a wrong impression. Also, they wrote [separate] stories of their own which I thought over-emphasized the Republican side, but I never saw anything that I considered a direct violation of the contract."[25]

Crossley in 1936 also called attention to what has become of one of polling's most enduring challenges—how to weed out nonvoters from the pool of survey respondents. It's a defiant conundrum about which Crossley spoke throughout his years in election polling. At the close of the 1936 campaign, for example, he noted that "even an eleventh-hour poll cannot answer one question satisfactorily: What proportion of each class of voters—farm and city, white collar and brown shirt—will actually cast ballots? Upon this much depends" on Election Day.

Crossley's final estimate was that Roosevelt would win 53.8 percent of the popular vote.[26] That matched Gallup's final estimate: 53.8 percent for Roosevelt. Gallup figured Roosevelt would win at least than 315 electoral votes and might even roll up an electoral vote landslide "comparable to that of 1932" when he won 472 electoral votes.[27]

The oddest election estimate was Roper's, which was derived from his quarterly survey of forty-five hundred adults for *Fortune* magazine. In a news release distributed *after* the election, *Fortune* claimed that Roper's survey had "forecast the election of President Roosevelt by a popular preference of 61.7%," a discrepancy of less than a percentage point from the president's popular vote total.[28] Roper later explained that he arrived at this nearly spot-on estimate indirectly and by inference. His interviewers did not specifically ask respondents for whom they intended to vote; they asked them to select one of four characterizations about Roosevelt that ranged from whether his reelection was vital, to whether his winning another term would be about the "worst thing that could happen to this country."[29] From the responses, Roper made his estimate, which was described nowhere in the magazine before the election but appeared in the news release afterward.[30]

In an interview conducted a few years before his death in 1971, Roper said that he, Crossley, and Gallup were regarded as "overnight heroes" in 1936 because their polling had pointed to the election winner.[31] That clearly was an overstatement. They weren't received as heroes. Newspapers pointed out (before *Fortune* began circulating its post hoc claim of nearly spot-on accuracy) that none of the polls had come close to forecasting the outcome.[32] "Not one of them came anywhere near discovering the true depth and scope of the tidal wave that was in the making," the *New York Herald Tribune* said.[33] Crossley conceded as much, writing, "The actual fact is that the polls in general did not forecast this election with anything like the degree of accuracy that should be achieved when they are perfected."[34]

But Gallup was having none of that. He sought to establish himself and his emergent polling franchise as preeminent in the embryonic field of quasi-scientific opinion research,[35] and he insisted that Roosevelt's victory had corroborated the soundness of his polling techniques. "Scientific sampling of public opinion came of age this week," Gallup declared soon after the election, declaring that his client newspapers "presented their readers with an exclusive forecast that predicted the reelection of Franklin D. Roosevelt and indicated the dimensions of his landslide."[36] The results, Gallup later said, provided "a glimpse of how accurate the new science of public-opinion measurement might become."[37]

Such claims were generous interpretations of a final poll that underestimated Roosevelt's vote by seven percentage points. The claim that his survey had "indicated the dimensions" of Roosevelt's landslide signaled Gallup's inclination to spin, or interpret favorably, election results in a way most flattering to his polling. It was a tendency that became more pronounced over the years.

Interestingly, as late as October 1936, Gallup had declared the Roosevelt-Landon race to be very close, that the Republican needed only to pick up Michigan, Minnesota, and Ohio to win the Electoral College. It wouldn't take much to swing the election, Gallup said at the time. A "campaign 'incident,' a rousing speech, a fighting phrase—almost anything could do it."[38] Gallup's first head-to-head poll of the campaign, reported in July 1936, also indicated a tight race—that Landon was slightly behind Roosevelt in the popular vote but slightly *ahead* in electoral votes, by 272 to 259.[39] The poll's findings corresponded to a sense that summer that the election would be close. The president's wife, Eleanor, thought as much, too, at the time.[40]

The competition among the *Digest* and its upstart rivals came as no small interest to the country's press. Walter Lippmann, a prominent syndicated columnist, wrote as Election Day approached that there "have been times when it has seemed as if the election was not a contest between Landon and

Roosevelt but between 'The Literary Digest' poll and Dr. Gallup, between the old tyrant and the young pretender. For 'The Literary Digest' has reigned as a kind of absolute monarch of political strategy . . . and now its supremacy is challenged."[41]

The *Boston Globe* said, "The battle of the pre-election polls commands almost as much public interest as the election itself."[42] And the *Los Angeles Times* declared, "Straw vote results and analyses have intrigued public interest more than the arguments of rival candidates."[43]

One episode in July 1936, weeks before the *Digest* mailed any of its postcard-ballots, revealed the edginess and audacity of the competition. Over the years, this episode has been characterized by Gallup's organization as an act of memorable courage.[44] Here's why: Gallup claimed that if the *Digest* were to report its final poll results then, in mid-summer, "Landon would be shown receiving about 56 percent of the popular vote, to 44 percent for Roosevelt." This seemingly brash claim appeared near the end of a lengthy report to Gallup's client newspapers. Gallup said he was qualified to make such a claim because his Institute had sent "part of its ballots to the same lists covered by the Digest," allowing him "to predict with a high degree of accuracy the sentiment the Digest would find in the different sections of the United States."[45]

The *Digest*'s editor, Wilfred Funk, was little amused by Gallup's claim, obscurely made though it was. Funk, whose father, Isaac Kaufman Funk, had founded the magazine in 1890, sputtered that no one had ever challenged the *Digest* in such a "gratuitous" manner. "I am beginning to wish," Funk stated in a letter to the *New York Times*, "that the esteemed Dr. Gallup would confine his political crystal-gazing to the offices of the American Institute of Public Opinion and leave our Literary Digest and its figures politely and completely alone." Funk further wrote: "We've been through many poll battles. We've been buffeted by the gales of claims and counter-claims. But never before has any one foretold what our poll was going to show before it was even started."[46]

For years afterward, Gallup recalled the episode with great pride. In *The Pulse of Democracy*, a book he coauthored in 1940, Gallup indirectly complimented himself for having "foreseen the [*Literary Digest*] disaster long before it actually happened."[47] In 1944, he told a congressional committee that "we, in 1936, predicted that the *Digest* would go wrong and almost by the exact percentage by which they went wrong."[48] He made a similar boast in 1957 in an article in *Public Opinion Quarterly*, writing, "The *Digest* was not only wrong, but its error was almost exactly what we said it would be."[49] In 1979, Gallup told his would-be biographer, "The boldest thing we ever did was meet the challenge of the Literary Digest."[50]

It seemed no one was immune to polling fever that fall. Scores of straw polls were conducted by newspapers, specialty magazines, and radio stations. Many of them were statewide in scope.[51] Never, said the *New York Times*, "had there been so much sampling, so many straw votes, so many confident prognostications."[52] To the *Los Angeles Times*, it was "a time of polls gone mad."[53]

Near the end of the campaign, the trade journal *Editor and Publisher* conducted what it called a "50-yard-line" poll of 68 correspondents who spent time on the campaign trains of Roosevelt and Landon. The president was favored overwhelmingly: all 30 reporters aboard Roosevelt's train pegged him to win, as did 31 of 38 correspondents on Landon's train, *Editor and Publisher* reported.[54]

The British news service Reuters also caught polling fever, surveying its correspondents across America and privately sharing the results with the White House. The Reuters canvass of its correspondents was completed in early October and found that Roosevelt led in thirty-two states—and was ahead in the electoral vote count, 314 to Landon's 217. The Reuters chief correspondent in the United States, A. Bernard Moloney, shared his writeup about the poll with a White House aide and said in an accompanying letter, "God forbid that I, as a foreigner, should be so lacking in correct etiquette as to attempt to prejudge the result of the election."[55]

The established "straw polls" signaled Alf Landon's victory. Among them was that of the *Farm Journal*, which had never erred in forecasting the winner since beginning its presidential poll in 1916.[56] The magazine conducted a door-to-door canvass of 164,000 rural residents in thirty-four states and reported that Landon was ahead, 277 electoral votes to 160.[57] A mail-in poll conducted by the Publishers' Autocaster Service Company mostly in rural portions of thirty-nine states showed Landon well in the lead.[58] The "poll of all polls"—a sort of proto-aggregation of state and national surveys compiled by the *Cleveland News*—pointed to Landon's winning at least 310 electoral votes.[59]

Easily the most reputable and prominent of all the straw polls was that of the *Digest*. In a burst of hubris of the sort that has infected pollsters periodically ever since, the magazine declared that if "past experience is a criterion," its poll would reveal "*to within a fraction of 1 percent* the actual popular vote" in the Roosevelt-Landon race.[60] The *Digest* mailed some ten million postcard-

U. S. ELECTION SEEN CLOSEST SINCE '16 RACE

Large Mid-West Area Called Key to Result; Eve of Tense Poll Test Finds Big Guns of Both Sides Trained on Group of Doubtful States; Both Confident

New England Found Republican, While Solid South Stays Solidly Democratic; Industrial East Leans to Landon; G. O. P. Minimum Set at 209 Electoral Votes

By JOHN M. CUMMINGS

The Presidential election next Tuesday, in the opinion of most observers, should provide the closest result since 1916 when Woodrow Wilson squeezed out a victory by virtue of belated returns from California.

Whether President Franklin D. Roosevelt, heading the Democratic ticket, or Governor Alf M. Landon, the Republican nominee, will be the next occupant of the White House depends almost entirely on what happens

FIGURE 6. The conflicting findings of pre-election polls was an important reason many newspapers like the *Philadelphia Inquirer* expected the 1936 presidential election to be the closest in twenty years. (Credit: Library of Congress)

ballots in late summer, of which 2.35 million were returned. Partial results were published weekly in the *Digest* beginning in early September and the final tabulation appeared in the issue dated October 31, 1936. It projected that Landon would unseat Roosevelt by a large margin.

The profusion of polls may have stimulated popular interest,[61] but they also offered a confusing and "jumbled picture of the probable outcome," as the *Chicago Tribune* pointed out.[62] There was some expectation that the Roosevelt-Landon race would end as "another 1916," a close race decided when late returns from California swung the election to Woodrow Wilson over Charles Evans Hughes. Newspapers backing Landon emphasized that prospect.[63] Notable among them was Hearst's flamboyant *American*. "This looks to be another 1916 with the result hanging on any one of a half dozen major states," the *American* declared on its front page two days before the election.[64]

More reserved observers also anticipated a 1916 redux. William Lyon Phelps, a seventy-one-year-old author, scholar, and educator who had taught English for more than thirty years at Yale University, invoked that possibility in a short essay published on Election Day. Phelps wrote that "just as in 1916

[when] the voters went to the polls in complete uncertainty as to the outcome, so in the same frame of mind they are voting today."[65]

Other commentators expected a close election. Arthur Krock of the *New York Times* predicted a few weeks before the election that "Roosevelt's big majorities are over."[66] David Lawrence, a widely read newspaper columnist who had accurately predicted the outcomes of presidential elections since 1920, forecast a narrow victory for Roosevelt, by 270 electoral votes to 261. Lawrence—who said he had traveled twenty thousand miles during the three months before the election to assess popular sentiments—noted that Roosevelt's margin was so slim that he could ill afford to lose states that had "a question mark on them," such as Indiana or Minnesota.[67]

A week before the election, Arch Crossley met for lunch in Manhattan with thirteen other men conversant in, or writing about, politics and polling. Around the table, they surveyed themselves about the election's likely winner. Seven men picked Roosevelt; seven said Landon would win. When they turned to discuss state-by-state outcomes, the pundits gave Landon 273 electoral votes, seven more than a majority.[68]

The expressions of uncertainty about the election's outcome were not unfounded or contrived. After all, the Great Depression that had begun in 1929 was easing but far from over. Several million Americans were out of work. The defection of leading conservative Democrats from Roosevelt and his New Deal also contributed to pre-election uncertainty.[69] Hearst was just one of the prominent apostates. Other defectors were the party's ill-fated presidential nominees in 1924 and 1928—John W. Davis and Alfred E. Smith, respectively.[70]

Moreover, it seemed risky to dismiss or disregard the *Digest*'s poll. Its record of polling accuracy was formidable and the results it reported in 1936 could not be taken lightly.[71] As Crossley pointed out, "Many people relied implicitly upon the *Literary Digest*."[72] The magazine was scarcely modest about its polling successes. "When better polls are built," it boasted after its success in 1932, "*The Digest* will build them."[73] And as its poll got underway in late summer 1936, the magazine declared: "In election after election, as the public knows so well, The Literary Digest has forecast the result long before Election Day. For this journalistic feat and public service it has received thousands of tributes during many years."[74]

The *Digest* relished publishing such compliments. It referred to them as "press bouquets."[75] Among the "bouquets" was a comment by William Allen

White, publisher of the *Emporia Gazette* in Kansas, which the *Digest* printed after forecasting that Herbert Hoover would easily win in 1928. "The *Digest's* poll," White said, "was the first absolute proof of political clairvoyance that America and the world has ever witnessed."[76]

Not only had its nationwide poll accurately forecast the winner in four successive presidential races, the *Digest* had identified the winner in gubernatorial races in California and New York. And it had conducted national polls

---

BOX 2. "PRESS BOUQUETS" FOR *LITERARY DIGEST* POLL

The *Literary Digest* reveled in the supposed "uncanny" accuracy of its straw polls. Following the presidential election of 1928, the magazine devoted nearly a page to what it called "press bouquets"—compliments from American newspapers about its poll. The *Digest* accurately predicted Herbert Hoover's victory that year, but overestimated his popular vote by 5.1 percentage points. Even so, the compliments were many. Here is a selection:

- "Before election *The Digest*'s poll looked to be too good to be true. Now we see it was both good and true."—*San Francisco Chronicle*

- "It was so close to the actual result as to be uncanny."—*Wichita Beacon*

- "In view of the accuracy of *The Literary Digest*'s polls in 1924 and 1928, it might be a good idea hereafter quadrennially to quit holding elections and accept *The Digest*'s polls as final. It would save millions in money and in time."—Josephus Daniels, editor, *Raleigh News and Observer*

- "It appears that *The Digest*'s reputation is safe."—*Springfield* [MA] *Union*

- "The *Digest*'s poll was the first absolute proof of political clairvoyance that America and the world has ever witnessed."—William Allen White, *Emporia* [KS] *Gazette*

- "The poll is an extraordinary demonstration of what can be accomplished in the way of political prediction by careful planning and efficient execution."—*Boston Transcript*

- "One of the shining victors in this campaign is *The Literary Digest*. The result justified the integrity and accuracy of its remarkable straw vote."—*New York Evening Post*

- "If *The Literary Digest* ever takes another poll, it should be a guide for newspapers, political leaders, and election-betting rings alike."—*Helena* [MT] *Independent*

- "We congratulate *The Digest*'s straw-gatherers once more on a prodigious success."—*New York Herald Tribune*

- "Four years hence there will be less disposition to question the accuracy of the poll if *The Literary Digest* sees fit to repeat it."—*Washington Post*

about Prohibition and Roosevelt's New Deal. As prestigious as it was, the *Digest*'s poll had notable, even fairly obvious, defects. Its lead time for receiving, compiling, and counting ballots meant that the effective cutoff date for returning a ballot in time to have it counted was about two weeks before the election.[77] As such, the *Digest* was unable to detect late-in-the-campaign shifts in popular sentiment, which Gallup claimed took place in 1936.[78]

More problematic was that the *Digest* had no control over who responded and had little understanding of the respondents and their political leanings, beyond asking them to report state of residence and for whom they had voted in the previous presidential election. As the editors realized, the poll's success rested in part on good fortune. They acknowledged, for example, that "the almost magical accuracy" of the *Digest*'s forecast in the 1932 election "was due to errors . . . that canceled each other."[79]

As critics noted, the *Digest*'s poll tended to oversample Republicans.[80] The magazine was aware of this flaw and puzzled by it, conceding that it had often wondered "why we were getting better cooperation in what we always considered as a public service from Republicans than we were from Democrats. Do Republicans live nearer mail-boxes? Do Democrats generally disapprove of straw polls? We don't know that answer."[81]

Curiously, the pages of the *Literary Digest* reveal scant interest in modifying, refining, or explaining in detail its mass-polling technique. It rejected the statistical adjustment of data known as weighting, saying it preferred avoiding anything that could be interpreted as compromising the poll's impartiality, or what the *Digest* called "our well-earned reputation for scrupulous bookkeeping."[82] The magazine that developed the most respected straw poll of the early twentieth century was not so much interested in embryonic survey research as in using its poll as a device to encourage participants to subscribe.[83]

Crossley worked at the magazine's market research department in the 1920s and later recalled that *Digest* polls "were conducted by the Circulation Department with the . . . purpose of selling more subscriptions. With each ballot that went out there was attached a card invitation to subscribe." Crossley said that millions of ballot-postcards were sent "purely because they had discovered that the more they mailed out the more subscriptions they would get in and the rate would be on a known and pretty much fixed basis. The method used was to hire a lot of men to do nothing but address envelopes and check in the results."[84]

Twenty million postcard-ballots were mailed in 1932. In what no doubt was a sign of the magazine's declining financial health, half that number went out in 1936. By then, the *Digest* was a fading publication, past its zenith. From 1910 to 1930, as *Time* magazine later acknowledged, the *Digest* was "far & away the most successful current events magazine in the U.S."[85] Its peak of 1.5 million subscribers was reached in the early 1920s. But with competition from the likes of *Time*—which was founded in 1923 and promised an edgier, more provocative, more opinionated treatment of the week's news—the *Digest*'s circulation had dwindled to about 685,000 in 1936.[86]

The newsroom of the *Digest* had become an unsettled place. In 1933, Arthur Stimson Draper, an editor at the *New York Herald Tribune*, was brought in to run the magazine. He lasted two years, during which time he sent Edward Price Bell, a Chicago journalist, on a round-the-world mission to interview Hitler,[87] Mussolini,[88] and other leaders in a quixotic campaign to promote peaceable international relations.[89] Wilfred Funk, son of the magazine's founder, took over when Draper left. Funk's editorship was likewise rocky. He reportedly sought funds to review and supplement the poll's mailing list, but the publisher turned him down.[90]

As the 1936 poll was underway, turmoil rippled through the newsroom. Amid rumors of disputes about how the poll was being run, the managing editor, Morton Savell, quit a month before the election.[91] By then, more than five hundred thousand ballots had been returned and counted in the *Digest*'s poll, and they showed Landon well ahead of Roosevelt.

There is little doubt the *Digest*'s poll and its reputation for accuracy injected optimism into the Landon camp while stirring at least mild concern among some Democrats.[92] James Hagerty, who covered the Landon campaign for the *New York Times*, wrote in the campaign's closing days that the *Digest*'s survey was "the principal source of hope" among Landon's top advisers and that results had "been very encouraging to Governor Landon. He is understood to hold, in company with his close friends, that, inasmuch as this poll has always previously pointed to the winner, there is no reason to doubt its accuracy now."[93] Similarly, Arthur Sears Henning, Washington bureau chief for the pro-Landon *Chicago Tribune*,[94] wrote that "Republicans find themselves fortified by the Digest poll which beginning in 1920 has never failed to forecast the outcome of a presidential election with amazing accuracy."[95] Frank R. Kent of the *Baltimore Sun* noted in late October 1936 that the *Digest* poll "is the main thing that buoys up the Republicans."[96]

John D. M. Hamilton, chairman of the Republican National Committee in 1936, cited the *Digest*'s poll in predicting on the Sunday before the election that Landon would roll up at least 320 electoral votes.[97] If anything, Hamilton said, the *Digest*'s poll was too conservative and had failed to capture a late swing to the Republicans. Even so, he commended the *Digest* for conducting "the only poll in the history of this country which has a 100 per cent record for accuracy in predicting the result."[98]

Hamilton's claim that Landon would win no fewer than 320 electoral votes was not only well off-target; it may have been disingenuous bluster. In an oral history interview thirty years after the election, Hamilton offered conflicting views about the importance of the *Digest*'s surveys. At one point in the interview, Hamilton said the poll was a factor in his believing that Landon could win. Elsewhere in the interview, however, Hamilton said he told Landon privately two days before the election—on the same day of Hamilton's bravado public prediction, in fact—that the governor would carry no more than five or six states.[99]

Final results of the *Digest*'s survey were cited in a campaign diary kept by Victor Anderson, Landon's "attendant" or bodyguard.[100] Anderson's diary entry for October 28, 1936, described a huge turnout for Landon's appearances in New York City and said: "The tide is turning beyond a doubt. I wonder if it is starting soon enough. The opposition are on the run." Anderson seemed somewhat subdued the next day, writing, "Everybody has the jitters. The Literary Digest Poll reports today show Landon to win. All the newspaper men on our train, with the exception of one, are for Roosevelt. I understand that the President is expecting a landslide in his favor." Anderson added, perhaps dutifully: "Oh, well, I still think we have a fighting chance—and if we get New York—it's in the bag."[101]

It didn't take long on Election Night to sweep away notions that Landon would unseat Roosevelt, or that the vote would be close. The early returns from Republican strongholds in Connecticut and Pennsylvania—states that had resisted the Roosevelt landslide in 1932—signaled a lopsided victory for the President.[102] New York State went overwhelmingly to Roosevelt. By 11 p.m., the "superlandslide" was sweeping the country and the governor had given up and gone to bed.[103]

The outcome irreparably shattered the *Literary Digest*'s reputation. "American citizens had come to look upon this poll as an authentic sampling of popular opinion," the *Philadelphia Inquirer* observed, adding: "What a crash of faith, what a shattering of idols, the election returns brought!"[104] The *New York Herald Tribune* wrote: "Over the rout and wreck of 'The Literary Digest's' once proud infallibility it is perhaps kinder to draw the veil."[105]

No one seemed more baffled by the landslide than Funk. He suggested that perhaps "the public had a revolution against the Republican candidates in the last few weeks when it was too late to show in our poll."[106] He noted "the last returns" in the *Digest's* poll had been received weeks before the election and in the interval, "there may have been a shift in voting sentiment."[107] Funk's bewilderment found expression as well in the *Digest's* post-election issue, which said: "We used precisely the same method that had scored four bull's eyes in four previous tries. And we were far from correct. Why? We ask that question in all sincerity, because *we want to know.*"[108]

The absence of clear answers allowed others, notably Gallup, to interpret the polling debacle. That interpretation emerged quickly and hardened into conventional wisdom that endures to this day. The interpretation rested on conjecture,[109] but seemed plausible enough. It argued that the *Digest's* methods were hopelessly skewed to well-to-do voters because the list the magazine used to send its ten million ballots was drawn largely from telephone directories and automobile registration rosters. Voters who had telephones and owned cars were comparatively affluent, the argument went, and the affluent tended to favor Landon. Put another way, the mailing list effectively excluded the mass of lower-income voters who didn't have phones or cars but supported Roosevelt. Gallup, who was eager to establish himself and his emergent polling franchise as preeminent in opinion research,[110] likened the *Digest's* polling technique to a boy who samples only the best portions of a lemon meringue pie: "he eats the meringue on top and the lemon in the middle, but ignores most of the crust on the bottom."[111]

Gallup was scarcely alone in arguing that the *Digest's* surveying technique was irredeemably flawed. Claude E. Robinson, a Gallup associate and author of the pioneering work *Straw Votes: A Study of Political Prediction,* wrote in September 1936 that the *Digest* poll was a "canvass not of the whole electorate, but of the telephone and automobile owning portion of the electorate, giving the returns the political bias of voters in the higher income levels. People who do not own a telephone or an automobile are excluded from participation in the straw vote, which means that low income voters are not represented in the Digest sample in correct proportion to their voting strength."[112]

Similarly, Harold Gosnell, a political scientist at the University of Chicago, wrote that the *Digest's* "sample was overloaded with persons in the high income groups because the [mailing] lists were made up largely from telephone books and automobile registrations."[113] James Farley, chairman of the Democratic

National Committee, said after the election, "I always contended that The Literary Digest only covered adequately those in the upper income brackets and that the great masses of people, the people of small salaries, who supported President Roosevelt, didn't receive ballots in the same proportion as those in the upper income brackets."[114]

In meek rebuttal, the *Digest* argued "the 'have-nots' did not reelect Mr. Roosevelt. That they contributed to his astonishing plurality, no one can doubt. But the fact remains that a majority of farmers, doctors, grocers and candlestick-makers *also* voted for the President."[115] "Besides," the *Digest* said, "we *did* reach these so-called 'have-not' strata." The magazine noted that it sent ballots to one out of three registered voters in Chicago, every other registered voter in Allentown, Pennsylvania, and every registered voter in Scranton, Pennsylvania. But even from those cities, the polling returns were far off target: most respondents favored Landon, but voters went overwhelmingly for Roosevelt.[116]

The *Digest* did not emphasize its argument about having reached "have-not" voters. So it was left to Gallup, who often pushed *his* interpretation about the magazine's flawed approach. In a self-congratulatory, year-end appraisal published in the *Washington Post*, Gallup wrote: "The Digest straw votes have customarily depended on mere numbers—millions of straws scattered without pre-arrangement. Almost every time, as it actually turned out, Digest ballots went to persons of superior income, because the available list of names—chiefly telephone directories and automobile lists—overrepresent wealthy people. This method leaves an important stratum of people with little income—or no income—almost untouched."[117]

Gallup returned to this argument in a journal article published in 1938, writing: "With the exception of a few cities, the Digest sampled only owners of automobiles and telephones. It neglected for the most part the very poor and those with little purchasing power. Before 1936, political sentiment in the upper income groups was sufficiently representative of the whole voting population to enable the Digest to get by. But in 1936 the lines of political cleavage were severely drawn between the haves and the have-nots, and the income bias in the Digest sample resulted in a disproportionate number of Landon votes."[118]

That explanation, or slight variations on it, solidified into conventional wisdom about the *Digest's* epic failure. But that interpretation has been disputed in recent years in imaginative analyses that have drawn on data collected in 1937 in an otherwise little-recalled Gallup poll. These studies have pointed to what is a more plausible explanation for the polling debacle—that opponents of Roosevelt who received the *Digest*'s postcard ballots were eager to participate in the *Digest*'s survey and did so in numbers far greater than supporters of the president. Such a disparity is called "nonresponse bias."

Interestingly, suggestions that Roosevelt's foes were more motivated to participate in the *Digest* poll than were his supporters emerged soon after the election in 1936. "What seems to have happened," the *Editor and Publisher* trade journal said, "is that [postcard ballots] were returned in larger numbers by those who regarded four years more of Roosevelt as death and damnation than by the followers of the man in the White House. This is a situation for which the Digest technique provides no control: it was the fatal defect in the poll."[119]

Arch Crossley likewise hinted at nonresponse bias in an article that analyzed the election for *Public Opinion Quarterly*. Crossley noted that the *Digest* depended "for its accuracy not only upon its mailing list, but more especially upon the degree to which each class of voter returns the postcards. . . . The *Digest* with its millions of postcards offers an ideal medium for an expression of protest" by "those who possess an urgent desire to register their opinions."[120] Crossley surmised that the *Digest* greatly overestimated support for Landon "probably because of the anti-Roosevelt feeling among those who returned the cards."[121] In other words, thousands of respondents seized on the *Digest* poll as a means of registering deep disapproval of Roosevelt and his New Deal policies.

That interpretation stirred little sustained discussion and soon fell dormant. It was resurrected in 1976 in an essay by Maurice Bryson, a statistician at Colorado State University. Bryson dismissed the conventional explanation of the *Digest*'s poll failure as "inherently implausible." He pointed out that telephone ownership was "not all that unusual" during the Depression and that Landon received his greatest support in rural states outside the South "where telephones were relatively scarce."[122] Bryson suggested that the *Digest*'s poll fell victim to its reliance on the "voluntary response" of its participants, adding that "it seems clear that the minority of anti-Roosevelt voters felt more strongly about the election than did the pro-Roosevelt majority." He conceded that his arguments represented "scanty proof" of his claim but said nonetheless they "should be enough to make one suspicious" of the conventional interpretation.[123]

Twelve years later in *Public Opinion Quarterly*, Peverill Squire presented more intriguing evidence of nonresponse bias—evidence drawn from questions about the *Digest*'s survey that had been included in a Gallup poll in 1937.[124] "This survey is the best tool for determining why the *Literary Digest* poll failed," Squire asserted, while acknowledging that several shortcomings made the Gallup poll a less-than-ideal sample.[125] Even so, Squire argued that if all ten million recipients of ballots in the *Digest*'s poll in 1936 had participated, "the results would have, at least, correctly predicted Roosevelt a winner."[126]

In a superb analysis that also drew on the 1937 Gallup poll data, Dominic Lusinchi presented in 2012 a highly persuasive case that nonresponse bias was indeed the main culprit of the *Digest*'s polling failure.[127] Writing in *Social Science History*, Lusinchi acknowledged, as Squire had, that the 1937 Gallup data are "limited and imperfect" but nonetheless are quite revealing when statistical adjustments are applied, a process known as "weighting."

Lusinchi reported that "Landon's supporters were much more likely to return their straw ballots than Roosevelt's"—a finding central to the hypothesis of nonresponse bias—and that poll "respondents and nonrespondents favored opposite candidates." Much of the *Digest*'s error "can be attributed to nonresponse bias," Lusinchi wrote, adding, "Had everybody on the original *Digest* [mailing] list returned his or her straw ballot, the magazine would have been in a position to forecast the correct winner of the election: Roosevelt."[128]

He also reported finding that people who owned either cars or telephones *supported* Roosevelt, thus challenging the conventional interpretation that Gallup and others had popularized. "If relying on telephone directories and car registration lists was not the problem" for the *Digest*'s poll, Lusinchi pointed out, "then the cause of the *Digest*'s poll blunder must lie elsewhere"— that is, in nonresponse bias.

Lusinchi's work was a *tour de force* that ought to have reset popular and scholarly understanding about the *Digest*'s poll debacle. But as Lusinchi noted in his article, the conventional explanation established long ago "does not seem to want to go away. Like other myths . . . it has acquired a life of its own."[129]

The polling failure of 1936 introduced themes and established patterns that have reemerged periodically in presidential elections in the eighty years that followed. Notably, the *Digest*'s debacle stands as an enduring reminder that polling inaccuracy has deep roots. The *Digest*'s failure was so unambiguous— and occurred so early in the modern history of survey research—that it introduced a sense of nagging doubt about polling, its methodologies, and its effectiveness in estimating election outcomes. After all, if the greatest election oracle of its time could spectacularly fail, then why wouldn't other polls sometimes go awry as well?

What's more, the clash of the *Digest* vs. Gallup and the other upstarts introduced an emphasis on the competitiveness of election polling, about which poll was most accurate. The competitive ethos endures. Pollsters often are eager to call attention to their surveys that come close to estimating election outcomes. It's become a point of pride.

At the same time, the 1936 election brought endorsement of the presumed value of "shoe-leather" reporting, of assessing the likely outcomes on the basis of observation, interviews, and intuition. As we've seen, reporters assigned to the respective campaign trains accurately and overwhelmingly expected Roosevelt to win. Even more impressive was James Farley's spot-on prediction. Farley, who in 1936 was chairman of the Democratic National Committee, estimated that Roosevelt would win all but two states, Maine and Vermont.[130] For his accuracy, Farley was hailed in the inaugural issue of the *Public Opinion Quarterly* as "the best predictor of them all."[131]

In developing his prediction, Farley relied on reports, estimates, and impressions submitted at his instruction by hundreds of Democratic party officials, officeholders, activists, and patronage workers across the country. Often, those estimates understated the expected scope of Roosevelt's victory.[132] To be sure, not all qualitative assessments that year were quite so close to the mark. David Lawrence, the syndicated columnist, traveled widely during the campaign and brought to bear what he called "investigation plus judgment" in making his forecast that Roosevelt would win, but narrowly.

The polls in the 1936 campaign were the targets of unflattering commentary by some prominent journalists who doubted the value and accuracy of election polls. These spasms of early poll-bashing deepened to hostility in presidential elections to come. For example, Frank Kent of the *Baltimore Sun* wrote after the election: "If the last election means an end of nation-wide polls and straw ballots by newspapers, magazines, and other agencies, a good many people will rejoice. To a vast number these polls have been an irritation and annoyance. Even when they correctly forecast the result they do not seem to serve any very useful purpose."[133]

The *Philadelphia Inquirer* assailed "the purported predictors" for having "failed lamentably to give the voters a reasonably accurate intimation of what was about to happen." The *Inquirer* further declared, "If the election proved anything other than that the country wanted Mr. Roosevelt to go on being president, it was that straw votes and delphic prognostications don't mean much in American politics."[134] The *New York Times* questioned "whether the public interest is actually well served by unofficial polls which attempt to reflect the shift of American opinion on matters of great political importance."[135]

The *Times* also anticipated the demise of the *Digest* poll, saying in a post-election editorial: "It will scarcely venture to show its face again in the Congressional elections of 1938 or the Presidential campaign four years from now. . . . It certainly will never be again the bogy or oracle as which it had so long figured in our elections."[136] The *Times* was right. The *Digest* never polled again. The magazine hinted that it might resume its polling in posing this rhetorical question shortly after the 1936 election: "Should the University of Minnesota, with the greatest record in modern football, give up the sport because it finally lost a game, after a string of twenty-one victories?"[137] Minnesota's unbeaten streak had been snapped by Northwestern University in an upset, 6–0, four days before the election. The implication was that the *Digest* wouldn't give up, either.

But less than a year after its polling debacle, the *Digest* was sold, reportedly for two hundred thousand dollars,[138] to the owners of the *Review of Reviews*, a monthly journal that had been established in 1891. The combined weekly publication was called *The Digest*. Its former name, *Literary Digest*, was restored when the magazine was sold again, in 1938, to a group headed by George F. Havell, who announced that the magazine would no longer conduct opinion polls.

Havell appealed for donations to keep the magazine alive, saying the *Digest* was a national institution. But the contributions became entangled in disputes with creditors and were scarcely enough to keep the magazine afloat. The *Digest* suspended publication in early 1938 and in May that year was acquired and absorbed by *Time*. By then, its subscriber base had dropped to 250,000.[139]

The *Digest* fell victim not so much to its dramatic polling failure as to flagging circulation and upstart competition.[140] "It lost out," the *New York Times* said, "because it couldn't adapt its formula to a jazzier lot of young people, whose attention is usually there when one wants it here."[141] What readers "want in this age," said the *Topeka State Journal*, "are large pictures and short paragraphs."[142] The *Digest* emphasized neither.

Funk, the editor at the time of the polling debacle, remained in the publishing business, launching a magazine in 1937 called *Your Life* and later starting

FIGURE 7. Wilfred J. Funk, editor of the *Literary Digest* at the time of its 1936 debacle, said he had "a very good chuckle" when pre-election polls badly misfired in the 1948 presidential race. (Credit: Associated Press/Harry Harris)

a book-printing company. In 1948, reporters looked him up for comment about the errant polls in that year's election. It was a fiasco that became more famous than the *Digest*'s debacle, in which President Harry Truman prevailed against all polling forecasts. "I get a very good chuckle out of this," Funk said soon after the 1948 election, adding, "nothing malicious, mind you. We were told by contemporary pollsters [in 1936] that we had been unscientific. I'm afraid they made the same mistakes. I'm afraid the word 'science' isn't going to be used with a poll for a long time."[143]

CHAPTER 3

"The Defeat of the Pollsters"

The Epic Fail of 1948

An undying myth of the 1948 presidential campaign, when Harry S. Truman won reelection to the presidency in a smashing upset, is that pollsters ended their fieldwork prematurely and thus failed to detect popular sentiment flowing decisively away from the odds-on favorite, Republican Thomas E. Dewey.[1] It's a plausible alibi for an epic polling failure. But that's not quite how it was.

Alone among the nationally prominent quasi-scientific pollsters of the time, Elmo Roper *did* conduct a survey in the week before the election. He decided against publishing the results because they showed nothing new. They reinforced what Roper had already detected and reported nearly two months earlier: Dewey held an insurmountable lead and was destined for victory. Besides, Roper had said on September 9, 1948, that he would publish no further poll results on the election unless a "political miracle" intervened.[2] His poll taken during the closing week of October showed slight movement toward Truman and slight movement away from Dewey. But those tendencies were hardly enough to suggest an upset was in the making, hardly enough to qualify as a political miracle.[3]

Roper's record in forecasting presidential elections was unsurpassed among the trio of prominent pollsters who included George H. Gallup and Archibald Crossley. Roper's polling closely anticipated the outcomes in the elections of 1936, 1940, and 1944, coming within a percentage point each time in projecting Franklin Roosevelt's victories. Roper's polls came with an asterisk, though. He oversampled Democratic voters in the South (then solidly for Democratic candidates) and oversampled Republicans elsewhere. The point was to cancel out sizable regional errors in order to report what were strikingly accurate national estimates.[4]

It was a called a compensating sample, a dicey technique that's almost unheard of nowadays. In retrospect, it was a method that seemed certain to fail Roper one day. But in 1948, Roper projected a sense of weary confidence as he polled his fourth presidential election. After the successes of the three previous elections, he figured polling had little to prove. Election polling by 1948 had come of age.

Roper said as much on *Where the People Stand*, his fifteen-minute Sunday afternoon show on CBS radio.[5] His program on September 12, 1948, was notable for Roper's casual confidence about the Truman-Dewey race and for his dismissal of the value of pre-election polling. "So right here and now," Roper said that afternoon, "I'd like to finish off my share in this whole business by predicting the election of Thomas E. Dewey by a heavy margin. I'd like to say that's that, and turn my attention to other and more valuable considerations. Don't misunderstand me—I'm not saying that our choice of a President of the United States in unimportant.

"But I am saying that presidential polls are unimportant. It seems absolutely unimportant to check every few minutes to see if Truman has gained six-tenths of a percent as a result of his whirlwind campaign on Labor Day." The previous three elections, Roper said, had confirmed the validity of election polling. "It's true that in the past, presidential polls did serve a useful function in proving and publicizing the value of the new science of public opinion research," he said, adding, "But that science is no longer young. It has come of age and proved its accuracy and worth."[6]

Election polling, he said, had become something of "a stunt, like balancing cocktail glasses on top of each other or tearing a telephone book in two. It's impressive. It has a certain fascination. But it tells us very little that we wouldn't find out even if poll-taking had never been invented."[7] It was a remarkable soliloquy that traced the upper reaches of pollster cockiness in 1948 while scoffing that the practice itself was of little value. Roper's pronouncement contributed as well to the gathering sense that Dewey's triumph and Truman's repudiation were inevitable. That outcome *was* inevitable, just a matter of time, Roper said that September afternoon. Over the two months that followed, no pundit, journalist, or pollster offered anything beyond muted dissent.

Roper seemed an unlikely detractor of opinion polling. He was, after all, a leading figure in the still-emerging polling landscape, probably second only

FIGURE 8. Cigar-smoking Elmo Roper, a failed jeweler who became prominent in opinion research, sometimes expressed misgivings about election polls. Before the election in 1948, he likened them to the stunt of tearing a telephone book in two. (Credit: Leonard McCombe/ Getty Images)

to Gallup in pollster name recognition. His columns about opinion polling were syndicated to sixty-six client newspapers in 1948, about one-quarter of Gallup's subscriber base.[8] The column, together with his polling for *Fortune* magazine and his weekly spots on CBS radio, enabled Roper routinely to reach millions of Americans.

Even so, Roper tended to suffer in comparison to Gallup. Roper's name never became synonymous with polling, as Gallup's did. Gallup, who was taller and heftier than Roper, cut the more imposing figure. Roper was dapper, though. He wore his suits well. But he peered a bit warily from behind wire-rimmed glasses perched on his roundish face, and he spoke with a nasal intonation. Often jammed in a corner of his mouth was the stub of a cigar.

Roper's smug confidence about Dewey's prospects in 1948 also reflected a mistaken interpretation, drawn from the three previous presidential elections, that campaigns mattered little. They did not change election outcomes.[9] Unexpected events might have that effect, Roper said, but not campaign oratory. In presidential elections, voter preferences were believed to be solidified by Labor Day. Roper underscored that notion the day before the election, in a front-page report in the *New York Herald Tribune*. "Apparently," he wrote, "three years of *performance* are a more determining factor with voters than three months of campaign oratory." Dewey, he wrote, "is in." Roper predicted Dewey would defeat Truman by 15 percentage points. "If he runs for re-election in 1952," Roper said, "he should know that the public's judgment will be on Dewey the public servant, not Dewey the campaigner."[10]

Roper may have been extreme in his certainty, but his confidence in Dewey's victory was widely shared. Arch Crossley, who also doubted that campaigns mattered much in voters' preferences,[11] declared in his final pre-election report: "If every adult citizen in the United States turned out on Election Day, the best Truman could have hoped for would be a tie." Crossley said Dewey was "assured of victory" and figured he was ahead by 5 percentage points.[12]

Gallup likewise estimated Dewey's lead was 5 points as the campaign neared its end—and noted that his polls had never erred in a national election.[13] His final pre-election polling report, released on Halloween, was unambiguous. Dewey, the report said, "will win the presidential election with a substantial majority of electoral votes."[14] Gallup's statement did not mention that his estimates were derived from combining the organization's final two pre-election polls in October, a bit of methodological sleight of hand that produced a larger overall sample of voters, presumably to enhance the prospect of an accurate reading.[15]

There was nonetheless abundant reason for the pollsters' confidence: Truman, who had become president on Franklin Roosevelt's death in April 1945, was not particularly popular, not an engaging speaker, and often dismissed as a political accident. He was earnest enough, but did not quite seem up to the job. "There is no question that Mr. Truman has done his best, given everything that is in him to his office," the *Miami Herald* said in an election-eve editorial. "But the country needs more than what Harry S. Truman can give."[16] Truman was nominated for a full term in 1948 after some Democrats, including Franklin Roosevelt's three sons, tried to persuade Dwight D. Eisenhower, America's World War II hero-general, to accept the party's nomination. Truman even flirted with the idea of Eisenhower's leading the ticket, privately proposing in 1947 that the general run for president while he, Truman, would again be the candidate for vice president.[17]

That idea, which was floated as a contingency to thwart General Douglas MacArthur's prospective candidacy on the Republican ticket, faded away in

1948. But strife still convulsed the Democratic party. In January, Henry Wallace, the vice president during Roosevelt's third term, announced his candidacy for president on the newly formed Progressive party ticket. The Democrats split again in July, at their nominating convention in Philadelphia. A Southern-based states' rights faction—segregationists commonly called the Dixiecrats—walked out to protest the party's civil rights platform, which proposed the integration of the U.S. armed forces. Soon afterward, the Dixiecrats nominated Strom Thurmond, the South Carolina governor, as their presidential candidate.

Meanwhile, Republicans were exceedingly confident. They had won control of both houses of Congress in the 1946 midterm elections. After a spirited primary campaign in 1948, Dewey gained the party's nomination for president. Dewey was battle-tested and competent. He had easily won reelection as New York governor in 1946. He had been the party's presidential nominee in 1944 but lost to Roosevelt after running an aggressive campaign. It was perhaps too aggressive: at one point, Dewey had called Roosevelt a traitor for not better preparing for the Japanese sneak attack at Pearl Harbor in December 1941. In the 1948 campaign, Dewey was persuaded to give up aggressive tactics for a cooler, smoother, more presidential approach.[18]

Given the schisms among the Democrats, the momentum of the Republicans, and the emphatic polling data, predictions that Dewey was headed to victory drew little dispute. Dewey's victory seemed to be as close to a sure thing as American politics could offer. Prominent and otherwise, journalists offered no serious challenge to the poll-driven narrative that Dewey was destined to win, and win easily.

If anything, their expressions of confidence in Dewey's victory became more unshakable as the election neared. For example, George Van Slyke, a veteran political reporter for the New York Sun, began his front-page preview of the election by writing: "Gov. Thomas E. Dewey tomorrow will be elected thirty-third president of the United States. The Republican sweep . . . assures the G.O.P. nominee a minimum of 345, and a probable 365, electoral vote[s]. The majority in the electoral college is 266."[19]

The Detroit Free Press in an Election Day editorial speculated on whether Truman would cooperate with the new president-elect. "Seventy-nine days will elapse between the election of Thomas E. Dewey as President of the United States and his inauguration on Jan. 20, 1949," the newspaper said. "They may be the most critical 79 days in the world's history. The extent to which President Truman permits President-elect Dewey to share in the decisions of the next 11 weeks may be decisive for our own future as well as for that of free governments everywhere."[20]

Fred Othman, the Hollywood columnist for the United Press wire service, wrote a sentimental sendoff to Truman. "The ballots haven't been counted at this writing," Othman said in a column written for publication on Election Day, "but there seems to be no further need for holding up an affectionate farewell to Harry Truman, who will go down in history as the President that nobody hated. . . . We're going to miss Li'l Ole Harry."[21] The *Kiplinger Washington Letter* said in its pre-election edition that Dewey's election would be clear by midnight on Election Night, and predicted he "will be in [office] for eight years, until '57."[22]

Drew Pearson's post-election syndicated column, written before the election for publication on the day afterward, considered the likely makeup of a Dewey administration, writing: "The men around Dewey who will take over the White House . . . are an exciting, hard-working, close-knit clique who function with almost too much perfection and are loaded with calculated coordination."[23] The *Washington Post* and many other subscribing newspapers published the column.[24] The *Daily Sentinel* of Hanford, California, did not. That small newspaper left blank the space where Pearson's column was to have appeared. The empty space was embroidered by a thick black rule and an explanation appeared nearby: the empty space was "In memory of Drew Pearson's column on 'President Dewey.'"[25]

Meanwhile, the country's fifty leading political reporters, surveyed by *Newsweek* magazine three weeks before the election, unanimously picked Dewey to win.[26] *Newsweek* noted that its survey of political reporters had "always correctly picked the winner." The gossip columnist Walter Winchell said of that prediction: "*Newsweek* has 50 political writers forecasting a Dewey sweep. Do you have to be an expert to predict that? It's like forecasting a rooster will crow at daybreak."[27]

Among the journalists who participated in the *Newsweek* survey was Frank Kent, a veteran political columnist for the *Baltimore Sun*. He mused in his Election Day column about the unlikelihood of miracles in presidential elections. "Someday, of course, the political miracle may happen," he wrote. "Someday the prophets, polls, experts, analysts and 'trained observers' may all turn out to be wrong and the Presidential candidate whom all the 'authorities' agree is a beaten man will come suddenly from behind and tear across the line a victor." Such an upset had never happened in a U.S. presidential election, Kent noted, suggesting that nothing of the sort was in the offing. It "would seem a political miracle, indeed, if Mr. Truman could win today against any Republican candidate."[28]

Nor did other prominent journalists consider the prospect of an upset. The brothers Joseph and Stewart Alsop declared in their syndicated column written before but published the day after the election, "The first postelection question is how the Government can get through the next 10 weeks. . . . Events will not wait patiently until Thomas E. Dewey officially replaces Harry S. Truman."[29]

Early editions of the *Washington Post* published a glowing, day-after-the-election profile of Dewey, whom the newspaper called the "president-elect." The article said: "A vigorous trait, rooted in the traditions of our pioneer forefathers, dominates the scintillating success story of Thomas Edmund Dewey, yesterday elected to become the thirty-third president of the United States. That trait is persistence." The profile declared in closing, "This same trait, victorious Republicans believe, will make him a great president."[30]

Faint challenges to the campaign's dominant narrative arose here and there before the election. These objections were typically muffled, or offered whimsically. In mid-July 1948, Earl Wilson, the *New York Post*'s gossip and nightlife columnist, polled one hundred New Yorkers and tourists at restaurants, bars, and cafes near Broadway. Wilson reported that his impromptu survey had Truman in the lead, 45–41. The survey, unrepresentative though it was, "is guaranteed to be as accurate as the Gallup Poll or a Ouija board," Wilson wrote.[31]

Another murmur came from Jennings Perry, a liberal columnist for the *New York Star*. A week before the election, Perry wrote that "the vote is going to be closer than you think" between Dewey and Truman. He offered no evidence for his assessment, beyond his impressions that the president had probably narrowed the gap "by being peppery, by sticking to his guns, by getting out of the White House and taking his show on the road. . . . He no longer appears futile, no matter what the polls report, since he has made himself the symbol of the real virility of his party."[32]

On Election Day in William Randolph Hearst's *New York Journal-American*, the writer Paul Gallico gave expression to vague qualms about the Dewey-will-win narrative, saying: "It would be very funny if everybody read the signs wrong and Truman got in again. Ha ha! Very funny! Have I got a sense of humor! Kills you with laughs. Can't you see all the poll-takers leaving town by the first bus? I will be able to see them all right, because I will be on the same bus. This Department [his column] has been writing as though Dewey had been president for the last three months. You know, wise guy. Dewey can't lose."[33]

Occasionally during the campaign, the mildly contrarian views of Louis H. Bean popped up.[34] Bean was an Agriculture Department economist who early in 1948 brought out *How to Predict Elections*, a thin monograph containing passages that suggested a Democratic victory in the presidential election that year wasn't out of the question.[35] In early October, Bean said the race was tighter than polling indicated, that Dewey was probably ahead of Truman by 52 percent to 48 percent.[36]

After the election, a minor media myth emerged, alleging that Bean had *predicted* Truman's victory—a myth propelled by Bean's book publisher and by an article in the *New York Herald Tribune*, the newspaper that syndicated Roper's polling column. "Fame of a sort tapped at the door of Louis H. Bean, a government economist, this week," the article stated, adding that Bean had predicted months earlier that the Democrats would retain the presidency.[37]

Roper, whose column was syndicated by the *Herald Tribune*, was so irritated about the article that he wrote to the managing editor to complain. Roper argued that Bean had presented no unequivocal prediction in *How to Predict Elections*. Moreover, Bean had told a reporter for the Scripps-Howard news service that "it would take a turnout of 60 million voters to even give Truman a fighting chance."[38] The 1948 election brought out 48.8 million voters. *Newsweek* magazine also sought to puncture the extravagant claims about Bean's forecast, noting that he had said Truman would carry only nine states if turnout was no greater than 51 million voters and only eighteen states if turnout reached 58 million.[39] Truman carried twenty-eight states.

Bean's private correspondence further undercuts the notion he accurately predicted the election. Theodore Rosenof reported in a journal article in 2007 that in a letter dated October 29, 1948, Bean said he was "inclined to think that the poll experts will turn out to be right . . . that this campaign will bring about relatively little change in attitudes and that voters will behave on election day about as they said they would some weeks or months back."[40] The myth of Louis Bean nevertheless proved tenacious. In its obituary about Bean, who died in 1994, the *New York Times* said the economist "became nationally known for a book that predicted Harry S. Truman's surprise victory in the 1948 Presidential election."[41] That's not what the book said, and Bean during the campaign did not insist, publicly or privately, that Truman was headed for victory.

The pollsters, meanwhile, brushed aside late-campaign warnings about their polls. Four days before the election, Senator J. Howard McGrath, chairman of the Democratic National Committee, sent Arch Crossley a lengthy telegram saying the pollster's state-by-state figures were suspect and should be revised. McGrath argued that when adjusted to account for Crossley's state-by-state polling errors in the 1944 campaign, Crossley's final poll result would stand at 47.5 percent for Dewey, 47.2 percent for Truman, "which is practically a tie." McGrath added: "These are not my opinions that I am expressing, but your own figures properly adjusted and correctly interpreted." The advantage, McGrath argued, "is with Truman, not Dewey."[42]

Crossley said in reply that McGrath's wire had not been received until the day before the election and that he "would have been glad to show you at any time during the campaign the details of our findings." Crossley said he was certain that McGrath "would have drawn [the] conclusion that [Truman's] election is and has been in recent weeks extremely unlikely."[43]

McGrath sent a similar notice to Gallup, saying, "Your polls this year do not tell a complete story nor give an accurate interpretation of your own findings." The warning was answered with a cocksure response. Gallup, according to the Associated Press, said "the only answer to Mr. McGrath will come on next Tuesday." He said that while "we've never reached the point yet where we claim infallibility," on Election Day "the whole world will be able to see down to the last percentage point how good we are."[44]

The president also insisted the polls were misleading. In whistle-stop railway tours that crisscrossed the country, Truman likened the polls to sleeping pills, "designed to lull the voters into sleeping on election day. You might call them sleeping polls."[45] He predicted that "there will be more red-faced pollsters on Nov. 3 than there were in 1936 when they had to fold up the Literary Digest." He added, pointedly, "You can throw the Gallup poll right into the ashcan."[46]

Truman was right. The election of 1948 was the most shocking polling fiasco in American political history, an outcome more stunning, even, than Donald Trump's Electoral College victory in 2016. Truman, as it turned out, was his own best pollster. According to one of his campaign aides, Truman figured he would win 340 electoral votes.[47]

Truman carried 28 states and 303 electoral votes, winning the popular vote by 4.5 percentage points. Dewey's strength was confined to the Northeast and a band of states from North Dakota to Kansas. The president swept most other heartland states as well as the West and several states in the South. He

FIGURE 9. No image in U.S. election history is more famous than that of President Harry Truman posing with the edition of the *Chicago Tribune* that declared he had lost the 1948 race. Truman called the newspaper's error "one for the books." (Credit: Associated Press/Byron Collins)

took a clear lead in early returns on Election Night, and never relinquished the advantage.

Even well into Election Night, some news outlets clung to expectations of Dewey's victory. H. V. Kaltenborn, who had one of the most distinctive voices on radio, declared late in the night that the slow-to-report rural vote surely would turn the election in Dewey's favor.[48] The *Washington Post* published several editions during the night, including two special or "extra" editions that said in banner headlines that the House of Representatives might have to decide the outcome, the election seemed that close.[49] It wasn't. And famously, an early edition of the *Chicago Tribune* proclaimed—in one of the most memorable banner headlines in American journalism—"Dewey Defeats Truman."

The *Tribune* headline was immortalized in photographs taken two days after the election as Truman triumphantly displayed the newspaper from the back of a train in St. Louis. "That," Truman said of the headline, "is one for the books."[50] It is the best-known image of the 1948 election, one indelibly associated with journalistic blunder.[51] Truman's biographer, David

McCullough, said the photograph captured "the spirit of both the man and the moment as almost nothing else would."[52]

Less well-known is a similar photograph, taken the same day, of Alben W. Barkley, the vice president-elect, posing at his breakfast table with the *Tribune* in hand. He beamed for the camera. Nearly as stunning as the *Tribune* front page was the election reporting in the *Merkur* newspaper in Munich, Germany. Well before the outcome was certain, the *Merkur* went to press with front-page news about Dewey's victory. A thick black headline across the *Merkur*'s front page read: "Thomas E. Dewey Amerikas neuer Präsident." The *Merkur* told of Dewey's delivering a triumphant radio address to the nation. It told of crowds thronging to Times Square to cheer Dewey's victory. It was all fiction.

The next day, the *Merkur*'s publisher, Felix Buttersack, blamed pollsters and pundits for the imaginative report in his newspaper. "All your American experts—your opinion poll takers, your political analysts—have been reporting a Dewey victory certain for months," Buttersack was quoted as saying, "so I thought it would be perfectly safe to go ahead as soon as the polls closed with the story I prepared in advance. How could I have known this would happen?"[53]

Almost immediately, the pollsters came in for wisecracks and withering scorn. In thick black type on its front page, two days after the election, the *Detroit Free Press* declared: "Truman: 304, Pollsters: 0"—a reference to the president's tentative electoral vote total. (A faithless elector in Tennessee reduced Truman's final total to 303 votes.) Roper was an easy target, and this barb made the rounds after Election Day: "Give a candidate enough Roper and he'll hang himself."[54] Bill Gold, a columnist for the *Washington Post* known for writing "good humor and bad puns,"[55] offered this gibe: "Last summer, Elmo Roper was so sure Dewey would sweep to victory that he said there was no use of his taking any more polls. A great many people are now ready to agree with Mr. Roper's conclusion."[56] Another insult aimed at pollsters went this way: "Harry is the first president to lose in a Gallup and win in a walk."[57] And a columnist for the *New York Sun* wrote an epitaph for pollsters: "Here he lies / 'Neath flowers fair: / He saw too much / That wasn't there."[58]

More than a few newspapers, not surprisingly, stopped carrying the Gallup and Roper polling reports. The *Chicago Daily News* explained its decision this way: when "a man breaks into dance after being pronounced dead, the doctor can reasonably expect to lose a few patients."[59] The *Akron Beacon Journal* ended its subscription to the Gallup poll, saying the feature had "killed itself, at least

FIGURE 10. Harry Truman rolled up more than three hundred electoral votes in winning reelection in 1948. The outcome inspired this headline in the *Detroit Free Press* that ridiculed the pollsters' predictions of Truman's certain defeat. (Credit: Library of Congress)

for the time being."[60] The editor of the *Peoria Journal* said he "would not have faith in any Gallup Poll findings from now on" and canceled the newspaper's subscription.[61] The *Pittsburgh Post-Gazette* announced it was dropping the Roper poll, declaring, "We won't pay attention any more to 'scientific' predictions, and we don't think our readers will. So, Mr. Roper's column will no longer appear in the *Post-Gazette*."[62]

In the year after the election, net income at Roper's company tumbled sharply—to $18,300 in 1949, from $77,300 in 1948.[63] Although the bulk of Roper's work was in market research for commercial and industrial clients such as Ford Motor Company and Philip Morris, predictive failure in the Truman-Dewey race doubtless contributed to the falloff in profits.

Journalists, meanwhile, eagerly assailed the polls, sometimes with glee. "One of the satisfying results of the election is that the professional pollsters fell flat on their faces," the *Washington Evening Star* said in an editorial.[64] "Perhaps it's a healthy thing that the polls were so convincingly off base," said the *Philadelphia Inquirer*. "Any feeling that they offer a reliable substitute for the ballot box in determining American political sentiment must disappear. For the present, the poll-takers join the astrologers, the crystal-gazers, and other dubious prophets of the future. They've earned their place in this company."[65] The *Bakersfield Californian* observed that "nothing is so foolish as a poll gone wrong."[66] The public, said the *Newark Star-Ledger*, "takes genuine delight in the defeat of the pollsters. . . . There is an element of the intolerable in being informed in advance how we are to exercise our free will."[67]

Syndicated columnist Marquis Childs acknowledged polling's role in set-ting the campaign's narrative that Truman had no chance. "We were wrong, all of us, completely and entirely, the political editors, the politicians—except for Harry S. Truman," he wrote. "And no one believed him. The fatal flaw was [our] reliance on public opinion polls. No amount of rationalization ever can explain away this mistake by Gallup, Roper & Co. It is nearly as complete and disastrous as the fiasco of 1936 when the Literary Digest poll predicted the election of Alf Landon over Franklin D. Roosevelt."[68] E. B. White, the essay-ist, declared in the *New Yorker*: "The total collapse of the public opinion polls shows that this country is in good health. . . . We are proud of America for clouding up the crystal ball, for telling one thing to a poll-taker, another thing to a voting machine. This is an excellent land."[69]

Expressions of figurative crow-eating became commonplace. "The cold, gray dawn of the day after the election is about to break and on my new electric stove I am boiling a crow," Othman, the Hollywood columnist, wrote in a day-after column. "My only consolation," he added, "is that I can't possibly feel as silly as the Messrs. George Gallup, Elmo Roper and Co. . . . Whether these gentlemen go out of business, I don't know. . . . The weird thing is that everybody, with the exception of Harry Truman, himself, was taken in by the poll takers."[70]

An amusing and imaginative expression of contrition was published two days after the election in a sendup on the *Washington Post*'s front page. Dis-played prominently was the facsimile of a mock-serious telegram to Truman, inviting him to a "crow banquet" at which he would be served turkey while pollsters, political reporters, editorial writers, columnists, and radio com-mentators would dine on "breast of crow en glace." Dress for the "crow ban-quet": white tie for Truman, sack cloth for the others. "We hope you will consent to deliver the address of the evening," the telegram said. "As the dean of American election forecasters (and the only accurate one) it is much desired that you share with your colleagues the secret of your analytical success."[71] (On the day of the election, the *Post* had said that "the polltakers and prog-nosticators would be forced into the greatest crow-eating debauch in the annals of American politics" if Truman won.)[72]

Truman said by telegram in reply: "I know that we could all have a good time together, but I feel I must decline. . . . I have no desire to crow over any-body or to see anybody eating crow, figuratively or otherwise. We should all get together now and make a country in which everybody can eat turkey whenever he pleases."[73] Three days after the election, Truman and Barkley arrived by train to a jubilant celebration in Washington. From Union Station to the White House, upward of 750,000 people lined the streets to cheer the winners.[74] En route, Truman's open-top limousine passed the *Washington Post* building. Displayed above the entrance was a bedsheet adorned with the image of a dead crow on a plate. "Welcome home from the crow-eaters," the makeshift banner declared.

While Truman was gracious, pollsters in the days after the election were the embodiment of stunned befuddlement—Roper especially so. He seemed nearly as flummoxed as Funk had been twelve years earlier. "I could not have been more wrong," Roper conceded. "The thing that bothers me most is that at this moment I don't know why I was wrong." But he added that "there is one thing that I do know. That is President Harry S. Truman proved to be a far better election predictor . . . than the professional pollsters, politicians and pundits."[75]

In his radio talk five days after the election, Roper said his face was "just as red as President Truman said it would be."[76] He told listeners he was "not sure why the polls went wrong," adding, "Perhaps all the people who said they were undecided finally cast their ballots for Mr. Truman. That may be it, but frankly I really don't know."[77] (The decisions of undecided voters were indeed a factor in the surprise outcome; many of them decided to support Truman. Gallup suggested another explanation, that support for Henry Wallace's third-party candidacy withered as Election Day approached, and Truman was the beneficiary. Some Republican voters, thinking Dewey was sure to win, may have stayed home, figuring there was no need to vote.)

Arch Crossley said there were "at least fifty possible reasons" for the polling fiasco. The most likely explanation, Crossley said in a letter to John R. Buckley, editor of *Good Housekeeping*, was that the Democrats mounted a "very intensive, aggressive sales campaign to get out the vote in which the polls themselves were used as a tool." Crossley added, in what probably was a self-deprecating reference, "I am unwilling to believe even that Elmo, George and I are all lousy research men—one of us might be but I don't think all are."[78]

Separately, in an undated memorandum about the 1948 debacle, Crossley mentioned a challenge that pollsters have never fully surmounted—the inadequacy of pre-election polls to assess future behavior based on respondents' expressions of intent. Pollsters, he wrote, "quite obviously do not know how to measure the distinctions between what people say they *intend* to do, and what they *will* do. If the proportions of voters who said they were for Dewey actually voted, there is certainly no doubt of how the election would have gone." (Emphasis in the original.) Crossley also speculated that wide publicity given the pre-election polls "had the two-fold effect of making the Republicans overconfident, and steeling the Democrats to work harder."[79]

Privately, Crossley mentioned another, seldom-discussed drawback that pollsters faced in 1948—the expense of poll-taking and his reluctance to spend money for additional polling late in a campaign that he thought had long since been decided. Writing two months after the election, Crossley conceded: "I think we were dead wrong not to carry on polls much later than we did, but the fact is that money would have had to come out of our own pockets and, as you know, they are expensive."[80] To the sociologist Alfred McClung Lee, Crossley wrote, "We stopped our feidl [sic] interviewing three weeks before the election because while Truman was rising we didn't see how he could rise enough to win, and the cost of additional polls would have had to come out of our own pockets."[81] Crossley gave more detail years later, writing that because his polling operation ran up an operating loss of $22,000 (or about $230,000 these days), "our budget had no funds to pay for a final telegraphic poll,"[82] meaning a focused survey lasting a day or two in which field results were submitted by telegram to the home office.

Gallup's would-be biographer, Phyllis L. Gillis, asked him years after the election whether Truman's victory had prompted him to drink to inebriation. "God knows I wanted to," Gallup replied, according to her notes. "I don't think I slept a wink all week." The unexpected outcome, he told Gillis, "was a great traumatic shock. Not only had Dewey lost, but every poll and every commentator was also wrong—and we took the brunt."[83] Gallup was a friend and admirer of Dewey, and the outcome came as a personal blow to the pollster. In an interview with Gillis, Gallup said Dewey was "the most capable man I ever met in the history of politics. And the most honest one."[84]

As was his wont, Gallup took to spinning the poll results, saying his estimates really weren't so far off. His reasoning was tortured and went this way: the average error in his final poll, if calculated among the election's four leading candidates, was just 2.9 percentage points. "In short," Gallup later wrote, "the polls came through the election with about the same accuracy as they had previously achieved."[85] It was a dazzling attempt to obscure an altogether dismal performance. *Time* magazine was among the publications that punctured Gallup's reasoning: "What he did was to add up his errors on all four candidates and divide by four," producing a far more generous impression of his poll results. In terms of raw percentages, *Time* noted, correctly, "Gallup guessed 10% high on Dewey's share of the total vote and 10% low on Truman's. He predicted Wallace would get 4%, and Wallace got 2.4%. In Gallup's book, that was a difference of 1.6%; counted another way, he had overestimated [Wallace's share] by 40%."[86] The *New York Herald Tribune* also challenged Gallup's spin, saying in an editorial: "It is apparent ... that the poll-takers have laid claim to a degree of accuracy they [did] not achieve."[87]

Gallup complained as he spun. "In no other field do one's sins find him out so inevitably," he said in a speech to members of the American Marketing Association, meeting in Cleveland in late December 1948. "His accuracy is known down to the last decimal point. A doctor can bury his mistakes. A lawyer can rationalize his. A market researcher can always blame something else. . . . But, a public opinion researcher must stand naked before the world, his shame recorded for posterity. Well, let's take a look at this whole problem of polling accuracy. Probably in no other field of research, at least where mass behavior is concerned, has such a high degree of accuracy been achieved." He claimed the average polling error was 3.9 percent points in 404 pre-election polls conducted over the years "by some twenty different organizations in twelve different nations."[88] Such claims likely were of thin comfort in the aftermath of the 1948 debacle. For a year afterward, Gallup claimed, he "couldn't turn on the radio without hearing some joke about me or the Gallup Poll."[89]

To his credit, Gallup did not duck scrutiny in the aftermath of the election. Twelve days after the election, he went on NBC's *Meet the Press* interview program, where he was promptly asked whether he was giving up poll-taking. "Absolutely not," Gallup snapped. "Why should I?" His interlocuter referred to the *Literary Digest* debacle and said, "You folks are about in the same boat, aren't you?" No, Gallup replied. "We've lost the battle but not the war." He added: "It's a good thing to get kicked around now and then. It's good for us and it's good for everybody." Besides, Gallup said, the *Digest* erred by nearly 20 percentage points in 1936.[90]

Gallup also appeared after the election on the NBC radio show *Living 1948*, where he cracked a few tame, self-deprecating jokes, saying, for example, that "the people are right about my being caught with my 'figures' down—I was plain wrong." Probably unwittingly, he borrowed an analogy from the *Literary Digest*, which, after its fiasco in 1936, asked rhetorically whether the power-house University of Minnesota football team would give up the sport because it finally lost a game. On *Living 1948*, Gallup invoked Joe DiMaggio, and asked whether the baseball star, "upon striking out in a crucial game with the bases full," would give up the sport. "Of course not," Gallup said, "and neither does a medical researcher looking for the cause of a disease. They go on and learn from their mistakes. I certainly intend to do the same thing, to go right on and learn from mine. The minute you think you have all the answers, that's when you're on dangerous ground." Gallup suggested his polling went bad because it failed to anticipate who would vote and who would stay home, because it assumed that most undecided voters would not go to the polls, because many respondents who said they were for Wallace ended up voting for Truman, and because Democratic candidates at the bottom of the ticket may have given a boost to Truman.[91]

Gallup was straightforward if platitudinous on the show. He acknowledged the inaccuracy of his poll and presented plausible-sounding explanations for failure. An audience research report shared with Gallup indicated that a plurality of listeners felt he had offered credible explanations; a majority said Gallup's answers didn't "sound twisted" to them. Another question included in the report was: "Do you feel the Gallup Poll can give an accurate forecast of how people are going to vote?" Only 2 percent of the audience replied "yes."[92]

It wasn't long before the pollsters turned their criticism on journalists. "It seems grossly unfair for the newspapers to lay all the blame on the pollsters," Roper complained, adding that they should "admit frankly that they abdicated their own journalistic functions, and that they don't seem to be willing to do."[93] Crossley, for his part, blamed newspaper editors for pressuring him to make a prediction. "The choice of making a forecast was one made entirely of my own free will," he wrote in a speech for delivery at Babson College. "I didn't have to do it, but considerable pressure was brought to bear on all sides and we simply yielded to that pressure. In the first place, there seems to be a pretty widespread feeling among newspaper editors, and I suppose also among the general public, that pretty nearly the worst sin a poll taker could commit would be hedging. I have since discovered there is a worse sin, and that is calling the election wrong, however close the election may be."[94]

Pollsters had set the pre-election narrative, but journalists had much to answer for. They were not blameless. They had missed one of the greatest political stories of the time. The newsmagazine *Time*—which conceded that it had been "just as wrong as everybody else"[95]—declared the press was "morally guilty" in its election coverage. "It was guilty of pride: it had assumed that it knew all the important facts—without sufficiently checking them," the newsmagazine said. "It was guilty of laziness and wishful thinking: it had failed to do its own doorbell-ringing and bush-beating; it had delegated its journalist's job to the pollsters."[96]

That characterization became a post-election refrain. No less a determined polling skeptic than Edward R. Murrow admonished the press, saying in a post-election broadcast over CBS radio: "Those newspapers that are pointing the finger at the polls should look at their own records and their own columns. Did the editors abdicate their job of reporting and analyzing in favor of Messrs. Roper and Gallup? As a matter of fact the press of this country, if you figure in terms of percentages, has gone to bat five times without getting a hit. During the last five Presidential elections the majority of them, generally a substantial majority, have [editorially] advocated the election of the losing candidate."[97]

Roy A. Roberts, president and editor of the *Kansas City Star*, said journalists had become complacent in accepting the findings of pre-election polls, an affliction the portly old newspaperman called "politis." Roberts, in a speech prepared for the national convention of Sigma Delta Chi, an organization of professional journalists, extolled the presumed virtues of "shoe-leather" journalism and advised journalists, "In the future, don't get politis. Pay more attention to the basic facts and get down to the grass roots . . . with hardboiled reporters searching for changes in mass thinking."[98]

James Reston, a prominent Washington-based correspondent for the *New York Times*, rebuked his profession for being "far too impressed by the tidy statistics of the polls" that pointed to Dewey's victory. Reston's was a broad indictment of the press, which the *Times* published in its letters column two days after the election. American journalism's failure in the 1948 election, Reston wrote, was "as spectacular as the President's victory, and the quicker we admit it the better off we'll be." He said journalists had "overestimated the tangibles and underestimated the intangibles; we relied too much on techniques of reporting that are no longer foolproof; just as [Dewey] was too isolated with other politicians, so were we too isolated with other reporters; and we, too, were far too impressed by the tidy statistics of the polls."[99]

As often is the case when journalists err because of their reliance on pre-election polls, Reston invoked the timeless appeal of "shoe-leather" journalism, stating that reporters should have spent more time "wandering around talking to the people. We tend to assume that somebody else is doing the original reporting in that area, and if the assumptions of the political managers, or the other reporters, or the polls are wrong (as they were in this campaign), then our reports are wrong."[100]

Years later, Reston returned to his criticism of the reporting of the 1948 campaign, writing in a memoir that the news media "misjudged Harry. We saw him through the eyes of the pollsters, rather than through the eyes of the people in the freight yards. After Roosevelt and the other wartime giants, he seemed just another little guy who had stumbled into the presidency with no visible qualifications for the job. On the back platform of a train, however, he was 'Give-em-Hell-Harry' to all the other little guys."[101]

A related criticism aimed at journalists said they were so eager to point to Truman's shortcomings that they overlooked qualitative indicators of his popularity. Frank Conniff, a columnist for the *New York Journal-American* writing after the election, said many reporters accompanying Truman during the campaign "were so busy poking fun at the President, ridiculing his halting speech, itemizing his various errors of judgment, that they missed the genuine enthusiasm his words kindled. They underestimated the intelligence of the American voter. Those huge crowds were not composed merely of curiosity gawkers; they were citizens anxious to hear the issues discussed before making up their minds."[102]

But qualitative indicators such as crowd size and reaction are not easily interpreted; they can be teasing, deceptive indicators. The lengthy reports that Richard Rovere wrote for the *New Yorker* in 1948 indicate how problematic the analysis of crowds can be. In early fall 1948, Rovere traveled aboard Truman's campaign train on a westward swing to California, and then switched to Dewey's "Victory Special" train and a trip East. "For judging crowds," Rovere wrote after spending time on both trains, "the ear is probably a more reliable instrument than the eye. Its verdict, I would say, favored Dewey almost everywhere. No Truman crowd that I heard responded with more than elementary courtesy and occasionally mild and rather weary approval. Partly, no doubt, this was because the President has a lamentable way of swallowing the very lines he ought to bellow or snarl, and partly, I think, it was because he simply didn't have his audience with him."[103]

A week earlier in the *New Yorker*, Rovere had written this about Truman: "It would be going too far to say that the crowds, either in the small towns or in the large cities, respond enthusiastically to his appeals for support. They don't. . . . Nobody stomps, shouts, or whistles for Truman. Everybody claps. I should say that the decibel count would be about the same as it would be for a missionary who has just delivered a mildly encouraging report on the inroads being made against heathenism in North Rhodesia. This does not necessarily mean that the people who come out to see him intend to vote against them—though my personal feeling is that most of them intend to do exactly that."[104]

Elsewhere in that dispatch, Rovere wrote charitably of Truman, saying: "Travelling with him, you get the feeling that the American people who have seen him and heard him at his best would be willing to give him just about anything he wants except the Presidency."[105]

Rovere, who later gained recognition as one of American journalism's most perceptive political correspondents, was thirty-three years old in 1948 and clearly impressed by the reassuring competence of Dewey's campaign, where everything seemed "slick and snappy," in decided contrast "to the general dowdiness and good-natured slovenliness of the Truman campaign." Presidential candidates, he wrote, "notoriously promise better than they ever perform, but if Governor Dewey manages the Presidency half as well as he is managing his campaign for it, we are about to have four, eight, twelve, sixteen years of cool, sleek efficiency in government."[106]

The news media were not inclined to focus for long on their failure to detect, or even to suspect, Truman's resurgence. *Time* said, "Many newspapers decided . . . they should wipe it up and say no more about it."[107] On the radio program *CBS Views the Press*, commentator Don Hollenbeck wondered aloud whether "the American press has learned anything from its lesson beyond the simple fact that it was monstrously wrong" in anticipating Dewey's victory. "A few newspapermen around the country have learned wherein they erred and why, but not many," Hollenbeck said. He mentioned Reston's post-election letter to the *Times*—which was reprinted in the trade journal *Editor and Publisher*[108]—and said that "even in the newspaper business itself, it received little attention."[109]

Eight days after the election, a committee of experts was empaneled by the Social Science Research Council (SSRC) to conduct a detailed examination of why the polls had gone wrong. Crossley, Gallup, and Roper promptly pledged cooperation and said they would share their technical data with the committee. The panel's chairman was Samuel S. Wilks, a Princeton University mathematics professor whom the pollsters knew fairly well. Other members included: Frank Stanton, president of CBS; Samuel A. Stouffer, a sociology professor at Harvard University; James Phinney Baxter III, president of Williams College; and Isador Lubin, chair of the Committee on Statistical Standards of the American Statistical Association.

A sense of urgency, even crisis, drove the committee's deliberations. The fear was, Peter Odegard of the University of California at Berkeley later wrote, "that a crude but immensely promising instrument of the social sciences—that is, the sampling survey—might suffer a serious set-back, if not irreparable damage" because of the polling failure in the presidential campaign.[110] "Quick action seemed necessary," wrote Frederick Mosteller, a Harvard statistician who was the committee's chief of staff. "An authoritative factual inquiry was needed to terminate the growing controversy or to focus discussion upon specific issues at the earliest possible moment."[111] The committee conferred with Gallup, Roper, and Crossley at its first meeting and, by the end of December, had completed a preliminary report that was notable for its detailed analysis and its enduring relevance. To read the findings more than seventy years later is to be impressed by their contemporary resonance and applicability.

Notably, the report said the pollsters in 1948 had "attempted the spectacular feat of predicting the winner without qualification. The presentation of the results gave the impression of certainty as to the outcome. . . . Statements of conditions under which different outcomes of the election might occur were dropped almost completely before the end of the campaign."[112] Analogous criticism arose about the 2016 election campaign, when poll-based statistical forecasters declared the probability of Hillary Clinton's election victory at upwards of 99 percent.[113]

Moreover, the SSRC committee report said a major source of predictive error in 1948 was the pollsters' failure "to detect shifts in voting intentions during the later stages of the campaign,"[114] a conundrum that has reemerged since then. Roper erred, the committee said, "by assuming that voting intentions would not change during the campaign, as evidenced by his announcement" in September. "Crossley and Gallup made no attempt to detect the shift in voting intentions in the last two weeks of the campaign."[115] As we'll see, the 2016 campaign gave rise to a similar failing, in that some pollsters in swing states such as Wisconsin completed fieldwork in the week or two before the November election, too soon to detect late shifts to Donald Trump—shifts that were crucial to his winning the presidency.[116]

The SSRC committee also noted, "The prediction of human behavior from an expression of intent is, in the present state of knowledge, and particularly with the actual methods used, a hazardous venture."[117] It further observed that "the public placed too much confidence in polls before the 1948 election and too much distrust in them afterwards."[118] Both observations remain pertinent, decades later. In its recommendations, the committee said it was "very important for the public to be effectively informed about the limitations of poll results so it can interpret them intelligently." It called for expanded research into social psychology and political science, noting that "we now know too little about voting intentions, factors affecting change in opinion, prestige effects, and similar topics to predict who will translate his opinion into actual voting."[119]

The committee was pointed in advising pollsters to embrace "better techniques now available, particularly in sampling and interviewing." By that the committee meant that pollsters would do well to substitute their quota-control methodologies with probability sampling techniques. In quota sampling, poll respondents are chosen according to criteria or characteristics such as age, gender, race, occupation, geographic location, and economic standing.[120] Quota surveys typically can be completed faster, and with less expense, than probability-based surveys. Crossley, for one, thought probability sampling was "very difficult to use right,"[121] given that pollsters following the method were obliged to keep trying and trying to reach respondents who were selected at random but proved to be elusive. That procedure, known as "call backs," added to the time and expense required to conduct probability samples.

In quota sampling, interviewers exercised considerable discretion in selecting would-be respondents, which was a well-known source of potential error.[122] Choosing respondents could be anything but random. "The advantage of the probability method of sampling, advocated by some statisticians, lies primarily in the fact that the errors introduced by selection of respondents by the interviewer can be reduced to a minimum," the SSRC committee said.[123]

The committee's work was impressive, especially as it was completed under severe time constraints. It attracted only passing attention in the press, however,[124] and pollsters did not receive it warmly. Crossley complained that the committee had found pollsters "honest but stupid."[125] Gallup's prickliness in confronting criticism was evident at a conference in Iowa in early 1949 that brought together pollsters and polling experts. The SSRC report was a topic of discussion. "I think the committee itself felt that it had to point an accusing finger at the pollsters," Gallup said. "Now I may be unfair, but it is my impression that committees of this type believe they will be attacked by their fellow academicians as not being objective if they praise anything."[126] Privately, Gallup criticized the report as "pretty naïve" in "many places."[127] As he did often in his career, Gallup brought up at the Iowa conference the *Literary Digest* polling debacle, recalling that the magazine's mail-in poll "had an error of nineteen percentage points in the election of 1936. If we are ever half that wrong," Gallup declared, "I will take up some other profession, probably plumbing."[128]

Grudgingly perhaps, the pollsters took to heart the committee's criticism that they had been too cocky, that they had too eagerly projected "certainty as to outcome." Extreme caution characterized the pollsters and their messaging during the presidential election in 1952. "Remember '48" in effect was their guidance.[129] But extreme caution would not keep them from another polling embarrassment. Hesitation born of restraint led to their failure to detect a landslide.

CHAPTER 4

A Tie "Would Suit Them Fine"

The 1952 Landslide Pollsters Did Not Foresee

Five days before the 1952 election, an overflow crowd gathered at the Belmont Plaza Hotel in Manhattan to hear the country's best-known national pollsters discuss that year's presidential race. The luncheon program, organized by the New York chapter of the American Marketing Association, was confidently titled "Why the Polls Won't Go Wrong in 1952."

The conviction embedded in that title was hardly matched by the presentations that midday. The pollsters were still reeling from the polling debacle of 1948. That fiasco still weighed on them, and they had no intention of making bold predictions, as they had done four years earlier. Wariness and equivocation shaped their discussions about the race between the Republican candidate, General Dwight D. Eisenhower, and his Democratic rival, Illinois governor Adlai Stevenson. They wouldn't be wrong this time because they would offer no unambiguous forecast.

Eisenhower seemed to be narrowly in the lead, the pollsters agreed. But they also agreed that Stevenson was closing fast.[1] "It could be a landslide [in electoral votes] for either candidate," Elmo Roper reportedly told the luncheon-goers. "The outcome is unpredictable," said Archibald Crossley. "I'm not going to guess," declared George Gallup.[2]

The portrait of restraint and vacillation they exhibited at the Belmont Plaza typified their analyses throughout the Eisenhower-Stevenson campaign. They heeded some of the lessons of the 1948 fiasco, which meant no premature end to fieldwork—Gallup completed the bulk of his polling days before the election in 1952[3]—and no "predicting the winner without qualification," for which a committee of the Social Science Research Council had chided them. But their wariness and circumspection was so pronounced in 1952 as to invite ridicule. So determined were they not "to be caught out on a limb," wrote a humor columnist named Henry McLemore, that a tie between Eisenhower and Stevenson "would suit them fine."[4]

William Henry Chamberlain of the Wall Street Journal said the pollsters in 1952 "were as coy as the Delphic Oracle (remembered in history for its skill in framing answers which would be right no matter what might happen)."[5] Joe Williams, a sports columnist for the New York World-Telegram and Sun, mocked the pollsters for "the most prodigious mass demonstration of fence straddling in the long and honorable history of crystal balling."[6] Arthur Krock of the New York Times referred to the pollsters as "those burnt children of 1948" who "shrank in 1952 from the possibility of getting singed again in the fires of political prophesy."[7] Frank Kent of the Baltimore Sun wrote that they had allowed themselves in 1952 "more loopholes, rope ladders and fire escapes than ever before."[8]

The pollsters couldn't afford to be wrong again, Kent reasoned, writing, "Obviously, and naturally, they are restrained by memory of their unhappy experience in 1948, [and] clearly realize that another such [disaster] will put them permanently out of business."[9] That admonition was not uncommon during the 1952 campaign. "In a very real sense, the professional poll-takers are on trial this year," said the Reporter-News newspaper in Abilene, Texas. "Another blunder like that of 1948 would just about finish them off."[10] McLemore wrote, "Another such failure as they had four years ago and they'll have to fold their tents and slip quietly away, as did the Literary Digest."[11] Business Week magazine noted early in 1952, "For almost four years, they have had to eat endless portions of crow; they have had to accept the unkind fact that political polling . . . has earned them little but ridicule. Now they have a second chance."[12]

The pollsters had lost esteem and newspaper clients following the embarrassment of 1948. Four years later, they had not fully recovered their client base. Roper had 54 client newspapers, compared to 66 in 1948. Crossley claimed 152 newspaper subscribers in 1948 and said most of them were still clients in 1952. Gallup said he had 206 newspaper subscribers for his polling reports in 1952, down from 226 four years earlier.[13] The Akron Beacon Journal in Ohio was one of the newspapers to resume its subscription to Gallup's poll in 1952 after dropping it in 1948. "We believe these reports between now and

Election Day will be of sufficient news interest to warrant a place in the paper," the *Beacon Journal* said in an editorial in August 1952. "Readers can take the reports with any number of grains of salt that they desire."[14]

To the end of the 1952 campaign, the pollsters were the picture of equivocation. Their final assessments said that either candidate could win, that the election was a tossup, given the substantial number of undecided voters. It "can still go either way," Crossley said in releasing his final pre-election poll, which showed Eisenhower ahead. The winner's popular-vote margin, Crossley added, "is likely to be narrow."[15] Although he would later insist that he had offered no prediction, Roper also said the presidential race would be close. He went on his Sunday afternoon radio program on NBC two days before the election and declared that either Eisenhower or Stevenson could win, that "there are enough people still undecided to throw this election either way."

Roper, who privately was a friend and admirer of the Democratic candidate,[16] said that "if there are any of you listening who want Governor Stevenson to win, you'd better make sure you translate that wish into a vote at the polls. If his followers can realize a slightly greater turnout at the polls and if he can pick up a goodly share of these undecided people—most of whom are normally Democratic anyhow—he too could win."[17] In one last nod to caution, Roper did not share his final poll data widely. Newspaper accounts before the election contained no reference to Roper's figures. The Associated Press, in its roundup of polling results compiled and distributed the day before the election, said "Roper did not give any overall breakdown of this year's probable vote."[18] Roper later said he had presented his final pre-election figures, over NBC radio, on the Sunday before the election. He said they showed Eisenhower ahead, 49 percent to 37 percent for Stevenson, with 14 percent undecided.[19]

Gallup also was guarded and emphasized the prospect of a close election. He said the race would turn on the outcomes in California, Illinois, New York, and Ohio, states his polling indicated were too close to call. Gallup's final poll had Eisenhower leading by 47 percent to Stevenson's 40 percent. But 13 percent of poll respondents said they were undecided. By allocating the undecided vote on a 3-to-1 basis to the Democrat—which is how Gallup figured the undecided population had voted in 1948—the final poll results showed that Eisenhower and Stevenson were tied, 50–50.[20] Were Stevenson to continue to make gains as the campaign wound down, Gallup said, he could win "a majority of the popular vote on election day."[21]

Despite their equivocation and the ridicule it prompted, the national pollsters again set the pre-election narrative: this time it was to be a close race, a race that could tip either way. An informal poll of fifty leading political writers on the eve of the election found that twenty-six of them thought Stevenson would win; twenty-four picked Eisenhower.[22] Walter Trohan, the *Chicago Tribune*'s Washington bureau chief, wrote: "Most politicians, pollsters, and experts agree that the contest appears to be close. Yet, all are hedging by saying the voting could end in an electoral landslide for either Gen. Eisenhower or Gov. Stevenson."[23] Dewey L. Fleming of the *Baltimore Sun* said two days before the election that the Eisenhower-Stevenson race "has shaped up as one of the most unpredictable in the nation's history. Extraordinary doubt as to the outcome persists in all quarters."[24]

The *New York Times* reported a similar finding in releasing its final preelection roundup of sentiment in the country, sentiment gleaned by correspondents in all forty-eight states. The outcome on the eve of the presidential election, the *Times* said, was "highly uncertain" and neither candidate "can be regarded as of now as certain of election." The *Times*'s roundup, drawn from "talks" with political leaders, as well as state and local polls, and other interviews, found that Eisenhower was "reasonably certain to carry eleven states with seventy-three electoral votes" and that Stevenson was "equally sure to carry ten states with 100 electoral votes."[25]

The presidential race was believed so close that the Associated Press addressed an unlikely though not improbable scenario in which the outcome might not be decided for more than two weeks after election day, given a quirk in California state law that did not permit absentee ballots to be opened right away. If the election was to be decided by the returns in California, and if the race there was "neck-and-neck" as pollsters had reported,[26] the state's thirty-two electoral votes—and thus the national election—could remain undecided until absentee ballots were counted well after Election Day.[27] The statewide California Poll said in its final pre-election report that Stevenson had "come thundering down the home stretch" in a way reminiscent of "the eleventh hour surge of popularity for President Truman in 1948." As such, the race in California was "a virtual tie."[28]

Perceptions of a tight race nationally gave rise to speculation about a split verdict—that Eisenhower could win the popular vote but lose the electoral vote. Such scenarios tend to arise, not surprisingly, when polls indicate a close election. Samuel Lubell, a reporter for the Scripps-Howard chain of newspapers who doggedly went door-to-door in fifteen states interviewing would-be voters, raised such a prospect on the eve of the election. Lubell hypothesized that Eisenhower could win the popular vote nationally but lose the Electoral College were Stevenson to prevail by narrow margins in populous states such as New York, Illinois, and California, Pennsylvania, or Michigan. "If that happens," Lubell said, "I would not be surprised if General Eisenhower actually got more popular votes through the whole country, while losing out on the electoral count."[29]

Arthur Krock, an influential columnist and Washington bureau chief for the *New York Times*, also raised the prospect of a divided outcome. He wrote in a column published on Election Day that the combination of close outcomes that polls were signaling in battleground states such as California, Illinois, New York, and Ohio, along with tight races in some Southern states, "could put Eisenhower first but futilely in the popular vote." That is, Eisenhower might carry the popular vote while Stevenson could win an electoral majority and thus the White House. If "the next President is the choice of a popular minority, and the majority looks for its national leadership to his competitor in the campaign," Krock wrote, "it will require all the luck, genius and common sense of the American people to keep the Ship of State on its course."[30]

The split-verdict scenario was active even as the votes were being counted and as Eisenhower built a solid lead in early returns. Elmo Roper went on NBC's Election Night television and radio programs to describe how Eisenhower could win the popular vote but lose the Electoral College. Roper said that outcome was possible though not probable.[31]

In some respects, the election of 1952 was the first modern presidential election: it was the first in which television figured prominently.[32] Richard Nixon kept his place as vice presidential candidate on the Republican ticket owing to an emotional, televised speech in September 1952 in which he denied being the beneficiary of a campaign slush fund. Eisenhower, the American hero of World War II, took to television late in the campaign to declare, "I shall go to Korea" to seek an honorable end to the bloody war that had claimed more than one hundred thousand American casualties.[33] And CBS News, on its television program reporting the returns on Election Night, incorporated predictions generated by a mainframe computer called the UNIVAC, for Universal Automatic Computer.

The UNIVAC stumbled badly in its televised debut. At one point late on Election Night, the computer spit out a prediction of a split verdict: that both

IKE LANDSLIDE SETS RECORD!

See GOP Rule in Congress

FIGURE 11. Pollsters never saw this coming: they figured that Dwight Eisenhower and Adlai Stevenson were locked in a tight race for president in 1952. Eisenhower won in a landslide—surprising news that commanded huge headlines in the *New York Journal*. (Credit: Library of Congress)

candidates would carry twenty-four states, and that Eisenhower would win a narrow electoral majority but Stevenson would win one million more popular votes. The projection astonished almost everyone on the CBS set, given that returns tabulated throughout the evening had shown Eisenhower with a lead. The projection prompted correspondent Charles Collingwood, the computer's on-air minder, to say in jest, "If you ask me, UNIVAC is beginning to act like a pollster."[34]

UNIVAC, and the pollsters, were wrong. The election wasn't close, not nationally, not in the battleground states. Eisenhower received more than 34 million popular votes, the most by any presidential candidate to that time. His victory margin was 6.7 million votes, or nearly eleven percentage points (55.2 percent to 44.3 percent). Eisenhower won 39 states and 442 electoral votes to Stevenson's 9 states and 89 electoral votes. Eisenhower carried eighteen states that Democratic candidates had won in every presidential election since 1932 and made deep inroads in the South, which was once solid for Democrats.[35]

It was a landslide that pollsters never saw coming. The outcome was no replica of the fiasco of 1948. But the poll failure of 1952 had the similar effect of misleading and surprising the public. It was an outcome that ought to have been another humiliation for the pollsters. But Gallup, especially, was not of that mind. He was not about to eat crow. He sought earnestly to place a most favorable interpretation on the dissonance between his polling and the surprise outcome. For Gallup, this reaction was to confirm an inclination he had shown in the weeks and months after the 1948 polling fiasco. He spun.

As he had done in 1940 and 1944, Gallup took out a full-page advertisement after the election in *Editor and Publisher*, the newspaper trade journal, as if to proclaim a triumph. In the ad, Gallup declared himself "happy" with his polling of the 1952 race. "It is nicer," the ad read, "to eat pheasant than crow"—a line that Gallup had tried out in polling a statewide race three years earlier.[36] The ad's centerpiece was a box displaying three sets of figures. One was the topline from Gallup's final pre-election report: Eisenhower, 47 percent; Stevenson, 40 percent, and undecided, 13 percent. Next to those figures was a breakdown for what Gallup called "decided voters only," which, he said, showed Eisenhower ahead, 54 percent to 46 percent. To the right of those figures were the election results, Eisenhower, 55 percent, Stevenson, 45 percent.[37] The implication was that Gallup had called the election within one percentage point. It was sleight of hand.

The advertisement in *Editor and Publisher* made no reference to Gallup's pre-election hedging. It conveniently ignored passages in Gallup's final pre-election report about how Stevenson was closing in, how the election appeared to be "a tight race for the popular vote majority," how it was a 50–50 proposition if undecided voters went for Stevenson by a 3-to-1 margin. The ad made no reference to states Gallup had identified as pivotal to the electoral vote outcome—California, Illinois, New York, and Ohio, in all of which, he said, the candidates were "running virtually even." The outcome was close in none of those states: Eisenhower won California by 14 percentage points, Illinois by nearly 10 points, New York by almost 18 points, and Ohio by 13.5 points. An editorial in a small-town Kansas newspaper referred to the ad, saying, "If that is Gallup's idea of eating pheasant, he is welcome to it. The fact remains that he and every other pollster missed the mark by a country mile, not a one having the temerity even to suggest the Eisenhower landslide that took place."[38]

Gallup in his spinning didn't confine himself to an ad in a trade journal. He told reporters he was "satisfied" with the performance of his polling, adding, "The only crime in this business is to be on the wrong side."[39] He took aim at Truman, no doubt remembering the president's barbed claim during the 1948 campaign that Gallup's poll was worthy only of the ashcan. "We'll let President Truman eat the crow this year," Gallup said. "It's good to be on the right side."[40]

Few, if any, media analysts, columnists, and editorial writers embraced Gallup's spin and some, like Raymond Moley, were antagonistic. Moley, an architect of the New Deal in Franklin Roosevelt's first administration, turned to column-writing after breaking with the president. "With George Gallup, life is just one bad prediction after another, followed by one alibi after another," Moley wrote in the election's aftermath. "It grows monotonous."[41] Gladstone Williams, a Washington correspondent for the McClatchy chain of newspapers, ridiculed Gallup and other pundits for predicting "a drizzle whereas a cloudburst descended." He wrote that Gallup's final pre-election poll had "left the way open for either an Eisenhower or a Stevenson victory, though shading his findings to the Republican side. Where he failed utterly, as did the other professionals, was in not sensing and predicting a landslide result."[42]

Missing the landslide was a major misstep, and other newspaper analyses relished jeering at the pollsters' failure. It was an open question, said the *Amsterdam Recorder* in New York, "as to whether the Democrats or the pollsters took the worst beating" in the election.[43] The *Berkshire County Eagle* in Massachusetts scoffed that pollsters had shown themselves "unable to tell a tidal wave from a photo finish."[44] The television writer for the *Chicago Tribune* wrote two days after the election that "pollsters should confine themselves in the future to such objectives as testing the popularity of cigarets or determining the relative status of Milton Berle and Red Skelton," comedians who were popular on radio and television at the time.[45] "The people who went down to absolute defeat in [the] general election were ... the 'expert' pollsters and samplers of public opinion," declared the *Huronite and Plainsman* newspaper in South Dakota.[46]

"None of the principal pollsters even hinted at a landslide," the *Troy Record* in New York observed. "And in failing to do so they discredited themselves even more thoroughly than when guessing wrong four years ago. ... After 1948 and 1952, we are obliged to conclude that polls may be interesting and helpful but they cannot command confidence."[47] "How can it be said that they do anything but mislead the public?" asked a letter-writer to the *Chicago Tribune*.[48] And a reader's letter published in the *Washington Post* suggested that "in the light of the Eisenhower landslide," the newspaper drop Gallup's syndicated polling report for "a good bridge column."[49]

The landslide the pollsters missed also was seen as a repudiation of polling's soundness and rationale. "Questions arise concerning the function and value of opinion polls when results are so different from forecasts," declared an analysis in *U.S. News and World Report,* adding, "Whole regions went to Eisenhower. The landslide was nationwide. Big polls did not catch it."[50] Some of the rejoicing in the press was tied to a belief that surveys were presumptuous and prying—unwelcome intrusions on private thoughts and beliefs. Americans, such arguments ran, were too diverse and idiosyncratic for their views to be pigeonholed by the obscure mechanisms of opinion polls.

A prominent exponent of such views was the legendary broadcast journalist Edward R. Murrow. On his CBS news program the day after the election, Murrow declared: "Yesterday the people surprised the pollsters, the prophets, and many politicians. They demonstrated, as they did in 1948, that they are mysterious and their motives are not to be measured by mechanical means."[51]

Murrow's assessment resonated in the American media. The election outcome "may be discouraging news for Messrs. Gallup, Roper, etc., but we like the independence demonstrated by the voters," declared the *Record-Chronicle* in Denton, Texas. "The American voter is an independent critter— and more power to him. He may say in advance how he intends to vote but reserves the right to change his mind. That is one great stumbling block for pollsters. Another lies in the individualism of the American voter."[52] In his post-election assessment, Chamberlain wrote in the *Wall Street Journal* that the "unpredictability of the American election is a good thing for the Republic. It shows that many voters are still individualists who cannot be placed in any political camp because of occupation, religion or ethnic origin. . . . It is significant that the only elections in which the outcome can be forecast with complete certainty are those held in the Soviet Union and its satellite states."[53]

Roper received the script of Murrow's on-air critique of the pollsters and fired off a letter rebuking the broadcaster for his "statement that the polls—and by inference, therefore, our poll—were as wrong as they were in 1948 [which] is demonstrably false."[54] The pollsters' failure in 1952 was different from that of 1948: it was an error of timidity rather than of excessive confidence. But the upshot was similar: the election outcome was shocking, a surprise.

Somewhat disingenuously, Roper after the election insisted that he had made no forecast and never said the race was close.[55] Roper may not have specifically identified a probable winner, but he said quite clearly on his radio program two days before the election that the race could go either way. Roper also groused that pre-election polling was a money-losing proposition for him. "If I had to depend on our proceeds from this kind of work," he said in a letter to the sociologist Floyd Albert Spencer, "I should not only have starved to death during 1952—and every other election year—but was actually out of pocket a little more than $20,000 this year. This $20,000 came from what is fortunately a very lucrative industrial research business."[56] Crossley also felt the pinch of polling the campaign. To save money, Crossley said privately that his final survey was based on fresh polling in twenty-six states and on older data, gathered before Labor Day, in the other states.[57]

If anything, Roper's irritation about using polls to forecast election outcomes deepened in 1952. The risk of doing so, he said, was that poll-based forecasts could influence the results of elections that polls were trying to predict—a scenario of "the measuring rod influencing the thing they were trying to measure."[58] He also argued that polls were socially useful as tools of analysis, in exploring "the issues that were uppermost in people's minds."[59] Using them for purposes of prediction ran the keen risk of alienating social scientists who "look down their noses at us as sensationalists who are more interested in headlines than in sound diagnostic work."

But if pollsters abstain from using survey results for predictions, Roper added, "the editors of American [newspapers] deride us and think the work is of no use. . . . In 1952, we won back the respect of the social scientists but not the editors. Is there any way of doing both?"[60] Roper made clear that he preferred the favor of social scientists, writing in a letter to the sociologist and media theorist Paul Lazarsfeld, "Any time I have to choose between the respect of men like you . . . and the plaudits of newspaper editors, I will quickly choose the former!"[61]

Roper's long-standing differences with Gallup about the usefulness of poll-based predictions became more pronounced after 1952. Gallup argued that pre-election polls represented an "acid test" of survey methodology. The "only justification of an election forecast," he said, "is to test polling methods."[62] Gallup didn't always speak favorably about pre-election polling, however. At the end of 1952, Gallup likened the polling to having created a "Frankenstein" monster, according to an account in the *Chicago Tribune*. Gallup was speaking at a conference of the American Statistical Association and the *Tribune* reported that "he doubted that opinion surveyors would be able to get out of election predicting much as they want to. He said, 'We reared this Franken-stein [monster] about 1936' and implied they were stuck with it.'"[63]

The disagreement between Roper and Gallup went public in May 1953, at the annual conference of the American Association for Public Opinion Research, convened at a retreat in Pennsylvania's Pocono Mountains. The discussion was informal and devoted to the polls and forecasts of the 1952 election. Given his antagonism toward journalists, and his eagerness to court the favor of social scientists, it was unsurprising that Roper upbraided the news media in his remarks, saying, "We learned that the press is not ready to handle the survey tool properly." He reiterated his view that pre-election polls were best used as instruments for probing and assessing voters' views of problems. "If this valuable analysis is discontinued or ever thrown out the window because your prediction is off, then polling is in danger," Roper said, adding, "Our problem is to get the press to accept polls as analytical and speculative, not as predictive tools."[64]

Gallup spoke next, and disagreed with Roper, saying that advances in polling methodology were more likely to come from making predictions rather than avoiding them. "You pay a terrible penalty for your mistakes if you're wrong," Gallup said, "but that's how you move ahead in research." He added that he found "little social value in election forecasting, but it is still the best way to test, and perfect, our techniques."[65]

The Roper-Gallup exchange was not heated and, according to the report of the conference proceedings, "No conclusion was reached; indeed perhaps none could be." The conference report also noted, perceptively, that when "polltakers themselves disagree on these points, the public may be pardoned for being somewhat confused about the true role of political polling."[66]

A prominent political analyst of the time, the syndicated columnist David Lawrence, sided with Roper. The pollsters' "proper role is assembling data—not making predictions," Lawrence wrote shortly after the election. "Thus instead of trying to allocate the vote of those who were undecided and noncommittal, the polls might better have made no allocations of their own whatsoever, but instead might have supplied the reasons for noncommittal attitudes. It isn't essential for them to get a numerical percentage figure for the Nation as a whole."[67]

Lawrence spoke as something of a hero in the American press, given his largely accurate forecast of the 1952 election. In what may be thought of as "shoe-leather" reporting from an armchair, Lawrence late in the campaign mailed 1,169 questionnaires to newspaper editors in every state, soliciting opinions about which presidential candidate was most likely to carry the state.

Lawrence maintained that "an editor knows his own city and State, for he or his reporters are in everyday contact with the politicians and the community leaders. . . . The editors [who responded to the questionnaire] had better collective judgment than the public-opinion experts had in the polls."[68]

Lawrence reported receiving 1,150 replies from editors.[69] Based on those returns, he concluded that Eisenhower would win handily and said as much in a column just before the election. He projected Eisenhower would win 32 states and 357 electoral votes while Stevenson would carry 14 states and 149 electoral votes. Two states were too close to call.[70] Lawrence's forecast in a way was faintly reminiscent of James Farley's survey of Democratic party leaders and activists in 1936, a canvassing that allowed him to predict Roosevelt's landslide with impressive accuracy.

Although not quite as striking as Farley's spot-on call, Lawrence's projection stood out amid the timorous, poll-based assessments of 1952. And Lawrence was lauded by fellow journalists. Krock of the *New York Times*, for example, wrote in an Election Day column that "only Mr. David Lawrence has ventured this year on an unreserved prophesy."[71] Raymond Moley, the syndicated columnist, praised Lawrence's survey of editors as "an excellent way of forecasting the result," asserting that "the best judges [of an election's outcome] are the newspapermen in the various States. They supply the common sense of which 'scientific' polls are in need."[72]

Lawrence seemed to revel in the accolades. He pasted several congratulatory columns and editorials into a small scrapbook he called a "'Memory Book' on 1952." One of the tributes came from Carl E. Brazier, an editor at the *Seattle Times*, who wrote:

> Four years ago, the pollsters took a terrible beating: they all agreed on a definite Dewey-victory prediction. Ever since, the polls have been fighting desperately to justify their existence and trying to regain public confidence . . . . The professional pollsters [in 1952] . . . rode the fence straight down the middle so they wouldn't be hurt too much either way. Such lack of courage is hardly calculated to win back that public confidence they lost four years ago. Particularly in comparison with David Lawrence, who had the courage to give forth with a definite prediction and who proved to have such accurate state-by-state information.

Perhaps, Brazier concluded, "the polls should confine their interviews to newspaper editors."[73] Also pasted into Lawrence's "Memory Book" was an editorial in the *Tulsa Tribune*, which said: "Without slide rules, electronic brains or tea leaves Dave stuck his neck out like a giraffe in a phone booth.

Fearlessly he gave Eisenhower 357 electoral votes to 149 for Stevenson. It was the closest shot we've seen."[74] The *Morning Call* in Paterson, New Jersey, credited Lawrence for "sampling the unbiased, clear-thinking opinions of newspaper editors throughout the nation," producing "the most reliable estimate of the probable electoral vote we have seen."[75]

Lawrence was an intriguing character. He was the founding editor of *U.S. News and World Report* magazine and wrote Washington-based columns from 1919 until his death in 1973. He seldom took vacations, deplored the expansion of the federal government during Franklin Roosevelt's terms, opposed the atomic bombing of Japan, abhorred communism, and for a time supported Senator Joseph R. McCarthy's campaign to expose communists in government. Lawrence thought of himself as a "conservative liberal."[76] And he was something of a contrarian. "No matter in which direction the tide may choose to flow," a journalist friend said of Lawrence, "Dave is more inclined to buck it than float with it."[77]

Lawrence was no poll-basher. A collection of his papers at Princeton University reveal that he and Gallup carried on a cordial, intermittent correspondence for years. Lawrence was no flawless oracle, either. He had, after all, predicted Dewey's election in 1948 "by a substantial majority in the Electoral College."[78]

The 1952 campaign brought a measure of prominence to another exponent of "shoe-leather" reporting. He was Samuel Lubell, a journalist who developed an exhaustive technique in which voting data were springboards for in-depth, in-person interviews in key wards and precincts around the country. In 1952, Lubell spent four months at the grassroots, conducting interviews in twenty-six cities and sixteen rural counties across fifteen states. He said what he "found around the country convinced me that most of the pollsters and forecasters were hedging. They were feathering their nests with two alibis—first, that there was a big undecided vote, and, second, that there was a possibility of a last-minute shift. My house-to-house conversations with voters all over the country persuaded me that the big swing against the Democrats took place long before the campaign started."[79] In the end, though, Lubell did suggest that Eisenhower could win the popular vote but lose the electoral vote.

Lubell was friendly, garrulous, and earnest in reviewing voting records to determine where in the country to conduct his in-depth interviews. "He was a master interviewer," one admirer wrote, "adept at steering any conversation with a stranger, who was also blessed with a scholarly mind and a . . . fascination with old election records."[80] Lubell honed his intensive-interviewing technique while writing a syndicated column. He also published six books, including *White and Black: Test of a Nation*, an historical assessment of U.S. race relations in which he wrote that "we are like two warring nations on this issue. . . . It is time we started thinking of how to make racial peace among ourselves."[81]

For all his productivity, Lubell and his techniques are rarely recalled in journalism or polling circles, no doubt because his interviewing model was too intensive, time-consuming, and singular to be widely adopted. It was a technique not readily transferable. At heart, Lubell was wary of pollsters and their quantitative ways. Philip Meyer, a former journalist who promoted the use of social science techniques in newsgathering, recalled the advice Lubell shared about pollsters and survey researchers at a conference of the American Association for Public Opinion Research. "Don't become one of these people, Phil," Meyer quoted him as saying. "Stay an honest man."[82]

In the history of polling's predictive failures, the landslide of 1952 is often overlooked. While it was much-discussed and ridiculed at the time, the polling failure in the Eisenhower-Stevenson race wasn't quite like the out-of-the-blue thunderclap of 1948. It prompted no soul-searching or crow-eating among pollsters, no hand-wringing, no urgent investigation by a special committee of the Social Sciences Research Council. After all, survey research had become more entrenched than ever by 1952, certainly for commercial, marketing, and government purposes.

Perceptive newspaper commentary observed that polling certainly wasn't doomed by polling failure. "Undoubtedly we'll go right on having these polls as important elections approach in the future," Winston Phelps, survey editor for the *Providence Sunday Journal* in Rhode Island, wrote after the 1952 election. "For we humans are impatient. We have an insatiable desire to peer into the future and anticipate the outcome of prize fights, football games—and elections. The pre-election forecasts, whether accurate or not, have a wide appeal."[83]

The pollsters' error in 1952 was conspicuous but could be interpreted as one of degree. For all its hedging and equivocation, Gallup's final pre-election poll did have Eisenhower slightly ahead. So did Crossley's final poll, as well as the one Roper revealed on the eve of the election. But none of the pollsters expressed great confidence in their pre-election forecasts. They were mindful perhaps of a key finding of the SSRC committee report in 1948, which criticized pollsters for predicting the outcome "without qualification."[84] Crossley pointed to another explanation for timidity, acknowledging after the 1952 election that "we were still suffering from the shell shock of 1948" and "didn't quite dare to trust our own data" in the Eisenhower-Stevenson race.[85]

The final pre-election polls did not detect particularly well the qualitative factors that propelled the landslide—factors such as Eisenhower's engaging personality and prestige as war hero, Stevenson's limitations as a campaigner,[86] and the broad desire for a change after twenty years of Democratic rule, not to mention popular dissatisfaction with the stalemated war in Korea and with corruption in government. The "mess in Washington" was a theme of *both* major party campaigns in 1952.[87] In retrospect it seems clear, wrote one historian of the campaign, that "there was virtually nothing that Eisenhower could have done in the fall to lose the election, short of being caught in a personal scandal (and one wonders if even *that* would have allowed Stevenson to break ahead)."[88]

Exasperation with the polls and their predictive failure ran deep but the sentiment was not long sustained. Critics were unable to present what Amy Fried has called "a coherent argument or a united, mobilized community" in opposition to election polling.[89] And prospective alternatives—such as Lubell's intensive grassroots interviewing or a somewhat similar experiment in "shoe-leather" reporting that the *New York Times* pursued in 1956—proved to be less than rousing successes.

The *Times* pursued its experiment to lessen a dependency on polling data. It dispatched four teams of reporters to twenty-seven states during the 1956 campaign to assess attitudes and trends in the presidential and congressional races.[90] Their reporting was supplemented by part-time correspondents in the twenty-one other states. Max Frankel, who spent fifty years at the *Times* and retired in 1994 as the newspaper's executive editor, was in 1956 a young reporter assigned to one of the roving teams. He recalled that the *Times* had "lost confidence in polls." So he went knocking on doors "to gather voter sentiment. I drove through odd precincts of Milwaukee and Austin, Arlington [Virginia] and St. Joseph [Missouri], feeding notes to William S. White," under whose byline several team-based reports appeared.[91] This commitment in time and "shoe-leather" reporting reached a fairly obvious conclusion: in his rematch with Stevenson, Eisenhower was going to win reelection easily—

although, the *Times* said, probably not by margins as sizable as those of 1952.[92] In fact, Eisenhower's popular vote margin was much greater. In 1956, he exceeded his popular vote plurality of four years earlier by more than 2.8 million.

Even though it was not accompanied by the stunning repercussions of the Dewey-Truman failed call, the election of 1952 was a little-recognized turning point in public opinion research, a pivotal moment in election polling's checkered past. Major change was afoot. As we will see, polling's reach, techniques, and relationship to journalism were to change markedly in the years after 1952. Newcomers such as Louis Harris and Warren Mitofsky brought dimension and controversy to election polling.

The 1952 election was the last stand for one of the Original Three pollsters. Arch Crossley, who said the Eisenhower-Stevenson election had brought him little more than red ink and headaches,[93] gave up polling presidential elections. His principal reason for leaving the field, Crossley wrote years later, was expense along with the fact that Gallup's widely used polls had left him little room to compete for newspaper clients.[94] "The quadrennial series of syndicated presidential polls that had begun in 1936 ended in 1952," Crossley wrote, "chiefly because the cost of a reliable job considerably exceeded what newspapers not carrying the Gallup Poll could pay for."[95]

Crossley sold his company in 1954 to a subsidiary of the market research firm Stewart, Dougall & Associates, forming Crossley SD Surveys Inc. He retired in 1961 and thereafter was regarded as a "grand old man" of election polling.[96] Roper, meanwhile, expressed reluctance about resuming presidential election polling in 1956, telling a reporter for the *Wall Street Journal* months before that election, "Those pre-election polls are money-losing propositions. I haven't decided whether to poll in 1956 or not."[97] In the end, he did. Roper's son, Burns, explained during the campaign: "I guess the main reason we do these election polls at all is to prove we're not yellow."[98]

For reasons unclear, Roper did not publicize its poll results. Roper's internal records indicate that he estimate the 1956 Eisenhower-Stevenson rematch at 60 percent to 40 percent in favor of the general,[99] which did not diverge dramatically from the popular vote outcome of 57.4 percent to 42 percent. Roper came even closer in forecasting the John F. Kennedy–Richard Nixon race in 1960. But his final poll that year pointed to the wrong winner. The volatility of 1960 race made for "a forecasting nightmare," Roper said almost two weeks before election, adding then that "either candidate could win in a landslide."[100]

At the end, Roper's poll signaled a narrow win by Nixon, 49 percent to 47 percent.[101] Gallup's final poll, on the other hand, placed Kennedy ahead, 51 percent to 49 percent, among respondents who had made up their minds.[102] Just three days earlier, Gallup had reported that Kennedy was ahead by six percentage points.[103]

Although Kennedy's razor-thin victory became clear on the day after the election, Burns Roper (by then a one-third partner in his father's firm) said in an internal memorandum that Nixon still could win the popular vote and cautioned the staff: "I'm not about to take any malarkey about having 'picked the wrong man.'"[104] But that's what the firm had done. Nixon lost by almost 113,000 votes.

Four years before the Kennedy-Nixon race, Roper's company had been rocked by the departure of Louis Harris, a partner and protégé of Elmo Roper, who left to set up his own opinion research firm in the Empire State Building. Harris was short, brash, and energetic, and believed himself unappreciated and overworked at Roper's company.[105] When he left, he took three Roper clients with him, which infuriated Elmo Roper.[106] Later, Roper was told that Harris had been actively recruiting clients before quitting Roper's firm.[107]

Harris may have been devious and sly in leaving Roper. He was certainly sluggish and sloppy in fulfilling a commitment to contribute to a study, led by Paul Lazarsfeld, about the effects of McCarthyism in American education in the 1950s.[108] Lazarsfeld was a prominent sociologist and media theorist at Columbia University who had helped finance Harris's 1954 book *Is There a Republican Majority?*[109] On the education study, Harris's contribution not only was late, Lazarsfeld said in a scathing letter, but also was "so wide of the mark!" He told Harris, "I think we should terminate the agony of trying to keep you in touch with the study." Lazarsfeld added that "you must understand how gravely you have hurt the study and me: a highly embarrassing delay in the publication schedule; heavy expenses for which there is not yet any budgetary coverage; and most of all a terrific strain on my own time and strength in the course of an academic year. I do not want to blame you, but I also cannot afford to keep on smiling and discussing with you what you might one day do."[110] Lazarsfeld shared a copy of the letter with Roper. In reply, Harris blamed his sluggishness on "getting my new firm underway and rolling." He disputed the claim that tardiness had caused Lazarsfeld "heavy expenses" and suggested that in making the charge the sociologist "must surely have been swept away by the welling emotion" that characterized his letter.[111]

In time, Harris steadied himself and made a reputation as the pollster for John Kennedy during the 1960 presidential campaign. Afterward, *Newsweek* published a flattering cover story that said it was "hardly a secret that Harris is close to Mr. Kennedy and that the President has real affection for Harris. They're bound together by mutual love of politics and close association through the 1960 primaries, when Harris joined the Kennedy inner circle."[112]

The reality, though, was more nuanced. And less kind. "Harris' success is built on illusion," Michael Wheeler wrote in *Lies, Damn Lies, and Statistics,* an entertaining if often critical look at pollsters published in 1976. "The quality of the polls he did for Kennedy was spotty at best, and, in the end, Kennedy gave his surveys little weight." Publicly, the Kennedys praised Harris and his polls, Wheeler wrote, but "privately they laughed behind his back."[113]

His association with Kennedy and his private polling in dozens of other political campaigns propelled Harris to launch his own public poll in 1963, begin a weekly column on public opinion research, and eventually become the most prominent rival to George Gallup as the country's best-known political pollster.[114]

Wheeler wrote that being "the second best-known pollster apparently grate[d] on Harris and may have caused him to make some mistakes of judgment in an effort to scoop Gallup."[115] A case in point, according to Wheeler, was the miscall of the 1968 presidential election, a three-way race between Nixon, Vice President Hubert H. Humphrey, and Alabama governor George Wallace. Humphrey trailed Nixon throughout the campaign, in part because he was tied to President Lyndon Johnson's prosecution of an unpopular war in Vietnam.

In the campaign's waning hours, Humphrey vaulted into a lead of four percentage points, according to a poll Harris took two days before the election. The poll was a stunning development, a surprising twist to the campaign's trajectory. Nixon's campaign manager, John N. Mitchell, accused Harris of revealing his partisan sympathies in the last-minute poll. He called Harris "the former Democratic pollster" and said, "The voting public has long ago become aware of the inaccuracies of the Harris polling record."[116]

Harris had overreached. Nixon won the election by less than one percentage point, which, for Harris, meant a miscall of nearly five points. He later said he "was chagrined" by the result, insisting that it came down to "a matter

FIGURE 12. Outspoken and brash, pollster Louis Harris reported that Hubert H. Humphrey had overtaken Richard M. Nixon as Election Day neared in the race for president in 1968. Harris's poll was off target by about five percentage points. (Credit: Associated Press)

of judgment—is there a surge here for Humphrey? He had been gaining, closing ground all the way through."[117] Had Harris's final poll been accurate, "he would have been the hero and Gallup the goat," Wheeler wrote, "but the opposite was the case."[118]

Harris made another misguided prediction two days after the election, declaring that when all ballots were counted, Humphrey likely would be ahead in popular votes but would lose the Electoral College tally.[119] But when all ballots were counted, Nixon led by more than five hundred thousand votes.

For Gallup, the 1968 race brought one of his best-ever predictions. His poll estimated the popular vote breakdown to within mere fractions of a percentage point of the result.[120] The *New York Times* reported that "operators of the Gallup Poll" were jubilant about their predictive success.[121] "We're floating on air," exclaimed Gallup's son, George Jr.[122] Even Harris declared himself ready "to take my hat off to Dr. Gallup for a final poll that was indeed accurate."[123]

Much had changed for Gallup since missing the landslide of 1952. He gradually moved away from quota-control sampling in favor of procedures that incorporated elements of probability sampling, as critics had long recommended.[124] Gallup called these techniques "pinpoint" or "precinct" sampling, and they focused on states and election districts that tended to reflect national voting patterns. "Pinpoint" sampling had its drawbacks, but Gallup declared himself reasonably satisfied. "We don't know," he wrote in 1957, "whether a better system will be developed or not."[125]

But far more significant developments in polling were in the offing. The late 1960s and '70s were a notably fertile time for innovation in opinion research. Decisive developments of those years had the effect of upgrading and invigorating the field, and finally untethering it from the sluggish and expensive process of conducting interviews in person. Figuring prominently in the developments of those years was a brash, bearded newcomer named Warren J. Mitofsky, who was hired in 1967 to head the polling operation for CBS News.

Mitofsky, who had pursued but never completed doctoral studies at the University of Minnesota, was a statistician who joined CBS from the U.S. Census Bureau. He wasn't the network's first choice, as he later acknowledged. CBS, he said, wanted to hire Morris Hansen, a well-regarded statistician who was nearing retirement from the Census Bureau.[126] Mitofsky then was in his early thirties and proved to be a colorful, outspoken, and sometimes acerbic character who seemed never to shrink from a good quarrel.

Murray Edelman, a colleague of Mitofsky at the Census Bureau and later at CBS News, recalled that "people in the field knew Warren for his creativity, his dedication, and his passion ... and they have the scars to prove it."[127] Mitofsky "didn't tolerate fools, poseurs or corporate tools, and he delighted in telling them so," wrote Richard Morin, the *Washington Post*'s longtime polling director, adding that even allies thought Mitofsky "began too many sentences with the words, 'Here's why you're wrong.'" Shortly after taking the job at the *Post*, Morin introduced himself to Mitofsky, who smiled an off-kilter smile and said, "Congratulations, I've never heard of you."[128]

Mitofsky had a sense of the history of opinion research, which many pollsters tend to lack or ignore. For example, a collection of Mitofsky's papers at the University of Connecticut include yellowing news releases about topics such as CBS coverage of the 1948 presidential election, the memory and lessons of which he sometimes cited. Mitofsky was a resolute advocate of probability-based sampling and brought that methodology to CBS.[129]

Among his most consequential contributions was developing in the 1970s an efficient and reliable way of conducting telephone surveys using random-digit dialing techniques. This development eventually enabled telephone surveys to replace face-to-face interviewing, which was much more expensive. Polling conducted by random-digit dialing became the industry's gold-standard sampling technique for two decades or more—until landline phones gradually became less common and people who had them became less inclined to take calls.

In collaboration with Joseph Waksberg, his former boss at the Census Bureau, Mitofsky developed a procedure that allowed pollsters to reach households having unlisted numbers, which expanded the coverage and reli-ability of telephone surveys, while undoubtedly annoying more than a few would-be poll respondents.[130] In any case, random-digit dialing helped make opinion polling faster, and a good deal less expensive, than door-to-door surveying.[131]

Mitofsky was better known as "the father of exit polling,"[132] those surveys of voters as they left polling places on Election Day, the results of which help newscasters and analysts to project election outcomes and explain why they turned out as they did. Participants in exit polls are randomly selected and invited to complete a questionnaire asking for whom they voted, and why. Mitofsky borrowed the idea from surveys conducted of movie patrons as they left theaters.[133] In 1967, he introduced the first full-fledged exit poll, in the governor's race in Kentucky.[134] At first, the surveys of voters were called, not "exit polls," but rather "election day polls."[135] The objective was to allow CBS to identify and explain trends in voting as returns were being counted, giving the network an analytical and interpretative edge in the highly competitive coverage of Election Night.

In the 1968 elections, CBS expanded exit polling to twenty-one states and rival networks had developed similar operations of their own by 1980.[136] That year on Election Night, NBC News systematically used its exit polls to declare that Ronald Reagan had won a sweeping victory in the presidential election—a call that was made long before CBS's projection, and hours before the polls closed in many Western states. NBC's early and unequivocal projections stirred indignation and resentment, especially in California, where voters were said to have left lines at polling places in droves. Although scant firsthand evidence was ever produced to support such claims,[137] the controversy became the first of many to bedevil exit polling.

Mitofsky also figured prominently in the first of several collaborative ventures by leading news organizations to share costs and resources and become prominent forces in opinion polling.[138] CBS News launched its polling partnership with the *New York Times* in 1975, ahead of similar ventures by the Associated Press, ABC News, the *Washington Post*, NBC News, the *Wall Street Journal*, CNN, and *USA Today*, all of which have remained prominent in public opinion research. The CBS News/*New York Times* polling collaboration lasted more than forty years.

Given Mitofsky's principal role, the first months of the CBS News/*New York Times* partnership were turbulent, perhaps predictably so. Mitofsky couldn't stand Gary Orren, the Harvard professor whom the *Times* hired as its consultant on the polling arrangement, and he stopped attending meetings where Orren was present. Mitofsky found Orren arrogant and difficult, according to David Moore's account in *The Superpollsters*. For his part, Orren was put off by Mitofsky's forceful self-confidence. "He never sees an issue as gray, but always as black or white," Orren complained of Mitofsky. "And he thinks he is always right. He *never* makes a mistake."[139]

Their disputes emerged partly from conflicting expectations about opinion polls: the *Times* wanted more detailed questions on each survey topic while CBS favored fewer questions with more topics. Eventually, a compromise was reached by designating major and minor topics in the joint surveys.[140]

The CBS News/*New York Times* collaboration not only heralded joint ventures by other large news outlets; it was emblematic of a broad, newfound interest in polls and survey research among journalists in the late 1970s.[141] Promoting this interest was *Precision Journalism*, a book by Philip Meyer, a journalist who encouraged news organizations to adopt the tools and methods of social science.[142] By doing so, he argued, "we journalists would be wrong less often" in understanding major issues.[143]

Precision Journalism was a clear challenge to time-honored reliance on "shoe-leather" reporting. Only by accident, Meyer noted, would reporters who venture out to interview handfuls of people at random accurately capture the views and opinions of any larger group.[144] *Precision Journalism* was a dense, proselytizing book that declared "journalism must become social science in a hurry,"[145] and outlined how that could be done in practice.

Of course it's impossible to say how profoundly the book's guidance and encouragement influenced and altered newsroom practices. It did not necessarily revolutionize journalism. But the growth in opinion polling—and in data-rich studies prepared from computer-based analysis—were real enough among news organizations. By 1979, "dozens of large news organizations" were reported to "have made major commitments to precision journalism," including sample surveys.[146] Meyer noted that the "tools of sampling, computer analysis, and statistical inference increased the traditional power of the reporter without changing the nature of the mission—to find the facts, understand them, and explain them without wasting time."[147]

The *New York Times* reported that the 1970s had seen an "extraordinary expansion" in opinion polling[148] but also noted the growth included no small amount of slipshod work. The *Times* quoted Mitofsky as saying in early 1980 that his polling unit at CBS News was aware of 147 discrete opinion polls, 43 of which had been launched in 1978 and 1979. Fewer than half of the 147 polls were grounded in reliable methodology, Mitofsky said.

This prevalence of sloppy poll-taking, he added, raised the prospect that the 1980 presidential election would be a replay of 1948.[149] The 1980 election pitted President Jimmy Carter against Reagan and a strong third-party candidate, former congressman John Anderson. As it turned out, the 1980 election was no 1948 redux. It much more resembled the outcome of 1952, a lopsided runaway that pollsters—Mitofsky and Gallup, among them—did not see coming.

CHAPTER 5

The "Close Race That Never Happened"

Miscalling the 1980 Election

Just after 5 in the afternoon, Eastern time, on Election Day 1980, veteran CBS News anchorman Walter Cronkite broke into a talk show airing on the network to report that Republican candidate Ronald Reagan was winning the presidential election. And winning handily.

"As the balloting continues," Cronkite said, "the CBS News/New York Times survey of voters across the country shows Ronald Reagan with a substantial lead nationwide over Jimmy Carter," the Democrat and incumbent. "While the race is closest in the East," Cronkite went on, "Reagan is leading in the other three regions of the country." In wrapping up the bulletin, Cronkite said, "To repeat, the CBS News/New York Times exit poll shows Ronald Reagan with a substantial lead nationwide over Jimmy Carter."[1]

Cronkite repeated the news about ninety minutes later, at the outset of the CBS evening newscast. He referred broadly to national exit polls conducted separately by the country's three broadcast networks and declared: "Even with the polls still open across the country in this presidential election, there was the smell of victory in the air for Republican Ronald Reagan. The three television networks each poll voters as they leave polling places in randomly selected precincts, and all three of the networks showed substantial leads for Reagan."[2]

Cronkite's "smell of victory" pronouncement that evening—it was still midafternoon on the West Coast—was among the first signs the pre-election polls of 1980 were way off, that instead of the eyelash-thin outcome they had anticipated,[3] Reagan was going to win easily, in a rout unforeseen by pollsters.

The election was turning out to be "a close race that never happened," as the *Washington Post*'s in-house critic later wrote.[4]

The breaking news from Cronkite, who that night reported presidential election returns for the last time before retirement,[5] anticipated a controversy that broke a few hours later. The controversy centered around a rival network's unprecedented use of exit polling to project the outcome of a presidential race. At 8:15 p.m. Eastern—with only about 5 percent of the national vote counted—the NBC network outright declared Reagan had won, even though polling places had not closed in California, New York, Rhode Island, and many other states. NBC's projection was based principally on results from exit polls—the first time such surveys had been used systematically to call the outcome of a presidential race. Not long after NBC's projection, Carter went on television to acknowledge his defeat.

The early and accurate projection of Reagan's victory was a singular coup for NBC in network television's brutal competition to report presidential election results.[6] But NBC irritated would-be voters in the West where, supposedly, many of them stepped out of lines at polling places and headed home in disgust once Reagan's victory was known.[7] The early call was said to have trimmed turnout and, in turn, purportedly affected results of closer races down ballot. In addition, the early call touched off a dispute about the uses of projections and exit polling in presidential elections that percolated for years.

The 1980 election also illuminated once again long-standing tensions between "shoe-leather" reporting and pre-election opinion polls, tensions between qualitative and quantitative assessments of public opinion. The news media's emphasis on, and participation in, election polling reached new heights in 1980. "Virtually every major news organization wanted to have a poll to call its own," the *Washington Journalism Review* noted.[8] But the polls never quite captured what was happening on the ground as the election neared. And the sweep of Reagan's victory seemed to suggest that journalists were well-served by practicing "shoe-leather" reporting.

It was undeniable that pollsters had missed badly. Again, they had failed to give Americans a reasonably accurate sense of what was in store. No published pre-election poll had anticipated what would happen in the race between Carter, Reagan, and John B. Anderson, a maverick Republican congressman running as an independent. No prominent pollster came close to suggesting a rout was in the making. Afterward, pollsters quarreled openly and disagreeably about what had caused their predictive failure. Was it a late, sudden, and

'I DON'T KNOW ABOUT YOU, BUT I'M GOING BACK TO TEA LEAVES AND EYE OF NEWT.'

FIGURE 13. Award-winning newspaper cartoonist Tony Auth poked fun at pollsters after their failure in 1980 to anticipate Ronald Reagan's sweeping election victory over President Jimmy Carter. (Credit: AUTH ©The Philadelphia Inquirer; reprinted with permission of Andrews McMeel Syndication. All rights reserved.)

dramatic shift in voter preferences that broke open a tight race? Or was it a matter of a steady, more gradual accretion of popular support in the campaign's last week that padded a slender lead for Reagan and made him a winner by nearly ten percentage points?

Pollsters squabbled at length over such questions, but couldn't agree.[9] Postmortems went on for years[10] before sputtering out without reaching a consensus. The unresolved dispute about what had gone wrong did nothing to burnish pollsters' reputations or that of their industry. Compounding the embarrassment was that the private pollsters for the respective campaigns— Patrick Caddell for Carter[11] and Richard Wirthlin for Reagan—had pegged the election far more accurately. Their final internal polls estimated Reagan would win by ten percentage points, or nearly so.[12] They disagreed only about when or how quickly Reagan built that advantage.

Bewilderment about the errant polls was pervasive and questions about what had happened arose as votes were counted on Election Night. "We have here what I think reasonably could be called a landslide, or certainly something approaching a landslide," David Brinkley, the veteran NBC News anchorman, said on the air on Election Night. "Where did it come from? Nobody antici-pated it. No polls predicted it. No one saw it coming. How did that happen?"[13] His colleagues on the set, John Chancellor and Tom Brokaw, had no conclu-sive answers for him.

As we have seen, journalists take their lead from polls and tend to be unforgiving when polls surprise them in a presidential election. So it was in 1980. Journalists traded in expressions of dismay and derision. Michael Gart-ner, the nationally prominent editor of the *Des Moines Register*,[14] suggested: "Maybe the polls have outlived their usefulness. . . . Nobody expected what happened."[15] The pollster and political commentator Michael Barone con-ceded that the "polls had not prepared most of us for what happened."[16] The 1980 election, said Richard Leonard, editor of the *Milwaukee Journal*, was "not one of the glorious moments for polling. It is an art that leaves much to be desired."[17] The *Washington Post*'s ombudsman, Bill Green, wondered in print whether "the experience of 1980 will lead the press to turn its back on polls."[18] A report by the Knight News Service said the country's "pollsters, part of the American political priesthood, have found themselves defrocked by an elector-ate whose performance at the ballot box Tuesday confounded most of the predictions."[19]

The unexpected and lopsided outcome demonstrated anew, wrote Robert G. Kaiser of the *Washington Post*, "the voters' right to inflict surprises on all the experts." The results, he said, revealed "a good deal about the fallibility of pollsters and . . . the persistent unpredictability of the American electorate."[20] His observations about the electorate's "unpredictability" were echoes of remarks by Edward R. Murrow the day after the election in 1952, when the polls also missed a runaway result.

The miscall of 1980 was a bad one. Martin Plissner, the CBS News politi-cal director, pointed out that the discrepancy that year between the CBS News poll and the election results were comparable to Gallup's "when he forecast Dewey defeating Truman." Like Gallup in 1948, Plissner noted, CBS News had company in 1980.[21] The CBS News/*New York Times* final poll gave Rea-gan a one-point lead, 44 percent to 43 percent, with 8 percent for Anderson. The final Gallup poll had Reagan ahead, 44 percent to 43 percent, with 7 percent for Anderson; its next-to-last poll, released in late October, indicated Carter held a three-point advantage. The *Washington Post* released two con-flicting polls during the final week of the campaign. One showed Carter in the lead by four percentage points; the other, a survey of 1,800 would-be voters

FIGURE 14. Rival pollsters Warren J. Mitofsky, left, and Louis Harris, right, posed with George Gallup at the National Press Club in Washington, DC, a few days before the vote in 1980. It was Gallup's last presidential election before his death. (Credit: John Metelsky/ National Press Club Archives)

who had been polled in September and were re-interviewed in late October, gave Reagan a three-point edge.[22]

The closest any published poll came in the closing days of the campaign was the ABC News/Lou Harris poll, which estimated that Reagan was ahead by five percentage points. Five points was the largest discrepancy in any final presidential poll that Harris had ever conducted. Harris also forecast that Carter would win 140 electoral votes; he won 49. But still, Harris crowed. "My neck was out a mile," Harris said, adding, "I was the only pollster to say that Ronald Reagan would win."[23]

The other published polls, Harris asserted, had the combined effect of misleading an "army of political reporters in the news media" and those polls together represented "one of the most massive hedges in the history of political reporting."[24] Harris touted his telephone-sampling methods as superior, saying his interviewers called back would-be respondents as many as three times to complete a survey. "Most polling organizations do not pursue this strict call-back procedure," Harris declared.[25]

His haughtiness grated, and surely deepened Harris's unpopularity in the polling fraternity.[26] "Being the best of the worst is not something I would go around bragging about," said Warren J. Mitofsky of CBS News and one of Harris's most persistent adversaries. "All this self-serving nonsense about how well Harris did—his results are only slightly less dreadful than ours."[27] No pundit or pollster, Mitofsky said, "really caught what was going to happen" in the 1980 election.[28] That included Mitofsky. He had said at the National Press Club in Washington shortly before the election, "If there's one clear conclusion from most of the nation-wide polls showing Carter and Reagan running neck-and-neck, it is that the electoral vote margin for the winner will also be small."[29] Reagan rolled up an electoral vote landslide, 489 to Carter's 49.

Mitofsky, who never seemed reluctant to indulge in a good feud, resumed his criticism of Harris and his polling at a conference of pollsters and survey researchers in 1981. Harris, he said, "has regularly had post-election praise for his own work—regardless of its accuracy—for as long as he has been in the business. . . . Harris' self-serving claims following the 1980 election would make you think his final poll was exactly the same as the national popular vote. When in fact he was further off the final margin than he has ever been in any presidential election since he started in the business."[30]

The biting remarks not only confirmed Mitofsky's prickly competitiveness; they also exposed the latent nastiness of the rivalries among pollsters who, over the years, usually succeeded in masking their antagonisms. George Gallup, after all, had mostly concealed his reservations about Elmo Roper. The miscall of 1980 brought pollsters' antagonisms into public view.

The Reagan-Carter-Anderson campaign was Gallup's last presidential election before his death in July 1984. The failure to detect Reagan's overwhelming victory brought Gallup another opportunity to spin the outcome, to insist on the reliability of his polling techniques despite what was a second successive defective estimate in a presidential race. In 1976, Gallup's final pre-election poll pointed to a one-point victory by President Gerald Ford. Carter won by two percentage points. The failure in 1980 "to determine the full dimension of Reagan's vote," Gallup insisted, was due not "to a flaw in the polling mechanism, but was a matter of timing."[31] But Gallup was well aware of the importance of surveying voters to the end of the campaign; he surely knew that "timing" was crucial to an accurate election forecast. He and fellow

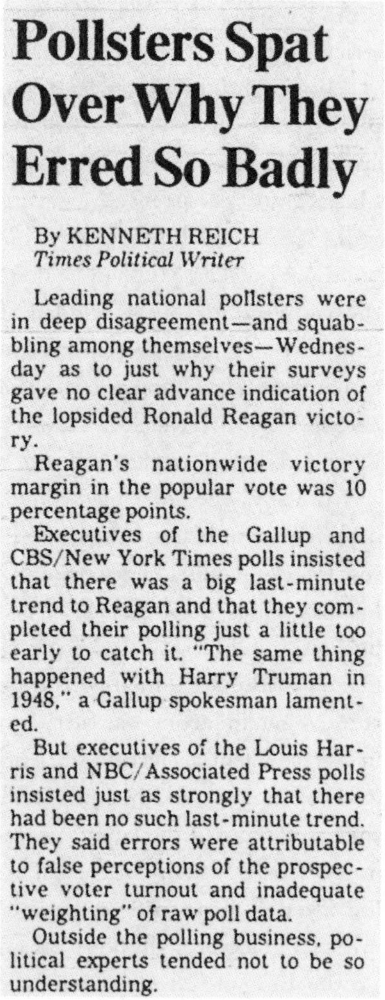

Pollsters Spat Over Why They Erred So Badly

By KENNETH REICH
Times Political Writer

Leading national pollsters were in deep disagreement—and squabbling among themselves—Wednesday as to just why their surveys gave no clear advance indication of the lopsided Ronald Reagan victory.

Reagan's nationwide victory margin in the popular vote was 10 percentage points.

Executives of the Gallup and CBS/New York Times polls insisted that there was a big last-minute trend to Reagan and that they completed their polling just a little too early to catch it. "The same thing happened with Harry Truman in 1948," a Gallup spokesman lamented.

But executives of the Louis Harris and NBC/Associated Press polls insisted just as strongly that there had been no such last-minute trend. They said errors were attributable to false perceptions of the prospective voter turnout and inadequate "weighting" of raw poll data.

Outside the polling business, political experts tended not to be so understanding.

FIGURE 15. Pollsters usually have kept to themselves the disputes arising from their rivalries. Not so in the aftermath of their miscalls of the 1980 election, when antagonism spilled into public view. (Credit: Library of Congress)

pollsters had absorbed that stern lesson in 1948, when ending fieldwork well before Election Day contributed to a polling debacle.[32]

Like Gallup, Mitofsky embraced the notion that an early end to polling caused him to miss the runaway outcome. "I could kick myself," Mitofsky said. "Clearly *our* mistake was not to have polled in the last two days" before the election.[33] Mitofsky was acutely aware of the importance of the final pre-election poll. Ten months earlier, he had pointed out in an internal memorandum that "that last poll must be devoted almost exclusively to producing the best outcome possible. This means a larger sample (about 2,500) with the concentration of questions devoted to obtaining the likelihood of voters turning out on election day and their candidate preferences."[34]

There may have been sound, practical reasons not to squeeze in one last poll during the campaign's final days. Personnel who helped conduct the CBS News/New York Times poll, for example, required preparation time for Election Night duties. "They had lots to do over that final pre-election weekend besides another night of polling," Martin Plissner noted.[35]

Even more important, perhaps, was the expense of another round of polling. The principal reason most pollsters did not survey right up until the last moment "is simple," Time magazine said. Doing so "would have cost too much." Another nationwide survey of at least 1,500 people would cost about $22,500, Time said, noting that Carter's private pollster, Caddell, spent about two million dollars on polling during the fall campaign, far more than public pollsters.[36] Another factor was a misguided "underlying assumption," as Mitofsky put it, "that not much will happen in those final days of the campaign to produce any significant movement of the public from what they will do on Election Day." But 1980 proved to be different, Mitofsky claimed, in that "the only significant movement by the public did occur in the last week" of the campaign.[37]

But the alibis about a premature end to fieldwork seemed to blur the more insistent questions: How could the polls have missed such a one-sided result? How could they have not come close to detecting Reagan's winning margin? Stopping too soon was a plausible but still incomplete explanation for the big miss. Burns Roper, speaking a few years after the 1980 election, rejected the alibi of timing. Roper said he was "very disturbed by the failure of the polls to indicate the magnitude of the Reagan victory in 1980" as well as their overstating the prospects of gubernatorial and senate candidates in 1982 elections.[38]

Presumably, Roper said, "our polling techniques have gotten more and more sophisticated, yet we seem to be missing more and more elections. Why? Many pollsters think it is simply a matter of timing [that] polls are not done quite late enough to catch last minute trends. I seriously question whether there was any last minute trend to Reagan in 1980. I know some pollsters point to evidence that there was a late trend to Reagan. I think there is at least equally strong evidence that there was not."[39] Roper added: "I cannot say why the polls are missing, but I would say to my colleagues, 'don't assume that merely polling 48 hours later will solve all of the problems.' I'm not at all sure that's where the problems lie."[40]

Officials at the Harris Poll, which continued surveying until the day before the election, said they detected no strong movement toward Reagan as the campaign closed. "There was no trend" in the closing hours, said David Neft, then executive vice president for the Harris Poll.[41]

One of the comparatively better polling performances in the overall woeful showing in 1980 was the final pre-election poll jointly conducted by NBC News and the Associated Press. That survey was completed eleven days before the election and showed Reagan ahead by six percentage points. The poll, in other words, indicated that Reagan had built a significant lead *before* the crowded final days of the campaign, before he and Carter convened their only face-to-face debate, and before the Iranian authorities announced conditions for releasing U.S. diplomatic personnel they had held hostage since November 1979.

Carter broke away from the campaign trail on the weekend before the election to return to the White House and monitor the prospective release of the hostages. According to his memoir, he realized that his "political future might well be determined by irrational people on the other side of the world over whom I had no control."[42] It turned out cruelly. The hostages were kept in captivity and "a wave of disillusionment swept the country" shortly before the election, Carter wrote in his memoir,[43] an interpretation reflecting the analysis of his campaign pollster, Patrick Caddell. The hostages were not set free until the day in January 1981 when Reagan was inaugurated.

Carter and his administration officials sought to portray Reagan as unproven and unpredictable—a warmonger, even.[44] Such rhetoric may have contributed to what Burns Roper suggested was a covert or shy Reagan effect that contributed to the polls failing to detect the depth of his support. In other words, respondents declined to tell pollsters they were going to vote for Reagan, a former Hollywood actor before serving two terms as California governor. Many lifelong Democrats could not abide voting for Carter in 1980, Roper said, but they "weren't about to admit they could actually bring themselves to vote for Reagan, saying they would probably end up voting for Carter, when in fact they knew they were going to vote the other way."[45]

Other analysts also pointed to evidence that suggested a "shy Reagan" effect. Fred Barnes, a political commentator then writing for the *Baltimore Sun*, noted that even as a gubernatorial candidate in California, Reagan typically had run "better on Election Day than in pre-election polls, which suggests that some voters are shy about admitting their support for an ex-actor but not as hesitant about voting for him."[46]

The campaign's turbulent closing week no doubt depressed support for Carter and widened Reagan's advantage, as many voters decided that the incumbent didn't deserve another term in office. "Given the choice between an incumbent with a poor job rating and a challenger with little experience, voters will naturally hesitate before making a decision," Michael Barone wrote after the election. "But if the challenger performs reasonably well, there is little question what that decision will be."[47]

Turnout in 1980 was the lowest in a U.S. presidential election since 1948, which was attributable in part to neither candidate's seeming especially appealing.[48] But it also reflected decisions by Democratic voters and independents to stay home because they could not countenance voting for Carter, not after the late-campaign reminders of his presidency's most humiliating failing—the hostage crisis, the first anniversary of which fell on Election Day.

Carter figured that the Iran-hostage crisis was key to his reelection prospects. "If the hostages were released," he wrote in a memoir, "I was convinced my reelection would be assured; if the expectations of the American people were dashed again, there was little chance I could win."[49] A post-election survey by CBS News and the *New York Times* reported that failure to win release of the hostages "was a major element" in shifts of voter sentiment away from Carter,[50] who was criticized for not standing up to the Iranian authorities and their late-campaign intrusions. "What did not come from the White House," wrote Suzanne Garment, a columnist for the *Wall Street Journal*, "was the one act that would have stopped the circus: a definitive statement on just where, for the moment, they could stuff this assault of theirs on the integrity of American elections."[51]

The lackluster, inflation-battered American economy was another important factor in Carter's defeat. The so-called misery index—a sum of the rates of inflation and unemployment (a reading that Carter had invoked in 1976 to pummel Ford)—climbed during his presidency. The misery index stood at 12.5 percent when Carter was elected; at one point in 1980, the index approached 22 percent.

The closing days of the campaign were turbulent but produced clues nonetheless to the election's outcome—clues that news reports seemed to detect more readily than the polls. In a post-election review of campaign news coverage, the *Los Angeles Times* noted that journalists in the days before the election "pictured an increasingly confident Ronald Reagan and an ever-more-worried Jimmy Carter." While the polls were signaling a race too close to call, the *Times* said, "the Republican challenger looked more and more like the winner as the [final] week wore on."[52]

The lone debate of the campaign between major party candidates came during that week, and it brought what widely was recognized as another setback for Carter. As Robert Kaiser wrote in the *Washington Post*, "It was Carter who built up the image of Reagan as some sort of political ogre; when it came to the debate, all Reagan had to do was stand up and smile to shatter the entire Carter strategy."[53] Reagan was more than genial and reassuring. He skewered Carter with the most memorable passages of the debate, saying in closing: "Are you better off than you were four years ago? Is it easier for you to go and buy things in the stores than it was four years ago? Is there more or less unemployment in the country than there was four years ago? Is America as respected throughout the world as it was? . . . This country doesn't have to be in the shape that it is in. We do not have to go on sharing in scarcity, with the country getting worse off, with unemployment growing."[54]

Given the troubles and setbacks that beset Carter's campaign, it seems fairly remarkable that the published polls almost entirely failed to detect his fading support. The 1980 election was, to be sure, a case of polls gone bad, and then some. It also was something of a watershed in the interplay of journalism and opinion polling. It was the first presidential election for a number of media partnerships that conducted or commissioned pre-election polls. The number of polls during the 1980 presidential campaign proliferated markedly, at the national, regional, and state levels.[55] Not only did these new media partnerships bring fresh dimension to pre-election polling; their entry into polling stirred controversy as well.

Critics like syndicated columnist Nicholas Von Hoffman regarded media-sponsored opinion polling as ethically questionable, a hazard to well-intentioned and evenhanded journalism. News organizations, Von Hoffman complained, "are making their own news and flacking [or promoting] it as though it were an event they were reporting on over which they had no control, like an earthquake or a traffic accident." He conceded that it was "too much to hope that news organizations will get out of the business of making news and confine themselves to reporting it. The answer is to teach our politicians to be like the population at large, which has long since decided to discount polls as harmless hullabaloo."[56]

Von Hoffman was waging a losing battle. Spurred by works such as Philip Meyer's *Precision Journalism*, many American news organizations had embraced the argument that social science research methods, including opinion polls, represented another tool to enhance, deepen, and differentiate their news reporting. Media polling was especially attractive because it generated "a political news story that nobody else is going to have," Glenn H. Roberts, director of polling for the *Des Moines Register*, was quoted as saying. "It's a chance to get some exclusive news."[57]

In a way, the popularity of "precision journalism" was not unlike the fads that have swept the field from time to time.[58] This one arose in the immediate aftermath of the Watergate scandal, in which investigative journalism had figured prominently though far from decisively. But "precision journalism" techniques, especially the use of computers to assemble and evaluate statistical data, produced analytical reporting on topics such as school desegregation, election campaign contributions, and the content of local television news.[59]

By 1980, the trend in newsrooms to embrace practices of "precision journalism" had reached what one writer termed a "stampede."[60] That characterization probably was an exaggeration, but the surge in poll-taking by media organizations was notable and, according to Albert E. Gollin, seemed to place the news media and the polling profession "in the same lifeboat, with all the risks that additional passengers pose for its stability."[61]

Inevitably, some polls "were of high quality; others were an embarrassment," the *Washington Journalism Review* noted after the election.[62] One emerging embarrassment was halted in mid-October 1980. That was when the *Rockford Register Star* repudiated[63] its "Illinois Poll" four days after publishing results of a survey of 816 respondents that showed Reagan defeating Carter in the state by eighteen percentage points.[64] Another poll conducted about the same time for the *Chicago Tribune* showed a much tighter race in Illinois.

The "Illinois Poll" sampled many more Republicans than Democrats, and 93 percent of respondents said they were white. These aspects of the poll prompted skepticism inside the newspaper. One of its columnists publicly scoffed at the survey, writing that it was probably a "polling gaffe."[65] The newspaper's executive editor, Charles Morris, acknowledged: "We can't say for sure the poll is inaccurate but we have enough doubts to discontinue publishing further poll stories."[66] In the end, Reagan carried Illinois in 1980 by eight percentage points. The final pre-election poll in the *Tribune* said the race in Illinois was deadlocked.[67]

The tension between the quantitative and qualitative approaches, between polling-based methods and "shoe-leather" reporting, was vividly if unintentionally depicted on page one of the *Washington Post* two days before the election. Side by side on the newspaper's front page that Sunday were two assessments of the coming election. One was based largely on the *Post's* polling; the other, a roundup that mostly reflected traditional political-reporting techniques, such as tapping the judgments and opinions of politicians and correspondents around the country.

The *Post's* poll-based report told of "an extraordinarily close" race[68] in which Carter held a lead of four percentage points, according to a survey of registered voters the *Post* had completed a few days earlier. "American voters remain narrowly divided in their choice for president and unusually volatile," the article said. The adjacent, more qualitative-based report appeared beneath the headline "Reagan Is in the Driver's Seat" and said the Republican had "the pieces in place and the machinery to deliver a Republican presidential victory."[69]

The dissonant, side-by-side assessments at the close of the campaign were jarring and offered anything but clarity. Neither article insinuated that a rout was in the offing, but both contributed to the befuddlement that marked the election's run-up and its aftermath. "It is clear that the decisions made in the privacy of voting booths were too intimate for the blunt instruments of journalism to detect in advance," the newspaper's in-house critic, Bill Green, observed after the election.[70] Green also speculated whether the news media just might give up on election polls.

That was rather what Haynes Johnson of the *Washington Post* suggested after the election, in a post-election commentary that proved ironic. "For the press," Johnson wrote, "the lessons are obvious. Polls are no substitute for hard reporting. In many cases, as it turns out, reporters [covering the 1980 campaign] would have been better served by relying on their own legwork, which in turn produces their own political instincts, than on the presumably scientific samples of voters supplied by the pollsters."[71]

Johnson's remarks were an obvious endorsement of the virtues of "shoe-leather" journalism—and of his own labors. Johnson spent weeks crisscrossing the country in the fall of 1980, stopping in disparate places like Boston, San Diego, Youngstown, and Orangeburg, South Carolina, filing long, exhaustive reports about Americans' views of the presidential race—reports that described worries, troubles, and apprehension about the state and direction of the country.

The installments of Johnson's periodic series typically were published on Sundays in the *Post* and appeared with the logo "American Portraits 1980." They were the quintessence of direct-observation, "shoe-leather" reporting in the 1980 campaign. As he traveled the country, Johnson sometimes sneered at opinion polls, saying he didn't like them because they "just don't pick up the complexities of people."[72] But intensive "shoe-leather" journalism did not necessarily lead to acute or accurate insight. Asked on the PBS show *Washington Week in Review* for a bottom-line prediction a few days before the election, Johnson offered a muddled forecast. "I really don't know," he said, adding, "I think all my bones tell me Reagan is going to win, but I think somehow that Carter is going to slip through" and be reelected.[73]

Johnson afterward didn't dwell much on his failed prediction. But he grumbled about the conspicuous role public opinion polls had taken in national elections. He likened them to "pseudo-science," writing that politics "has taken on more of the trappings of a science, or shall we say, pseudo-science: we rely heavily on, and quote approvingly from, the latest of the endless outpourings of authoritative (we pretend) survey data from the national opinion people. Stories about the game [of politics] are buttressed— or based entirely—on the findings of the pollsters."[74]

The 1980 election, Johnson noted, "saw this process reach new heights with more polls than ever, many commissioned by news organizations, more journalistic reliance on them to take the daily, if not hourly, political temperature readings—and more mistakes than at any point in a generation. Misreading the election as 'too close to call' even as citizens prepared to vote will be the polling mistake most remembered" from 1980.[75] He made no mention of his own misprediction.

The election's aftermath brought other demonstrations of the appeal and shortcomings of "shoe-leather" reporting. In Chicago, Anne Keegan, a local columnist for the *Chicago Tribune*, went out into the city, seeking reactions from what she called "the ordinary people." Keegan's foray produced an intriguing if undeniably post hoc qualitative assessment of attitudes of urban working-class voters. Reagan's sweeping victory, Keegan wrote, may have surprised journalists, pundits, and commentators, but it was not at all shocking to the people with whom she spoke. The outcome was no surprise, she wrote, "because they've been listening"—not to the polls and not to the "endless political talk that journalists inflict on one another." No, Keegan wrote, "they'd been listening to the people. The ordinary people. The 'I make $14,000 a year, work six days a week, and am rearing three kids on that and am not making it anymore' people. The people who quietly created the avalanche" for Reagan.[76]

Keegan, who at her death in 2011 was described by the *Tribune* as perhaps "the best female reporter/writer in the history of Chicago journalism,"[77] spoke with, among others, Walter "Duke" Bingham, a former Marine known familiarly in his neighborhood as "Duke the bookkeeper." "I called this election long ago," she quoted Bingham as saying. "It was Reagan. It was obvious."[78]

Bingham also told her: "The guys [reporting election results] on television last night, they acted surprised. But who've they been talking to? And the pollsters? They'd better get off their butts and get among the multitude. They'd better listen. . . . The pollsters were all wet because they never understood the feelings of America right now."[79] It was easy, of course, to claim prescience and insight after the election, easy to assail the pollsters and pundits once the votes had been counted.

However limited and impressionistic, Keegan's reporting did hint at the wider discontent and frustrations with Carter that propelled Reagan's victory. At the same time, Keegan's reporting signaled the limitations of "shoe-leather" journalism, in that it can be haphazard, hazy, even misleading. The tone of her post-election account suggested otherwise, but Chicagoans in 1980 voted overwhelmingly for Carter.

The controversies in polling and political reporting in 1980 went beyond the rout that was missed. ABC News was roundly criticized for its post-debate phone-in poll in which viewers were asked to call and register opinions about whether Reagan or Carter "gained more from his participation" in the late October encounter. Callers were charged 50 cents to place the call, a method professional pollsters scoffed at as unscientific and probably misleading. More than seven hundred thousand people participated in ABC's dial-a-poll and the callers favored Reagan 2 to 1.

"No credence at all should be given to the figures," said George Gallup, who did not hesitate to recall the *Literary Digest* poll failure of his salad days. "The procedures used in the ABC survey have long since been discredited," Gallup said. "It has all the faults of the Literary Digest procedures of 1936, in which postcard ballots were sent to people who had car registrations and were listed in the telephone book, which biased the sample toward people with higher income levels and more interest in the issues."[80]

ABC executives readily conceded the survey was unscientific but said there was no attempt to deceive, given that disclaimers were aired as viewers called in their preferences. Roone Arledge, president of the network's news division, defended the call-in poll as "comparable to reporting early election returns on Election Day. They don't prove anything, but there is an interest in them."[81] The instant poll had other defenders. A commentary published after the election by the *Baltimore Sun* noted that "the ABC poll, like the real thing, required people to get out of their armchairs and make an effort to support their man. It may not have been scientific, but it did give an indication that Mr. Reagan was moving toward an impressive margin of victory—which is more than the sophisticated 'scientific' polls could do."[82]

Far more controversial were the Election Night projections, especially those of NBC News, that were based in part on exit polls and signaled Reagan's easy win while voting was still underway in a significant number of states, most of them in the West. The projection was a competitive feat for NBC—and was bitterly remembered years afterward by journalists and producers at rival networks, especially CBS, which had become accustomed to winning the ratings on Election Night.[83] CBS News was far more deliberate—inexplicably so—in projecting Reagan's victory, doing so as votes were counted. More than forty minutes *after* Carter had gone on television to concede defeat, CBS finally felt confident enough in its assessments to declare Reagan the winner.[84]

Even though he accepted a measure of blame, the network's news division president, Bill Leonard, was livid in private. "I felt like a damn fool when the President of the United States gets on television and congratulates the next President and we are still droning along implying that the Election has not been decided," he wrote in a scathing memorandum to Ernest Leiser, the CBS executive in charge of political coverage. Leonard complained that "we sat there *knowing* that Reagan had been elected, and yet, even after the President of the United States conceded the election, like ostriches with our heads in the sand, we stuck to our petty little [projection] system. And not until it told us what the whole country knew and had known for hours would we go on the air and say that Reagan had been elected."[85] In reply, Leiser conceded that CBS had been "beaten and bloodied by the speed of NBC's Election Night calls based on exit polling in key states."[86]

What Mitofsky thought of Leonard's upbraiding isn't known. But he said he regretted not pointing out to his CBS colleagues on the afternoon of Election Day that "the big popular vote margin for Reagan in our Election Day

Poll meant an electoral vote landslide. Perhaps that would have triggered a change in the flow of the broadcast."[87] Perhaps CBS would have gone beyond Cronkite's tantalizing "smell of victory" remarks on Election Night.

Mitofsky also said he thought NBC took acute risks in calling the election as quickly as it did. More significantly, NBC's early call for Reagan renewed and deepened the dispute about whether or to what extent projections drawn from exit polls depress turnout late on Election Day. Anecdotal accounts abounded about would-be voters in California and elsewhere leaving polling places in droves because the top-of-the-ticket race had already been decided. An editorial in the *Wall Street Journal* said as much: "Reports from California indicate that once the news broke [about Reagan's certain victory], long lines disbanded at polling places as disgusted voters drifted home. Indeed, many polling places in California were nigh empty, hours before the booths were set to close. Undoubtedly, many who intended to vote during the evening stayed home once they'd heard the news during dinner."[88]

Supporters of some losing candidates such as Al Ullman, a twelve-term Democratic congressman from Oregon, blamed the projections for deterring voters, thus resulting in their defeat by narrow margins.[89] Even Republicans in California complained about the effects of the network projections and close races their candidates lost. "I think that it probably hurt us as much as it hurt the Democrats," the Republican state chairman in California, Truman Campbell, said on the *PBS NewsHour* program. "I think the analogy is that nobody goes to a ball game in the ninth inning when the score's 100 to nothing. And that's just about what happened here."[90]

That network projections of presidential races can depress voter turnout is a powerful and compelling tale, especially in what are expected to be close elections. But it is a tale more often invoked than confirmed. Although the presumed effect seems plausible and gave rise to considerable debate about imposing restraints on television networks,[91] it appears to be mostly a myth, one of several myths about election polling the news media have promoted. Martin Plissner reported that CBS News, in the weeks and months after the 1980 election, "tried with little success to document those reports of lines at polling places melting away after the NBC call—or after President Carter's concession speech an hour and a half later. Some of us who give speeches on the West Coast would ask if anyone in the audience had ever decided not to bother voting because of a network call or could tell us of someone else, or actually saw people on line at polling places leaving in disgust. No verifiable example has ever turned up."[92] Besides, Plissner wrote, "no one ever explained why, among voters already at the polls when they heard of NBC's call, there should have been more Democrats than Republicans declaring that their vote 'no longer counted.'"[93]

The definitive findings about the effects of early television projections appeared twenty-five years after the Reagan-Carter election, in a book by William C. Adams of George Washington University. Adams reported on a series of studies—including those in counties on either side of time zones—that found almost no evidence that network projections deterred voters or diluted turnout at the polls. In one large survey around Portland, Oregon, for example, most nonvoters "never heard any projection news before polls closed," Adams reported. Focus groups conducted with registered voters in California, Oregon, and Washington turned up "no first-hand knowledge of people abstaining because of projections." What's more, Adams noted that other studies on voter turnout indicated that "by the time Election Day arrives, citizens already have many complex, lifelong personal and structural influences on their decision to vote or not to vote. Those propensities are not easily transformed by happening to hear projection news."[94]

In the end, the polling failure of 1980 was a rout that no pre-election poll foresaw. It wasn't a replay of the epic polling failure of 1948, although some commentators in 1980 invoked the Truman upset in characterizing Reagan's sweeping victory. *Time* magazine, for example, said the lopsided outcome of the Carter-Reagan race was such a surprise that it "touched off the most skeptical examination of public opinion polling since 1948." Carter in fact had invoked the lesson of 1948 in the exhausting final hours of campaigning, when his defeat seemed increasingly likely. During a speech in Springfield, Missouri, he held up a reproduction of the *Chicago Tribune*'s "Dewey Defeats Truman" front page[95] and said, "As you know, the pollsters were wrong in 1948."[96] His indulgence in nostalgia set something of a tone for underdog candidates in presidential elections to follow.

It is striking how often the lessons of 1948—especially the reassuring notion that the candidate who trails badly in the polls and seems destined to lose in a landslide can mount a stunning comeback—offered thematic connections to presidential campaigns of the 1980s and 1990s. A succession of losing candidates, Democrat and Republican, invoked Truman's surprise victory, finding in it a reservoir of distant hope amid despairing prospects and woeful polling data. Whether or not they truly believed history was bound to repeat

FIGURE 16. Long-shot presidential candidates often have found encouragement in recalling the surprise outcome of 1948. Democratic candidate Walter Mondale did so in 1984. He claimed the polls were "dead wrong" and declared he had "an excellent chance of winning." Mondale lost in a landslide. (Credit: Associated Press/John Duricka)

itself on Election Day, the reminder of Truman's 1948 surprise victory was seductive. It is an undying vision that has beckoned and teased woebegone candidacies.

In 1984, during the final days of his ill-fated run against Ronald Reagan, Democrat Walter Mondale lashed his desperate candidacy to the lesson of 1948, saying at a stop in San Francisco, "There's something going on in this country and the pollsters aren't getting it. Nobody who's been with me for the last few days and has seen these crowds, seen their response, seen their enthusiasm, seen the intensity of their response and how they respond to these issues, no one who's been where I've been, can help but believe that there's something happening in this country."[97] Asked whether his campaign's private polling was signaling certain defeat, Mondale replied, "I think that these polls are dead wrong. I think we've got an excellent chance of winning."[98]

A torchlight parade and rally in Chicago marked a spirited high moment late in the campaign, and Mondale took the occasion to declare that the pre-election polls were missing the movement of voters to his candidacy. To underscore the point, Mondale held up a reproduction of the *Chicago Tribune's* "Dewey Defeats Truman" front page. "The pollsters and the slick magazines are trying to tell us that the election is over," Mondale said, sounding themes reminiscent of Truman's in 1948. "Well, I've got a little message for them: Public opinion polls don't count at all. People vote, public opinion polls don't vote, and we're going to win!"[99]

Embracing the trappings, sentiments, and rhetorical flourishes of 1948 may have been heartening,[100] but the gestures were misplaced, as Mondale probably understood by the campaign's end.[101] He lost to Reagan in a forty-nine-state landslide.[102] Four years later, Democrat Michael Dukakis turned to the Truman memory in his losing race against Vice President George H. W. Bush. Dukakis, who often came across as wooden and aloof, asked at a rally late in the campaign. "You remember that famous *Chicago Tribune* headline in 1948, 'Dewey Beats Truman'? Well it was Harry who won."[103] Dukakis lost to Bush by nearly eight percentage points.

Bush sought to align himself with the memory and strategies of Truman during his failed run for reelection in 1992. As Truman had, Bush placed a sign on his desk that declared, "The buck stops here." As Truman had in 1948, Bush blamed Congress for his difficulties. Bush's interest in Truman seemed quite obvious, as syndicated columnist Mona Charen pointed out. Truman, she wrote, was the only president "within living memory who was in deep, deep trouble as an incumbent running for reelection, who managed—against all the odds and against all the polls, in the last few weeks of the race—to run against Congress, which was then dominated by the other party, the Republicans, in Truman's case; and succeeded in rallying the people to his side. This is George Bush's only hope now of reelection, that he can somehow manage to persuade the American electorate that, just like Harry Truman, his troubles stem from a recalcitrant Congress."[104]

Bush echoed some of the poll-bashing flourishes of Truman's campaign, telling supporters at one point in mid-October, "Forget about all these polls. Forget people telling you how you think."[105] Bush was trailing Bill Clinton in the polls at the time by as much as eighteen percentage points;[106] he lost by less than six points in a three-way race that included independent candidate H. Ross Perot.

In 1996, Republican Bob Dole even more conspicuously summoned the trappings and reminders of Truman's victory. He made appearances in the final hours of his ill-fated campaign with a reproduction of the "Dewey Defeats

Truman" front page, an artifact that seemed to cheer him.[107] "I may be the Harry Truman of 1996," Dole declared.[108] "I'm like Harry Truman," he said on another occasion. "I'm from the Midwest and I'm plainspoken, and I'm going to win, whether you like it or not!"[109]

One of Dole's last campaign stops in the hours before dawn on Election Day, was in Truman's hometown, Independence, Missouri. Standing before a statue of Truman near the county courthouse, Dole quoted from Truman's closing campaign speech, telling supporters, "The tide is rolling. All over the country, I have seen it in other people's faces. The people are going to win this election."[110] Dole lost to Bill Clinton by 8.5 percentage points—a humbling margin, to be sure, but an outcome considerably closer than the forecasts of many pre-election polls.

The final CBS News/*New York Times* poll before the 1996 election was almost ten percentage points too high. It had pegged Clinton's lead at eighteen percentage points. The Pew Research Center estimated Clinton's advantage at fourteen points at campaign's end—and its director, Andrew Kohut, said Dole's chances were so remote that his winning the election "would make Truman and Dewey look like a minor slip."[111] The Harris and the ABC News/ *Washington Post* polls gave Clinton a twelve-point lead.[112]

Not all pollsters were so off target. A maverick pollster named John Zogby was almost spot-on in estimating that Clinton's lead was 8.1 percentage points. That forecast was so accurate that Richard Morin of the *Washington Post* was moved to declare, in print: "All hail Zogby, the pollster who conquered the 1996 election. *And may you burn in the fires of polling hell, you lucky dog*, hiss his competitors, who say John Zogby is the newest bad boy of survey research. They criticize some of his polling techniques as little more than method-ological malpractice." In polling, Morin added, "getting it right is the best revenge. And that's exactly what Zogby did" in his campaign polls conducted for the Reuters wire service.[113]

Zogby's unexpected success was far from being the most anomalous turn in opinion polling that year. A few weeks after the election, Everett Carll Ladd, a political scientist known for his analyses of opinion polls, declared in the *Chronicle of Higher Education* that the pollsters' performance in 1996 had been more dreadful than that of 1948. "Election polling had a terrible year in 1996," wrote Ladd, the executive director of the Roper Center for Public Opinion Research, which then was at the University of Connecticut. "Indeed, its over-all performance was so flawed that the entire enterprise should be reviewed by a blue-ribbon panel of experts—from academe, commercial polling firms, and the news media—who should recommend ways to improve the accuracy of polling and of news reports about the surveys' findings."[114]

Ladd also wrote, "The sheer volume of pre-election polls . . . contributed to the idea that the presidential election was settled well before Election Day." He added, "Of late, both pre-election surveys and exit polls on Election Day have missed the mark by margins well in excess of the Gallup results in 1948."[115]

In calling for a blue-ribbon panel, Ladd seemed to have in mind the committee empaneled by the Social Science Research Council following the 1948 debacle. Ladd's proposal went nowhere, however. Some polls in 1996 had estimated that Clinton's victory would be far more comfortable than it was, but none of them pointed to the wrong winner. The election brought no surprise outcome; it was no 1948 redux. As such, Ladd's characterization was easily refuted, and the polling fraternity's response was punishing. Not one to shrink from a dispute, Mitofsky conspicuously took Ladd to task.

For years Mitofsky kept displayed on a wall the famous photograph of Truman in victory, holding up the *Chicago Tribune* front page. In an article in *Public Opinion Quarterly*, Mitofsky eviscerated Ladd's assertions. "After the ballots were counted in the 1996 presidential election," he wrote, "there were no pictures of a victorious Bob Dole, gleefully holding a newspaper with the erroneous headline, 'Clinton Defeats Dole.' We saw no postelection speeches in which President-elect Dole ripped into the liberal media polls that had declared him prematurely dead. . . . There were no press conferences in which pollsters expressed regret and confusion about what could have led them to think that Bill Clinton would win. And a humbled Clinton did not opine that the lead he had in pre-election polls must have lulled his supporters to sleep on election day."[116]

Mitofsky added: "We saw none of these things because, in concert with the estimates from all of the media pre-election polls, Clinton won the 1996 presidential election. . . . [T]he 1996 polls were unanimously correct in predicting that Clinton would win by a safe margin."[117] Mitofsky presented a variety of measures to demonstrate that the polls in 1996—although they mostly overestimated the extent of Clinton's victory—were nothing akin to those of 1948. Among the measures he cited was the difference between the final polling margin and the vote margin. In 1948, the discrepancy in the Gallup and Crossley polls was nine percentage points; among the final pre-election polls in 1996, only the CBS News/*New York Times* survey had an error that large.

"By this measure" alone, Mitofsky wrote, "the polls of 1996 were clearly better than the polls of 1948."[118]

It was a tour de force refutation, which Mitofsky closed by declaring: "One can only speculate as to why Ladd chose to make demonstrably erroneous and unsupported claims. . . . If he really meant to improve polling practice, one cannot imagine a less effective means of achieving the goal. Certainly, in view of his less-than-rigorous analysis, Ladd's call for a 'blue-ribbon' commission to investigate poll performance cannot be taken seriously."[119]

Little was heard again about a blue-ribbon panel to investigate the polls of 1996. But the debacle of 1948 remained a compelling point of reference in assessing the interplay of polling and the news media. Just four years later, a post-election analysis for CBS News described the bizarre and deeply flawed Election Night coverage as nothing less than "television's own version of 'Dewey Defeats Truman.'"[120]

CHAPTER 6

"Television's Version of 'Dewey Defeats Truman'"

The Trifecta of 2000

It was nearly two months before the election of 2000, but to Will Saletan, a political writer for the online magazine *Slate*, the polls already were signaling a winner in the race for president.

By then, the Democratic nominee, Al Gore, had slipped ahead of his Republican rival, George W. Bush, in most opinion polls. To Saletan, that was enough to declare "the race is over." In theory, "Bush could win," Saletan wrote. "The stock market could crash. Gore could be caught shagging an intern. Bush could electrify the country with the greatest performance in the history of presidential debates. But barring such a grossly unlikely event, there is no reason to think Bush will recover."[1]

In offering his prediction, Saletan referred to Bush's swagger and character defects and declared: "A candidate who puts pride before prudence, refuses to learn from his mistakes, and is capable of living for days in an alternate political universe can only survive while he's ahead. Once he falls behind, there's no reason to think he's up to the task of correcting his course and regaining control of the race."[2]

Stick a fork in Bush, Saletan declared. "He's done."[3]

Saletan's supremely confident political obituary for Bush was published at about the same point in the campaign as Elmo Roper's supremely confident declaration in 1948 that Thomas Dewey was as good as elected president. Both prophesies proved premature and, in retrospect, Saletan's prediction represents a fitting start to a memorably wrong fall election campaign in 2000, a bizarre time when it seemed opinion polls had never been more numerous, erratic, or unhelpful.

Everything about 2000 seemed a bit off, and unprecedented: the polls, the predictions, the television coverage on Election Night. The national election essentially was a dead heat between Bush, the gaffe-prone governor of Texas, and Gore, the tightly wound vice president who deliberately kept his distance from Bill Clinton, the scandal-tainted yet still-popular president.[4]

Neither Bush nor Gore was particularly inspiring or popular. Bush was widely regarded as a political lightweight forever stepping on his own message, Gore as a stiff who couldn't help but exaggerate his accomplishments, such as claiming to have taken "the initiative in creating the Internet." *Newsweek* magazine likened their race to "the world's largest student-body election, a low-stakes affair pitting the gregarious chairman of the Inter-Fraternity Council [Bush] against the earnest president of the Science Club [Gore]."[5] Ralph Nader and Patrick Buchanan were in the presidential race, too, as crabby public figures, beyond their prime and without a chance of winning.

The outcome turned on the knife's-edge result in Florida. On Election Night, the television networks in rapid succession awarded the state to Gore, and then, a little more than two hours later, retracted their projections almost in unison. Several hours after that, and again in rapid succession, the networks called Florida—and the presidency—for Bush. Within two hours, they all had recanted those projections, leaving everything in an electoral Twilight Zone. A report for CNN called the networks' coverage a "debacle"[6] and a report for CBS said it was television's equivalent of the Dewey-defeats-Truman miscall of 1948.[7]

That night, there was "no script. Things kept happening that had never happened before," wrote David Von Drehle in a lengthy account that reconstructed Election Night 2000 for the *Washington Post*.[8] Al Gore called George Bush to concede defeat. Then Gore called back to retract his concession. Florida's outcome was in dispute and the election brought no clear winner. Bush was ahead in electoral votes, and narrowly ahead in Florida. Gore led the national count of popular votes and was close enough to winning Florida, and the presidency. For thirty-seven days, the outcome of the Florida vote remained unsettled, tied up in disputes and legal maneuvers that were finally dissolved when the U.S. Supreme Court, in a five-to-four decision, effectively awarded the state, and the election, to George Bush.

The unscripted plot twists of Election Night played out on network television, and the protracted legal drama and uncertainty that followed in Florida had the effect of obscuring what was rather poor election polling. It was a time of error, surprise, miscalls, and confusion across three subgenres of election polling, serving to confirm anew the fragility of polls and their potential to sow confusion and frustration.

The polls in 2000 were more numerous and inescapable than ever— amounting to "a relentless barrage," as the *American Journalism Review* saw it. "Americans were polled, polled, and repolled. And the media reported what were often two- and three-point statistically insignificant leads faithfully. And with vigor."[9] Some two hundred polls on the presidential campaign were released in a little more than two months, from early September to early November. That came to about three fresh polls a day.[10]

Such abundance was attributable in part to the frequency of day-to-day tracking polls in 2000. At the end of the campaign, eighteen polling organizations released estimates about how the election would turn out; that compared to nine organizations in 1996 and six in 1992.[11] The blizzard of polls in 2000 grew so intense and distracting that Alison Mitchell of the *New York Times* took to the newspaper's opinion page in early October to suggest that polls ought to be banned in the four weeks before elections.

She decried the "numbing length . . . to which polling is consuming both politics and journalism." She deplored how "polls and focus groups have been creating an echo-chamber effect in politics where candidates all address the same issues and speak with the same poll-tested words until every candidate seems indistinguishable." She argued that the "emphasis on polling is now so pervasive within political campaigns that they may be actively deterring original ideas." She criticized the daily tracking polls, saying they attempt to measure "every tiny mood swing of the electorate. And the race is being reported on through the prism of polls."[12]

Mitchell's observations were not far-fetched, even if her suggestion about banning polls in the run-up to the election was. "If there is one bright spot this year," Mitchell wrote, "it may be that the voters themselves almost seem like they want to confound everyone. Just when Mr. Gore looked like he was out of the race, the public swung his way. When Mr. Bush appeared in danger of permanently falling behind, he caught up."[13]

The 2000 campaign gave rise to polling controversies that were remarkable in their variety. These controversies took shape on three fronts: The daily tracking polls, especially those conducted by Gallup for CNN and *USA Today*, were dizzying and seemingly implausible in reporting dramatic swings in

TABLE 2   EVALUATING POLLSTERS, PRESS IN
PRESIDENTIAL ELECTIONS

The public's grades for pollsters and the press reached lows in 2016. Since 1988, Pew Research Center has asked respondents for the grade they award pollsters and the press (among other entities) "for the way they conducted themselves in the campaign."

Grades for pollsters

Year	A	B	C	D	F	DK
2016	6%	15	24	**21**	**30**	5
2012	16	27	27	10	9	11
2008	**20**	**31**	23	6	8	12
2004	16	26	**33**	9	8	8
2000	7	22	28	15	14	14
1996	11	23	29	11	10	**16**
1992	15	**31**	27	9	6	12
1988	13	29	29	12	11	6

Grades for the press

Year	A	B	C	D	F	DK
2016	6%	16	19	**21**	**38**	1
2012	8	23	29	12	26	2
2008	9	**25**	26	15	24	1
2004	8	24	32	19	16	1
2000	6	22	31	18	20	3
1996	6	22	**33**	19	18	2
1992	**11**	**25**	29	16	15	**4**
1988	8	22	**33**	19	16	2

SOURCE: Pew Research Center.

NOTE: Not all rows add to 100% due to rounding. DK = Don't know. Numerals in bold signify the highest percentage in each category.

popular support for Bush or Gore. The tracking polls irritated more than they informed, and were criticized as too erratic to be believed.[14] The final pre-election polls—the showpieces of election surveys—correctly signaled a close vote. But most of those polls pointed the wrong way, to Bush's winning the popular vote. And errors in exit polls, which were conducted as the election was underway, contributed to the televised fiasco that Election Night became.

It was no salutary performance for election polling and, not surprisingly, the American public gave the polls and the news media low marks for their work in the campaign. In all, 29 percent of respondents to a Pew Research Center post-election survey assigned pollsters a "D" or "F" for their campaign coverage, their worst grades in years.[15] Pew also said that 38 percent of respondents assigned the news media similarly poor grades for their coverage in 2000.[16]

What surely helped drive down the grades were the head-scratching daily tracking polls, the swings of which attracted unflattering comment throughout the fall campaign.[17] Tracking polls sought to gauge day-to-day changes in sentiment as, presumably, voters made up their minds. Most likely, these shifts were phantom swings that did not reflect public opinion and did little to clarify or explain to Americans how the presidential race was unfolding. They suggested the electorate was more volatile and more inclined to rapid shifts in opinion than it really was.

As the name suggests, tracking polls are a series of consecutive, day-on-day surveys that are intended to detect and report shifting preferences in public opinion, supposedly reflecting developments in the campaign, such as sudden controversies and televised debates. Gallup's was not the only national tracking poll in 2000,[18] but given its famous brand—and the poll's fitful performance—it attracted the most commentary and criticism.[19] Gallup produced a rolling average based on the most recent three samples of four hundred likely voters, giving the poll an aggregated total of twelve hundred respondents. Each day, the oldest results were dropped and replaced by the newest. The effect, Gallup said, was to present "a continuously changing portrait of where the American public stands."

The picture, however, was obscured by what were remarkable fluctuations in Gallup's tracking poll, which was conducted from August to early November. It drew considerable attention in producing what Andrew Kohut, a former president of the Gallup Organization, called "loopy results that defied credibility."[20] Given its swings, some journalists took to calling it the "Nasdaq poll."[21]

As an example of those fluctuations, Kohut pointed in a post-election assessment to a five-day period in mid-September when Gallup's tracking polls swung from a ten-point led for Gore to a three-point lead for Bush.[22] And that wasn't even the most fitful phase of the tracking poll. Richard Morin, head of the *Washington Post's* polling unit, noted that over three days in early October, a period that included the first of three debates between the presidential candidates, Gallup's figures swung from an eleven-point lead for Gore to a seven-point advantage for Bush.

"A howl immediately went up from journalists, who expect Gallup's numbers to be much better behaved," Morin noted. "And it certainly didn't help when other polls . . . suggested a much tighter and less mercurial race."[23] Other pollsters, wrote Saletan at Slate.com, were "dismayed at Gallup's radical swings."[24] He noted that, in a three-day span in the second half of October, Bush's nine-point lead had evaporated, according to Gallup.

The swings of Gallup's tracking poll in 2000 were so marked that curiosity about them lingered for years after the election. Alan Abramowitz, a political scientist at Emory University, wrote in an essay for the *Huffington Post* in 2008: "Everyone remembers the 2000 presidential election with its excruciating post-election vote counting controversy in Florida and the Supreme Court decision that awarded the presidency to George W. Bush. But how many people remember the Gallup 2000 election tracking poll? I'm sure the Gallup folks would like us to forget it." Abramowitz noted that no other poll in 2000 "showed anything like the volatility of the Gallup tracking poll" and recalled his "favorite" swing in preference: "On October 24 Gallup had Gore ahead of Bush by one point. Three days later, on October 27, they had Bush ahead by 13."[25]

Frank Newport, the editor-in-chief at Gallup, said swings in the tracking polls were no surprise, given that they were intended to reflect uncertainty and indecision among would-be voters. Newport said in an interview in late October 2000 that "built into [the tracking poll] is the assumption that it's a very sensitive measure of Americans' changes from day to day. . . . There are a lot of uncommitted voters. People don't have to make up their mind from day to day, and they do shift back and forth." Newport added that Gallup's objective was "to allow viewers, readers, those interested, to really see those ups and downs that we think do occur in a fall campaign." He said the tracking poll was "an absolutely sound scientific model" for discerning voters' shifting views in the midst of a national campaign.[26]

Not many analysts embraced that explanation. "I would love to be tracking the election that Gallup is tracking," quipped Morin of the *Washington Post*, which conducted tracking polls during the closing three weeks of the campaign and reported less volatile results. "It's a lot more interesting election than the one I'm looking at. I see something far more stable than the Gallup numbers suggest."[27]

The zigzagging of Gallup's tracking polls eased somewhat as Election Day approached. But overall, the polls were puzzling. They projected an erroneous impression of instability in the electorate; they seemed to be measuring volatility when volatility wasn't there.[28] "People throw their hands up and dismiss the mystifying patterns in the polls," Kohut noted, and "with good reason."[29]

Morin said he suspected that Gallup's tracking polls weren't picking up any "real changes in the electorate, but merely changes in relative interest or enthusiasm of Republicans and Democrats."[30] Saletan suggested a more commercial explanation, saying that "CNN and *USA Today* are in the news business. They're paying Gallup for new numbers every day. If Gallup's numbers don't change, where's the news? So Gallup has an incentive . . . [in] allowing the winds of shifting partisan intensity to blow its numbers back and forth."[31]

The best explanation for the erratic performance of Gallup's tracking poll in 2000 was that it mostly was "an artifact of classification" rather than a reflection voters' inclination.[32] An article published in *Public Opinion Quarterly* a few years later reported that fluctuations in Gallup's tracking poll were due not to voters' shifting opinions and preferences but to Gallup's method of identifying and including "likely" voters as its principal targets. Screening for likely voters tends to be most effective in the days before the election, when voters' interest in the candidates and the campaign is most keen.[33] Gallup in 2000 was screening for likely voters weeks before Election Day. Had Gallup's tracking poll focused on preferences of registered voters, instead of seeking to identify "likely" voters, fluctuations in poll results may have been less marked, a subsequent study indicated.[34]

The disputed readings of Gallup's tracking poll represented one leg of polling's trifecta of controversy in 2000. Gallup's final pre-election poll, like most of the others, pointed to the wrong popular-vote winner—to Bush, not Gore. Of the nineteen final pre-election polls evaluated by Michael W. Traugott for *Public Opinion Quarterly*, fourteen reported a lead for Bush at the close of the campaign. Five of the fourteen polls—including the joint CBS/*New York Times* survey—estimated Bush's lead on the eve of the election to be five percentage points or more. Three of the final polls figured the race to be a tie. Only two of the nineteen final polls showed Gore in the lead.[35] Gore won the popular vote by 543,000 votes, or one-half of a percentage point, 48.4 percent to 47.9 percent.

The two pollsters who at campaign's end estimated that Gore was ahead were John Zogby, who conducted the Reuters/MSNBC poll and who was closest in predicting Bill Clinton's margin of victory in 1996, and Kathleen Frankovic, polling director for CBS News and a chatty former protégé of Warren Mitofsky, who had left the network in 1990. Zogby's final poll showed Gore with a two-point lead, 48 percent to 46 percent; Bush had led by as many as five percentage points in the days before. The final CBS News poll estimated Gore was up by a point, 45 percent to 44 percent.

"You know," Zogby said in an interview afterward, "I sweat an awful lot" in close races. "Give me one of those old McGovern-Nixon races," he said, referring to Richard Nixon's landslide victory over George McGovern in 1972. "But I called it right again," he said, "and I'm knocking on wood."[36] Zogby was a colorful character and, among pollsters, a bit unconventional. On the Saturday before the 2000 election, he had his call center in Utica, New York, pose what he called the "Wizard of Oz" question: "You live in the land of Oz, and the candidates are the Tin Man, who's all brains and no heart, and the Scarecrow, who's all heart and no brains. Who would you vote for?" The result, he said, was a tie: 46.2 for the Tin Man and 46.2 for the Scarecrow.[37] "Tin Man" obviously was a proxy for Gore; "Scarecrow," a stand-in for Bush. Eccentric though the question was, the result was further confirmation of a tight race.

Frankovic acknowledged feeling anxious on the morning of the election with the release of a stand-alone CBS poll, showing Gore had taken a narrow lead. She said her "hugest fear was that I would have to spend the next four years explaining why our preelection poll was 10 points off or something horrible like that." She added: "It turned out that the final preelection poll numbers we released had Gore up by one point over George W. Bush, and that one point was actually a function of rounding. If you look at it to the tenth of a decimal point, our poll had Gore up over Bush nationally by that half a percentage point. So, I feel pretty good about that."[38]

Zogby and CBS were the outliers. Most pre-election polls at the end had Bush slightly ahead in the popular vote, although many of those estimates were within margins of sampling error. Gallup, for example, said in its final poll taken for CNN and *USA Today* that Bush was leading by 48 percent to 46 percent. The final poll of the well-regarded Pew Research Center likewise showed Bush ahead by two points, 49 percent to 47 percent.

The first large-scale experiments in internet polling were conducted in 2000, when only about half of Americans were online, either at home or at work. The results were mixed. The Harris Poll Online, conducted over the final seven days of the campaign, estimated the race was tied at 47 percent. Another online survey, conducted by Knowledge Networks over the closing two weeks of the race, placed Bush ahead by 46 percent to 44 percent.

From its earliest days, internet polling had its derisive critics. They pointed to inherent socioeconomic biases in such polls, given that internet use was not distributed evenly across the country. And they noted that respondents were not easily or always selected by random sampling.[39] Advocates of online polling waved off the criticism. "All research is going to migrate to the internet," Gordon Black, chairman of Harris Interactive, said in 1999. He noted that internet poll data could be adjusted to compensate for disparities between users and nonusers. "It's a funny thing about scientific revolutions," he said. "People who are defenders of the old paradigm generally don't change. They are just replaced by people who embrace new ideas."[40] Harris also conducted more traditional, telephone-based polling in 2000. Like its online counterpart, the telephone poll showed the race tied at 47 percent.

There were some way-off howlers among the pre-election polls. Farthest from the mark was the final Hotline Bullseye poll, which estimated that Bush had a seven-point advantage. The final poll of the Marist College Institute for Public Opinion said Bush was ahead by five points.[41] Both polls completed fieldwork five days before the election, meaning they were unable to detect late movements to Gore.[42]

The wrong-winner indications of most final pre-election polls hardly made for an outstanding showing. Traugott wrote that it was "a cause for concern that the vast majority of the polls expected Bush to receive a majority of the popular vote."[43] Even so, Traugott noted, the performance of pre-election polls in 2000 prompted no calls for a national review, which was in decided contrast to 1996, when pollsters had accurately forecast Clinton's victory over Republican Bob Dole—although usually by margins much greater than Clinton's winning advantage of 8.5 percentage points.[44]

Some of the final polls in 2000 were completed too soon to capture the effects of the disclosure, five days before the election, that Bush in 1976 had been arrested for, and had pleaded guilty to, driving under the influence of alcohol near his family's summer compound in Kennebunkport, Maine. The stunning revelation, which threw Bush's campaign into disarray, had been uncovered by Erin Fehlau, a twenty-seven-year-old local television reporter in Maine. She pursued a rumor she had picked up at the courthouse in Cumberland County, tracking down court records and locating the arresting officer to confirm Bush's arrest and guilty plea to a misdemeanor violation. He had been fined $150 and surrendered driving privileges for a time.[45]

Fehlau said she heard about the case from a local policewoman, who at first thought it was a joke. As she chased the lead, Fehlau spoke with Tom Connolly, a lawyer and local Democratic party gadfly who handed her a copy of the court docket about Bush's DUI offense. Connolly had been a Gore-supporting delegate to the 2000 Democratic National Convention. Learning of that connection, Bush's campaign cried foul, suggesting that Gore's campaign was behind the eleventh-hour disclosure. Gore's press secretary, Chris Lehane, insisted: "This is just not something the Gore campaign is involved with in any shape, way, or form." Fehlau said on the ABC News *Nightline* program that Connolly "did not hand this [information] to me; it was something that this police officer overheard, talked to me about it, and I just ran and asked him about it. . . . I'm confident that I wasn't set up" by the Gore campaign.[46]

Opinion polls about Bush's 1976 drunk-driving conviction indicated that not many voters were especially troubled by the disclosures, at least not right away.[47] Several pundits predicted Bush would win easily, even after the disclosures about his arrest.[48] But then, it would take only a comparatively few votes in a close national election to tip the popular vote[49] away from Bush, who had campaigned for the presidency on a message of personal integrity, good judgment, and morality—as a corrective to the tainted presidency of Bill Clinton, who had told falsehoods under oath to conceal a sexual dalliance with a White House intern. The drunk-driving disclosures shattered that pretense and prompted questions about the wisdom of Bush and his aides in not revealing the arrest, on their terms, early in the campaign.[50] "If Bush had mentioned the arrest months ago, perhaps buried deep in a speech about finding religion and giving up drinking, it would have lacked any eleventh-hour drama," *Time* magazine noted. "But by avoiding it, the campaign made itself vulnerable."[51]

Bush wrote in his memoir that not disclosing the drunk-driving case "on my terms may have been the single costliest political mistake I ever made." He noted that his senior political adviser, Karl Rove, estimated that more than 2.1 million people, "including many social conservatives, either stayed home or changed their votes."[52] News about his drunk-driving case surely contributed to Bush's slumping poll results in the campaign's closing days. And whatever the effect of the DUI revelation, the final pre-election polls encouraged speculation in the news media that Bush would win the popular vote but lose the electoral vote[53]—a turn of events that had not happened in a U.S. presidential election since 1888, when the incumbent, Democrat Grover Cleveland, lost to Republican Benjamin Harrison.

Despite its rarity, the split-decision scenario often has emerged as a topic of conjecture in presidential elections that were, or were thought to be, closely contested.[54] Speculation about a split decision in 2000 arose with some intensity in the final days of the campaign. Because Bush led in the national polls but Gore seemed to be edging ahead in battleground states such as Florida and Pennsylvania, a divided popular vote–electoral vote outcome seemed possible.[55] "The tightness of the race with so little time left has fueled speculation that the contest could end with Bush capturing the popular vote but Gore winning the electoral college vote—and the presidency," the *Detroit News* speculated two days before the election.[56]

Mark Siegel, a former executive director at the Democratic National Committee, went on MSNBC to declare that "it is very, very easy to configure an Electoral College map where Bush wins states like Texas and states in the Mountain parts of the United States, and in the South, by very, very large margins, while Gore is winning states like Florida, Michigan, Pennsylvania, Wisconsin, by two or three points. And at the end of the day, we could have Bush winning a 2 million or 3 million popular vote plurality, while Gore is hovering around 300 Electoral College votes," enough to win the presidency.[57]

Some journalists said they relished or were intrigued by the prospect of a popular vote–electoral vote discrepancy,[58] saying even that it would be the stuff of dreams. "Now we always talk about scenarios like this," Cokie Roberts said on NPR the day before the election, "and they are the kinds of things that those of us who want a good story dream about." Still, she added, "it's unlikely" the election would end in a split decision.[59]

But it did. That outcome wasn't confirmed until December 9, when the Supreme Court abruptly ended weeks of post-election wrangling and recounts in a five-to-four decision that effectively declared that Bush had carried Florida. His margin of victory in the state was 537 votes, out of nearly six million votes cast. Winning Florida and its twenty-five electoral votes gave Bush the presidency, 271 electoral votes to Gore's 267.

Election Night 2000 is best remembered for what happened on America's television networks—for their projections and retractions about the outcome in Florida, for the bewilderment and frustration they created. The second of two erroneous projections about the outcome in that state seemed decisive, prompting Gore to call Bush to concede the election, prematurely.

The complex interplay of journalism, polling, and presidential elections was never more vividly or inelegantly on display than it was that night. A report ordered by Tom Johnson, CNN's most senior executive, said it was "a news disaster that damaged democracy and journalism." The report was emphatic, colorful, and certainly dramatic in condemning television news organizations for having "staged a collective drag race on the crowded highway of democracy, recklessly endangering the electoral process, the political life of the country, and their own credibility, all for reasons that may be conceptually flawed and commercially questionable. Their excessive speed, combined with an overconfidence in experts and a reliance on increasingly dubious polls, produced a powerful collision between the public interest and the private competitive interests of the television news operations and the corporations that own them." The botched coverage, the CNN report said, "played an important role in creating the ensuing climate of rancor and bitterness" as the election outcome remained in limbo until early December.[60] The "news disaster" report reserved sharp criticism for exit polls, saying they had lost much of their value for projecting results in close elections.[61] In the networks' projections about the outcome in Florida, exit polls were a factor in their first[62] (but not the second) miscall of the race.[63]

Throughout Election Day, exit polls were conducted with randomly selected voters in key precincts. They were asked to complete a two-page questionnaire as they left polling places.[64] These results were fed into projection models that produced statewide or nationwide estimates. The exit polls in 2000 were administered by representatives of Voter News Service (VNS), a consortium of the five television networks and the Associated Press (AP) that was formed in 1994 by the merger of two predecessor organizations.

Voter News Service was a cost-sharing resource through which the networks and AP received exit-poll results and vote tallies. An obvious hazard of the collective arrangements was that faulty VNS data could corrupt the analysis of all the partners.[65] What's more, the partners did not routinely make clear that the data were gathered in a joint operation. Indeed, each network "created the illusion that it had its own independent polling operation when most of what each used was pooled VNS data with some special questions added for each network," one study of Election Night news coverage reported. It noted that the CBS anchor, Dan Rather, turned to this "rhetorical gambit" during the network's Election Night coverage: "As you and your neighbors have gone to the polls, we've been conducting our own national poll, part of our exit poll operation throughout the day."[66]

Voter News Service tabulated and shared the emergent exit-poll data in three waves, giving the partner organizations, as well as news organizations that subscribed to the data, periodic and updated insights as the election was

FIGURE 17. Election Night 2000 was an embarrassment for U.S. television networks, all of which miscalled the presidential race. Dan Rather of CBS News, shown here with a producer at left, said of the coverage errors, "We've lived by the crystal ball; we're eating so much broken glass. We're in critical condition." (Credit: Associated Press/Mark Lennihan)

unfolding. Since 1980, when they projected Ronald Reagan's sweeping victory, exit polls had gained a reputation for accuracy. Mistakes were made on occasion, but exit polls were believed to be very reliable, especially when augmented by partial vote returns from precincts where exit polls had been conducted.

Their presumed reliability had helped turn Election Night coverage into what Jeff Greenfield of ABC News called "a ritual of concealment." By that he meant that the networks' anchors and analysts knew from undisclosed exit-poll data who likely would be elected; on the air, these anchors and analysts tried to act none the wiser. That's because the "rules of the game," Greenfield said, "strictly forbade us from reporting to our viewers and listeners the facts that all of us knew, thus turning the whole Election Night into something of a dramatic recreation—a little like reporting the World Series *after* learning how every key moment of the game would turn out."[67]

But 2000 was markedly different. Exit polls that year went historically off target,[68] contributing to the networks' miserable Election Night performance. The estimates in some states were described as "stupendously bad."[69] The exit-poll estimate in Alabama, for example, placed Gore in the lead by 1.2 percentage points; Bush won the state by almost 15 points. The exit poll in Colorado showed Gore ahead by 3.1 percentage points; Bush won there by 8.4 points. In North Carolina, the exit poll had Gore leading by 3 points; Bush won the state by nearly 13 points.[70] Those estimates were so obviously off target that they were not used in making projections; decision teams at the networks waited for partial vote counts to be reported.

The flaws in exit polling were many. The surveys overstated the vote for Gore in twenty-two states and for Bush in nine states.[71] They pointed to the wrong winner in eight states.[72] Response rates dropped to 51 percent, meaning that just slightly more than half the voters approached by interviewers agreed to fill out the questionnaire. In 1996, the response rate was 55 percent; it was 60 percent in 1992. Refusals hardly were the only problem in 2000. Voter News Service was able to assign interviewers to 84 percent of the selected sample precincts in the country—meaning that many designated precincts went uncovered.[73] A large number of interviewers had no prior experience in conducting exit polls.[74]

New practices in casting votes before Election Day—by absentee ballot or at designated early-voting centers (or, as in Oregon, voting exclusively by mail)—presented significant challenges. Voter News Service markedly underestimated the extent of absentee voting in Florida, for example.[75] In addition, it was becoming evident that Republican voters were less likely than Democrats to participate in exit polls, perhaps reflecting suspicions about the media outlets that sponsored the surveys. Such imbalances risked injecting distortion into results.

"The number of people who decline to respond to exit polls, combined with the increase in the number of early and absentee voters who are not reached by exit polls, are making the results of such polls less reliable with each election cycle," the CNN report said, adding, "We believe the networks should return to reporting election outcomes based much more on actual vote counts and much less on the crystal ball of exit polls and sketchy returns."[76]

Election Night on television had begun confidently enough for the networks. So confidently that Dan Rather, the CBS News anchor, told viewers: "Let's get one thing straight right from the get-go. We would rather be last in reporting returns than to be wrong. If we say somebody has carried a state, you can pretty much take it to the bank, book it, that that's true." Rather's commitment, born of hubris and swagger, went unfulfilled.

The "take it to the bank" pledge was the first of many pretentious, ostensibly folksy aphorisms that Rather uttered that night. Occasionally, his remarks were mildly amusing. After Florida was called for Gore, for example, Rather quipped: "You can bet that Governor Bush will be madder than a rained-on rooster that his brother [Jeb Bush, the governor of Florida] wasn't able to carry this state for him."[77] But often, Rather's observations were weird or cringe-worthy,[78] rather like Election Night itself. Some of them were puzzling and a bit bizarre, like this comment: "If a frog had side pockets, he'd carry a handgun."[79]

Bush's chances of winning, Rather said at one point, seemed "shakier than cafeteria Jell-O." Later, as the night began unraveling after the retraction of Gore's victory in Florida, Rather said at bit sheepishly, "If you're disgusted with us, frankly, I don't blame you."[80] Over on CNN, Greenfield reacted to the withdrawn projection by blurting, "Oh, waiter! One order of crow!"[81]

By the end of the night, CBS, CNN, and the other networks had performed the exceptional feat of awarding the election's pivotal state, Florida, to Gore; then pulling back those projections, before awarding the state—and the presidency—to Bush. That call, apparently decisive, came shortly after 2:15 in the morning, and Rather sounded utterly confident about it all. "Sip it, savor it, cup it, photostat it, underline it in red, press it in a book, put it in an album, hang it on the wall—George Bush is the next president of the United States," he declared.[82] Over on ABC, Peter Jennings was only slightly more cautious. At about 2:20 a.m., Jennings declared: "Unless there is a terrible calamity, George W. Bush, by our projections, is going to be the next president of the United States."[83]

Not surprisingly, the candidates and their campaigns took their leads from the networks. Gore's telephone call to Bush at 2:30 a.m. conceding the election clearly was motivated by the projections; the thinking in Gore's inner circle was the networks had to be right.[84] "They were just so damn positive," Gore's brother-in-law, Frank Hunger, was quoted as saying.[85]

Bush's advantage, according to Voter News Service estimates, was fifty-one thousand votes. But this margin turned out to be inflated by data-entry errors and substantial underestimates of the votes remaining to be counted in Florida. A little more than an hour later, after the data-entry errors were corrected, Bush's lead in Florida had narrowed dramatically. Gore called back to rescind his concession.

"Circumstances have changed dramatically since I first called you. The state of Florida is too close to call," Gore said to Bush, according to the *Washington Post's* account of the exchange.

"Are you saying what I think you're saying?" Bush asked, incredulously. "Let me make sure that I understand. You're calling back to retract that concession?"

"Don't get snippy about it!" Gore retorted.[86]

It was then about 3:30 in the morning. Within thirty-five minutes, all the networks had revoked their second projection about Florida. The rollback prompted Peter Jennings, the anchor on ABC, to mutter on air, "We're not absolutely sure quite what to do next."[87]

Rather had this to say: "We've lived by the crystal ball; we're eating so much broken glass. We're in critical condition."[88]

Voter News Service lurched from the Election Night disaster in 2000 to near-total collapse in the midterm elections in 2002. Its rebuilt computer system was incapable of handling the information load of Election Day, and VNS said it could not vouch for the integrity of data collected in exit polls, which were not released. Vote tabulations were released slowly, usually well behind the tallies of the Associated Press. "The new computer system was not ready for the 2002 election," observed Warren Mitofsky,[89] who, along with his colleague Joe Lenski, was hired by the consortium to conduct exit polling and vote-counting in the 2004 election. Their joint venture was called the National Election Pool. Voter News Service was dissolved.

Soon after the 2000 election, William Saletan of Slate.com returned to his "Bush is toast" commentary, addressing why he erred, and offering something of a mea culpa. "My record as an election prognosticator is cooked. It's just as well," Saletan said, adding, "Most of us pundits suspect we're no better at predicting election results than the average intelligent person is. In my case, there's now proof." He conceded that he had based much of his "Bush is toast" argument "on polls that showed significant post-convention progress for Gore on measures such as honesty, management of the economy, and compatibility with voters on key issues." He also wrote: "Predictably—if I may use that word—I've been hounded and derided . . . by Bush supporters angry that I wrote off their candidate. They've accused me, rightly, of pretending to omniscience."[90]

"Bush is toast" became an inside joke at *Slate* in the years after the election. It was an informal rule among staffers never to call anyone "toast," the online magazine said in an article in 2016 that looked back at its greatest failures.[91] Even so, the "toast" metaphor was irresistible. In early August 2004, Saletan wrote that John Kerry's prospects of ousting George Bush in the upcoming election seemed very promising, that it was "Kerry's race to lose." The headline accompanying Saletan's commentary hinted at, but didn't exactly say, "Bush is toast."

This time the headline read:

"Warm bread."[92]

CHAPTER 7

"President Kerry"

Exit Polls Misfire in 2004

On Election Day 2004, Jimmy Breslin, the brash but celebrated New York writer who was said to have "inspired every emotion but indifference,"[1] abruptly quit his column for the Long Island newspaper *Newsday*. He did so in a rant, and with a botched prediction.

Breslin's swan song essay for *Newsday* anticipated the unfulfilled certainties of that day—a day of poll-driven confusion when, for a time, many people thought the incumbent president, George W. Bush, had been repudiated and the losing candidate, John Kerry, was headed to the White House. It also was the day when the barbed hostility that many prominent journalists had directed at pollsters over the years reached a peak.

Breslin—a rumpled, churlish, and fast-talking bard, "an intellectual disguised as a barroom primitive," he was once called[2]—contributed to that hostility. His Election Day column was written with the snarl of insult and breezy self-confidence that were traits of Breslin and his work.[3] He took a swipe at the polls as he restated the prediction he had put forward six months earlier, that Kerry was going to win the presidency. Easily.

The pre-election polls showing an edge for Bush had to be wrong, Breslin said, because they didn't fully capture the opinions of young people who mostly shunned landline telephones in favor of cellular devices. Such preferences put them beyond the reach of most pollsters in 2004. Polling cell phone–only users was a novelty then; few pollsters did so in part because of federal restrictions on random-dialing cell phone subscribers. Cell phone–only households

FIGURE 18. Fast-talking newspaper columnist Jimmy Breslin assailed the pre-election polls of 2004, declaring them surely wrong in pointing to George W. Bush's victory. Breslin predicted, wrongly, that John Kerry would win easily. (Credit: New York Daily News Archive/ Getty Images)

were comparatively few in 2004.[4] But to Breslin, omitting them utterly compromised the polls and rendered their results implausible.

"One-hundred seventy million cell phones [in the country] and you don't poll one of them," Breslin wrote. "The polls they are pushing at you in the news magazines, on the networks, in the big papers are such cheap, meaningless blatant lies that some of these television stations should have their licenses challenged."[5] Breslin said he was so sure Kerry would win "that I am not even going to bother to watch the results tonight. I am going to bed early. . . . Besides, if I was up, so many people, upon seeing every word I said of this election coming true on television in front of them, would be kissing my hands and embarrassing me with outlandish praise." And so, he wrote, obliquely announcing his leave-taking from *Newsday*, "I go to bed with total confidence. I will get up and stroll to other meadows. I invented this column form. I leave now, but will return here for cameo appearances. And I leave today as the only one in America who from the start was sure John Kerry would win by a large margin."[6]

For several hours that Election Day, it appeared as if Breslin had nailed it. The first waves of exit polls circulating that afternoon were promising for Kerry. Very promising.

These were preliminary results of interviews conducted with voters who were chosen at random as they left selected precincts across the country. They were asked to complete a two-sided questionnaire containing some twenty-five questions, the first of which asked for whom the respondent had voted moments earlier.

The exit surveys were commissioned by the television networks and the Associated Press wire service in a consortium called the National Election Pool. The fieldwork was designed, organized, and supervised by Warren J. Mitofsky and his former assistant, Joseph Lenski. Mitofsky was gruff, innovative, and widely respected. As we have seen, he pioneered exit polling at CBS News in the 1960s. After George Gallup's death in 1984, Mitofsky became the single most prominent American in survey research.[7] He was mindful of the affliction of pollster cockiness. For years, he kept displayed on a wall a photograph of the front page of the *Chicago Tribune* that declared Thomas Dewey's election victory in 1948—a reminder, Mitofsky said, "not to get too cocky at election time."[8]

Given the nature of exit polls—voters are asked to complete questionnaires right after having cast their ballots—they were not burdened with the uncertainties of pre-election polling such as identifying likely voters. So exit polls ought to have been on target. Or pretty reliable. But they were off in many places, overstating Kerry's lead in twenty-six states, including the election battlegrounds Pennsylvania, Virginia, Ohio, and Florida.

The depth and extent of errors in the exit polls didn't become clear until late on Election Day. By then, they had become the source of all sorts of convulsions, demonstrating in a concentrated if uncommon way the disruptive effects opinion polling may have. Exit polls in 2004 fueled an erroneous election narrative, causing the winner to think he had lost and prompting a top aide to call the loser "Mr. President." The exit-poll data triggered a drop of one hundred points on the New York Stock Exchange, caused the British prime minister to go to bed thinking Bush had lost, and set off powerful but never-proven allegations of conspiratorial vote fraud that lingered as an alternative explanation for the election's outcome. And exit polls—once thought to be the "crown jewel of political surveys"—were revealed to be "just another poll, with all the problems and imperfections endemic to the craft," as Richard Morin of the *Washington Post*'s polling unit noted.[9]

None of this was yet known when the President received word of the first round of exit polls. When he learned of them, he thought he was heading for repudiation, for a resounding defeat that he had not seen coming. Bush was aboard Air Force One, returning to Washington from a final foray to Ohio, the most decisive of the battleground states, when Karl Rove, his senior adviser, took a call and got word of the first exit polls. Bush peered over the aide's shoulder as Rove jotted down the numbers. "They're dreadful," Rove said. The effect was like a punch in the gut, the president would recall. "If the numbers were right," Bush wrote in his memoir, "I would suffer a landslide defeat."[10]

When he returned to the White House, Bush went to the second-floor quarters and, by his account, brooded. He moped around the Treaty Room. "I just couldn't believe it," Bush wrote. "After all the hard work of the past four years, and all the grueling months on the campaign trail, I was going to be voted out of office decisively," much as his father had been rejected in 1992 after a single presidential term.[11]

That afternoon and evening, Bush had plenty of company among people who had access to the exit polls, or portions of them, as they were compiled and shared among sponsoring media organizations—and leaked to other news outlets. The inclination to believe the exit polls, or at least to take them very seriously, was pervasive in newsrooms, among political pundits, and among the candidates and their aides. These were same-day data, drawn from voters across the country, which lent the exit polls a lofty reputation among some polling experts.[12]

On Election Day, there was no way such data would remain confidential, as their sponsors intended. The temptations were too strong and the data were too readily available. So they spread. The sponsors later agreed to quarantine the first wave of exit-poll results until 5 p.m. Eastern time. But that agreement came after the embarrassment of 2004, when details of the exit polls spilled into the public domain and circulated widely online.[13] The effect was to change "the entire tenor of the coverage," Bush's chief campaign strategist, Matthew Dowd, recalled a few weeks after the election. "Everybody in our campaign felt it. It was as if Kerry was going to go measure the drapes at the White House that afternoon."[14] By midafternoon, Jim Rutenberg wrote in the *New York Times*, "the likely outcome ... appeared clear. Polling data streaming into the broadcast and cable news networks indicated that nearly every state that had been in contention after eight months of hard campaigning was breaking for Senator John Kerry."[15]

FIGURE 19. Exit polls in the 2004 presidential election misled many people, including Bob Shrum, a senior adviser to Democratic candidate John Kerry. Shrum called Kerry "Mr. President" after receiving an update about the exit polls early on Election Night. (Credit: Associated Press/Susan Walsh)

Around 7 that evening, Kerry's senior campaign adviser, Bob Shrum, took a call from a journalist at one of the television networks who told him the latest exit polls looked so promising that there was no way Kerry would lose. Shrum at the time was with Kerry and Mary Beth Cahill, the campaign manager, at a hotel in Boston. Moments later, they entered a freight elevator, on their way out of the hotel and on to Kerry's home on Beacon Hill. At first, no one in the elevator said anything. Then Shrum broke the silence. He looked at Kerry and said: "Mr. President."

"Not yet," Kerry replied. "Not yet."[16]

There is a more dramatized version of that moment, one repeated by several sources,[17] including Kerry in the memoir he published in 2018. That version quotes Shrum as saying something to this effect: "May I be the first to call you Mr. President?"[18] Whatever Shrum said,[19] his sentiment was unmistakable. And soon enough, he said, Kerry, too, believed he was headed for victory. Back at his five-bedroom townhouse, Kerry and aides set to work on polishing a victory speech.[20] At that point in the evening, Kerry said in his memoir, he was working only on a "potential victory statement."[21]

By then other sources were signaling a win for Kerry. John Zogby—whose nearly spot-on predictions of the presidential elections in 1996 and 2000 earned him the alias "polling hero"[22]—announced late in the afternoon on Election Day that Kerry was sweeping to victory. He would carry the four major swing states—Florida, Ohio, Iowa, and New Mexico—and roll up at least 311 electoral votes to Bush's 213, Zogby declared.[23]

The day before, Zogby had released his final pre-election poll, which showed Bush ahead by one percentage point. His Election Day predictions of a sweeping Kerry victory, Zogby said, were based on indications that turnout by young voters was robust.[24] His new estimate was in line with the exit polls which, by one calculation, corresponded to Kerry's winning 302 electoral votes and Bush 236 votes.[25] Throughout the afternoon and evening, the exit polls consistently pointed to Kerry's winning the popular vote by about 51 percent to 48 percent. That was enough for Frank Luntz, a pollster for Republican candidates, to send an email to his clients, saying he anticipated a substantial win by Kerry. And Mark Mellman, Kerry's campaign pollster, went on a radio show early in the evening on Election Day and committed what he later said was "the cardinal sin of gloating, and gloating early and inappropriately," about what appeared to be Kerry's imminent triumph.[26]

On the cable news shows that evening, anchors and commentators made sly and knowing hints that a Kerry victory was in the offing. Sentiment at the Fox News Channel, the *New York Times* noted, was "that the race would be locked up long before midnight in Mr. Kerry's favor."[27] Susan Estrich, a Fox News analyst who ran Michael Dukakis's ill-fated presidential campaign in 1988, said on air: "The view in Boston is that if the exit polls are right, it's going to be very difficult for George Bush to win tonight." And in what the *Times* said may have been a Freudian slip, Martha MacCallum, one of the anchors on Fox News Channel, referred to Senator Kerry as "President Kerry," just after 8:30 p.m.[28]

But as the night wore on and votes were counted, it became clear that Kerry's victory in the exit polls was an illusion, a false dawn. It turned into what Louis Menand described in the *New Yorker* as "a very bad night for John Kerry and for the art of polling."[29] Kerry was not to be "Mr. President." Bush carried key swing states including Arizona, Missouri, and Iowa. Early on the day after the election, the networks called Colorado for Bush. Then Florida. Then Ohio.

By late morning, New Mexico was in Bush's column and Kerry conceded defeat. Bush had won with almost 51 percent of the popular vote, or sixty-two million votes. He carried thirty-one states, including the battleground states Zogby had said would go to Kerry. Bush's electoral vote margin was narrow but clear—286 to 252.

Some journalists were forceful, and even a bit gleeful, in criticizing the performance of the exit polls. "Exit polls were the scandal of this election," wrote conservative columnist Cal Thomas.[30] Conor O'Clery, then a correspondent for the *Irish Times*, observed that once the exit polls entered the public domain, "pro-Kerry partisans and many in the media believed them, because they desperately wanted to."[31] A posting at *Slate* magazine's *Kausfiles* blog poked fun at Kerry's "seven-hour presidency" while deploring the exit polls as "utterly dreadful."[32]

So what had gone wrong? The exit polls were a ten-million-dollar project conducted for the television networks and the Associated Press in the consortium headed by Mitofsky and Lenski. Both men were respected public-opinion researchers. They noted that the exit polls led to no mistaken calls by their clients, unlike the debacle in Florida in 2000.

Lenski seemed eager to blame blogs such as the *Drudge Report* and *Wonkette* and other internet sites for posting preliminary details from exit polls that had been leaked to them. "I'm not designing polls for some blogger who doesn't even understand how to read the data," Lenski snapped the day after the election. "It's like if you were graded by your readers on the first draft of your article."[33] To that, media critic Jack Shafer replied, "Lenski must know by now that the worst exploiters of exit polls are not bloggers but newscasters. The TV networks create exit-poll mania by cravenly hyping their importance in election after election while insisting that the figures stay under wraps. The election projection elite also lecture the public that the early exit-poll data is so flawed that viewers should be blocked from seeing it. But if that's the case, why is it collected and distributed to journalists in first place?"[34]

It was clear the 2004 exit-poll data skewed consistently in Kerry's favor. Even a late wave of data, distributed around 11 p.m., showed Kerry ahead. For newspapers like the *Washington Post*, which bought the data from the consortium, the erroneous exit polls caused "a real problem in our newsroom," said Steve Coll, the newspaper's managing editor. An important function of exit polls is to help news outlets plan their post-election coverage and explain the outcomes. "The last wave of national exit polls we received, along with many other subscribers, showed Kerry winning the popular vote by 51 percent to 48 percent," Coll said in an online discussion with readers on the day after the election. Such a margin, Coll added, was "surely enough to carry the electoral college, however the contested states in the Midwest broke down. The sample size was so large that it appeared beyond the usual margins of error in polling. Yet the poll was dead wrong. How can this be?"[35]

The discrepancies between the exit-poll estimates and the actual vote were significant and widespread, Mitofsky and Lenski acknowledged. On average, exit-poll results at the voting precinct level overstated Kerry's advantage over Bush by 6.5 percentage points—the greatest such discrepancy in any presidential election for which comparable data were available. What's more, the overestimate for Kerry was on average higher in states that were most competitive, including Colorado, Florida, Iowa, Nevada, New Mexico, Ohio, and Pennsylvania.[36] In twenty-six states, exit polls overstated the vote for Kerry, Mitofsky and Lenski reported. In only four states did exit polls overstate Bush's vote total.[37]

More Kerry than Bush voters agreed to participate in the exit polls, Mitofsky and Lenski said, adding, however, that it was not entirely clear why this occurred. "It is difficult to pinpoint precisely the reasons that, in general, Kerry voters were more likely to participate in the exit polls than Bush voters," they said.[38] Some blame fell to the interviewers, about fourteen hundred of whom were recruited for a single day's work. They were to stand outside polling places and approach voters as they left, asking them to complete the exit-poll form. Interviewers were to note the number of voters who refused to participate and the number they were unable to approach because of distance restrictions or other reasons.

More than three-quarters of the interviewers were novices, having never before worked as exit-poll interviewers.[39] More than half of them were younger than thirty-five, and most of them were white women.[40] The interviewers typically worked alone, without on-site supervision. More than 20 percent of interviewers who were questioned afterward gave low marks to the quality of their pre-election training,[41] which typically included instructions received by phone as well as a manual delivered by an express-parcel service.

In a memorandum for the steering committee of the National Election Pool, Mitofsky and Lenski said interviewer partisanship was "a significant factor" in the precinct-level discrepancies that favored Kerry.[42] They did not explain this effect in detail. But it suggests that pro-Kerry interviewers were inclined to approach people whom they suspected had voted for the Democrat, which could help explain why more Kerry voters were included in the exit polls.

This scenario seems even more plausible because Mitofsky later pointed to the failure of exit-poll interviewers to adhere to random-selection procedures in asking voters to participate. Interviewers were to make their approaches at fixed intervals—to select every third voter, say, or every fifth: the pattern varied by precinct. Not hewing to the selection pattern was "the biggest source of the vote problem," Mitofsky said at the 2005 conference of the American Association for Public Opinion Research, or AAPOR.[43]

A hint of interviewers' disregard for the selection pattern appeared in USA Today the day after the election. Walter Shapiro, a columnist for the newspaper, described participating in an exit poll outside his voting station in Manhattan. "My selection," he wrote, "was not part of a random sample. I merely walked up to a young man sitting by a ballot box on a folding table and asked if I could fill one out. His only restriction was the same rule used by many promotional giveaways: one to a family, so my wife was arbitrarily disenfranchised."[44]

It is likely that the indifference Shapiro described occurred elsewhere, and perhaps often, outside polling places in 2004. In some precincts, interviewers reported they had difficulty in approaching voters, another contributing factor in the exit polls' discrepancies. The greater the distance interviewers were required by local officials to keep from polling places, the greater the error rate, Mitofsky and Lenski reported. The length of the questionnaire, and the logos of the consortium's media partners that appeared on the face of the questionnaire, also may have deterred some voters, Mitofsky said.[45]

Explanations for the failure of the exits polls to include an adequate sample of Bush voters remained vague and amorphous. No single factor, or set of factors, was clearly identified as accounting for the errors that pointed to Kerry's victory in the afternoon, and well into the evening, on Election Day. "Maybe," said Kathleen Frankovic of the CBS News elections unit, the messy and misleading results "will undercut some of the blind faith in exit polls."[46] That surely was an effect. The misguided exit polls of 2004 were mentioned by critics for years. Writing in 2016, Nate Cohn of the New York Times recalled how "the exit polls showed John Kerry easily winning an election that he clearly lost."[47]

Mitofsky sought to spin the performance of the 2004 exit polls, saying the data had led to no erroneous on-air projections by the television networks in the National Election Pool. Of course, the television networks had pledged before the election to demonstrate greater caution and restraint than they had in 2000 in using exit-poll data to project state-by-state outcomes.[48] "I thought our goal was to make projections and produce analysis," Mitofsky told the 2005 AAPOR conference, "and I think we did that pretty well."[49]

But in fact, the exit polls' performance in 2004 was quite poor. They notably failed in the objective—not mentioned by Mitofsky in his remarks—of providing client news organizations with accurate indications about the election outcome while voting was underway, to allow them to plan their coverage accordingly.[50] "We think it wasn't worth the money we paid for it, that's for sure," Coll of the *Washington Post* said of the exit polls.[51] The misleading data generated confusion to an extent not fully realized until Bush, Kerry, and others reported in memoirs and in retrospective discussions how the deceptive exit polls had affected them on Election Day. The exit polls simply did not provide a sure understanding of what was happening as a closely contested national election unfolded.

Even worse, exit polls became the scaffolding for claims and suspicions—never proven—that the election had been stolen from Kerry, that the exit polls were accurate but fraud had altered the results in key states such as Ohio. Had Kerry carried Ohio and its twenty electoral votes, he would have won the presidency while perhaps losing the national popular vote.

Suspicions about vote fraud and corruption arose almost immediately after Kerry's concession speech and persisted for months. Skeptics scoffed at the idea that a broad and clandestine conspiracy to rig the election could have been organized and conducted in secret. They dismissed the argument that exit-poll results were evidence that Kerry had won the election and that his defeat was the result of massive fraud. The skeptics included Mitofsky who, as the *Washington Post* noted, "found himself in the peculiar position of arguing for the inaccuracy of his own 2004 exit poll."[52]

Mitofsky scoffed at conspiracy theories, saying he was "much more a believer in something practical, like incompetence."[53] Coll of the *Washington Post* put it this way: "Which is more likely—that an exit polling system that has been consistently wrong and troubled turned out to be wrong and troubled again, or that a vast conspiracy carried out by scores and scores of county and state election officials was successfully carried off to distort millions of American votes? I think the Kerry campaign concluded that the former is what happened."[54]

Advocates of the stolen-election thesis were persistent, however. In a lengthy article in *Rolling Stone* in June 2006, Robert F. Kennedy Jr. wrote that he had "become convinced that the president's party mounted a massive, coordinated campaign to subvert the will of the people in 2004. Across the country, Republican election officials and party stalwarts employed a wide range of illegal and unethical tactics to fix the election."[55] Kennedy's claim of a deeply embedded criminal conspiracy by Republicans was much discussed— and derided for its dubious assumptions, including those about exit polls and their precision.

"Over the past decades, exit polling has evolved into an exact science," Kennedy asserted, quoting as an authority Dick Morris, President Bill Clinton's former pollster. Soon after the 2004 election, Morris had written, "Exit polls are almost never wrong"[56]—an exaggeration, as polling experts pointed out.[57] In fact, exit polls in presidential elections since 1988 skewed slightly— and sometimes more than that—to the Democratic candidate. "Exit polls are never exactly right," Morin wrote in the Washington Post, pointing out that the national exit poll in 1992 had overstated Bill Clinton's advantage by 2.5 percentage points. "But Clinton won, so [the error] didn't create a stir."[58]

Among Mitofsky's papers at the University of Connecticut is a printout of Kennedy's article, marked up in red pen. The margin annotations, written in Mitofsky's hand, included comments such as: "Not true," "nonsense," "wrong," "they ignore all evidence of no fraud," and "the troubling part is his bad analysis."[59] Mitofsky wrote "Never happened" in the margin adjacent to this claim by Kennedy: "On the evening of the vote, reporters at each of the major networks were briefed by pollsters at 7:54 p.m. Kerry, they were informed, had an insurmountable lead and would win by a rout: at least 309 electoral votes to Bush's 174, with fifty-five too close to call."[60]

Kennedy's article was deeply flawed—and based on "claims that grossly distort reality or lack documented support," Mark Blumenthal, a polling analyst, wrote in one of several blog posts addressing the conspiracy claims.[61] But controversy about the outcome in Ohio did turn up cases of apparent voting irregularities in that state, including reports of the rejection of provisional ballots, of insufficient voting machines at precincts with heavy concentrations of minority and Democratic voters, and of claims that many African Americans in Cincinnati and Toledo had been suspiciously purged from voting rolls. Those and other accounts of irregularities were detailed in a Harper's Magazine cover article in August 2005, which berated the news media for treating suspicions of vote fraud with indifference.[62]

A more skeptical assessment was offered by Mark Hertsgaard, who, in Mother Jones magazine, wrote that "it remains far from clear that Bush stole the election."[63] He quoted the legal counsel for the Ohio Democratic party as saying that the claim that the election outcome was hijacked "relies on the assumption that the entire Republican Party is conspiratorial and the entire Democratic Party is as dumb as rocks. And I don't buy that."[64] Bush carried Ohio by a margin of 118,600 votes, out of 5.5 million cast.

Hertsgaard's article noted that the discrepancies in exit-poll results and the official vote count represented "a key part of the skeptics' argument," but added that "skeptics betray a poor grasp of exit polling, starting with their claim that exit polls are invariably accurate within tenths of a percentage point. In truth, the exit polls were wrong by much more than that in the 1988 and 1992 presidential elections."[65]

Kerry's campaign was little interested in pursuing vote-fraud allegations, which were briefly debated in Congress when time came to certify the electoral votes in the 2004 election. Representative Stephanie Tubbs Jones of Ohio and Senator Barbara Boxer of California objected to Ohio's twenty electoral votes being counted for Bush, given the reported voting irregularities in the state. Their objections set off debates and roll-call votes in both houses of Congress. In the end, the House rejected the challenge, by 267 votes to 31. The objection failed in the Senate, 74 votes to 1. Kerry was said to be opposed to the challenge. When the Senate voted, he was traveling in the Middle East.[66] Although the challenge went nowhere in Congress, suspicions of a criminal conspiracy to defraud the election swirled for months, demonstrating anew, and perhaps in an extreme way, how polling errors can produce powerful and enduring effects.

Paradoxically, the exit polls of 2004 were expected to be a vast improvement over those conducted by Voter News Service in 2000, when they were a source of erroneous projections about Florida, and in the midterm elections in 2002, when the exit-poll system crashed on Election Night. The successive debacles led the sponsoring consortium of the television networks and the Associated Press to dissolve Voter News Service and set up the National Election Pool, directed by the Mitofsky-Lenski team.

That the exit polls were problematic in 2004 made for a dismaying conclusion to what had been a tempestuous election campaign, one that brimmed with polling controversies and melodramatic excess. For pollsters and their critics, the 2004 campaign was a loud and combative time, the intensity of which prompted the pollster Zogby to call it the "Armageddon Election." By that, Zogby said, he meant the campaign was "the closest, most bitter election

I've ever seen. There used to be a center in politics but the center seems to be gone this year, and both side are convinced that if the other wins it will be the end of the world."[67]

"Armageddon" was more than a little exaggerated, of course, although the term did apply, somewhat, to Zogby. His reputation for accuracy in polling presidential elections was severely dented by his curious Election Day prediction that Kerry would win easily, with more than 300 electoral votes. The *New York Times* gave Zogby top billing among its prominent "losers" of the 2004 campaign—a roster that included exit pollsters. "I did something I shouldn't have," Zogby said of his Election Day call. "I am a better pollster than predictor."[68]

Nearly all the final pre-election polls in 2004 signaled a close race. Most of them, but certainly not all, showed Bush narrowly in the lead at the end of the campaign. "In the end," polling analyst Michael Traugott wrote, "the final estimates of the preelection polls, the bread and butter of the polling industry, were very good in suggesting it would be a close race, with Bush the likely winner."[69]

As always, there were notable outliers. *Newsweek's* final poll, completed four days before the election, showed Bush ahead by six percentage points. At the other extreme, a Harris online poll gave Kerry a three-point lead. Gallup estimated that the race was tied at 49 percent. The polls exhibited some erratic and puzzling swings during the campaign, prompting Rutenberg of the *New York Times* to observe: "What's going to happen on Election Day? It depends on which pollster you ask."[70] No conflicting readings were more perplexing than the separate results released at almost the same time in mid-September by Gallup and the Pew Research Center.

Gallup's poll gave Bush a lead of thirteen percentage points; the Pew survey showed the race was virtually a dead heat. David Moore, who then was the senior editor of the Gallup Poll, recalled that news media reaction to the conflicting results was "explosive." Moore said he and a fellow Gallup executive "were buried by calls from reporters around the country demanding an explanation for the differences between the polls." Eventually, Moore said, Gallup and Pew "agreed that the difference might well be attributed to 'timing'—the Pew poll was conducted over a five-day period, Gallup's over three days, and it was a volatile period of campaigning."[71]

The perplexity about the Gallup-Pew disparity was emblematic not only of instability of the polls during the campaign but also of the exceptional

FIGURE 20. Public controversies swelled around the election polls in 2004. The left-wing advocacy group MoveOn.org took out a full-page advertisement in the *New York Times* to assail aspects of the Gallup poll's methodology. (Credit: MoveOn.org)

controversies that surrounded them that year. Pollsters themselves were swept up in very public disputes.[72] Not long after the clashing Gallup and Pew poll results were released, the left-wing advocacy group MoveOn.org placed a full-page advertisement in the *New York Times* that impugned Gallup's polling methodology and implied that its results tilted toward Bush because of the religious views of its retired co-chairman, George Gallup Jr., the youngest son of the company's founder.[73]

"Gallup-ing to the right," read the headline of the MoveOn ad. "Why does America's top pollster keep getting it wrong?" The text questioned why the Gallup polls had so often favored Bush, suggesting the tilt was due to how it determined likely voters—and to the beliefs of Gallup Jr.[74] The advertisement was an astonishing display of hostility.[75] "Never saw anything like it," said Andrew Kohut, a veteran pollster who was formerly president of the Gallup Organization and founding director of the Pew Research Center. "People have their guns drawn to a greater extent than usual and they're shooting at us."[76]

However exaggerated, the MoveOn advertisement plainly stung Gallup. Frank Newport, its editor-in-chief, said, "We have a group that doesn't like that their candidate is behind in most polling, if not all polling, and therefore they're shooting out at the messenger." Newport also said the advertisement encouraged people to conclude "that Gallup Polls showing George W. Bush ahead were to be doubted." He said he was interviewed by many reporters after the ad appeared and was often "directly confronted with questions that assumed the allegations of Gallup bias were factual and correct."[77]

The MoveOn ad wasn't the only public protest against pollsters during the 2004 campaign. A simmering dispute between Republicans and the polling done for the Minneapolis *Star Tribune* spilled over into a demonstration outside the newspaper in September 2004. "There are good polling organizations out there—then there is the Strib," one of the protestors said, invoking the diminutive for *Star Tribune*. The demonstrators carried signs referring to the *Star Tribune* as the "Star and Sickle" and saying, "Strib polls are fibs."[78] They called for the dismissal of Robert Daves, the newspaper's polling director. They chanted, "Hey, hey, ho, ho, Rob Daves has got to go!"[79]

What sparked the protest was the *Star Tribune*'s survey that showed Kerry ahead by nine percentage points in Minnesota while other polls in the state suggested a closer race. The protest wasn't angry or hostile—the *Star Tribune*'s report said it "was relatively good-natured."[80] And the newspaper didn't dismiss Daves, who later reported that he had been the target of "e-mail campaigns that resulted in vile—even scatological—attacks" directed at him.[81] "It's tough being a pollster these days," Richard Morin, polling director for the *Washington Post*, observed, "even in Minnesota."[82]

The 2004 campaign marked the last, aggressive outbreak of hostility that prominent journalists had directed at pollsters over the years. No presidential campaign since 2004 has generated quite as much unconcealed poll-bashing. Among the most caustic poll-critics was Jimmy Breslin. "Anybody who believes these national political polls are giving you facts is a gullible fool," Breslin wrote in his *Newsday* column in mid-September 2004. "Any editors of newspapers or television news shows who use poll results as a story are beyond gullible. On behalf of the public they profess to serve, they are indolent salesmen of falsehoods."[83]

He added: "If you want a poll on the Kerry-Bush race, sit down and make up your own. It is just as good as the monstrous frauds presented on television and the newspaper first pages."[84] Breslin's principal complaint was that pollsters were ignoring cell phone–only households. He quoted John Zogby, who was something of a self-styled heretic in the polling industry, as saying that pollsters who conducted traditional telephone-based surveys were "in denial." They "try not to mention cell phones. They don't look or listen. They go ahead with a method that is old and wrong."[85]

Soon afterward, the *Washington Post* pointed out that Zogby himself conducted polls by telephone, which Zogby acknowledged a few days after Breslin's column was published. "I still conduct telephone polls," Zogby wrote. "The reality is that polling on the telephone is becoming more difficult."[86] In the end, not calling cell phone–only households apparently was not much of a factor in the accuracy of the pre-election polls in 2004.[87] Polling organizations soon devised ways of reaching those households in elections that followed.

Breslin was not alone in bashing the polls that year. "The polls are wrong," complained filmmaker Michael Moore. "They are all over the map like diarrhea. . . . You are being snookered if you believe any of these polls."[88] On the *Fox News Watch* program a few days before the election, panelist Jim Pinkerton declared that the polls "are as accurate and precise as human nature, which is to say they are not accurate and they are not precise. This is witchcraft."[89]

Arianna Huffington, the founder of the *Huffington Post*, renewed her intermittent hang-up-on-pollsters campaign in October 2004, telling NPR's *On the Media* program that "we are treating these polling results with the kind of reverence that ancient Romans gave to chicken entrails." She encouraged the show's listeners to pledge "that they will not talk to pollsters. They can talk to them, socially, but they should hang up on them if they call them at home, interrupting their dinner and asking them questions about this or any other election. If we can bring the response rate down to single digits, then even pollsters will have to admit that their results are pretty meaningless."[90]

It is striking that hostility toward pollsters has not reemerged with such virulence in elections since 2004. One explanation is that polling operations have become well integrated at leading media organizations. Polling units are not new to journalism, and they appear to be better accepted. AAPOR, the survey research organization, may have helped temper poll-bashing with its outreach program, begun in 2000, that was intended to help journalists better understand survey design and data analysis.[91]

Also factoring in the ebbing of poll-bashing has been the passing or the eclipse of journalists who were eager to assail election surveys. Mike Royko of the *Chicago Tribune*, who wrote columns encouraging people to lie to pollsters, died in 1997. Huffington's antipollster campaign sputtered out. Dan Rather of CBS News, a vehement critic of polling, left the network under an ethical cloud in 2005. He had made use on a *60 Minutes* program of what were determined to be bogus documents that suggested George Bush used family connections to enter the Texas Air National Guard and thus avoid serving in Vietnam.

The rise to prominence of data journalists and their statistics-based prediction models may also have helped curb poll-bashing. Best known among the data journalists is Nate Silver, who has developed an election forecasting model based on survey data. Silver became something of a celebrity after he accurately predicted the outcomes in forty-nine states in the 2008 presidential election. His status only deepened when he accurately projected how all fifty states would vote in 2012.

CHAPTER 8

"Gallup vs. the World"

Pointing the Wrong Way in 2012

High-profile failure in presidential elections can batter the reputations of venerable and well-regarded takers of pre-election polls. The *Literary Digest*, once the oracle of presidential elections, was shattered by its epic miscall in 1936, when its forecast was outdone by the new and more systematic methods that George Gallup, Elmo Roper, and Archibald Crossley brought to election surveys. The *Digest* never conducted another poll after 1936.

The 2012 election traced a strikingly similar narrative arc. This time, the venerable Gallup poll was acutely embarrassed. Its methods were challenged by an upstart data journalist armed with a powerful statistical model that aggregated pre-election polls to produce highly accurate state-by-state and national forecasts. And not unlike the *Literary Digest* in the landslide of 1936, Gallup was singled out for its failings in 2012, for consistently placing Mitt Romney, the Republican challenger, ahead of President Barack Obama. When the election was over, the upstart data journalist rated Gallup's polls the least accurate of all in 2012.

Gallup's final pre-election poll estimated that Romney held a one-point lead over Obama, a margin that had dwindled from as much as seven points in the weeks before Election Day.[1] Obama carried the popular vote by nearly four percentage points and the electoral vote by 332 to 206. For Gallup, the outcome represented a miss of almost five percentage points. Gallup acknowledged flaws in its methodology in a remarkable public mea culpa a few months after the election, and later announced it was retreating from presidential polling. It did not report its polling results in 2016 and said it will not do so in 2020.

Romney 49%, Obama 48% in Gallup's Final Election Survey

FIGURE 21. After miscalling the 2012 race between President Barack Obama and Republican Mitt Romney, the Gallup Organization dropped out of election polling. Gallup had begun its pre-election surveys seventy-six years earlier. (Credit: Peter Souza/Obama White House)

Parallels between the failures of the *Literary Digest* and the Gallup poll in 2016 are not entirely exact; they are not a case of history repeating, or rhyming.[2] No one should equate the dimensions of Gallup's miss in 2012 with the failing of the *Digest* in 1936. But the parallels are more than just a curiosity: the thematic connections are intriguing. The narrative arc of wayward polls bringing embarrassment to venerable and respected organizations holds true for Gallup in 2012 as it did for the *Digest* in 1936. Gallup, after all, long had been the most prominent name in public opinion research—much as the *Digest* was before its polling debacle.

An important distinction lurks in the storyline, however: whereas the *Digest* often was applauded before the debacle of 1936 for accurately forecasting presidential elections, Gallup's polling, as we've seen, had been a source of confusion and controversy in campaigns before 2012. Gallup had misfired in forecasting the popular vote winner in 2000, after attracting considerable criticism for its erratic daily tracking poll. In 2004, Gallup's final estimate was that the presidential race was tied; George Bush defeated John Kerry by 2.4 percentage points. In addition, Gallup's methods that year were publicly, if wrongly, attacked as favoring the Republicans. Gallup really had not had an outstanding polling performance in a presidential race since 1984 and its nearly spot-on estimate of Ronald Reagan's landslide reelection.

In the closing month of the 2012 campaign, Gallup's polls consistently showed Romney ahead of Obama, often by substantial margins. Romney led by seven percentage points in poll results released in mid-October, for example.[3] Because almost all other polls were showing a much tighter race, Gallup's survey became a source of reassurance for the Republican faithful—much as the *Digest*'s weekly reports of its polling results in 1936 had encouraged the hopes of Alf Landon's supporters.

For example, the Republican political strategist Karl Rove pointed out that no presidential candidate so late in the campaign had ever lost when he had scored better than 50 percent in Gallup's tracking poll of likely voters.[4] Five days before the election, Rove offered this prediction in his *Wall Street Journal* column: "Sometime after the cock crows on the morning of Nov. 7, Mitt Romney will be declared America's 45th president. Let's call it 51%-48%, with Mr. Romney carrying at least 279 Electoral College votes, probably more."[5]

Other right-of-center commentators expressed confidence in Romney's pending victory. It seemed almost unimaginable to them that Romney would lose to an incumbent whose record, especially on the sluggish domestic economy, was so mixed. Some analysts predicted Romney would win easily. Among them was Michael Barone, a veteran Washington political analyst. His prediction: Romney, 315 electoral votes; Obama, 223.[6] Barone figured that Romney would win Ohio, Pennsylvania, Wisconsin, Florida, Virginia, New Hampshire, Iowa, and Colorado—states that Obama had carried in 2008. Obama won them all again in 2012.

Peggy Noonan, a columnist for the *Wall Street Journal* and former speech-writer for Ronald Reagan, predicted Romney's victory based less on the polls than on hunches, impressions, and observations about the prevalence of campaign yard signs. "I think it's Romney," she wrote in her blog the day before the election. "I think he's stealing in 'like a thief with good tools,' in Walker Percy's old words. While everyone is looking at the polls . . . Romney's slipping into the presidency." She referred to crowds at campaign's end in Ohio and Pennsylvania that seemed genuinely enthusiastic for Romney.[7]

"There is no denying the Republicans have the passion now, the enthusi-asm," Noonan added. "The Democrats do not. Independents are breaking for Romney. And there's the thing about the yard signs. In Florida a few weeks ago, I saw Romney signs, not Obama ones. From Ohio I hear the same. From tony Northwest Washington, D.C., I hear the same."[8]

"Is it possible," she wondered, "this whole thing is playing out before our eyes and we're really not noticing because we're too busy looking at data on paper instead of what's in front of us? Maybe that's the real distortion of the polls this year: They left us discounting the world around us."[9]

At campaign's end, nearly all national polls were signaling a close race. The composite average of all presidential polls, calculated by the *RealClearPolitics* website, showed Barack Obama ahead by only 48.8 percent to 48.1 percent. Of the surveys taken during the campaign's closing week, only those by Pew Research and ABC News/*Washington Post* came within a percentage point of estimating Obama's winning margin. It was hardly a stellar performance by the pre-election national polls. Collectively, they offered no hint that Obama was heading to a fairly comfortable victory. By one count, just 8 of 113 polls conducted in the campaign's final month showed Obama ahead by 3 percent-age points or more.[10] He won by 3.9 points.

That outcome was enabled perhaps by the president's high-profile response to Superstorm Sandy, which brought severe flooding to New Jersey, New York City, and elsewhere in Northeastern states in the last days of October, causing more than one hundred fatalities and seventy billion dollars in damage.[11] The storm disrupted telephone service, too, prompting some election pollsters, such as Gallup, to suspend their work for several days. Pew Research noted that Obama had gained three percentage points in its poll during the cam-paign's closing days and said his "handling of the storm's aftermath may have contributed to his improved showing."[12]

The pre-election polls of 2012 were notable not for their pinpoint accuracy but for the variety of their sampling methods. The trend toward internet surveys— which are less expensive and usually less time-consuming to complete than telephone-based polling—was confirmed in 2012. Rand Corporation in Cali-fornia, for example, conducted a staggered, internet-based survey drawn from a panel of thirty-five hundred participants. Each participant was contacted once a week and paid a nominal sum to respond online to a small set of ques-tions about the presidential election.[13] The results were impressive; at the close

FIGURE 22. Gallup's bête noire of the 2012 election was Nate Silver, a data journalist whose polls-based model accurately predicted the outcomes in all fifty states. Gallup's editor-in-chief grumbled that Silver, in making his forecasts, just took "advantage of all the hard work" that pollsters had done. (Credit: Associated Press/Russell G. Sneddon)

of the campaign, the Rand panels estimated Obama was ahead by 3.3 percentage points.

But Gallup's estimates stood out in the campaign's closing days and weeks—and not because of the company's prominent name or because it was the oldest of all presidential election pollsters. Along with the Rasmussen Reports survey, which was conducted by automated robodialing and an online panel, Gallup was an outlier at the end, pointing to a narrow Romney win.

Just as the *Literary Digest* had no more high-profile detractor in 1936 than George Gallup, a thirtysomething former journalism professor, the Gallup poll in 2012 had no more intense or skeptical critic than Nate Silver, a thirtysomething data journalist whom a British newspaper called "Nerdstrodamus."[14] Before turning to poll-based election forecasting, Silver had made a name for himself by crunching statistics to predict performance of professional baseball players. Silver called his projection technique PECOTA, or Player Empirical Comparison and Optimization Test Algorithm.

Silver launched the *FiveThirtyEight* blog in 2008, taking the name from the total number of electoral votes in a U.S. presidential election. He burst into national prominence by correctly forecasting the outcomes in forty-nine of fifty states in that year's presidential election. He missed only on the outcome in Indiana, which Obama narrowly won.

By 2010, Silver had moved his blog and forecasting model to the *New York Times* under a three-year licensing agreement. As the 2012 election approached, *FiveThirtyEight* reportedly was responsible for 20 percent of all traffic to the *Times* online site.

Silver's technique essentially is to assess and aggregate national and state-level polls, then crank them through a statistical model that considers past performance of the polls and the rigor of their survey methodology, as well as factors such as job growth and inflation, among other variables. The reasoning is straightforward: "Averaging polls together increases their sample size— making them much more powerful statistically than any one poll taken alone," he wrote. Silver described his forecasting method as essentially "an Electoral College simulation, and therefore relies . . . heavily on state-by-state polls."[15]

In 2012, Silver exceeded his exploit of four years earlier, forecasting Obama's victory and picking the winning candidate in all fifty states. It was a tour de force that confirmed his reputation and enhanced his rather unlikely celebrity status. Silver was fêted as an oracle of election forecasting whose data analysis had outclassed bloviating pundits and their hunches and gut feelings. An "exalted journo-statistician," a blogger for the *Washington Post* called him.[16] "He's arguably the most famous person in American journalism at the moment," said the conservative columnist John Podhoretz, "and deservedly so."[17]

Silver is a self-described data geek who seems a bit uncomfortable in public appearances and television interviews—of which he did many before and after the 2012 election. It seemed as if he worried that a trick question of some kind were about to be sprung. Mannerisms aside, Silver comes across as deeply knowledgeable yet modest. He seemed eager to downplay his exploit of correctly calling the outcomes in all fifty states, referring to the forecast as "a lucky break."[18] In fact, Silver said, it was not "all that hard to figure out that President Obama, [who was] ahead in the overwhelming majority of nonpartisan polls in states such as Ohio, Pennsylvania, Nevada, Iowa and Wisconsin, was the favorite to win them, and was therefore the favorite to win the Electoral

College."[19] But had his 2012 forecast failed, Silver said, "I don't know if I would have been inclined to blog about politics for very much longer."[20]

Silver was hardly alone in analyzing polling data to forecast Obama's victory. He had company in his spot-on forecast. The *Daily Kos* blog, for which Silver used to write, claimed that its forecast was even more accurate. Samuel Wang of the Princeton Election Consortium, which focused on state-level polls, accurately predicted the outcome in forty-nine of fifty states, and one analysis found his overall forecast, including House and Senate races, even sharper than Silver's. But none of the rival poll-based forecasters cut the profile that Silver did. And none of them worked from the *New York Times*, where Silver and his techniques were rather more tolerated than admired or eagerly embraced.

No other forecaster turned out trenchant, sometimes-acerbic analyses with the frequency that Silver did. His analyses were lengthy but confidently written. And they were comprehensible to laymen. Silver's analyses offered an empirical, data-based check on mushy, impressionist punditry—and a counterpoint to conflicting and errant polls.

Silver considered himself "a counterweight to what seem like misinformed views about the presidential race"[21] and remained in that role months after the election. He revisited, for example, Peggy Noonan's pre-election essay that cited yard signs in predicting Romney's victory. Silver wrote that "a handful of anecdotal data points are not worth very much in a country of more than 300 million people. Ms. Noonan, and many other commentators, made a similar mistake . . . in their analysis of the presidential election, when they cited evidence like the number of Mitt Romney yard signs in certain neighborhoods as an indication that he was likely to win, while dismissing polls that collectively surveyed hundreds of thousands of voters in swing states and largely showed Mr. Obama ahead."[22]

Silver insisted that while the national polls were suggesting a close race between Obama and Romney, polls in battleground states such as Florida, Ohio, and Pennsylvania mostly showed Obama in the lead. Obama's persistent advantage in those states signaled he would win the Electoral College vote, Silver argued. He doubted there was much momentum toward Romney late in the campaign, especially after Obama's well-publicized response to the havoc of Superstorm Sandy. Even the Republican governor of storm-battered New Jersey, Chris Christie, had praised Obama after the storm, saying, "The President has been all over this. He deserves great credit."[23]

Romney would win the Electoral College only if crucial state polls were systematically in error, Silver said, adding that such a prospect was very unlikely. Silver did allow himself some wriggle room, however. He invoked a professional football analogy a few days before the election in saying, "Obama is not a sure thing, by any means. It is a close race. His chances of holding onto his Electoral College lead and converting it into another term are equivalent to the chances of an N.F.L. [professional] football team winning when it leads by a field goal with three minutes left to play in the fourth quarter. There are plenty of things that could go wrong, and sometimes they will."[24]

But Silver noted that "an N.F.L. team that leads by a field goal with three minutes left to go winds up winning the game 79 percent of the time. Those were Mr. Obama's chances in the FiveThirtyEight forecast" as of October 31, 2012: 79 percent.[25] (Silver's point, essentially, was this: if 79 blue ping-pong balls and 21 red ones were placed in a large bowl and someone, with eyes averted, chose one, it would not be deeply shocking if a red ball had been selected. In an election with those same probabilities, Romney clearly had a chance of winning.)

But by Election Day 2012, Silver had boosted his estimate of Obama's win-probability to 90.9 percent. Just as Gallup's polling reports brought cheer to Republican activists and pundits during the 2012 campaign, Silver's analyses were a source of relief to Democrats—a kind of anxiety-relief like Xanax, the *Hollywood Reporter* said.[26] A reporter for BuzzFeed News wrote that Silver "has become the most trusted source in polls, if you're an Obama supporter." His forecasts, she added, "are the answer to a welter of conflicting poll results and a Republican insistence that Mitt Romney is, in fact, winning."[27]

His analyses could be prickly and unsparing,[28] as the Gallup Organization learned to its discomfiture in 2012. In mid-October, as Gallup's tracking poll showed Romney with a seven-point lead over Obama, Silver posted a lengthy and scathing assessment that zeroed in on Gallup and carried the headline "Gallup vs. the World." He cast himself effectively as Gallup's bête noire.

Silver noted that Gallup's numbers were "deeply inconsistent with the results that other polling firms are showing in the presidential race." When Gallup diverged so markedly from the polling consensus, Silver wrote, it "has a history of performing very poorly." Silver reviewed that history, recalling that Gallup's final poll in 2008 gave Obama a lead of eleven percentage points over Republican John McCain. An eleven-point lead was well beyond the average of national polls, which showed Obama's margin was closer to seven percentage points. (He won the election by 7.2 percentage points.) The Gallup poll in 2008 missed by almost four points.[29]

Silver also recalled Gallup's overestimate in the midterm elections in 2010, when it reported that Republicans held a lead of fifteen percentage points on the overall national Congressional ballot. Republicans won the popular vote for the House of Representatives by about seven percentage points. That outcome, Silver wrote, represented "another big miss for Gallup." He also recalled the odd and "implausibly large swings" in Gallup's tracking poll during the presidential campaign in 2000, writing, "Apart from Gallup's final poll not having been especially accurate in recent years, it has often been a wild ride to get there."[30]

Silver closed his essay by suggesting that Gallup's survey methodology had an "endemic" problem in how it identified poll respondents who were most likely to vote. "I would *not* recommend that you literally just disregard the Gallup poll," Silver advised. "You should consider it—but consider it in context. The context is that its most recent results differ substantially from the dozens of other state and national polls about the campaign." It is far more likely, he wrote, that "Gallup is wrong and everyone else is right than the other way around."[31] "Gallup vs. the World" was pointed, scathing in places, yet a thoroughly reasonable analysis. It was faintly redolent of George Gallup's cheeky claim in midsummer 1936 about how the *Literary Digest*'s mail-in poll would turn out.

A few days after posting the "Gallup vs. the World" essay, Silver insisted that his objective in calling attention to polling outliers like Gallup was "not to browbeat them into changing their methods. Instead, as strange as this might sound, I would much rather that the pollsters paid no attention to FiveThirtyEight. When pollsters feel as though they are under pressure to conform to expectations about the race, they may herd toward the poll averages, which would reduce their independence and would therefore reduce the benefit of aggregating different polls together," he wrote.[32] Silver had suspicions about "herding," a difficult-to-prove tendency in which pollsters' end-of-campaign estimates converge to appear fairly similar.[33]

Gallup's final pre-election survey in 2012, released the day before the election, pointed to a much tighter race than its previous polls had estimated.

According to Gallup, Romney held a one-point lead, or what essentially was a statistical tie.

Even though his forecasts about the 2012 election were spot-on, the campaign was in some ways a rough time for Silver. Given his record, the certainty of his analyses, and his association with the *Times*, Silver became a target. Dylan Byers, a writer for *Politico*, suggested in the closing days of the campaign that Silver risked becoming "a one-term celebrity," should Obama lose. "Sure," Byers wrote, Silver "is the guy who correctly predicted the outcome of the 2008 election in 49 of 50 states, but this year's polls suggest a nailbiter."[34] (After the 2012 election, Byers praised Silver's "carefully curated aggregation of polling data" and said the accuracy of his pre-election forecast ranked among the top media stories of 2012.)[35]

The race also produced annoyances like the online site unskewedpolls.com and its author, Dean Chambers. The site, which Chambers long ago gave up, railed in 2012 against election polls and aggregators like Silver, and sought to "unskew" polls that were not favorable to Romney. Chambers, a conservative activist, mocked Silver as "a man of very small stature, a thin and effeminate man with a soft-sounding voice. . . . Nate Silver, like most liberal and leftist celebrities and favorites, might be of average intelligence but is surely not the genius he's made out to be. His political analyses are average at best and his projections, at least this year, are extremely biased in favor of the Democrats."[36] In the end, Chambers predicted Romney would win narrowly, with "50.67 percent of the popular vote and 275 electoral votes to President Obama's 48.88 percent and 263 electoral votes."[37]

Silver had no more prominent critic during the campaign than Joe Scarborough, a former Republican congressman and host of the *Morning Joe* program on MSNBC. Eight days before the election, Scarborough dismissed Silver and his forecasts as "jokes." "Both sides understand that it is close," Scarborough said of the election, "and it could go either way. And anybody that thinks that this race is anything but a tossup right now is such an ideologue, they should be kept away from typewriters, computers, laptops and microphones for the next 10 days, because they're jokes."[38]

Silver responded by saying his poll-based forecasts were "not wizardry or rocket science. . . . It's a pretty simple set of facts. I'm sorry that Joe is math-challenged."[39] Soon after, Silver proposed in a post on Twitter that he and Scarborough place a wager on the election's outcome: "If Obama wins, you donate $1,000 to the American Red Cross. If Romney wins, I do. Deal?" The prospective bet soon grew to $2,000 and brought a reprimand from Margaret Sullivan, then the *Times*'s public editor or in-house critic. Whatever the motivation, Sullivan wrote, "the wager offer is a bad idea—giving ammunition to the critics who want to paint Mr. Silver as a partisan who is trying to sway the outcome." Such a bet, she said, was "inappropriate for a *Times* journalist, which is how Mr. Silver is seen by the public even though he's not a regular staff member."[40]

Silver's offense seemed trivial. He said the wager offer was made half in jest at "a high-stress time" as the election approached. And he told Sullivan that Scarborough had "been on a rant, calling me an idiot and a partisan," prompting the suggestion that Scarborough back up his claims with some money. "I'm asking him to put some integrity behind it," Silver said. "I don't stand to get anything from it; it's for charity."[41]

Sullivan said in her dressing-down that she sympathized and recognized that Silver wasn't "covering the presidential race as a political reporter would. But he is closely associated with The Times and its journalism. . . . When he came to work at The Times, Mr. Silver gained a lot more visibility and the credibility associated with a prominent institution. But he lost something, too: the right to act like a free agent with responsibilities to nobody's standards but his own."[42]

Sullivan's reproach seemed fussy and exaggerated. And it set off a brief tempest. Hundreds of Silver's defenders sent her email or posted comments on her blog. Some of the messages, she later said, "questioned my intelligence, sanity or sense of fun." Or the logic of her criticism. But Sullivan doubled down on her complaint about Silver's wager, writing that it "may not be a true conflict of interest, but there is an appearance of one. And appearance matters—it affects credibility, which is at the heart of good journalism."[43] Months later, Sullivan conceded that her rebuke was "probably off-base."[44] And Joe Scarborough extended a sort-of apology to Silver, saying after the election, "I was too tough on him and there's an 84.398264 percent chance I will be less dismissive of his good work in the future."[45]

Its polling error of 2012 rattled the Gallup Organization on several fronts in the months after the election. It feuded with Silver. It saw its long-standing partnership with *USA Today* break up. It released an internal study describing how it had erred in polling the election. And it agreed to pay more than ten million dollars to settle a whistleblower lawsuit with the federal government that was unrelated to election polling but deeply embarrassing nonetheless.

Silver renewed his criticism of Gallup soon after the election, in an assessment of the performance of pollsters in 2012. "It was one of the best-known polling firms . . . that had among the worst results," he wrote. "In late October, Gallup consistently showed Mr. Romney ahead by about six percentage points among likely voters, far different from the average of other surveys." Gallup's final pre-election poll, which showed Romney leading by one point, "was slightly better, but still identified the wrong winner in the election," Silver wrote.[46] A table accompanying Silver's essay ranked Gallup dead last among the nearly two dozen pollsters that had conducted at least five surveys during the campaign's closing three weeks.

Silver's analysis—and his ranking Gallup as the worst-performing of all presidential pollsters—was blunt, stinging, and maybe something of a response to a lengthy statement issued the day before by Frank Newport, editor-in-chief of the Gallup poll. Newport argued that Gallup's final pre-election estimate wasn't far from the mark, saying the poll "gave a broadly accurate picture of what was, in fact, a very close popular vote."[47] It was an interpretation faintly evocative of George Gallup's labored claim that the polls hadn't been that much in error in 1948. It seemed a stretch to describe the Gallup poll in 2012 as "broadly accurate" when it pointed to the wrong winner and missed the popular vote margin by nearly five percentage points. .

Newport took an obvious if indirect swipe at Silver and his poll-based modeling, saying with some justification that it was less expensive—and less hazardous to one's reputation—to aggregate and analyze polling data that had been collected at considerable expense by others. It was a complaint that Newport had made previously. In a radio interview in September 2012, Newport said Silver was "in a wonderful position because he doesn't have to do any work in terms of day-by-day polling. He just takes advantage of all the hard work that the rest of us do and then he aggregates it into his numbers."[48]

Newport hinted in his post-election statement that Gallup just might quit election polling, saying that survey research companies that "go to the expense and effort to conduct individual polls could, in theory, decide to put their efforts into aggregation and statistical analyses of other people's polls in the next election cycle and cut out their own polling. If many organizations make this seemingly rational decision, we could quickly be in a situation in which there are fewer and fewer polls left to aggregate and put into statistical models."[49]

While Newport's post-election critique did not mention Silver by name, his target was clear enough. "It is impossible to read this as anything other than an attack on Nate Silver, who is by far the most prominent aggregator and analyzer of others' polls," wrote Andrew Leonard at the online magazine *Salon*. He added that Newport's complaint "simply reeks of sour grapes. During the campaign year, Silver consistently pointed out that Gallup's results were oddly inconsistent with what other pollsters were finding. And he was right—Gallup got it wrong. It is not inappropriate to point that out. But Gallup presumes too much when it effectively threatens to take its surveys home and just stop playing." Gallup was facing an "unhappy future," Leonard wrote. "If the company keeps getting the numbers wrong, the market will punish it. At that point, Gallup won't be able to blame its sorry fate on anyone but its own incompetence."[50]

Other assessments of the Gallup-Silver feud were snidely mischievous, such as the comment posted at the popular and gossipy *Wonkette* online site: "We feel vaguely bad for Frank Newport, truly, because he represents a stolid and storied organization and he's probably institutionally unable to give vent to his full-on snarky rage against his critics, as he'd like. Instead, he had to jam a bunch of passive aggression into a very serious blog post about how successful Gallup's polling was this year!"[51] An essayist in Minnesota surmised that "Gallup hates . . . Silver for the same reason the newspaper business hates Google. Both are aggregators that are undermining established business models."[52] And veteran journalist Walter Shapiro wrote in *Columbia Journalism Review* that "anyone organizing a post-election panel discussion might be wise to put a few chairs between *New York Times* polling guru Nate Silver and Frank Newport, the editor-in-chief of Gallup."[53]

The unraveling of Gallup's polling reputation resumed in early 2013, when its twenty-one-year partnership with *USA Today* was dissolved amid speculation that the newspaper had grown displeased with Gallup's polling results. Gallup and *USA Today* said the decision to split was mutual. Whoever initiated the breakup, the announcement of the split was an occasion to recall Gallup's recent poll failings. "In case you don't remember," the *Guardian* of London pointed out, "Gallup continuously and incorrectly showed the Republican presidential nominee, Mitt Romney, leading during the final month of the 2012 election."[54]

Nate Cohn, then of the *New Republic*, said about the divorce, "If *USA Today* pulled the plug because it was dissatisfied with Gallup's polling, then the paper made a wise move." He added that "the break-up with *USA Today* does not mean Gallup is done with political polling. Unlike many public pollsters . . . Gallup's public political polls are conducted at a loss, funded by revenue from Gallup's other private ventures like consulting for large corporations. So why does Gallup do it? The publicity these polls earn for the Gallup brand is priceless."[55]

The end of the Gallup/*USA Today* polling affiliation brought a few reminders that the partnership had once included CNN. The cable network left in a messy public split in 2006, highlighted by the leak of an internal memorandum about the breakup written by Jim Clifton, Gallup's chief executive officer. Clifton's memorandum reaffirmed Gallup's ties to *USA Today* but said CNN was attracting "far fewer viewers" than it had "in the past, and we feel that our brand was getting lost and diluted."[56] He also wrote that ending the partnership with CNN would likely result in Gallup's polling analysts being "invited on a wide variety of television shows rather than primarily linked to CNN. We believe with this newfound independence, we will get covered by more broadcast media because we are not the poll of their competitor."[57]

CNN said in response that Clifton's statements were "not only unprofessional but in every respect untrue." It was Gallup that wanted to end the relationship, CNN said, adding that "the CNN brand was so dominant that Gallup wasn't getting the attention for the polls that they wanted."[58] Interestingly, Gallup had reestablished its public profile in opinion polling by forging the relationship with CNN and *USA Today*, according to a former Gallup vice president, David W. Moore.

By the late 1980s, Moore wrote, "the Gallup poll had all but disappeared from most national news stories. Few major newspapers continued to subscribe to Gallup's polling service, because most newspapers got their poll results for free, recycled from the newspapers and television networks that conducted their own polls."[59] Linking up with CNN and *USA Today*, Moore stated, brought Gallup "back in the news" as its poll results "were immediately published on CNN and in *USA Today*. And the two media organizations benefited from the credibility of the Gallup poll."[60]

Seven months after the 2012 election, the Gallup Organization convened a news conference at its government division headquarters on F Street in downtown Washington, DC, to release a seventeen-page report about its pre-election polling in the presidential campaign. It was an extraordinary mea culpa by the venerable pollster. It also was, as the *Washington Post* observed, an acknowledgement "of the damage done to the poll's brand in the last election."[61]

Newport presented and discussed the findings of Gallup's report, which identified four factors that contributed to the miscall. None of the factors, alone, was decisive but collectively, they moved the poll results in Romney's favor, Newport said.[62] Notable among them was Gallup's procedure to identify who among poll respondents were most likely to vote—a long-standing conundrum of election polling. Included in Gallup's screening procedure was a question in which respondents were asked how much they had thought about the election. Removing that question while applying other tweaks would have improved Gallup's final estimate, the report said.[63]

The report also said questions posed to respondents about their race and ethnicity resulted in including a disproportionate number of whites and too few blacks and Hispanics in Gallup's samples. Another flaw was traced to Gallup's decision to call listed landline telephone numbers instead of making use of the more expensive random-digit dialing technique. Using listed numbers led to the inclusion of "more older and more Republican respondents" in its 2012 polls, Gallup acknowledged. In addition, Gallup said its pre-election polling at times underrepresented respondents living in portions of the Eastern and Pacific time zones. "Gallup's goal in presidential election environments," the report asserted, "is to reflect underlying voter opinions and sentiment accurately, and in its final estimate, to closely approximate the final popular vote outcome."[64]

Newport said modifications would be made to Gallup's survey methods so that when "the next presidential election rolls around, we think we'll certainly be in a position at the accurate end of the spectrum" of pollsters.[65] But there was to be no "next presidential election" for Gallup. In June 2015, the news broke that Gallup was retreating from polling presidential elections to focus on issue-oriented surveys about the public's views and opinions. The decision reflected not a lack of confidence in pre-election polling, Newport said, but rather a judgment about how to be "most effective in keeping the voice of the people injected into the democratic process."[66] The explanation vaguely evoked Elmo Roper's statements following the polling failure of 1952 that the best use of opinion polls was "to provide analysis of voter motivation, not to make predictions."[67]

Gallup's departure from election polling came as a shock in survey research circles. No other pollster, after all, had conducted election surveys as routinely or for as long as Gallup. Even critics like Silver's *FiveThirtyEight* blog were charitable in their reactions. Harry Enten wrote at *FiveThirtyEight*: "So Gallup was bad at horse-race polling, and it's good that it's stopping, right? Not really. Gallup uses rigorous polling methodologies. It employs live interviewers; it calls a lot of cell phones; it calls back people who are harder to reach. . . . Gallup rates as solidly average in FiveThirtyEight's pollster ratings in large part because of those techniques."[68]

Peter D. Hart, a prominent Democratic pollster, wrote that Gallup's departure was "a loss for the public when the opinion survey company with the longest tenure and the most stature decides to abandon the presidential election. As with so many issues, this is a time when leadership is most needed. It is disheartening, and a decision so unlike its organization's founder, George Gallup."[69] Leaving the field for issues-oriented polling seemed almost to be a repudiation of George Gallup's argument that pre-election polling, while a headache, nonetheless presented an "acid test" of the soundness of polling techniques. Pre-election polling was the means by which Gallup established himself in the 1930s and '40s as a leader in survey research. Pre-election surveys were crucial to Gallup's name becoming nearly synonymous with poll-taking.

Newport, though, characterized the departure from election polling as a move Gallup likely would have endorsed, saying, "Dr. Gallup probably would be rejoicing in his grave." Perhaps. But the field has had no more prominent name than "Gallup." While Roper and Archibald Crossley grew impatient with election polling or drifted away, George Gallup relished the attention that election polling brought him—even though he claimed it gave him stomach ulcers. Gallup, his cachet, and his eponymous poll outlived other crises and miscalls, such as those of 1948, 1952, 1976, and 1980.

The Gallup cachet outlived George Gallup, who was eight-two years old when he died in 1984. A little more than four years later, Gallup's heirs sold the company to a market research firm in Nebraska that took the Gallup name and transformed the company: it became a consulting and market research firm that also did some opinion polling.[70]

Humiliation swept the company in July 2013 when it announced it would pay the federal government $10.5 million to settle a whistleblower lawsuit. Gallup stood accused of bilking the U.S. mint and the federal passport agency by deliberately and substantially inflating no-bid contract work. The whistle-blower, Michael Lindley, had been hired in February 2008 as Gallup's director of client services, and according to documents submitted in the case, soon found that some company officials were overstating by two or three times the number of hours required to complete tasks related to the no-bid contracts.

Lindley said he tried unsuccessfully to persuade company officials to aban-don the overbilling practices and, according to court documents, warned his supervisor in July 2009 that he intended to report the misconduct to the Justice Department. The next day, Lindley was fired. He quoted Gallup's chief counsel as telling him, "When you start talking about going to the Department of Justice, we don't trust you anymore."[71]

Gallup denied wrongdoing and said it settled the lawsuit to "avoid further distraction and focus on serving its customers." The settlement also required Gallup to pay a fifty-thousand-dollar penalty on another ethics issue arising from Lindley's lawsuit—Gallup's receiving a lucrative contract at an inflated price from the Federal Emergency Management Agency while negotiating to give a job to the official who awarded the contract.[72] The litigation had noth-ing to do with Gallup's election-polling operation, but it was an acute embar-rassment nonetheless. "This is a company that has branded itself and has caused the American people to believe that it is the most trusted name in polling," Lindley's lawyer, David Marshall, said in an interview on NPR. "But as this lawsuit shows, the company was involved in fraud against the U.S. government, against the taxpayers."[73]

About the time Gallup was settling the fraud case, Silver announced he was moving his *FiveThirtyEight* franchise to ESPN, leaving the *New York Times* at the expiration of a three-year licensing contact. His departure followed lengthy discussions and no small amount of hand-wringing. It wasn't an especially nasty divorce, at least not on the surface. Margaret Sullivan, who had rebuked Silver for a public wager made a few days before the 2012 election, wrote a generous column describing him as "a thoroughly decent person" and favorably noting his patience and humility.[74]

But Silver never "really fit into the Times culture," Sullivan pointed out, adding, "I think he was aware of that. He was, in a word, disruptive. . . . Nate disrupted the traditional model of how to cover politics." She also wrote that a "number of traditional and well-respected Times journalists disliked his work," but didn't say who they were. She noted that the newspaper "tried very hard to give him a lot of editorial help and a great platform. It bent over backward to do so, and this, too, disturbed some staff members."[75]

The move to ESPN, Silver said, was "a dream job for me. I'm excited to expand FiveThirtyEight's data-driven approach into new areas, while also reuniting with my love of sports. I'm thrilled that we're going to be able to create jobs for a great team of journalists, writers and analysts. And I think that I've found the perfect place to do it."[76]

Silver also was asked about whether he would crank up his prediction model again in election seasons ahead. He replied that while it was tempting to "just mic-drop retire from elections forecasting, I expect that we'll be making forecasts in 2014 and 2016. Midterm elections can be dreadfully boring, unfortunately. But the 2016 G.O.P. primary seems almost certain to be epic."[77]

CHAPTER 9

"The Night That Wasn't Supposed to Happen"

The Shock Election of 2016

Nate Silver was right about the 2016 primaries: they were remarkable, if not exactly "epic." But he was quite wrong, too: his *FiveThirtyEight* blog dismissed Donald Trump's candidacy, insisting that the blustery Queens real estate tycoon and reality TV star stood no chance of winning the Republican nomination. Silver, the wonky data journalist who made a reputation with his pinpoint forecasts of presidential elections in 2008 and 2012, flubbed the Trump ascendancy, keeping company with many other media analysts, pundits, and presumed authorities.

"Our emphatic prediction," Silver wrote in August 2015, months before the Republican primary elections, "is simply that Trump will not win the nomination. It's not even clear that he's trying to do so."[1] Such breezy confidence emanated not from a poll-based statistical model of the kind that helped make Silver's reputation years earlier. It was mostly educated guesswork, as Silver later acknowledged. "Without a [statistical] model as fortification," he said, "we found ourselves rambling around the countryside like all the other pundit-barbarians, randomly setting fire to things."[2]

That miscall was an embarrassing prelude to November 2016 and "the night that wasn't supposed to happen"[3]—Trump's election to the presidency, an outcome predicted by almost no one. Nearly every sounding by pollsters, and poll-based forecasters like Silver, signaled Clinton would win, probably by a comfortable margin.

As in the presidential election of 1948, vague hints emerged here and there that the dominant narrative was flawed. Final estimates posted at the

TABLE 3   FINAL POLLS AND THE FOUR-WAY POPULAR VOTE
FOR PRESIDENT, 2016

Poll	Field dates	Clinton	Trump	Johnson	Stein	Spread
Voting results	—	**48.2%**	**46.1%**	**3.3%**	**1.1%**	**Clinton +2.1**
RealClearPolitics average	Nov. 2–7	45.5	42.2	4.7	1.9	Clinton +3.3
Bloomberg	Nov. 4–6	44	41	4	2	Clinton +3
Investor's Business Daily/ TIPP	Nov. 4–7	43	45	8	2	Trump +2
Economist/YouGov	Nov. 4–7	45	41	5	2	Clinton +4
ABC/*Washington Post*	Nov. 3–6	47	43	4	1	Clinton +4
Fox News	Nov. 3–6	48	44	3	2	Clinton +4
Monmouth	Nov. 3–6	50	44	4	1	Clinton +6
Gravis	Nov. 3–6	47	43	3	2	Clinton +4
NBC/*Wall Street Journal*	Nov. 3–5	44	40	6	2	Clinton +4
Reuters/Ipsos	Nov. 2–6	42	39	6	3	Clinton +3
Rasmussen	Nov. 2–6	45	43	4	2	Clinton +2
CBS News	Nov. 2–6	45	41	5	2	Clinton +4

SOURCE: RealClearPolitics.com.

RealClearPolitics site, which aggregates or combines poll results, indicated that Clinton led by only 272 electoral votes to 266, suggesting that an improbable victory for Trump was within reach. CNN's final Electoral College map showed that Clinton was one state shy of an electoral majority.[4] A report posted at *Politico* the day before the election declared, "Donald Trump is still in the hunt."[5]

But such contrarian notices seemed tentative. Ambiguous. A lengthy list of pre-election national polls, summarized and posted at *RealClearPolitics*, showed Clinton ahead by an average of 3.3 percentage points. The final poll of Monmouth University in New Jersey and the final joint poll by NBC News and the SurveyMonkey online tool were the most generous in their estimates, saying Clinton led by six points.[6] Of the nineteen polls that completed field-work in November and included in the *RealClearPolitics* lineup, just one had Trump ahead in the popular vote—that of *Investor's Business Daily*.[7]

Persistently, if at times narrowly, Clinton had maintained a clear overall advantage in the national polls since early August. Her aggregate lead ebbed and flowed, swelling to 7.1 percentage points on October 18, after her third face-to-face debate with Trump. The Republican narrowed the gap to 1.9 percentage points on November 2, days after James B. Comey, the then–FBI director, announced that federal investigators were reopening an inquiry closed months earlier related to the private, nonsecure electronic mail system installed at her home and used while she was secretary of state.[8] Two days before the election, Comey announced that the renewed inquiry was over. By then, Clinton's advantage had begun to grow again.

So there seemed ample reason to believe that Clinton would win. The consistency of the pre-election polls seemed persuasive and maybe even conservative. "If the polls are wrong they are more likely to be underestimating Clinton's support than overstating it," Matthew Yglesias, a political reporter for Vox.com, wrote on the eve of the election. He said that a "polling error that results in an unexpected landslide is a lot more likely than a polling error that results in a Trump win."[9]

If anything, the prospects of Clinton's victory brightened during the campaign's final hours. Silver's *FiveThirtyEight* data blog estimated that her chances of winning had improved in the two days before the election, from about 65 percent to 71.4 percent. *FiveThirtyEight* projected that Clinton would win 302 electoral votes and carry important swing states such as Florida, Michigan, North Carolina, Pennsylvania, and Wisconsin. Silver's forecast was more guarded and restrained[10] than the *Huffington Post*'s poll-based projection, which on election eve pegged the probability of Clinton's victory at 98.2 percent. The Upshot data blog at the *New York Times* gave her about an 85 percent chance of victory.[11]

The Princeton Election Consortium, directed by the neuroscientist Samuel Wang, estimated Clinton's probability of winning at 99 percent. In mid-October 2016, Wang declared on Twitter that the race was "totally over" and vowed to eat an insect on live television were Trump to win more than 240 electoral votes, or 30 votes short of the threshold for victory.[12]

None of the poll-based prediction models anticipated or advertised the prospect of a split decision, with Trump's winning the Electoral College while losing the popular vote. Silver figured the chances of that outcome were slightly better than 10 percent: not impossible, but far from likely. Even Trump figured he would lose. At a rally a month later, he said the polls on Election Day were not very promising and that he reckoned, "If I lose, I lose, and I'm going to have a nice easy life."[13]

Clinton and her entourage clearly thought she was bound for victory. Jeff Zeleny, who covered Clinton's campaign for CNN, recalled that in the hours before dawn on Election Day, the candidate's "blue and white campaign plane landed in White Plains, New York, after a final, midnight rally in North Carolina. "The Clinton staff wasn't just counting their chickens before a single vote was tabulated," Zeleny wrote, "they were popping the champagne. Jon Bon Jovi was aboard, holding court with Bill and Hillary Clinton. A couple dozen Clinton friends and top aides were too. As reporters watched from the back of the plane, their words were out of earshot, but their celebration was clear as they raised their glasses to what they over-confidently thought was a job well done."[14]

To celebrate on Election Night, Clinton's campaign rented the Jacob K. Javits Convention Center, a sprawling, glass-enclosed structure in the Hell's Kitchen neighborhood of Manhattan. The Javits Center was chosen not for its architecture, but for its glass.[15] Shattering the metaphoric glass ceiling of American politics was a defining objective of Clinton's campaign. Plans were to shower the party at the Javits Center with confetti in the shape of glass shards when the moment of victory came.

To say Hillary Clinton was going to win the presidency was neither out-landish nor extraordinary on November 8, 2016.[16] As the day wore on, she seemed to be carrying battleground states such as Florida, Iowa, Ohio, and Wisconsin—at least according to poll-based, turnout-derived estimates by VoteCastr, a Silicon Valley data startup. Its estimates were posted periodically online at *Slate* and *Vice News*.[17] VoteCastr's data boosted stock markets on the afternoon of Election Day, the *Wall Street Journal* reported.[18]

Exit polls, which were not released to subscribing news organizations until 5 p.m., Eastern time, also contributed to the sense that Clinton was ahead in key states like Florida and Wisconsin, and winning overall. When they came out, the first wave of exit polls "didn't flat out say Clinton was going to win," recalled Chris Wallace, an anchor and political commentator for Fox News. But "if you read it," he added, "you had to think Clinton was going to win."[19] Kristen Soltis Anderson, a Republican pollster and commentator, was more emphatic. The exit-poll data "really pointed to a difficult night for Republicans," she said.[20]

Reflecting such convictions, David Remnick, the editor of the *New Yorker*, drafted an essay about the first female American president, incorporating references to Elizabeth Cady Stanton, Frederick Douglass, and the suffrag-ettes. It was, Remnick recalled, "written in a mood of 'at long last' and, yes, celebration. The idea was to press 'post' on that piece, along with many other pieces by my colleagues at The New Yorker, the instant Clinton's victory was declared on TV."[21]

Remnick conceded he had not written anything in the event of Trump's victory, adding, "I don't think our site had anything, or much of anything, ready in case Trump won." After all, he said, the final pre-election polls "provided sufficiently promising news for Democrats in states like Pennsylvania, Michigan, North Carolina, and even Florida that there was every reason to think about celebrating . . . the election of the first woman to the White House."[22]

Omens of Trump's imminent defeat seemed everywhere and inescapable in the run-up to the election. Trump's sneering image was plastered in black and white on the cover of the election issue of *New York* magazine. Across the center of the image the magazine emblazoned the single word: "LOSER." The cover was to evoke comparisons to the *Chicago Tribune*'s "Dewey Defeats Truman" post-election banner headline in 1948.[23] And such comparisons were

---

BOX 3. OVERCONFIDENCE IN 2016

Among the dramatic mispredictions about the 2016 presidential election were these:

- "Donald Trump *will not* be the 45th president of the United States. Nor the 46th, nor any other number you might name. The chance of his winning the nomination and election is exactly zero."—James Fallows, *Atlantic*, July 13, 2015 (emphasis in the original)

- "'Trump' will likely join Goldwater, McGovern and Mondale as names forever associated with crushing presidential election defeats."—Anthony J. Gaughan, *Salon*, May 5, 2016.

- "There's every reason to think that Trump can pull off the near-impossible task of losing by more than 10 percent and possibly by much more."—Jeet Heer in *New Republic*, June 17, 2016

- "The race is not close. And it won't be on November 8th. 350+ electoral votes for Clinton."—David Plouffe, campaign manager for Barack Obama in 2008, on Twitter, June 29, 2016

- A "lot of people have no idea that Trump is headed for a historic defeat."—Bret Stephens, *Wall Street Journal* columnist, on MSNBC's *Morning Joe*, August 8, 2016

- "Clinton has created a robust, focused and deliberate grassroots operation with a laser-like focus on early vote and a diverse coalition of the willing that will get her to 270 electoral votes and beyond."—Buffy Wicks, in "How Hillary Clinton is going to win today," *Time*, November 8, 2016

- "In defeat, Trump will have much to get even about. Losing spectacularly before the eyes of the nation and the world will be a severe psychological blow, probably prompting a 'wounded animal' or 'cunning rat' response—or a mix of the two."—Paul McGeough, chief foreign correspondent, *Sydney Morning Herald*, November 8, 2016

- "In case I wasn't clear enough from my previous tweets: Hillary Clinton will be the next President of the United States"—Frank Luntz, Republican pollster, on Twitter, November 8, 2016

---

not far-fetched. Among pundits and journalists, certainty about Clinton's victory was on the order of 1948.

The polls and poll-based statistical forecasts had set an election narrative that the news media embraced and locked into place. The final polling estimates showed little to challenge the dominant narrative. The election might be close, but an upset? That seemed implausible.[24]

Yet, Trump was elected, carrying 30 states and 306 electoral votes to Clinton's 20 states and 232 votes.[25] Clinton won the popular vote, winning 2.87 million more votes than Trump, an advantage made possible by the crushing margins she piled up in California. Clinton carried the Golden State by nearly thirty percentage points, or a plurality of 4.27 million votes, which erased the margin Trump had built in the other forty-nine states. Absent his overwhelming defeat in California, Trump would have won the national popular vote by 1.4 million votes.

The split-decision outcome was envisioned a few days before the election in a brief, discerning, if little-noted analysis by Phillip Reese of the *Sacramento Bee*. While some polls showed tightening races in some battleground states, Clinton maintained a huge advantage in California, home to 55 electoral votes, the most in the country. Reese wrote, "Hillary Clinton has built up such a disproportionate lead in California that it's possible—should she end up losing a few key battleground states—that she could get more votes than Donald Trump but still lose the presidential race." Reese added, "It's not the most probable scenario." But Clinton's lead in California was "so huge," he wrote, that "it could keep her ahead in the popular vote," nationally.[26] Which is what happened.

As the outcome slowly became clear, the celebratory mood of the victory party at the Javits Center turned subdued, anxious, and then morose. As the evening began, there was "a sort of swagger about the place, then there was a little bit of anxiety, then deep depression, then total disbelief," Jon Sopel of BBC News recalled. "And this was played out in the course of three or four hours. People arriving six or seven in the evening, really upbeat; by nine o'clock, that's when the dawning realization came that they had failed, Trump had succeeded. Oh my goodness, what a night of misery."[27]

Journalists' initial response to Trump's victory was to concede how utterly dumbfounded they were. "This was an earthquake unlike any earthquake I've really seen since Ronald Reagan in 1980," Joe Scarborough said on his MSNBC program the morning after the election. "It just came out of nowhere. Nobody expected it." In opening the Election Night program on *The Daily Show* comedy program, host Trevor Noah said, "This is it, the end of the presidential race, and it feels like the end of the world. I don't know if you've come to the right place for jokes tonight because this is the first time throughout this entire race where I'm officially shitting my pants."[28] Nate Silver said that, broadly speaking, Trump's victory was "the most shocking political development of my lifetime."[29]

Remnick of the *New Yorker* went to a party at a friend's place that night. As the returns signaled trouble for Clinton's chances, Remnick took his laptop to a corner of what was a noisy room and set about to write in what he said was "a kind of strange state of focus that happens only once in a while." He produced a polemic that carried the headline, "An American Tragedy." It began this way: "The election of Donald Trump to the Presidency is nothing less than a tragedy for the American republic, a tragedy for the Constitution, and a triumph for the forces, at home and abroad, of nativism, authoritarianism, misogyny, and racism. Trump's shocking victory, his ascension to the Presidency, is a sickening event in the history of the United States and liberal democracy."[30]

Almost immediately, the seemingly errant national polls came in for censure. "It was a big polling miss in the worst possible race," the *Economist* magazine said the day after the election.[31] "Most polls clearly got it wrong," CBS News declared.[32] Even the country's largest organization devoted to survey research was quick with blame. "The polls clearly got it wrong this time," the American Association for Public Opinion Research, or AAPOR, declared in a statement issued the day after the election.[33] The Pew Research Center said the election results "came as a surprise to nearly everyone who had been following the national and state election polling, which consistently projected Hillary Clinton as defeating Donald Trump."[34]

On the day after the election, Jim Rutenberg of the *Times* alluded to the decades-old reality that polls set the election agenda for journalists, who, he wrote, "didn't question the polling data when it confirmed their gut feeling that Mr. Trump could never in a million years pull it off. They portrayed Trump supporters who still believed he had a shot as being out of touch with reality. In the end, it was the other way around." Rutenberg mused: "You have to wonder how different the coverage might have been had the polls, and the data crunching, not forecast an almost certain Clinton victory. Perhaps there would have been a deeper exploration of the forces that were propelling Mr. Trump toward victory."[35]

Natalie Jackson, the *Huffington Post* analyst who forecast that Clinton's chances of winning the presidency stood at 98.2 percent, wrote after the election that "when there are hundreds of polls all saying the same thing—as most polls did when they indicated Clinton would win—it's easy to develop a false sense of certainty and safety in concluding that that's what will happen."[36] Jackson later vowed never to "write another forecast model that's completely dependent on polls."[37] Speaking at an AAPOR conference several months after the election, Gregory Holyk, an analyst for the survey research firm Langer Research Associates, declared, "the credibility of the polling industry has taken a hit."[38]

But in the weeks and months after the election, the narrative about the polls began to shift: the national polls, at least, weren't so bad as all that, the revised narrative went. Overall, they came close to projecting the popular vote outcome. They certainly were closer to estimating the 2016 outcome than they had been in 2012, when the popular vote for Barack Obama exceeded the final polling average by more than three percentage points. Six months after the election, AAPOR declared in a report that the national polls of 2016 had been "highly accurate by historical standards,"[39] a characterization that seemed almost to suggest the polls collectively had turned in one of their all-time great performances.

Polling failure was not the story of the 2016 election, insisted Sean Trende, senior elections analyst for *RealClearPolitics*. Rather, he wrote, "It is a story of interpretive failure and a media environment that made it almost taboo to even suggest that Donald Trump had a real chance to win the election." What happened, Trende argued, "wasn't a failure of the polls. . . . [I]t was a failure of punditry." A failure of analysis. Don't blame the polls, Trende said. "Instead, blame the analysts and pundits, and their stubborn resistance to considering the possibility of a Trump presidency."[40]

So were the polls of 2016 in error, or not?

When Americans blamed the polls for having missed the election, they were rather more right than wrong: neither the polls nor the poll-based prediction models signaled Trump's upset victory. They pointed consistently to Clinton's winning, even if some projections—such as Silver's *FiveThirtyEight* model—were less bullish than those of the *Huffington Post* or the *Los Angeles Times*, which said she was a shoo-in.[41] Two weeks before the election, Silver wrote that "Hillary Clinton is probably going to become the president. But there's an awful lot of room to debate what 'probably' means."[42] (Silver said his final pre-election forecast showing Clinton with a 71.4 percent chance of winning was "the least inaccurate" among the poll-based statistical models.)[43]

As the 2016 campaign closed, no prominent polling estimate or poll-based forecast was warning insistently that a spectacular upset loomed just ahead. The pre-election polls were not sending mixed messages, and poll-based forecasters weren't pointing to plausible alternative scenarios that would place Trump in the White House. They were, for the most part, directionally harmonious, suggesting the race was Clinton's to lose. Clinton, herself, said she had not prepared a concession speech.

As we have seen, polling failures are almost never alike. The 2016 election brought surprise and disbelief that certainly rivaled the profound shock of Harry Truman's unexpected victory. But 2016 was not a replay of the epic polling failure of 1948. Unlike Thomas Dewey in 1948, Clinton in 2016 did not lose the national popular vote. Thanks to wiping out Trump in California, she carried the national vote by 2.1 percentage points,[44] which meant her final popular vote margin came close to the average estimate of the polls.

One way to judge polls for accuracy is to determine whether the polls during the campaign, and in the weeks just before the voting, collectively presented accurate clues as to what was going to happen on Election Day.[45] Were polls telling the right story along the way?[46] The answer in 2016 was not quite. The weighted average error for all polls conducted in the three final weeks of the 2016 presidential campaign, Nate Silver later reported, was almost five percentage points—larger than the average error of any of the previous four presidential elections.[47] In addition, Trump's final overall polling average, as compiled by the *RealClearPolitics* site, was just 42.2 percent—hardly an indication that he was on the cusp of a stunning upset victory.

The public largely expected Clinton to win the election, an expectation surely built upon the persistent indications of pre-election polls and forecasts.[48] "Whatever went wrong with the polls in this country," wrote John Cassidy of the *New Yorker*, "they inevitably colored perceptions." And the estimates of the poll-based prediction models, Cassidy added, "had a big influence on how many people, including journalists and political professionals, looked at the election."[49] The polls of 2016, said Alan Murray, a former president of the Pew Research Center, "misled analysts of all stripes."[50]

When Clinton failed to convert her unevenly distributed[51] popular vote advantage to an Electoral College victory, the outcome became a split decision in Trump's favor. With that, Election Night 2016 turned into "the night that

TABLE 4   WHICH PARTY WILL WIN?

Only four times since 1952 has the U.S. public, in surveys by American National Election Studies, failed to anticipate the winning party in presidential elections. Those years are highlighted. The most recent occasion was 2016. (Check marks indicate the party that won the election.)

	Democrat		Republican	
2016	61%		33%	✓
2012	64	✓	25	
2008	59	✓	30	
2004	29		62	✓
2000	47		44	✓
1996	86	✓	10	
1992	56	✓	31	
1988	23		63	✓
1984	12		81	✓
1980	46		38	✓
1976	43	✓	41	
1972	7		83	✓
1968	22		57	✓
1964	81	✓	8	
1960	33	✓	43	
1956	19		68	✓
1952	35		43	✓

SOURCES: American National Election Studies; FiveThirtyEight.com.

wasn't supposed to happen, that had almost no chance of happening," as Liz Spayd, the public editor at the *New York Times*, wrote the day after. "Having relied on major media, and the overflow of polls it fed readers on a near-daily basis," Spayd said, "the audience sat back and waited for a Democratic victory, possibly a rout."[52]

The American public was little pleased with the pollsters or the news media during the 2016 campaign. Fifty-one percent of respondents to a post-election survey by Pew Research Center assigned pollsters grades of "D" or "F"—their worst scores in eight presidential elections since 1988, when Pew began asking for grades. Fifty-nine percent of the respondents gave the media grades of "D" or "F." (See table 2, in chapter 2.)

Beyond the final averages of the national polls and beyond the projections of poll-based statistical models, there *was* clear polling failure in a more discrete sense in 2016: in key places, state-level polls were historically off-target,[53] demonstrating once again that poll-based election forecasts can misfire in a number of ways. Polling error in the 2016 election, Nate Cohn wrote in the *New York Times*, "was almost perfectly distributed across the battleground states," with the effect of maximizing the consequences for the election overall.[54]

Because the outcome pivoted on a handful of states, state-level polling is central to the interpretation that polls failed in 2016. These errors were most conspicuous in Pennsylvania, Michigan, and Wisconsin, all of which supposedly were sure to support Clinton. Had she won that trio of states, Clinton would have been elected president. Instead, Trump rolled up an electoral vote majority by narrowly winning those states and carrying other battlegrounds such as Florida, Iowa, North Carolina, and Ohio.[55]

Pre-election surveys in Pennsylvania, Michigan, and Wisconsin consistently placed Clinton ahead, often comfortably so. In Pennsylvania, she led in all but two of the dozen polls completed from the end of October to a few days before the election, according to the compilation by *RealClearPolitics*. Clinton led in *all* thirty-one discrete polls conducted in Michigan from July 2016 to just before the election. She led by comfortable margins in *all* nineteen polls conducted in Wisconsin between June 2016 and early November.

Pennsylvania, Michigan, and Wisconsin were fundamental elements of Clinton's presumptive "blue wall" of reliably Democratic Rust Belt states. No Republican presidential candidate had won *any* of those states since the 1980s. Pennsylvania always seemed tantalizingly out of reach for Republicans; it certainly was for Mitt Romney, who made a late push for votes there in 2012. Wisconsin simply seemed out of the question for Trump, given Clinton's composite lead there of six percentage points. Wisconsin seemed so secure that Clinton did not campaign there in the fall.

Michigan, though, provided hints that all was not locked up for Clinton. Three days before the election, the *Detroit Free Press* reported that a poll it commissioned showed Clinton's lead in Michigan had fallen to four percentage points. Trump had seized the momentum in a state that, the newspaper said, "was believed all but decided" for Clinton just a few weeks earlier.[56] A small Republican polling company, the Trafalgar Group, conducted the final pre-election poll in Michigan and reported that Trump was ahead by two percentage points. He won the state by 0.3 points. The director of the poll for the *Free Press* later said he regretted not conducting another survey over the weekend before the election.[57]

No statewide poll was taken in Wisconsin during the closing days of the campaign. The state's most respected survey, the Marquette University Law School Poll, completed fieldwork at the end of October and its final pre-election poll showed Clinton ahead by 6 percentage points. Trump carried Wisconsin by 0.7 points—which means the polling discrepancy was nearly 7 percentage points. "No one will ever say the Marquette Poll is 'never wrong' ever again," Charles Franklin, the poll director, acknowledged after the election. "We've now been wrong."[58] He said in an interview months afterward that the poll miss of 2016 "doesn't feel good."[59]

The dearth of late-in-the-campaign polling meant that few surveys in key states were positioned to pick up the swing to Trump in the days before the election. Late-deciding voters in Pennsylvania, Michigan, and Wisconsin appear to have tipped the outcomes in those states to Trump, who also received overwhelming support from white voters without college degrees. Most polls in battleground states did not adjust their data to account for this variable. They had too many college graduates in their sample, which may have contributed to exaggerating Clinton's support in states such as Pennsylvania, Michigan, and Wisconsin. That was a central finding of AAPOR's post-election report, which noted that voters' preferences in 2016 were strongly linked to education levels: the more formal education, the more likely the voter backed Clinton.[60]

Perhaps more important was the broad failure to recognize that voting preferences in Rust Belt states could be correlated, that a candidate's troubles, say, in Ohio could show up in states nearby, such as Michigan or Pennsylvania, that have roughly similar demographic makeups. The correlations were more striking *after* the election, but Nate Silver argued that not anticipating such connections represented a serious flaw in campaign news coverage. "No matter how many polls you have in a state, it's often the case that all or most of them miss in the same direction," he said, adding that "if the polls miss in one direction in one state, they often also miss in the same direction in other states, especially if those states are similar demographically."[61] In that sense, the outcome in Pennsylvania was related to those in Ohio, Michigan, and Wisconsin.

Polling error was notable in other battleground states. Clinton narrowly carried Nevada, even though some late polls showed Trump ahead in the state by as many as six points. In North Carolina, none of the three final polls estimated Trump was ahead there; he won the state by almost four percentage points. Late-campaign polls suggested the race in Ohio was much tighter than it turned out to be. One of them was the Dispatch Poll, a mail-in survey conducted by the *Columbus Dispatch* newspaper. That poll may have been a faint reminder of the surveys of the *Literary Digest* of the 1920s and '30s, but it had a reputation for being reasonably accurate in Ohio. Two days before the election, the results of the lone Dispatch Poll of the 2016 campaign were released, showing Clinton ahead in Ohio by one percentage point.[62] She lost Ohio by eight points.

State polls were particularly important to the prediction model developed by Samuel Wang, whom *Wired* magazine, on the eve of the election, touted as the "election data hero" of 2016 and the "new king of the presidential election data mountain." *Wired* said Wang "has been the intrepid election data explorer furthest out this election cycle, never once wavering from his certainty of a Clinton win."[63] Wang was wrong in his certainty. He conceded that his prediction model placed too much confidence in state-level polling, which he had previously regarded as "a gold standard for monitoring elections." In 2016, he said, "Polls failed, and I amplified that failure."[64]

Four days after the election, Wang made good on his vow to eat an insect on live television were Trump to win more than 240 electoral votes. Wang redeemed the pledge on a Saturday morning program on CNN, bringing with him a shallow white bowl of gourmet-style crickets doused with honey. "John the Baptist in the wilderness, he ate locusts and honey," Wang said. "So I regard myself as being in the wilderness a little. After all, I was wrong. A lot of people were wrong, but nobody else made the promise I did." With that, he dug out a dollop of cricket and popped it in his mouth. Wang seemed to wince slightly as he chewed. It tasted, he said, "kind of mostly honey-ish. A little nutty."[65]

Although no one made the connection, Wang's theatrical bug-eating was faintly reminiscent of Hugh S. Johnson's vow to eat his column if George Gallup's polls were accurate in forecasting Franklin D. Roosevelt would win a third term in 1940.[66] Johnson, a Roosevelt administration official who fell out of favor and became a syndicated columnist, acknowledged after the election, "I was sincerely but terribly wrong. . . . If it will please anybody, I am willing to eat that column. It would hardly give me indigestion. It is only 600 words."[67] In an interview, Wang said he had never heard of Johnson and the column-eating pledge. Wang said he ruminated about his forecast error until the first months of 2017 and then moved on to other commitments.[68]

The seeming certainty of poll-based forecasts like Wang's helped conventional wisdom to congeal for journalists, especially at elite news organizations. The polls and poll-based models confirmed for journalists that Clinton was headed for victory and that Trump, a vulgar and eccentric candidate, simply had no chance. But missing Trump's victory could not be blamed entirely on misleading polls or failed poll-based statistical models. The shock of Election Night 2016 signaled a profound media failure as well—one of the greatest in modern times, Kyle Pope, the editor-in-chief of the *Columbia Journalism Review*, declared the day after the election. "In terms of bellwether moments," he wrote, "this is our anti-Watergate."[69]

Too often, Pope added, "the views of Trump's followers . . . were dismissed entirely by an establishment media whose worldview is so different, and so counter, to theirs that it became chic to belittle them and wave them off. Reporters' personal views got in the way of their ability to hear what was happening around them."[70]

Many journalists at elite, mainstream news organizations certainly were thrown off stride by Trump's candidacy. They never fully grasped his appeal to aggrieved Americans in the heartland, never quite understood why his insulting and incendiary comments did not summarily collapse his candidacy. Some journalists came to think of Trump as an existential threat, which justified their unconcealed opposition to his candidacy. In this they found encouragement from the *Columbia Journalism Review* which, in a commentary published before Pope became the editor, declared that "when a politician's words go way beyond the pale," journalists can be excused for abandoning mainstream professional norms of detached impartiality. Trump had changed the rules, the logic went; therefore journalists must, too, in meeting the threat.[71]

The journalism review's commentary offered as a precedent the legendary television report in March 1954, when Edward R. Murrow denounced the red-baiting scare tactics of Senator Joseph R. McCarthy. The commentary declared: "If a politician's rhetoric is dangerous, Murrow implied, all of us, including journalists, are complicit if we don't stand up and oppose it." On Election Day, the commentary added, "we will be eager for signs to see if today's journalists pushing back against Trump actually stop him."[72]

The argument was smug and solipsistic. Why, after all, should *journalists* presume to decide whether "a politician's words go way beyond the pale"? Why should journalists presume to be empowered to "stop" any candidate? Not only that, but the example of Murrow's standing up to McCarthy was badly distorted. Murrow was hardly the quintessence of courage in taking on the senator; he did so only years after other journalists had begun calling attention to McCarthy's smears and vague charges about communist infiltration of the U.S. government.[73]

The argument that journalists could be justified in open hostility to Trump ignored that professional detachment brought journalists at least some measure of authority, and that once discarded, it was not easily retrieved. As David Zurawik, the media critic for the *Baltimore Sun*, observed in the campaign's closing days, "Once you accepted the need for new ways to cover Trump and bought into the logic of abandoning legacy standards [of detached impartiality], anything was possible—from calling him a liar on the front page of The New York Times to telling readers it's never a shame to storm the barricades set up around a fascist."[74] Zurawik was referring to the *Times's* deciding to label Trump's falsehoods as "lies" in news reports and analyses,[75] and to a Twitter post by an editor at the *Vox* news website that said, "If Trump comes to your town, start a riot."[76]

Shedding detachment in covering Trump no doubt deepened suspicions about the motives, practices, and ostensible fair-mindedness of the news media. Popular confidence in the media to report fairly and accurately dropped to new lows during the 2016 campaign, according to Gallup Organization polling.[77] *USA Today* reported that by nearly a 10-to-1 margin, respondents to a separate late-campaign poll believed the news media preferred Clinton to win the election.[78]

So the unforeseen outcome came "not just as an embarrassment for the press," as Jack Shafer, one of the country's leading media critics, wrote, "but as an indictment. In some profound way, the election made clear the national media doesn't get the nation it purportedly covers."[79] How, then, did this media failure happen? Why did journalists fail to alert the public to the prospect of a Trump victory? The narrative-shaping influence of the polls and poll-based forecasts was partly to blame. But explanations run deeper than that.

Many journalists were afflicted by an "unthinkability bias,"[80] believing that there was no way a repulsive and unsophisticated character like Trump could be elected. His winning the White House was simply unimaginable and some journalists were quite open in saying so. "We thought that it was unthinkable that someone who was insulting people, saying racist and xenophobic and sexist and misogynist things, could become the president," Margaret Sullivan, the *Washington Post's* media columnist, said after the election. "Many of us didn't really deal with the idea that this could be the case."[81] In its editorial about the election, the *New York Times* also invoked the unthinkability quotient, declaring: "President Donald Trump. Three words that were unthinkable to tens of millions of Americans—and much of the rest of the world—have now become the future of the United States."[82] In the opening sentence of a front-page article in the *Times*, Patrick Healy and Jeremy W. Peters declared Trump's victory "a once-unimaginable scenario."[83]

The sense that Clinton couldn't possibly lose took expression in confident if premature claims in leading newspapers as the campaign reached its closing weeks. In mid-October, for example, the *Washington Post* reported that Republicans were braced for Clinton's landslide victory and that some party leaders had concluded "it was probably too late to salvage his flailing campaign."[84] What triggered the purported spasm of pessimism was Trump's reluctance to say unequivocally during a televised debate with Clinton that he would accept the results of the election. "I'll keep you in suspense," he said.

Even after Clinton's campaign was jolted late in the campaign by news of the FBI's reopening its investigation into her private email server, some news reports strained to be reassuring. The *New York Times*, for example, declared a week before the election that while "Clinton's overall support has shrunk in recent days, she can easily assemble the 270 electoral votes she needs for a victory next Tuesday, given her broad base of voters in more demographically diverse states." The *Times* article further declared, "The loss of a few percentage points from Mrs. Clinton's lead, and perhaps a state or two from the battleground column, would deny Democrats a possible landslide and likely give her a decisive but not overpowering victory, much like the one President Obama earned in 2012."[85]

The *Times* account said the "most enduring obstacle" facing Trump was Clinton's "formidable position in the Electoral College, where Democrats and a significant cohort of Republicans believe she is close to locking down the 270 electoral votes required for victory."[86] That interpretation was in error. Clinton's strength in the Electoral College was scarcely "formidable." Her support was most pronounced on the coasts, particularly in California and New York, where she piled up enormous pluralities, and much weaker in Rust Belt states, where the election tipped to Trump.

The failure to anticipate Trump's victory also pointed to a profound and not-unknown shortcoming in mainstream journalism—a pack mentality, or a left-of-center like-mindedness that prevails in many newsrooms. "It's indisputable that America's newsrooms, especially its mainstream newsrooms, are not diverse with ideological opinion," Jim Rutenberg, the *New York Times* media columnist, said the day after the election.[87] Nate Silver called it journalistic "groupthink" and said "a pack mentality" had afflicted political journalism "since at least the days of *The Boys on the Bus*," Timothy Crouse's memorable book that described homogeneity in news coverage during the 1972 presidential campaign.[88]

"Events such as conventions and debates literally gather thousands of journalists together in the same room; attend one of these events, and you can almost smell the conventional wisdom being manufactured in real time," Silver wrote, adding that social media, especially Twitter, "can amplify these information cascades, with a single tweet receiving hundreds of thousands of impressions and shaping the way entire issues are framed." As a result, he added, "it can be largely arbitrary which storylines gain traction and which ones don't. What seems like a multiplicity of perspectives might just be one or two, duplicated many times over."[89]

Viewpoint conformity has long been noted, if not deeply studied, in American journalism. Years ago, Senator Eugene McCarthy likened newspaper columnists to blackbirds on a telephone wire. "As one flies away, they all fly away, when one comes back, they all come back," he said in 1963.[90] Michael Kelly, editor-in-chief of the *National Journal*, wrote in the *Washington Post* in 1999: "Reporters like to picture themselves as independent thinkers. In truth, with the exception of 13-year-old girls, there is no social subspecies more slavish to fashion, more terrified of originality and more devoted to group-think."[91]

After Barack Obama's election to the presidency in 2008, the *Washington Post*'s ombudsman, Deborah Howell, wrote that "some of the conservatives' complaints about a liberal tilt are valid. Journalism naturally draws liberals; we like to change the world. I'll bet that most Post journalists voted for Obama. I did. There are centrists at The Post as well. But the conservatives I know here feel so outnumbered that they don't even want to be quoted by name in a memo."[92] Pope of *Columbia Journalism Review* argued that reporters covering the 2016 campaign "depended on a small circle of sources and experts, most of whom were just like them. The result was journalistic groupthink on an industrial scale."[93] Journalists, wrote Silver, "*just didn't believe* that someone like Trump could become president. . . . So they cherry-picked their way through the data to support their belief, ignoring evidence—such as Clinton's poor standing in the Midwest—that didn't fit the narrative."[94]

This is not to say that campaign coverage was distorted and myopic without exception. Some searching accounts about discontent in the heartland, and about profound frustration with the U.S. political system, did appear in leading news outlets. Larissa MacFarquhar's deeply reported *New Yorker* article about Trump supporters in Logan County, West Virginia, was a notable example.[95] But as Will Rahn of CBS News wrote, news accounts about Trump supporters often "read like reports from colonial administrators checking in on the natives," reflecting an "assumption that Trump voters are backward, and that it's our duty to catalogue and ultimately reverse that backwardness."[96]

Some of the most senior editors in American journalism conceded after the election there had been too few serious-minded reports about Trump supporters or about the discontent his candidacy tapped. Marty Baron, the *Washington Post*'s executive editor, acknowledged that "we should have detected the depth of grievance and anxiety in America's working class well before Trump became a candidate. It's obviously our job to get out in the country and listen to people and to take the measure of the American public, and I don't think we did as well as we should have, and we need to make sure we learn that lesson and make it a regular responsibility to really understand America's working class."[97]

Baron's counterpart at the *New York Times*, Dean Baquet, said his newspaper "and the rest of the press corps weren't completely in touch with, or understood the Trump voter. . . . I think we could do better writing about the people who voted for Donald Trump, understanding what drove them, their anxiety. I think it's too simplistic to just see them as crazy people or deplorables. There aren't *that* many deplorables in the United States."[98] His reference was to Clinton's sneering claim in September 2016 that half of Trump supporters held such repellant views they belonged in a "basket of deplorables."[99]

The election outcome brought a brief burst of self-analysis among journalists. Everyone, Jack Shafer wrote, "acknowledges Trump's election really was a bad miss and if the media doesn't figure it out, it will miss the next one, too."[100] Pope argued that "the entire journalistic enterprise needs to be rethought and rebuilt."[101] Nothing quite so dramatic took place in the election's aftermath. The media's introspection about how they covered the 2016 campaign didn't last long. "There was never much of a learning process after the election," Silver wrote. The news media were far more interested in "finding various scapegoats for the surprising result . . . instead of examining whether there was some deeper problem with their reporting methods."[102]

Soon enough, journalists shifted from the election shock to chase suspicions that Trump and his campaign had denied Clinton victory by entering into a traitorous conspiracy with Vladimir Putin's Russia to influence the election. It may have been a tempting narrative, surely the stuff of awards, but it came a cropper when a special counsel's nearly two-year investigation turned up no evidence of collusion among Trump, his campaign, and Russia.[103]

American journalism seldom engages in sustained introspection when it errs in major ways on major stories. There is little interest in such self-analysis. "The rotten truth," Shafer once observed, "is that media organizations are better at correcting trivial errors of fact—proper spellings of last names, for example—than they are at fixing a botched story."[104] Pursuing suspicions that Trump had conspired with Russia enabled journalists to excuse themselves from analyzing why they had erred so badly, why they failed to assess the depth of popular frustration and resentment that helped drive Trump's victory. As Matt Taibbi wrote in *Rolling Stone*:

> The 2016 campaign season brought to the surface awesome levels of political discontent. After the election, instead of wondering where that anger came from, most of the press quickly pivoted to a new tale about a Russian plot to attack our Democracy. This conveyed the impression that the election season we'd just lived through had been an aberration, thrown off the rails by an extraordinary espionage conspiracy between Trump and a cabal of evil foreigners. This narrative contradicted everything I'd seen traveling across America in my two years of covering the campaign. The overwhelming theme of that race, long before anyone even thought about Russia, was voter rage at the entire political system. . . . A cloak-and-dagger election-fixing conspiracy therefore seemed more likely than it might have otherwise to large parts of the domestic news audience, because they hadn't been prepared for anything else that would make sense.[105]

Some elite outlets, like the *New York Times*, showed little tolerance for persistent internal criticism about its reporting. Notably, Liz Spayd, the newspaper's public editor, on occasion wrote scathingly of the newspaper's coverage of Trump, often basing her piercing critiques on calls, letters, and email correspondence from readers. Spayd brought impressive credentials to the position of in-house critic at the *Times*—she had been managing editor at the *Washington Post* and editor and publisher of the *Columbia Journalism Review*. A writer for *Esquire* called Spayd "the embodiment of traditional journalistic standards."[106] The *Times* publisher said in hiring her that Spayd was "an exceptionally accomplished journalist."[107]

FIGURE 23. As the public editor at the *New York Times*, Liz Spayd offered tough-minded criticism of the newspaper's election reporting in 2016. She told of finding "a searing level of dissatisfaction out there with many aspects of the coverage." (Credit: Joe A. Mendoza/ Colorado State University)

Spayd wasn't out to trash the *Times* but to insist that it be more evenhanded and accountable in its political reporting. She was severe in her post-election assessments of the *Times*'s coverage of the campaign which, she wrote, left an impression "of a juggernaut of blue state invincibility" that dismissed the prospect that Trump could win the White House.[108] Certainly, she said, the *Times* wasn't "the only news organization bewildered and perhaps a bit sheepish about its predictions coverage. The rest of media missed it too, as did the pollsters, the analysts, the Democratic Party and the Clinton campaign itself. But . . . I hope its editors will think hard about the half of America the paper too seldom covers." The *Times*, she added, "would serve readers well with fewer brief interviews" of Trump supporters and with "fewer snatched slogans that inevitably render a narrow caricature of those who spoke them."[109]

It was tough-minded criticism of a kind that appeared seldom in mainstream American media. It was blunt, and it was on target. Spayd renewed her critique of the *Times* with greater vigor in a column twelve days after the election that described "a searing level of dissatisfaction out there with many aspects of the coverage"—based on the enormous volume of calls, letters, and email her office had received. The newspaper's readers, she said, "complain that The Times's attempt to tap the sentiments of Trump supporters was lacking. And they complain about the liberal tint The Times applies to its coverage, without awareness that it does." She wrote that the news media were "at fault" for turning Trump's often-inflammatory rhetoric "into a grim caricature that it applied to those who backed him. What struck me," she added, "is how many liberal voters I spoke with felt so, too. They were Clinton backers, but they wanted a news source that fairly covers people across the spectrum."[110]

Spayd acknowledged that during the campaign, the newspaper's national desk correspondents had "filed a steady stream of compelling stories from voters between coastal America. And yet between the horse race and the campaign drama, much of their work was simply drowned out. That left many of the readers I spoke with feeling like The Times was a swirl of like-mindedness."[111]

Spayd took on other controversies, such as one stirred by the provocative debut essay of Bret Stephens, the *Times's* conservative columnist, whose inaugural effort raised doubts about climate change, provoking the anger of many *Times* readers and staffers. "I support the general principle of busting up the mostly liberal echo chamber around here," Spayd wrote in a column about Stephens. "I stand among the readers who worry that Stephens is minimizing the serious risk of climate change," she further wrote, adding: "But I believe steadfastly that The Times should be giving readers a range of views—not just from conservatives but also populists left and right, women, blacks, Latinos and Asians. All are in short supply."[112]

Her advocacy and insistence on traditional principles and standards of impartiality in reporting proved at odds with the *Times's* post-election oppositional coverage of the Trump administration.[113] Less than a year after taking the job, Spayd was unceremoniously dismissed and the public editor's position—which had been established in 2003 in the wake of a staggering plagiarism scandal at the *Times*—was abolished.[114] She did not go in evident anger, but she wasn't quiet about leaving, either. In her swan song column,

Spayd wrote that she worried that mainstream news organizations risked forfeiting their impartiality to "morph into something more partisan, spraying ammunition at every favorite target and openly delighting in the chaos." She wrote that she was

> plenty aware that I have opinions—especially about partisan journalism—that don't always go over well with some of the media critics in New York and Washington. I'm not prone to worry much about stepping in line with conventional thinking. I try to hold an independent voice, to not cave to outside—or inside—pressure, and to say what I think, hopefully backed by an argument and at least a few facts. In this job, I started to know which columns would land like a grenade, and I'm glad to have stirred things up. I'll wear it like a badge.[115]

She also said: "Derision may feel more satisfying, but in the long run stories that are measured in tone are more powerful. Whether journalists realize it or not, with impartiality comes authority—and right now it's in short supply."[116]

Conclusion

Will It Happen Again?

Election polling's great fear is also an abiding obsession: will the polls be wrong again?

Almost surely, they will. At some time. As George Gallup observed after the polling fiasco in 1948: "With the same certainty that we know we can be right most of the time, we know that we will be wrong some of the time. It has to be that way. We live by the law of probabilities."[1] As suggested by the cases examined in this book, the next polling failure in a U.S. presidential election may well be unique, and not a facsimile of a flub of the past. As we have seen, polling failure hews to no singular pattern. There is no garden-variety type of polling failure.

Some people in the polling business say they fear the 2020 presidential election may give rise to polling errors akin to those that dramatically upended expectations in 2016. Their fear is that state-level polls, which failed to signal Donald Trump's popular vote strength in crucial swing states such as Pennsylvania, Michigan, and Wisconsin, may flop again. Courtney Kennedy, director of survey research for the Pew Research Center and lead author of a report about polling's performance in 2016, has spoken publicly about this fear. "I don't see forces that are going to fix this," she said at a conference of the American Association for Public Opinion Research, or AAPOR, adding, "We need more high-quality polls at the state level, conducted close to the election."[2]

In her remarks, Kennedy was underscoring a key passage of the report, prepared for AAPOR, about polling in the 2016 presidential election. "Errors in state polls like those observed in 2016 are not uncommon," the report stated. "With shrinking budgets at news outlets to finance polling, there is no reason to believe that this problem is going to fix itself. Collectively, well-resourced survey organizations might have enough common interest in financing some high quality state-level polls so as to reduce the likelihood of another black eye for the profession."[3] Elections of the recent past are, of course, seldom predictors of what will happen next time. Given the attention directed to the misleading state polls of 2016, a comparably shocking failure in 2020 may be unlikely.

It is certain that polling in 2020 will be different from polling of elections in the recent past. Gallup's polls will be absent again, as they were in 2016. The organization last conducted and publicized voter-preference surveys in 2012. The company has made it clear that it will devote resources to issues polling, and with a more pronounced international perspective.[4] Pew Research is unlikely to return to horse-race polling. It, too, skipped the 2016 election and has preferred to concentrate on issues research. One of Pew's senior executives said privately that election polling has become too expensive and, given the number of companies conducting surveys of U.S. presidential elections, it is difficult for any single poll to stand out. HuffPost, after its embarrassing failure in 2016, has said it will not forecast the 2020 election in a poll-based statistical model. The regionally prominent Field Poll of California was shut down in late 2016, after sixty-nine years of conducting surveys.[5] The mail-in poll begun in 1980 by the *Columbus Dispatch* newspaper in Ohio has been discontinued. It fell victim to rising costs and staff cutbacks.

As those departures suggest, an ethos of churn and change characterizes election polling. So, too, does an impulse to experiment and innovate: this spirit endures despite, or perhaps because of, the reverses and uncertainties in the field. The 2020 presidential election will be accompanied by fresh competition in the controversial practice of exit polling. The Associated Press and Fox News Network have split away from the consortium known as the National Election Pool, which used to conduct exit polling alone. The rival operation, AP VoteCast, was rolled out in the 2018 midterm elections.[6] Competition has been long overdue in exit polling, which, as we've seen, has not infrequently produced results that were at odds with election returns.

The 2018 midterms were the occasion for another experiment in polling, one that highlighted a serious limitation in contemporary election surveys: during the two months before the elections, the *New York Times* and its polling partner, the Siena College Research Institute, conducted nightly telephone polls of competitive House and Senate races across the country. It was an experiment in "live polling," as it was called, and was devised to allow anyone to follow online, in real time, as polling was conducted and as results were gathered and weighted for factors such as age, race, gender, and educational attainment.

"No media organization has ever tried something like this, and we hope to set a new standard of transparency," the *Times* said as its "live polling" was about to get underway. "You'll see the poll results at the same time we do. You'll see . . . where we're calling and whether someone is picking up."[7] The polling was conducted from five call centers in North America where operators placed more 2.8 million calls to landline and cellular phones, drawing on voter-registration lists. The "live polling" experiment was imaginative, easy to follow, and revealing. It demonstrated that contemporary opinion polling is time-consuming, expensive, and highly uncertain. It further underscored how infrequently would-be respondents answer the phone—a problem that has vexed and confounded poll-takers for years. The reported response rate to the *Times*/Sienna polling was 9 percent. That means that 91 of every 100 calls went unanswered, or the person who took the call declined to participate.

A reported response rate of less than 10 percent is no longer a surprise among poll-takers, given how casually would-be survey participants screen calls from spammers and telemarketers, or ignore calls from numbers they do not recognize. In reaction to the anemic response rates in telephone surveys, a good deal of election polling during the 2020 fall campaign will be done online, extending a trend that began taking shape some twenty years ago.

Online polling can be conducted in a variety of ways: recruiting a large panel of respondents willing to complete periodic online questionnaires is a popular and not unreasonably expensive option. Online polls can be completed more quickly than telephone polls. Some pollsters incorporate automated techniques such as robocalling, or Interactive Voice Response, into their polling. But response rates can be even lower than with traditional, live-interviewer phone surveys. And telephone polls conducted by trained interviewers have fared better than online and automated polls, according to assessments by Nate Silver, the data journalist who runs FiveThirtyEight.com.[8]

Some pollsters, meanwhile, are testing ways of including data drawn from social media platforms. But as Stephanie Slade, managing editor of the libertarian magazine *Reason*, has noted: "The biggest problem with trying to use social media analysis in place of survey research is that the people who are active on those platforms aren't necessarily representative of the ones who aren't."[9]

Polling's abundant methodologies signal that the field is in the midst of a paradigm shift, but a dominant method, a new "gold standard"—the one that will replace live-interviewer telephone surveys—has yet to become clear.[10] It may be a phone/online hybrid of some sort. Such hybrids are becoming more common.[11]

Rather than ruminating about the technique that will become polling's next great methodology, it may be more intriguing and relevant to consider why election polls are still with us, given the flubs, fiascoes, and miscalls over the years. Predictive failure clearly has not killed off election polling. So what accounts for its tenacity and resilience?

The answer, somewhat paradoxically, lies in election polling's status as a modest component of a multibillion-dollar industry broadly known as opinion and market research. Polling on issues and policy (not to mention polling about consumer preferences and for marketing purposes) is far more common than election surveys. Just as it would be implausible for polling not to figure in national elections, it would be difficult to imagine day-to-day life without polls of many kinds—even if they are imperfect instruments that can produce conflicting, distorted, and superficial impressions about American life and society.[12]

After the debacle of 1948, Rensis Likert, one of Gallup's most pointed and thoughtful critics, observed that in fewer than fifteen years, "the public opinion poll [had] become thoroughly established in this country" and predicted that the use of polls was "likely to continue to increase," given that "well-executed polls" could offer insights difficult to obtain otherwise.[13] Similarly, Sarah Igo noted that by 1948 polling had made itself "indispensable" in many facets of American society. By then, Igo wrote in *The Averaged American: Surveys, Citizens, and the Making of a Mass Public*, polling had put down "deep roots in the broader society: as an academic pursuit, a well-funded means of data collection by corporations and the government, and a popularly recognized form of social knowledge."[14]

If a fiasco like the "Dewey defeats Truman" election couldn't uproot opinion polling, probably nothing would. Serious suggestions about prohibiting election polls were floated in the fiasco's aftermath. Stuart Chase, a prominent economist and prolific writer, suggested that AAPOR oversee a ban on the polling of presidential elections. Chase said in an essay for *The Nation* that "'scientific' polling of Presidential elections" may be an "impossible objective. It may be beyond the competence of the art." He added he "would be glad" if such polls were "utterly abandoned. I do not believe it is necessary for Congress to pass a law. Let the American Association for Public Opinion Research make the ban part of its ethical code."[15] Chase's suggestion apparently received no serious consideration.[16]

Polling also has survived election miscalls because the practice has intrigued generations of American journalists. This is due, in part, to polls projecting a sense, or illusion, of data-based precision, which is alluring in journalism, where practitioners routinely encounter ambiguity and inexactitude. "The world is a complicated place," Silver has noted, "and journalists are expected to write authoritatively about it under deadline pressure,"[17] in tidy, seemingly coherent packages. Polling data can help journalism appear authoritative. Journalists long have been wedded to elections polls because they tell them something about the rhythm of campaigns and who is likely to win. In that sense, Chris Matthews, the voluble former host of MSNBC's *Hard Ball* program, wasn't much exaggerating when he observed in 2008 that "we live by polls."[18]

In the end, the best explanation for polling's tenacity may be as simple and straightforward as the public's being "very interested in learning about itself." Timothy Johnson, then president of AAPOR, made that observation at the organization's conference in 2018. At the same time, he warned about efforts to "delegitimize" polling and survey research, saying that "sociological, technological, and political pressures" were "converging in a perfect storm" to undermine and discredit the field. He said "Americans do not especially trust public-opinion researchers,"[19] noting a McClatchy–Marist College Poll in 2017 that reported 61 percent of respondents said they had little to no trust in public opinion polls, a reading just slightly better than perceptions of the media.

For such an unflattering assessment, Johnson said, polling of the 2016 presidential election deserved some blame. Seldom a day passes, he said, "when you are not obliged to correct the declaration of a friend, an acquaintance, or a university administrator that 'the surveys got it wrong in 2016.' This is going to be with us for a long time."[20] Johnson didn't mention, although he might have, that polls *were* in error in 2016 in key Midwestern states, disrupting expectations of Hillary Clinton's victory. Johnson didn't mention, but might have, the statement AAPOR issued on the morning after the election that declared, "The polls clearly got it wrong this time."[21]

Johnson's remarks seemed aligned with a tendency to absolve political polls in the wake of surprises such as Trump's victory and Britain's referendum in 2016 to leave the European Union—and perhaps were a response as well to critical commentaries such as Cliff Zukin's essay in the *New York Times* in 2015. "Election polling is in near crisis," Zukin, a former AAPOR president, declared. He said that pollsters "are less sure how to conduct good survey research now than we were four years ago, and much less than eight years ago," and predicted that, given troubles such as declining rates of participation, "polls and pollsters are going to be less reliable."[22]

More sanguine appraisals have been offered since then. Notable among them was an ambitious study published in 2018 that focused on results of polls taken during the closing weeks of 220 election campaigns in thirty-two countries from 1942 to 2017. The study's authors, Will Jennings and Christopher Wlezien, reported that "if anything, polling errors are getting smaller on average, not bigger." They also said that while "claims about the demise of pre-election polling have become common in recent times, we find little basis to support them. In fact, some of our findings point to just the reverse."[23]

The authors acknowledged, though, "We have not considered all possible explanations of polling error" in the study.[24] And as we have seen, polling failures spring from no single template. Election polls can be inaccurate in a variety of ways. Assessing the discrepancies between final pre-election polls and election outcomes, as Jennings and Wlezien did, is just one measure of error. And even then, national polls can collectively signal a close election while pointing to the wrong winner—as nearly all of them did in the 2000 presidential election.

As Nate Cohn of the *New York Times* has observed, "there's no shortage of reasons why the polls could be wrong."[25] These confounding factors include flaws that arise innocently enough, from question order or gender of the interviewer—peculiarities not related to sampling methodologies. And they tend to be among the flaws that pollsters don't often advertise or much discuss.

It is nonetheless certain that opinion polls will drive the election narrative for the news media in 2020, much as they have in most presidential elections since 1936. Not infrequently have polls encouraged conventional wisdom among journalists to congeal and take hold, only for conventional wisdom to be upset. That happened in 1948. And 1952. And 1980. And 2004. And 2016.

So, what to expect in 2020 from the interplay of journalists, polls, and pollsters? Expect surprise, especially in light of the Covid-19 coronavirus pandemic that deepened the uncertainties of the election year. And whatever happens, whatever polling controversy arises, it may not be a rerun of 2016. Voters in 2020 are well advised to regard election polls and poll-based prediction models with skepticism, to treat them as if they might be wrong and not ignore the cliché that polling can be more art than science. Downplaying polls, but not altogether ignoring them, seems useful guidance, given that polls are not always in error. But when they fail, they can fail in surprising ways.

NOTES

INTRODUCTION

1. Natalie Jackson, "HuffPost forecasts Hillary Clinton will win with 323 electoral votes," *Huffington Post* (November 7, 2016); accessed February 25, 2018, at: https://www.huffpost.com/entry/polls-hillary-clinton-win_n_5821074ce4b0e80b02cc2a94

2. Natalie Jackson, "Why HuffPost's presidential forecast didn't see a Donald Trump win coming," *Huffington Post* (November 10, 2016); accessed September 27, 2017, at: https://www.huffpost.com/entry/pollster-forecast-donald-trump-wrong_n_5823e1e5e4b0e80b02ceca15

3. Jackson, "Why HuffPost's presidential forecast didn't see a Donald Trump win coming," *Huffington Post*.

4. See "Here's (some of) the best political journalism of 2016," Poynter Institute (November 7, 2016); accessed October 19, 2019, at: https://www.poynter.org/reporting-editing/2016/heres-some-of-the-best-political-journalism-of-2016/

5. Jamelle Bouie, "There is no horse race," Slate.com (August 24, 2016); accessed October 19, 2019, at: https://slate.com/news-and-politics/2016/08/there-is-no-clinton-trump-horse-race.html. Bouie also wrote: "Clinton's odds of *losing* this election amount to the general chance of an unimaginable black-swan event that transforms the political landscape. If you think there's a 10 percent chance that the American economy collapses before November, then that is roughly the chance that Donald Trump wins this election."

6. Mack C. Shelley II and Hwarng-Du Hwang, "The mass media and public opinion polls in the 1988 presidential election: Trends, accuracy, consistency, and events," *American Politics Quarterly* 19, 1 (January 1991): 61.

7. See David Gelman, "Polls and the pollsters," *New York Post* (October 17, 1980): 23.

8. George Gallup, remarks at National Press Club (October 30, 1980); transcript prepared from National Press Club audio recording.

9. See, for example, Will Jennings and Christopher Wlezien, "Election polling errors across time and space," *Nature Human Behavior* 2, 4 (April 2018): 276–283.

10. Even key details of the epic miss of 1948 can be misremembered. For example, an essay posted in 2018 at the right-of-center PJ Media online site recalled that pollsters in 1948 "predicted a narrow win for Republican Thomas Dewey. They were wrong. It is generally believed that their error was one of methodology, in that they relied too heavily on telephone polling. Private telephones in 1948 were a luxury many, especially in urban areas, could not afford." The statement errs in two respects: The pollsters predicted a comfortable-to-overwhelming victory for Dewey. And few polls that year were conducted by telephone. See Avner Zarmi, "The far left is driving a possible blue tsunami," PJ Media (February 9, 2018); accessed February 10, 2018, at: https://pjmedia .com/trending/far-left-driving-possible-blue-tsunami/

11. "The opinion polls always fascinate the press, even when they're irritated by them, and they make politicians nervous whether they're ahead or behind in the polls," Eric Sevareid, a veteran CBS News commentator, said in 1968. "There is something vaguely wrong about a weekly array of statistics telling us the political state of mind of the people, before the people have expressed their state of mind in the voting booth. Nobody seems exactly sure why it's wrong." Sevareid's observations were made September 20, 1968, and are quoted in Richard Craig, *Polls, Expectations, and Elections: TV News Making in U.S. Presidential Elections* (Lanham, MD: Lexington Books, 2014), 85.

12. Quoted in Will Lester, "Pollsters recall 'Dewey' mistake," Associated Press (October 18, 1998); retrieved from LexisNexis database.

13. See, for example, Nate Cohn, "No one picks up the phone, but which online polls are the answer?" *New York Times* (July 2, 2019); accessed July 2, 2019, at https:// www.nytimes.com/2019/07/02/upshot/online-polls-analyzing-reliability.html. See also Nate Silver, "Which pollsters to trust in 2018?" FiveThirtyEight.com (May 31, 2018); accessed June 20, 2019, at: https://fivethirtyeight.com/features/which-pollsters-to-trust-in-2018/

14. Peter Odegard, "Review: *The Pre-Election Polls of 1948,*" *American Political Science Review* 44, 2 (June 1950): 461. Odegard, a political scientist at the University of California at Berkeley, noted that pollsters' "talk of quota versus area sampling, of coding, stratification, regression equations, modes, quindimensional analysis, and so forth, was incomprehensible to the layman," who, he added, "was mystified by it all and more than a trifle suspicious of what he did not understand." Odegard's critique remains strikingly relevant, seventy years on. The jargon of pollsters seems incomprehensible to the uninitiated.

15. "General Eisenhower wins," *Berkshire County* [MA] *Eagle* (November 5, 1952): 22.

16. Gaps in the years considered in this study do not suggest that polls in the missing years were spot-on. The principal focus of this study is on *prominent* polling missteps and errors in presidential elections.

17. See "'Pullet Poll' had it right, but ashamed to announce it," *Abilene* [TX] *Reporter-News* (November 6, 1948): 1.

18. Irving Crespi, *Pre-election Polling: Sources of Accuracy and Error* (New York: Russell Sage Foundation, 1988), 4.

19. See "Hurja poll," *Time* (May 22, 1939): 25. The article stated: "Dr. George Horace Gallup, punditical pollster of public opinion, last week received at his home in Princeton, N.J. a postcard asking him to choose among the ten leading Presidential candidates. It was from Emil Edward Hurja, the sly, plump ex-newspaperman from Michigan and Alaska who used to dope elections expertly for the Democratic National Committee and now operates his own 'political analyst' office in Washington, D.C. for business clients."

20. " 'Digest' poll machinery speeding up," *Literary Digest* (August 29, 1936): 5.

21. Elmo Roper, "On the public mind," text of speech delivered October 21, 1948, New York, NY: Box 36, folder 2260, Elmo Roper papers, Thomas J. Dodd Research Center, University of Connecticut, Storrs.

22. Quoted in Carrell Phillips, "And the polls: What went wrong?" *New York Times* (November 7, 1948): B4.

23. Archibald M. Crossley, "The public wants," unpublished manuscript (1969): Archibald Crossley papers, Thomas J. Dodd Research Center, University of Connecticut, Storrs.

24. Quoted in "Losers," *New York Times* (November 7, 2004): N34. Zogby also was quoted as saying about his Election Day prediction, "I did something I shouldn't have. I am a better pollster than a predictor."

25. Quoted in Michael Shulson, "Meet a polling analyst who got the 2016 election totally wrong," *Pacific Standard* (November 17, 2016); accessed October 27, 2018, at: https://psmag.com/news/meet-a-polling-analyst-who-got-the-2016-election-totally-wrong. Wang was further quoted as saying, "I underestimated the amount of uncertainty that was present in the home stretch."

26. See Alexandrea King, "Poll expert eats bug after being wrong about Trump," CNN (November 12, 2016); accessed March 20, 2019, at: https://www.cnn.com/2016/11/12/politics/pollster-eats-bug-after-donald-trump-win/index.html

27. See "Nate Silver rages at Huffington Post in 14-part tweetstorm," *Politico* (November 5, 2016); accessed December 10, 2017, at: https://www.politico.com/story/2016/11/nate-silver-huffington-post-polls-twitter-230815. Silver referred to the *Huffington Post*'s forecast of a near-certain Clinton win and declared in one of his tweets that "a model showing Clinton at 98% or 99% is not defensible based on the empirical evidence."

28. Ryan Grim, "Nate Silver is unskewing polls—all of them—in Trump's direction," *Huffington Post* (November 5, 2016); accessed March 20, 2019, at: https://www.huffingtonpost.com/entry/nate-silver-election-forecast_us_581e1c33e4b0d9ce6fbc6f7f

29. See Taylor Gee, "15 October surprises that wreaked havoc on politics," Politico.com (October 4, 2016); accessed July 10, 2018, at: https://www.politico.com/magazine/story/2016/10/october-surprises-214320. Gee wrote, "An 'October surprise' can be happenstance or deliberately orchestrated; international (e.g. the outbreak of war) or domestic (e.g. a massive economic rally)."

30. The *New York Times* in 2018 concluded that the Trump-Clinton election was so close that "anything and everything could have been decisive." See Nate Cohn, "Did Comey cost Clinton the election? Why we'll never know," *New York Times* (June 14, 2018); accessed June 15, 2018, at: https://www.nytimes.com/2018/06/14/upshot/did-comey-cost-clinton-the-election-why-well-never-know.html?smtyp=cur&smid=tw-upshotnyt

31. Dewey's gaffe was not prominently reported at the time. The *New York Times* mentioned it deep in its coverage of Dewey's speech on foreign policy given in Louisville. The *Times* quoted Dewey as saying about the train episode, "Well, that's the first lunatic I've had for an engineer. He probably ought to be shot at sunrise, but I guess we'll let him off because nobody was hurt." See "Dewey pledges end to U.S. 'wobbling' in foreign affairs," *New York Times* (October 13, 1948): 1, 17. See also Richard Norton Smith, *Thomas E. Dewey and His Times* (New York: Simon & Schuster, 1982), 532. "Dewey's outburst," Smith wrote, "roused lethargic reporters [on the campaign train], handing them a colorful tidbit to at last break the tedious perfection of his campaign."

32. As the veteran polling analysts Michael W. Traugott and Paul J. Lavrakas have noted, "There are many possible threats to the accuracy of a survey." See Traugott and Lavrakas, *The Voter's Guide to Election Polls* (Morrisville, NC: Lulu Publishing Services, 2016), 108.

33. Stephanie Marken, remarks at panel program, "Best polling practices: Contemporary polling and reporting methods among industry leaders," Association for Education in Journalism and Mass Communication (August 8, 2018), Washington, DC.

34. See Elmo Roper, oral history interview with Robert O. Carlson (August 14, 1968): 18: "Roper at 50" folder, Warren J. Mitofsky papers, Thomas J. Dodd Research Center, University of Connecticut, Storrs.

35. See Aaron Zitner, "Why the 2020 Democratic polls are so different," *Wall Street Journal* (October 24, 2019); retrieved from Factiva database.

36. See, for example, Harry Enten, "'Shy' voters probably aren't why the polls missed Trump," FiveThirtyEight.com; accessed January 22, 2019, at: https://fivethirtyeight.com/features/shy-voters-probably-arent-why-the-polls-missed-trump/. If the "shy Trump" theory were correct, Enten wrote, "we would have expected to see Trump outperform his polls the most in places where he is least popular—and where the stigma against admitting support for Trump would presumably be greatest.... But actual election results indicate that the opposite happened: Trump outperformed his polls by the greatest margin in red states, where he was quite popular."

37. "In other words," as D. Sunshine Hillygus wrote, "it is an unknown population [about] whom pollsters are trying to generalize because we do not know who will show up on Election Day." See Hillygus, "The evolution of election polling in the United States," *Public Opinion Quarterly* 75, 5 (2011): 966.

38. See Joel David Bloom and Jennie Elizabeth Pearson, "Reliable compared to what? A probability-theory based test of the reliability of election polls," in Fritz J. Scheuren and Wendy Alvey, eds., *Elections and Exit Polling* (Hoboken, NJ: John Wiley, 2008), 282.

39. Andrew McGill, "How to spot a likely voter," TheAtlantic.com (January 11, 2016); accessed June 11, 2018, at: https://www.theatlantic.com/politics/archive/2016/01/likely-voter/423456/

40. Archibald M. Crossley, quoted in Gideon Seymour and others, "Should public opinion polls make election forecasts? A symposium," *Journalism Quarterly* 26, 2 (June 1949): 136.

41. "I guess the main reason we do these election polls at all," he once said, "is to prove we're not yellow." Quoted in "Polls point to an Ike victory but pollsters may hedge forecasts," *Wall Street Journal* (October 29, 1956): 1, 18.

42. Burns W. Roper, "Political polls: Some things that concern me," text of remarks to the American Association for the Advancement of Science (May 25, 1984): Box 11, Roper papers.

43. See Jon Cohen, "Our polls are on the mark. I think," *Washington Post* (November 2, 2008): B2. Cohen noted: "Even a few days away from an election, that group remains an unknown population. Not everyone who says that they will vote will actually do so."

44. Kyley McGeeney, "How do weighting targets affect pre-election poll results?" American Association for Public Opinion Research (AAPOR) panel presentation (May 18, 2018), AAPOR annual conference, Denver. Many likely-voter models are proprietary.

45. Nate Cohn, "Using same data, 4 pollsters arrive at 4 different results," *New York Times* (September 22, 2016): A3.

46. Cohn, "Using same data," *New York Times.* "Clearly," Cohn wrote, "the reported margin of error due to sampling . . . doesn't come close to capturing total survey error."

47. William Saletan, "Pollish sausage," Slate.com (October 27, 2000); accessed March 15, 2019, at: https://slate.com/news-and-politics/2000/10/pollish-sausage.html. Saletan also wrote: "Each pollster designs his survey to suit his preferences, and each gets the results he's looking for. Like the rest of us, pollsters have theories about who will vote and how. Polls don't confirm these theories. They incorporate them."

48. See Crespi, *Pre-election Polling,* 183.

49. Nate Silver, "The invisible undecided voter," FiveThirtyEight.com (January 23, 2019); accessed June 24, 2019, at: https://fivethirtyeight.com/features/the-invisible-undecided-voter/

50. Robert P. Daves and Sharon P. Warden, "Methods of allocating undecided respondents to candidate choices in pre-election polls," in Paul J. Lavrakas, Michael W. Traugott, and Peter V. Miller, eds. *Presidential Polls and the News Media* (Boulder, CO: Westview Press, 1995), 102.

51. George Gallup, "Gallup finds race tight in poll's closing survey," *Los Angeles Times* (November 3, 1952): 18.

52. Gallup, "Gallup finds race tight," *Los Angeles Times.*

53. Silver, "The invisible undecided voter," FiveThirtyEight.com.

54. George Gallup and Saul Forbes Rae, *The Pulse of Democracy: The Public-Opinion Poll and How It Works* (New York: Simon & Schuster, 1940), 77. They noted, "Even

though the most accurate polls took periodic measurements in 1936, all of them probably stopped polling too soon."

55. George Gallup, "Exclusive survey gave Landon 3 'sure' states," *Washington Post* (November 8, 1936): B1.

56. See Elmo Roper, "Pollster says Dewey practically elected," *Salt Lake Tribune* (September 9, 1948): 1.

57. Archibald M. Crossley, "The disparity between the polls and the elections," paper prepared for the Iowa Conference on Attitude and Opinion Research (February 10, 1949), Iowa City, IA: 8: Crossley papers.

58. Archibald M. Crossley, letter to Alfred M. Lee (January 4, 1949): Crossley papers.

59. Archibald M. Crossley, letter to Roy S. Forthingham (January 7, 1949): Crossley papers.

60. "An evaluation of 2016 election polls in the United States," American Association for Public Opinion Research (May 2017); accessed February 19, 2018, at https://www.aapor.org/getattachment/Education-Resources/Reports/AAPOR-2016-Election-Polling-Report.pdf.aspx

61. See "Now that it's over, pollsters say they saw landslide coming," *Philadelphia Inquirer* (November 5, 1980): 4-A.

62. See "From a conversation with George Gallup," *U.S. News and World Report* (November 3, 1980): 25.

63. George Gallup, "What happened to the polls?" *Washington Post* (November 12, 1980): 36.

64. Warren J. Mitofsky, memorandum to Ernest Leiser (January 2, 1980): Box 2, Mitofsky papers.

65. Kyley McGeeney, "Best polling practices: Contemporary polling and reporting methods among industry leaders," Association for Education in Journalism and Mass Communication (AEJMC) panel presentation (August 9, 2018); AEJMC annual conference, Washington, DC.

66. George Gallup, letter to David Lawrence (June 16, 1960): David Lawrence papers, Seely G. Mudd Manuscript Library, Princeton University, Princeton, NJ.

67. See "National pre-election polls and forecasts in 1952," in "Proceeding of the American Association for Public Opinion Research," *Public Opinion Quarterly* 17, 4 (Winter 1953–54): 532.

68. George Gallup, "Answering the poll critics," text of speech to members of the American Marketing Association (December 29, 1948), in *Collected Speeches of George Gallup through 1963*, volume 1, series 12, Gallup Organization Papers, University of Iowa special collections, Iowa City.

69. Thomas E. Patterson, "Of polls, mountains: U.S. journalists and their use of election surveys," *Public Opinion Quarterly* 69, 5 (2005): 718.

70. Crossley, letter to Gallup (September 27, 1948): Crossley papers.

71. See C. Anthony Broh, "Horse-race journalism: Reporting the polls in the 1976 presidential election," *Public Opinion Quarterly* 44, 4 (Winter 1980): 527.

72. Jack Shafer, "Why horse-race political journalism is awesome," *Politico* (January 9, 2019); accessed February 18, 2019, at: https://www.politico.com/magazine/story/2019/01/09/why-horse-race-political-journalism-awesome-223867

73. David Yepsen, "Shoe leather beats BlackBerries," *Nieman Report* (Spring 2004): 15.

74. Quoted in Steven J. Rosenstone, *Forecasting Presidential Elections* (New Haven, CT: Yale University Press, 1983), 27.

75. Thomas B. Littlewood, *Calling Elections: The History of Horse-Race Journalism* (Notre Dame, IN: University of Notre Dame, 1998), 181–182.

76. Gallup and Rae, *Pulse of Democracy*, 80–81.

77. Philip M. Meyer, "Presidential address: Polling as political science and polling as journalism," *Public Opinion Quarterly* 54, 3 (Fall 1990): 455.

78. Philip Meyer, "Commentary: Polls are predictions (so let's stop kidding ourselves)," *Newspaper Research Journal* 8, 3 (Spring 1987): 85.

79. See David W. Moore, *The Superpollsters: How They Measure and Manipulate Public Opinion in America* (New York: Four Walls Eight Windows, 1992), 278.

80. Mitofsky, typescript of undated speech titled "AAPOR plenary 1981," Box 10, Mitofsky papers.

81. Mitofsky, memorandum to Leiser (January 2, 1980): Mitofsky papers.

82. Charles K. Atkin and James Gaudino, "The impact of polling on the mass media," *Annals of the American Academy of Political and Social Science* 472 (March 1984): 121–122.

83. See Tom W. Smith, "The first straw? A study of the origins of election polls," *Public Opinion Quarterly* 54, 1 (Spring 1990): 21–36. Smith noted (31) that what he termed "the proto-straw polls" represented "a significant development in the assessment and quantification of public opinion and deserve a special place in the history of election polling."

84. See Roscoe Drummond, "Should polls decide?" *Washington Post* (August 22, 1959): A9. Drummond also wrote: "My complaint is not that we have these polls. It is that all of us voters, politicians, columnists, dentists, and taxi drivers, ought to be more determined not to become their prisoner."

85. "A warning to poll watchers," *Los Angeles Times* (October 12, 1952): B4.

86. Richard Morin, "Don't ask me," *Washington Post* (October 28, 2004): C1.

1. OF POLL-BASHING JOURNALISTS AND THE 'BABE RUTH' OF SURVEY RESEARCH

1. See "Gallup polls public opinion for 25 years," *Editor and Publisher* (November 5, 1960): 62. Gallup was quoted as saying thirty-five newspapers subscribed to his polling reports in 1935. "Thirty-five leading newspapers underwrote the costs of the Gallup poll in the beginning," he said. "These 35 included papers of all political views."

2. "Although Gallup's fees [in 1948] might range as high as $500 a week for a large newspaper, it was his far more lucrative commercial market-research business that continued to subsidize news polls," Thomas B. Littlewood noted in *Calling Elections:*

The History of Horse-Race Journalism (Notre Dame, IN: University of Notre Dame Press, 1998), 123.

3. See Barry Sussman, "George Gallup dies; was pioneer pollster," *Washington Post* (July 28, 1984): A1, A17.

4. Frank Newport, oral history interview, AAPOR Heritage Interview (May 13, 2016): https://www.youtube.com/watch?v=b4QQ7PbrZ_c&feature=youtu.be

5. George Gallup, remarks on CBS *Meet the Press* program (November 14, 1948); recording retrieved from Moving Image Research Center, Library of Congress, Washington, DC.

6. "Goddammit," Rather was quoted as saying, "I hate these fucking polls. . . . I hate polls. I've always hated polls. . . . I am famous or infamous inside our organization for hating polling." Quoted in Martin Schram, *The Great American Video Game: Presidential Politics in the Television Age*" (New York: Morrow and Company, 1987), 136. Schram wrote that Rather complained polling can "become the drivetrain that propels the journalistic coverage, especially when the journalistic organizations themselves get into the business of doing their own polling—which they then feel obliged to report at length with detail and importance."

7. See Christopher Hitchens, "Voting in the passive voice: What polling has done to American democracy," *Harper's Magazine* (April 1992): 45–52. Hitchens argued (46) that "polling was born out of a struggle not to discover the public mind but to master it."

8. "The battle of the straw men," *New York Herald Tribune* (November 5, 1936): 26.

9. Edward R. Murrow, CBS Radio script (November 5, 1952): Elmo Roper papers, Thomas J. Dodd Research Center, University of Connecticut, Storrs. Ellipses in the original. In a reply sent weeks later, Elmo Roper scoffed at Murrow's "obvious delight in thinking that it is impossible to gain any clues as to the motives of mankind. At a time when it seems to me to be of vital importance to throw whatever light can be thrown on what are the forces that make mankind tick, it would seem to me any searcher for the truth would welcome any effort that had any validity." Roper also disputed Murrow's assertion that the pre-election polls in 1952 "were as wrong as they were [in 1948]." Roper, letter to Murrow (January 27, 1953): Roper papers.

10. Edward R. Murrow, broadcast script, CBS Radio (December 27, 1948): Series 4, box 2, Gallup Organization Papers, University of Iowa special collections, Iowa City.

11. Eric Sevareid, "Most people have feeling of glee when the pollsters prove wrong," *Philadelphia Bulletin* (May 31, 1964): sect. 2, p. 1.

12. James Reston, "In defense of the pollsters," *New York Times* (June 26, 1970): 40. "With dependable polls," Reston further wrote, "governments would be relieved of the hard job of governing: All they'd have to do would be to take a poll and follow the result."

13. Mike Royko, "Annoy pollsters—resort to lying," *Chicago Tribune* (October 28, 1992): D3. Royko also wrote that he had grown "weary of countless pollsters telling 250 million people what they thought on the basis of the way 1,000 answered questions."

14. Mike Royko, "Small lie for poll, leap for mankind," *Chicago Tribune* (November 1, 1984): 3.

15. Royko, "Small lie for poll, leap for mankind," *Chicago Tribune*.

16. See "Exit lying," *Washington Post* (March 17, 1984): A16.

17. Timothy P. Johnson, "Legitimacy, Wicked Problems, and Public Opinion Research," 2018 presidential address, American Association for Public Opinion Research (May 17, 2018); transcript accessed May 21, 2018, at: https://www.aapor.org /About-Us/History/Presidential-Addresses/2018-Presidential-Address.aspx

18. Quoted in Bill Steigerwald, "Arianna Huffington finds a lot to laugh about in Washington," *Pittsburgh Post-Gazette* (May 18, 1998); retrieved from LexisNexis database.

19. Arianna Huffington, interview with *CNN Talkback Live* program (October 24, 2000); retrieved from LexisNexis database.

20. Arianna Huffington, interview with *On the Media* program (October 22, 2004); transcript accessed April 6, 2019, at: https://www.wnycstudios.org/story/130106-polls-be-gone. Huffington also said in the interview, "We are not going to end the addiction of politicians and the media to polls. The only thing we, the people, have control over is offering our opinion to the pollsters."

21. Arianna Huffington, "Say 'no' to pollsters!" *Huffington Post* (January 11, 2008); accessed August 18, 2017, at: https://www.huffpost.com/entry/say-no-to-pollsters-a-huf_b_81128

22. Quoted in Jeremy W. Peters, "Huffington Post acquires an opinion poll service," *New York Times* (July 8, 2010): B3.

23. Paul Trescott, "How polls can help newspapers," *Public Opinion Quarterly* 13, 1 (Spring 1949): 19.

24. Jay Rosen, "Good old fashioned shoe leather reporting," *PressThink* [blog] (April 16, 2015); accessed April 13, 2019, at: http://pressthink.org/2015/04/good-old-fashioned-shoe-leather-reporting/

25. For a discussion of the media-driven myths of Woodward, Bernstein, and Watergate, see W. Joseph Campbell, *Getting It Wrong: Debunking the Greatest Myths of American Journalism*, 2nd ed. (Oakland: University of California Press, 2017), 150–164.

26. See Timothy Crouse, *The Boys on the Bus* (New York: Random House, 1972), 33.

27. James David Barber, *The Pulse of Politics: Electing Presidents in the Media Age* (New York: W. W. Norton, 1980), 87.

28. Crouse, *Boys on the Bus*, 15.

29. Haynes Johnson, interview with Brian Lamb, C-SPAN *Booknotes* (March 3, 1991); transcript accessed April 13, 2019, at: http://booknotes.org/Watch/16899–1 /Haynes-Johnson

30. Haynes Johnson, "Polls," *Washington Post* (March 2, 1980): A3.

31. See "A political reporter's toolbox," *Nieman Reports* (Spring 2004); accessed December 18, 2018, at: https://niemanreports.org/articles/a-political-reporters-toolbox/

32. Quoted in Jim Rutenberg, "News outlets wonder where they stumbled," *New York Times* (November 10, 2016): A1.

33. Neal Gabler, "Five ways the media bungled the election," *Columbia Journalism Review* (January 24, 2017); accessed August 20, 2019, at: https://www.cjr.org/criticism/media_election_trump_fail.php. Gabler also wrote that after the 2016 election, "No one will ever believe Nate Silver or Nate Cohn or The Huffington Post aggregator or any other polling data ever again."

34. Nate Silver, "Ohio was a bellwether after all," FiveThirtyEight.com (January 25, 2017); accessed May 30, 2019, at: https://fivethirtyeight.com/features/ohio-was-a-bellwether-after-all/#fn-2

35. See Jeremy W. Peters, "In shift, Romney campaign approaches Pennsylvania with a new urgency," *New York Times* (November 1, 2012): A11. Peters wrote that "there is a tangible sense—seen in Romney yard signs on the expansive lawns of homes in the well-heeled suburbs, and heard in the excited voices of Republican mothers who make phone calls to voters in their spare time—that the race is tilting toward Mr. Romney."

36. See Walter Shapiro, "What if there are fewer polls in 2016?" *Columbia Journalism Review* (November 27, 2012); accessed March 8, 2020, at: https://archives.cjr.org/united_states_project/fewer_polls_in_2016.php

37. "Market research and polling services industry profile," Dun & Bradstreet First Research, n.d.; accessed November 9, 2019, at: http://www.firstresearch.com/Industry-Research/Market-Research-and-Polling-Services.html

38. Quoted in Michael M. Grynbaum, "2020 advice for reporters: Assume nothing," *New York Times* (April 17, 2019): B3.

39. Charles Franklin, remarks at panel, "At least a dozen things we learned from the 2016 election" (May 19, 2017); annual conference of the American Association for Public Opinion Research, New Orleans.

40. Elmo Roper, letter to his parents (November 13, 1952): Roper papers.

41. Quoted in "Pollsters poll selves on flop; see better day," *Chicago Tribune* (December 31, 1952): 5.

42. George Gallup, remarks at National Press Club (October 30, 1980); transcript prepared from National Press Club audio recording.

43. See George Gallup, *Sophisticated Poll Watcher's Guide* (Princeton, NJ: Princeton Opinion Press, 1976), 123.

44. "Gallup Poll sets another record for election accuracy," *Editor and Publisher* (November 11, 1944): 85.

45. See Daniel Katz, "The polls and the 1944 election," *Public Opinion Quarterly* 8, 4 (Winter 1944–1945): 481.

46. Quoted in "M'Grath calls on Gallup to adjust poll," *Salt Lake Tribune* (October 29, 1948): 2. The article was an Associated Press dispatch.

47. George Gallup, letter to Elmo Roper (November 18, 1940): Box 3, folder 134, Roper papers. Gallup's overture seemed another example of his eagerness in the early years of modern election polling to identify who was most accurate in his forecasts. Additionally, Gallup maintained that "accuracy of polls in a scientific sense should be judged solely on how closely they predict the actual division of votes on candidates or

the division of opinion on issues." Quoted in Frederick Mosteller and others, *The Pre-Election Polls of 1948* (New York: Social Science Research Council, 1949), 52.

48. Elmo Roper, letter to George Gallup (November 19, 1940): Roper papers. Scrawled across the face of the typescript of Roper's letter were the words "not sent."

49. On this point, see J. Michael Hogan, "George Gallup and the rhetoric of scientific democracy," *Communication Monographs* 64, 2 (June 1997): 166.

50. See Jean M. Converse, *Survey Research in the United States: Roots and Emergence, 1890–1960* (Berkeley: University of California Press, 1987), 88.

51. Quoted in Gideon Seymour and others, "Should public opinion polls make election forecasts? A symposium," *Journalism Quarterly* 26, 2 (June 1949): 141. Gallup also said that "standing up to the rigorous test of election forecasting has had the effect of improving methods and increasing our knowledge of voting behavior." See George Gallup, "The changing climate for public opinion research," *Public Opinion Quarterly* 21, 1 (Spring 1957): 25.

52. Hogan, "George Gallup and the rhetoric of scientific democracy," *Communication Monographs*, 167.

53. Gallup declared in 1946, for example, that "Mr. Eugene Meyer was one of our earliest sponsors in organizing the Gallup Poll and has given us much aid and encouragement throughout the decade of our operation." See George Gallup, "Dr. Gallup salutes Post poll," *Washington Post* (November 17, 1946): B2.

54. Eugene Meyer, "A newspaper publisher looks at the polls," *Public Opinion Quarterly* 4, 2 (June 1940): 239.

55. See Susan Ohmer, *George Gallup in Hollywood* (New York: Columbia University Press, 2006), 4.

56. See Bernard Roshco and Irving Crespi, "From alchemy to home-brewed chemistry—polling transformed," *Public Perspective* (April/May 1996): 11.

57. Phyllis L. Gillis, typescript notes of interview with Jack Tibby, n.d.: Series 2, box 1, Gallup Organization Papers. Tibby was a senior Gallup employee who later became news editor and assistant managing editor at *Sports Illustrated* magazine.

58. Converse, *Survey Research in the United States*, 114.

59. Gillis, typescript notes of interview with George Gallup (September 26, 1979): Series 2, box 1, Gallup Organization Papers.

60. William J. Gaskill, letter to Elmo Roper (December 18, 1947): Roper papers.

61. Elmo Roper, letter to William Gaskill (January 7, 1948): Roper papers.

62. Frank Stanton to Elmo Roper (January 10, 1948): Box 5, folder 278, Roper papers.

63. For example, Gallup wrote in 1957: "I can remember addressing a meeting on a college campus where I advanced the idea that the common people of the country display an extraordinary amount of good sense about the issues of the day. The left-wingers in the group nearly stoned me from the campus. . . . The extreme right wing was equally bitter in its views. Through the years the *Chicago Tribune* never missed an opportunity to flail us." See Gallup, "The changing climate for public opinion research," *Public Opinion Quarterly*, 24.

64. Rensis Likert, "Public opinion polls," *Scientific American* (December 1948): 7.

65. Likert, "Public opinion polls," *Scientific American*, 8, 9.

66. Pollsters and market researchers were aware of the potential for adverse interviewer effects as early as the 1930s. Roper in 1938 cited "careless fieldwork" as a potential flaw in market research, for example. See Converse, *Survey Research in the United States*, 98. Converse wrote, "The solitary work of interviewers, their minimal training, their skeletal supervisory staffs, the supervision by mail—most of these factors were likely to increase the chances of error and possible deception."

67. George Gallup, "Answering the poll critics," text of speech to members of the American Marketing Association (December 29, 1948): "Collected speeches of George Gallup through 1963," volume 1, series 12, Gallup Organization Papers.

68. Gallup, "Answering the poll critics," Gallup Organization Papers.

69. Lindsay Rogers, *The Pollsters: Public Opinion, Politics, and Democratic Leadership* (New York: Alfred A. Knopf, 1949), 17.

70. George Gallup, "A reply to *The Pollsters*," *Public Opinion Quarterly* 13, 1 (Spring 1949): 179, 180.

71. See Gallup, "The changing climate for public opinion research," *Public Opinion Quarterly*, 24. Gallup added (25): "Professor Rogers obviously has a keen mind. But his lack of knowledge about the operation of polls and their findings destroys his effectives as a critic of polls. His assumptions, beautifully stated though they be, can be 'murdered by a gang of facts.'"

72. See "The black & white beans," *Time* (May 3, 1948): 21. *Time* said Gallup was a "big, friendly, teddybear of a man with a passion for facts & figures."

73. "The black & white beans," *Time*, 23.

74. David Ogilvy, *An Autobiography* (New York: Wiley, 1997), 74.

75. Ogilvy, *An Autobiography*, 73. Gallup and Rae shared bylines on the book, *The Pulse of Democracy: The Public-Opinion Poll and How It Works*, which came out in 1940.

76. Ogilvy, *An Autobiography*, 74.

77. George Gallup on CBS program *Meet the Press* (November 1948); sound recording accessed at Library of Congress, Washington, DC.

78. David W. Moore, a former vice president at the Gallup Organization, observed, for example, "The hard truth is that on most policy issues, large proportions of the public know or care little about the specifics, and thus have developed no meaningful opinion about them." See Moore, *The Opinion Makers: An Insider Exposes the Truth behind the Polls* (Boston: Beacon Press, 2008), 18.

79. "The serious observer of public opinion on scores of issues," he once wrote, "cannot fail to come away with a feeling of intense admiration for the honesty and common sense with which an enormous number of ordinary people in all walks of life and at all levels of the economic scale have continued to meet their obligations as citizens." See George Gallup and Saul Forbes Rae, *The Pulse of Democracy: The Public-Opinion Poll and How It Works* (New York: Simon & Schuster, 1940), 287.

80. See, for example, Gallup, "The changing climate for public opinion research," *Public Opinion Quarterly*, 27. "The public is almost always ahead of its leaders," he wrote.

81. George H. Gallup, typescript of interview with Edward R. Murrow, *Person to Person* television program, CBS network (April 13, 1956): Series 14, box 1, Gallup Organization Papers. Gallup once described Americans as "intellectually immature," asserting: "What we need most in this country, in my opinion, is an intellectual renaissance." He also said the country's "educational system is admirably designed to keep the Nation mentally immature." See George Gallup, "America needs to read a book," *Washington Post* (October 19, 1952): B3.

82. See Michael Wheeler, *Lies, Damned Lies, and Statistics: The Manipulation of Public Opinion in America* (New York: Liveright, 1976), 39.

83. "George Gallup, pollster who found the pulse of democracy," *New York Times* (July 26, 2016); retrieved April 28, 2019, at: https://www.nytimes.com/interactive/projects/cp/obituaries/archives/george-gallup

84. See, for example, Williston Rich, "The human yardstick," *Saturday Evening Post* (January 21, 1939): 8–9, 66, 68–71. Rich wrote of Gallup, "This brash young fellow who makes a profession of climbing out on a limb, teetering there amid cheers and jeers, and then bringing back the apple, is a farm boy, now thirty-seven years old."

85. Ogilvy, *An Autobiography*, 73.

86. Phyllis L. Gillis, letter to Jack Tibby (May 19, 1980): Series 2, box 2, Gallup Organization Papers.

87. Phyllis L. Gillis, letter to Ellen Levine (November 24, 1980): Series 2, box 2, Gallup Organization Papers.

88. No prominent pollster, in fact, has been the subject of biographic treatment. Lou Harris said in 1997 that he had been approached by several people, "including a few literary agents, [who] have suggested that I ought to sit down and write my memoirs on my relationship with Kennedy, Nixon, Humphry [sic], Ford, Reagan(!!), and, lately, Clinton (in a strange way). And, also, my career in polling. I have resisted all such entreaties (let me quickly add no publisher has come to my door with a big advance in hand, which puts all that flattery in proper perspective!)." Louis Harris, letter to Lee Hills (May 12, 1997): Box 80, Louis Harris papers, Wilson Library, University of North Carolina, Chapel Hill.

89. Ohmer, *George Gallup in Hollywood*, 73.

90. Converse, *Survey Research in the United States*, 118.

91. See "Gallup poll analysis of the election" (advertisement), *Editor and Publisher* (November 8, 1952): 25. "It's nicer to eat pheasant than crow," Gallup's ad declared. See also George Gallup, "Gallup finds race tight in poll's closing survey," *Los Angeles Times* (November 3, 1952): 1.

92. George Gallup, "A second look at the 1948 election," text of speech delivered to Iowa conference (February 1949): "Collected speeches of George Gallup through 1963," Gallup Organization Papers.

93. See Committee on Analysis of Pre-Election Polls and Forecasts of the Social Science Research Council, "Report on the Analysis of Pre-Election Polls and Forecasts," *Public Opinion Quarterly* 12, 4 (Winter 1948–49): 608, 609.

94. See Joseph Lelyveld, "Gallup fondly recalls friendship with Dewey," *New York Times* (May 20, 1971): 33.

95. Gillis, typescript notes of interview with George Gallup (July 10, 1980): Series 2, box 1, Gallup Organization Papers.

96. Gillis, typescript notes of interview with George Gallup (December 12, 1979): Series 2, box 1, Gallup Organization Papers.

97. See George Gallup, "Exclusive survey gave Landon 3 'sure' states," *Washington Post* (November 8, 1936): B1.

98. See "Leaders in many walks of life here congratulate Post on poll results," *Washington Post* (November 6, 1936): X15.

99. In his profile in the *Saturday Evening Post* in 1939, Williston Rich said Gallup became so worried he might be wrong about the Roosevelt-Landon race that he "began to suffer insomnia" and his wife took him to Sarasota, Florida, "for a rest. He didn't get it." See Rich, "The human yardstick," *Saturday Evening Post*, 66.

100. John K.M. ("Jack") Tibby, letter to Marvin McIntyre, assistant secretary to the president (November 4, 1936): Franklin D. Roosevelt papers, Franklin D. Roosevelt Presidential Library and Museum, Hyde Park, NY.

101. Marvin McIntyre, letter to John K.M. ("Jack") Tibby (November 9, 1936): Roosevelt papers. McIntyre wrote that "the President has been glad to place his signature on one of these copies, and I take pleasure in returning it to you herewith."

2. 'A TIME OF POLLS GONE MAD'

1. See "Superlandslide: Voters smash records everywhere in plumping for Roosevelt," *Literary Digest* (November 14, 1936): 10.

2. See Si Sheppard, *The Buying of the Presidency? Franklin D. Roosevelt, the New Deal, and the Election of 1936* (Santa Barbara, CA: Praeger, 2014), 193.

3. Willard Edwards, "Roosevelt to meet Bell on budget plans," *Chicago Tribune* (November 7, 1936): 6. Also cited in William Manchester, *The Glory and the Dream: A Narrative History of America, 1932–1972* (Boston: Little, Brown, 1973), 145.

4. As the *Literary Digest* noted in publicizing the results, the poll "has always previously been correct. Even its critics admit its value as an index of popular sentiment." See "Landon, 1,293,669; Roosevelt, 972,897," *Literary Digest* (October 31, 1936): 5, 6.

5. Quoted in "Bourbon landslide astounds editor of Literary Digest," *Salt Lake Tribune* (November 4, 1936): 21.

6. See, for example, "The Digest Poll," *Chicago Tribune* (October 30, 1936): 14. "The significance of this poll cannot be shirked," the *Tribune* said in its editorial. "The Digest has taken polls for over a quarter of a century, has developed in that experience the most reliable methods, and has earned the reputation of 'uncanny accuracy.'"

7. See Maurice C. Bryson, "The Literary Digest poll: Making of a statistical myth," *American Statistician* 30, 4 (November 1976): 184.

8. Roper's partners were Paul T. Cherington, formerly a professor at Harvard University's School of Business, and Richardson Wood, an advertising agency executive. See Elmo Roper, oral history interview with Robert O. Carlson (14 August 1968): Box 20, "Roper at 50" folder, Warren J. Mitofsky papers, Thomas J. Dodd Research Center, University of Connecticut, Storrs.

9. See Jean M. Converse, *Survey Research in the United States: Roots and Emergence, 1890–1960* (Berkeley: University of California Press, 1987), 115.

10. "The Institute's purpose," he wrote in 1940, "was to perform the function of fact finding in the same general way as the Associated Press, the United Press, and the International News Service functioned in the realm of events." See George Gallup and Saul Forbes Rae, *The Pulse of Democracy: The Public-Opinion Poll and How It Works* (New York: Simon & Schuster, 1940), 46.

11. See Roper, oral history interview, Mitofsky papers. George Gallup privately conducted fifty-four trial polls before reporting the results of his first weekly survey, called "the National Weekly Poll of Public Opinion," in October 1935. See "54 polls taken before offering weekly project," *Washington Post* (November 3, 1935): B1.

12. Dominic Lusinchi, "Straw poll journalism and quantitative data," *Journalism Studies* 16, 3 (2015): 417.

13. Gallup and Rae, *The Pulse of Democracy*, 74–75.

14. Gallup and Rae, *The Pulse of Democracy*, 75.

15. Archibald M. Crossley, "Straw polls in 1936," *Public Opinion Quarterly* 1, 1 (January 1937): 33.

16. Of these criteria, Roper said, economic standing was "the most important." See Elmo Roper, "Sampling public opinion," *Journal of the American Statistical Association* 35, 210 (June 1940): 327. A top Republican party official, Harrison E. Spangler, criticized quota-control methods as leading "to error rather than accuracy. They divide the American people into classes and then by various means attempt to find out the political preference of a very few in each class or group. Such a method is based on a false assumption at the outset. The American people cannot be regimented or classified in this way when it comes to appraising their political views." Quoted in "G.O.P. leader terms Institute poll inaccurate," *Washington Post* (November 1, 1936): M17.

17. See "Roosevelt bags 41 states out of 48," *Literary Digest* (November 5, 1932): 8.

18. "'The Digest' presidential poll is on!" *Literary Digest* (August 22, 1936): 4.

19. For example, the magazine said in the run-up to its presidential poll in 1932, when it mailed twenty million postcard-ballots: "All who have borne a share in the varied and far-flung labors of a *Literary Digest* poll know the kick that comes with the preparations to start it off under a full head of steam. Twenty million envelops [*sic*] to be addrest [*sic*] by hand. Twenty million ballots to be printed. Twenty million letters to be prepared, folded, and inserted in those envelops [*sic*]. Forty thousand extra square feet of floor space to be provided, making a total of 60,000 square feet devoted entirely to the preliminaries of the job of finding out who will be the next President of the

United States." See "Tuning up for 'The Digest's' Presidential Poll," *Literary Digest* (September 3, 1932): 1. Four years later, the magazine reported: "This week, 500 pens scratched out more than a quarter of a million addresses a day. Every day, in a great room high above motor-ribboned Fourth Avenue in New York, 400 workers deftly slipped a million pieces of printed matter—enough to pave forty city blocks—into the addressed envelops. Every hour, in the Digest's own Post Office Substation, three chattering postage metering machines sealed and stamped white oblongs; skilled postal employees flipped them into bulging mail-sacks; fleet Digest trucks sped them to express mail-trains." See "'The Digest' presidential poll is on!" *Literary Digest*, 3.

20. See "Fortune Magazine survey conducted over nine months period most closely approximated election results," *Fortune* news release, n.d.: Box 61, folder 7, Alfred M. Landon papers, Kansas State Historical Society, Topeka.

21. See "The outcome of the election by W. R. Hearst," *New York American* (November 1, 1936): 1, 2. Landon, on the other hand, "is the kind of man you would select to leave in charge of whatever savings you have been able to accumulate for your wife and children," Hearst wrote. In August 1936, Hearst declared: "The race will not be close at all. Landon will be overwhelmingly elected, and I'll stake my reputation as a prophet on it." Quoted in "So they said: Clipped from the files," *Washington Post* (November 6, 1936): X13.

22. A. M. Crossley, "Landon needs only Michigan to win election, poll shows," *New York American* (October 11, 1936): 1.

23. Archibald M. Crossley, "Presidential race tightens as Election Day draws near," *New York American* (October 18, 1936): 1.

24. A. M. Crossley, "Poll shows present campaign one of closest in U.S. history," *New York American* (November 1, 1936): 2. In a later edition of the *American*, the headline was revised: "Closest contest in U.S. history."

25. Archibald Crossley, letter to Charlton R. Price (March 17, 1949): Archibald M. Crossley papers, Thomas J. Dodd Research Center, University of Connecticut, Storrs. Crossley added in the letter: "We have often found that when we released a story which was in line with the newspaper's policies it would turn out on the front page with glowing headlines, but if contrary to that policy would get small space and some headlines on an inside page. We never felt that we could do anything about this."

26. Archibald M. Crossley, "Crossley poll gives its final vote analysis," n.d.: Series 10, box 1, Gallup Organization Papers, University of Iowa special collections, Iowa City, Iowa.

27. See George Gallup, "Roosevelt polls 55.7% of major party vote," *Washington Post* (November 1, 1936): B1. Gallup estimated that Roosevelt would receive 53.8 percent to Landon's 42.8 percent and Lemke's 2.2 percent. In the two-party vote, Gallup figured the President would win 55.7 percent.

28. See "Fortune Magazine survey conducted over nine months period," *Fortune* news release, n.d.: Landon papers. Although it carried no date, the news release was clearly prepared shortly after the 1936 election.

29. Roper briefly discussed how he arrived at his 1936 estimate in "Sampling public opinion," *Journal of the American Statistical Association*, 331. See also "Fortune Quarterly

Survey: VI," *Fortune* (October 1936): 130. That article presented findings from the *Fortune* survey and included several data tables, among them a compilation indicating that 59.2 percent of the survey's respondents agreed that Roosevelt's election was "essential" or that "there is no one else who can do as much good." The combined response to two negative statements—that Roosevelt's "usefulness" was mostly over and that it would be nearly "the worst thing" for the country were he reelected—was 36.7 percent. That breakdown was more akin to measuring Roosevelt's favorability rating than to forecasting his race against Landon, however. The article included other data indicating that nearly 70 percent of the survey's respondents believed Roosevelt would win reelection; just 22 percent felt Landon would win. That result, *Fortune* said, "spells dark defeatism among Republicans." See "Fortune Quarterly Survey: VI," *Fortune*, 131.

30. "Fortune Quarterly Survey: VI," *Fortune*, 130.

31. Roper, oral history interview, Mitofsky papers.

32. See, for example, Robert P. Post, "Polls in disfavor as voters' guides," *New York Times* (November 8, 1936): E5.

33. "The battle of the straw men," *New York Herald Tribune* (November 5, 1936): 26.

34. Crossley, "Straw polls in 1936," *Public Opinion Quarterly*, 26. "It should be possible," Crossley added, "so to improve the polls that accuracy could be achieved almost to one percentage point."

35. On this point, see Dominic Lusinchi, "'President' Landon and the 1936 *Literary Digest* poll," *Social Science History* 36, 1 (Spring 2012): 24–25.

36. George Gallup, "Exclusive survey gave Landon 3 'sure' states," *Washington Post* (November 8, 1936): B1.

37. Gallup and Rae, *The Pulse of Democracy*, 75.

38. George Gallup, "Minnesota, Delaware swing to Democrats," *Washington Post* (October 4, 1936): B1.

39. George Gallup, "Great shift in vote nation-wide in scope," *Washington Post* (July 12, 1936): B1. Years later, Charles Michelson, a former publicity director for the Democratic National Committee, sarcastically recalled Gallup's report in July 1936 about Landon and 272 votes, writing, "Obviously, nothing happened between that date and election day that could explain why, when the votes were counted, the Kansas Governor got only eight electoral votes." See Michelson, "Michelson, the former chief of publicity for Democrats, says the surveys have no useful purpose and frequently err," *New York Times* (May 23, 1944): 20.

40. See Eleanor Roosevelt, "Memo from Mrs. Roosevelt" (July 16, 1936): Franklin D. Roosevelt papers, Franklin D. Roosevelt Presidential Library and Museum, Hyde Park, NY. "My feeling is that we have to get going and going quickly," she wrote, adding, "More and more my reports indicate that this is a close election and that we need very excellent organization."

41. Walter Lippmann, "At the end of the campaign," *Ogden* [UT] *Standard-Examiner* (November 2, 1936): 5.

42. "Public excited by battle between two straw polls," *Boston Globe* (November 2, 1936): 28.

43. Chapin Hall, "National straw vote season nearing end," *Los Angeles Times* (November 1, 1936): 1.

44. Frank Newport, former editor-in-chief of the Gallup poll, said in an oral history interview in 2016 that Gallup had acted "courageously" in estimating the *Literary Digest's* erroneous final result before the survey had even begun. See Frank Newport, "Heritage interview," American Association for Public Opinion Research (May 13, 2016); accessed May 12, 2019, at: https://www.youtube.com/watch?v=b4QQ7PbrZ_c&feature= youtu.be

45. See "'Landon still gaining?' parties ask," *Oakland* [CA] *Tribune* (July 19, 1936): B3. See also, "'Is Landon still gaining in presidential poll?' both parties ask," *Washington Post* (July 19, 1936): B1. Several months earlier, Gallup had anticipated the results of a *Digest* poll about Roosevelt's New Deal policies. Gallup was quoted as saying in November 1935 that the *Digest* would find 60 percent opposed. Final figures reported by the magazine in January 1936 said 62 percent of respondents opposed the New Deal. See "Press to keep opinion polls, claims Gallup," *Washington Post* (November 22, 1935): 9.

46. Quoted in "Dr. Gallup chided by Digest editor," *New York Times* (July 19, 1936): 21. Some newspapers sided with Funk in criticizing Gallup's cheek. For example, the *Alton Evening Telegraph* in Illinois praised the *Digest* for having "performed a great service in the past and the hope persists it will continue long to relieve our minds of uncertainty." The newspaper also said, "Dr. Gallup and his kind may think they know how to run a straw vote but, we agree with Editor W. J. Funk that the Literary Digest really does know." See "Blown-in-the-bottle prophet," *Alton* [IL] *Evening Telegraph* (July 22, 1936): 4.

47. Gallup and Rae, *The Pulse of Democracy*, 44.

48. George Gallup, testimony, in *Hearings before the Committee to Investigate Campaign Expenditures, House of Representatives*, part 12 (December 28, 1944), 1278.

49. George Gallup, "The changing climate for public opinion research," *Public Opinion Quarterly* 21, 1 (Spring 1957): 24. He also wrote, "The sampling polls were on the right side, and by this fact could lay claim to superiority over the straw poll methods which had prevailed up to that time."

50. Phyllis L. Gillis, typescript of interview notes with George Gallup (October 11, 1979): Series 2, box, 1, Gallup Organization Papers.

51. George Gallup's papers indicate that he kept tabs on several straw polls, including those conducted by newspapers in Columbus, Toledo, Cincinnati, Salt Lake City, and Portland, OR. See "Summary of other polls, October 20, 1936," Series 10, box 2, Gallup Organization Papers.

52. "Landslide," *New York Times* (November 8, 1936): E1.

53. Hall, "National straw vote season nearing end," *Los Angeles Times*, 1, 2. "The straw vote has become one of the great campaign institutions of this country," declared the editorial board of the *Baltimore Sun* shortly before the election. See "Straws in the wind," *Baltimore Sun* (October 31, 1936): 12.

54. See "Special train correspondents see Roosevelt 1936 'landslide,'" *Editor and Publisher* (October 31, 1936): 4.

55. A. Bernard Moloney, letter to Stephen Early (October 6, 1936): OF 857, "Straw votes," Roosevelt papers.

56. See Sheppard, *The Buying of the Presidency?* 119.

57. See "Farm Journal's vote forecast," *Delaware County Daily Times* [Chester, PA] (November 2, 1936): 12. The *Farm Journal* canvass was restricted to farmers and rural residents and included states with large urban centers, such as New York, New Jersey, Ohio, Pennsylvania, Michigan, and California.

58. See "Gov. Landon leads in rural vote," *Santa Ana* [CA] *Register* (October 21, 1936): 1.

59. "Landon wins with 310!" *Cleveland News* (October 26, 1936): 4. The newspaper did not explain its aggregating methodology clearly or well, beyond saying "the poll of all polls" was based on results of 3,009 straw polls conducted by U.S. newspapers and magazines. The *News* did not conceal its preference for Landon, noting it sponsored 150 billboards around Cleveland with the message, "Go Ahead with Landon." See "Go ahead with Landon," *Cleveland News* (October 1, 1936): 4.

60. "'The Digest' presidential poll is on!" *Literary Digest.* Emphasis in the original. The *Digest*'s boast echoed its confident assertions in earlier campaigns. In 1924, for example, the magazine said it had "promised, through a journalistic enterprise, including the largest Presidential straw vote ever attempted, to anticipate this most important news [the election outcome] 'not by minutes, or even by days, but by weeks.'" See "2,386,052 straws forecast Tuesday's tempest," *Literary Digest* (November 1, 1924): 5.

61. Hadley Cantril, a Princeton University psychologist, wrote in the *New York Times* as the campaign neared its end: "The excitement centered around public-opinion polls has reached a new high in the current campaign. Dozens of polls, both local and national, are whetting the voter's political appetite." See Cantril, "Straw votes this year show contrary winds," *New York Times* (October 25, 1936): E3.

62. "Politics," *Chicago Tribune* (November 1, 1936): 9B.

63. See, for example, John M. Cummings, "U.S. election seen closest since '16 race," *Philadelphia Inquirer* (November 1, 1936): 1.

64. Cole R. Morgan, "Biggest vote in U.S. history seen in nip and tuck election," *New York American* (November 1, 1936): 1.

65. William Lyon Phelps, "Election Day," *Washington Post* (November 3, 1936): X9.

66. Arthur Krock, "Republican comeback brings memories of 1930," *New York Times* (September 18, 1936): 22. Krock also estimated that the Republicans "will poll a far larger popular and electoral vote than in 1932," when Herbert Hoover lost overwhelmingly to Roosevelt.

67. David Lawrence, "Nine uncertain states hold key to election on Tuesday," *New York Sun* (October 31, 1936): 6.

68. Crossley, "Straw polls in 1936," *Public Opinion Quarterly,* 24. Crossley also wrote about the lunchtime predictions in an article for Hearst's *New York American*; see Archibald M. Crossley, "Poll experts concede Landon victory with electoral votes,"

New York American (October 26, 1936): 4. Crossley did not disclose the identities of the other diners beyond describing them as "open-minded men, exceptionally well-informed about the background and 'inside' of the polls, their own as well as their rivals'."

69. See Arthur Sears Henning, "Doubt clouds election; party lines twisted," *Chicago Tribune* (November 1, 1936): 8A. Henning further wrote: "This criss-crossing of party lines through which is discerned a definite tendency of conservatives to gravitate to the Republican party and of radicals of every shade to flock together under the banner of New Deal is the seat of the difficulty in forecasting the outcome of the election. The old party landmarks are missing on every side, and what will come out of the confusion of allegiances is anybody's guess."

70. See "Party bolters," *Literary Digest* (October 10, 1936): 9.

71. See Hall, "National straw vote season nearing end," *Los Angeles Times*, 2.

72. Crossley, "Straw polls in 1936," *Public Opinion Quarterly*, 24.

73. See "Our poll is O.K.—what price Pennsylvania?" *Literary Digest* (November 26, 1932): 6.

74. "'Digest' poll machinery speeding up," *Literary Digest* (29 August 1936): 5. The *Digest* was occasionally criticized for its self-congratulatory comments. The *Miami Herald*, for example, said after the 1924 campaign, "One of the worst features of the election is the way The Literary Digest will crow about its straw ballot." Quoted in "Accuracy of 'The Digest's' big poll," *Literary Digest* (November 22, 1924): 12.

75. See "Press bouquets for 'The Digest's' straw vote," *Literary Digest* (November 17, 1928): 9.

76. Cited in "Press bouquets," *Literary Digest*.

77. This estimate is in Gary L. Britton's doctoral thesis. See Britton, "A History of Some Recent Applications of Survey Sampling for Human Populations," Ph.D. dissertation, University of Northern Colorado (Summer 1983), 117.

78. Gallup claimed that the *Digest* in 1936 "failed to catch the move of political sentiment toward Roosevelt in the last stages of the campaign." See Gallup and Rae, *The Pulse of Democracy*, 49.

79. "How the Digest Poll came out," *Literary Digest* (November 19, 1932): 6. The magazine noted: "The straw vote showed Hoover leading in Massachusetts, Rhode Island, and New Jersey, which went for Roosevelt on Election Day, and showed Roosevelt leading in Pennsylvania and Delaware, which went for Hoover. These errors almost balanced."

80. The *Digest* oversampled Republicans in every state in 1928, for example.

81. "What went wrong with the polls?" *Literary Digest* (November 14, 1936): 7.

82. "What went wrong with the polls?" *Literary Digest*, 8. Researchers Sharon L. Lohr and J. Michael Brick noted, "A large part of the reason that the *Literary Digest* chose not to weight the results was that the unweighted results had worked well for the 1932 and 1928 elections." See Lohr and Brick, "Roosevelt predicted to win: Revisiting the 1936 *Literary Digest* poll," *Statistics, Politics and Policy* 8, 1 (2017): 73.

83. The *Digest* said in 1924 that "the cost of these huge polls . . . is more than met through new subscriptions, increased newsstand sales, wide-spread publicity and advertising." See "Accuracy of 'The Digest's' big poll," *Literary Digest*, 13.

84. Archibald Crossley, letter to Charlton R. Price (March 17, 1949): Crossley papers.

85. "Digest overhauled," *Time* (July 10, 1933): 32.

86. See "Digested Digest," *Time* (June 28, 1937): 48.

87. See Edward Price Bell, "'Nobody in Germany wants war'—Hitler," *Literary Digest* (May 11, 1935): 11. The first paragraph of Bell's article referred to Hitler's "violet-tinged eyes and rugged features."

88. Although Bell was a veteran journalist, he seemed inclined to take the dictators at their word. For example, Bell began his article about Mussolini this way: "'*I will not break the peace.*' Signor Mussolini lifts his eyes—large, luminous dark eyes, now softened by much thought—from a piece of paper on which some questions are written, and fixes them on his visitor. '*I will not break the peace*' he repeats, uttering the words clearly and slowly in English, and continuing to hold his eyes steadily on his visitor, as if watching to see the statement sink in." Edward Price Bell, "Mussolini vows not to break the peace," *Literary Digest* (April 27, 1935): 11.

89. Arthur S. Draper, letter to Edward Price Bell (April 25, 1935); Edward Price Bell papers, Newberry Library, Chicago. Atop the letter, which Draper wrote on *Literary Digest* letterhead, Bell typed, "I did 39,000 miles in Europe, Asia, and America for this editor and this magazine." He fell seriously ill in Asia while on the assignment.

90. "Editor's afterthoughts," *Time* (November 16, 1936): 85.

91. See "Savell quits Literary Digest; refuses to blame straw poll," *Brooklyn Eagle* (October 3, 1936): 1. See also "Lurton is Digest M.E.," *Editor and Publisher* (October 17, 1936): 54.

92. On the Democrats' response to the *Digest*'s poll, see Franklyn Waltman, "Literary Digest poll indicating Landon as victor, makes Democrats uneasy," *Washington Post* (October 16, 1936): X2. Waltman wrote: "The one fly in the Democratic cup of joy and cheer at this time is the Literary Digest poll, which indicates Gov. Alf M. Landon as the victor in the Presidential contest. Even though they publicly scoff at the Digest figures, many Democratic leaders feel uneasy over them. The thought that constantly haunts them is that the Digest polls have never failed to indicate the trend."

93. James A. Hagerty, "Hope in Landon camp," *New York Times* (November 1, 1936): E4. Hagerty also wrote, "Intimate friends of Governor Landon admit privately that if he should be elected it will be by a narrow margin." Three years after the election, syndicated columnist Raymond Clapper wrote about a dinner conversation in New York with an aide to Landon who had spent the afternoon at the *Digest*'s offices, "inspecting the work sheets behind that poll which showed that Governor Landon would be elected easily over Mr. Roosevelt. This Landon adviser was convinced that the Literary Digest poll was correct." See Clapper, "Straw votes disturb politicians,"

Syracuse Journal (November 20, 1939): 16. Biographer Donald R. McCoy described Clapper as "one of Landon's closest newspaper friends." See McCoy, *Landon of Kansas* (Lincoln: University of Nebraska, 1966), 328.

94. The *Tribune* asserted in a front-page editorial that Election Day 1936 would be "the most fateful day in the history of the American people. Do not consider that statement an exaggeration. If Landon is not elected you may have seen the last of free government as you have known it. . . . Roosevelt can be snowed under if the people are aroused to save their country." See "An editorial: Paul Revere must ride again," *Chicago Tribune* (November 2, 1936): 1.

95. Henning, "Doubt clouds election," *Chicago Tribune*.

96. Frank R. Kent, "The great game of politics: Swope's Law," *Baltimore Sun* (October 25, 1936): 1.

97. "Landon's victory predicted with 320 electoral votes; Democrats claim 46 states," *New York American* (November 2, 1936): 1.

98. See "Hamilton holds a landslide sure," *New York Times* (October 31, 1936): 2.

99. Hamilton said in the interview he told Landon he would win only five states but he named six states when asked to name them. They were Maine, Vermont, North Dakota, South Dakota, Nebraska, and Kansas. See "Typescript of interview with John D. M. Hamilton" (November 22, 1966): John D. M. Hamilton papers, Manuscript Division, Library of Congress, Washington, DC.

100. See McCoy, *Landon of Kansas*, 277 n.27.

101. [Victor Anderson,] "Observations of the campaign," undated typescript: 40: Landon papers.

102. See Sheppard, *The Buying of the Presidency?* 195, 198.

103. See Sheppard, *The Buying of the Presidency?* 197.

104. "A bad year for straw polls," *Philadelphia Inquirer* (November 6, 1936): 8.

105. "The battle of the straw men," *New York Herald Tribune*. See also Arthur Ross, "Shop talk at thirty," *Editor and Publisher* (November 7, 1936): 48. "The *Literary Digest's* reputation for infallibility took an awful licking," Ross wrote.

106. Quoted in "Digest editor is astonished," *Santa Ana* [CA] *Daily Evening Register* (November 5, 1936): 1.

107. Quoted in "Digest to seek reason for failure of poll," *New York Times* (November 4, 1936): 4.

108. "What went wrong with the polls?" *Literary Digest*, 7. Emphasis in the original.

109. Critics such as Dominic Lusinchi have noted that the conventional explanation was "mere conjecture." See Lusinchi, "'President' Landon and the 1936 *Literary Digest* poll," *Social Science History*, 33.

110. On this point, see Lusinchi, "'President' Landon and the 1936 *Literary Digest* poll," *Social Science History*, 24–25.

111. Gallup and Rae, *The Pulse of Democracy*, 64.

112. Claude E. Robinson, "Digest's polls fail to portray clear picture," *Washington Post* (September 14, 1936): X9.

113. Harold F. Gosnell, "How accurate were the polls?" *Public Opinion Quarterly* 1, 1 (January 1937): 103.

114. Quoted in "Farley to finish his cabinet term," *New York Times* (November 5, 1936): 2.

115. "What went wrong with the polls?" *Literary Digest*, 7.

116. "What went wrong with the polls?" *Literary Digest*, 7.

117. See George Gallup, "Science and journalism partners in second year of polls," *Washington Post* (December 27, 1936): B1.

118. George Gallup, "Government and the sampling referendum," *Journal of the American Statistical Association* 33, 201 (March 1938): 139.

119. Ross, "Shop talk at thirty," *Editor and Publisher*.

120. Crossley, "Straw polls in 1936," *Public Opinion Quarterly*, 27.

121. Crossley, "Straw polls in 1936," *Public Opinion Quarterly*, 28.

122. Bryson, "The Literary Digest poll," *American Statistician*, 184–185.

123. Bryson, "The Literary Digest poll," *American Statistician*, 185.

124. Peverill Squire, "Why the 1936 *Literary Digest* poll failed," *Public Opinion Quarterly* 52, 1 (Spring 1988): 125–133.

125. Squire, "Why the 1936 *Literary Digest* poll failed," *Public Opinion Quarterly*, 129. Among the shortcomings of the 1937 Gallup poll, Squire wrote, was that it overrepresented the percentage of owners of telephones and automobiles and overstated the number of people who had received a mail ballot from the *Digest* and returned it. Moreover, the polling methodology Gallup used then was quota sampling, which is not a probabilistic methodology.

126. See Squire, "Why the 1936 *Literary Digest* poll failed," *Public Opinion Quarterly*, 130. Squire's conclusion (131) was a bit muddled, in that he blamed the *Digest*'s mailing list *and* response-related problems for having "produced the wildly erroneous forecast" in 1936.

127. Lusinchi, "'President' Landon and the 1936 *Literary Digest* poll," *Social Science History*, 44.

128. Lusinchi, "'President' Landon and the 1936 *Literary Digest* poll," *Social Science History*, 38.

129. Lusinchi, "'President' Landon and the 1936 *Literary Digest* poll," *Social Science History*, 45.

130. "Farley sees 46 states 'safe' for Roosevelt," *New York American* (November 2, 1936): 4. Chapin Hall of the *Los Angeles Times* reported after the 1936 election that Farley "told me last March, four months before the conventions, that the result was 'in the bag' and that Roosevelt would be re-elected by a greater popular and electoral vote than in 1932," which he was. See Chapin Hall, "Farley beat all polls in predicting result," *Los Angeles Times* (November 5, 1936): 7. See also Farley's account in his memoir, *Behind the Ballots: The Personal History of a Politician* (New York: Harcourt, Brace, 1938), 324–326.

131. See Gosnell, "How accurate were the polls?" *Public Opinion Quarterly*, 100. The *New York Times* declared, "Farley's was the only accurate prophesy of the election."

See Arthur Krock, "History's largest poll," *New York Times* (November 5, 1936): 2. A few days after the election, Farley received a letter from an admirer in Sea Cliff, NY, who wrote, tongue in cheek: "How much is a subscription to your political forecasting service? I have been paying the Literary Digest four Dollars ($4) per annum, and this year I didn't get my money's worth. I am thinking of making a change." See M. A. Workman, letter to James A. Farley (November 5, 1936): O.F. 300, 1936 campaign: general, Roosevelt papers.

132. To take one example, John J. Cochran, a Missouri congressman, reported, "The consensus of opinion of well informed people, including newspaper men who can be looked upon as capable of analyzing the situation, warrants the statement that the President will carry Missouri by a majority estimated anywhere between 200,000 to 300,000 votes." Roosevelt won the state by more than 400,000 votes. Cochran's estimate is in the file titled "Democratic National Committee," O.F. 300, box 40, Roosevelt papers.

133. Frank R. Kent, "The great game of politics: Policing the polls," *Baltimore Sun* (November 24, 1936): 4.

134. "A bad year for straw polls," *Philadelphia Inquirer*.

135. "Straw ballots," *New York Times* (November 13, 1936): 22.

136. "They will never be missed," *New York Times* (November 6, 1936): 24.

137. "What went wrong with the polls?" *Literary Digest*, 8.

138. That figure was quoted by *Time* magazine in its report about the *Digest*'s sale. See "Digested Digest," *Time*.

139. "Literary Digest acquired by Time," *New York Times* (May 12, 1938): 21.

140. George Gallup said years after the magazine ceased publication that "it's pretty naïve to believe that the *Literary Digest* went out of business because of its wrong prediction in 1936. It was going out of business long before the 1936 prediction. What killed the *Literary Digest* was an upstart magazine called *Time*." Quoted in Gideon Seymour and others, "Should public opinion polls make election forecasts? A symposium," *Journalism Quarterly* 26, 2 (June 1949): 142. Nonetheless, the notion has endured that predictive failure in 1936 killed off the *Digest*.

141. "The Digest marches off," *New York Times* (May 14, 1938): 14.

142. Quoted in "Thanks," *Literary Digest* (July 17, 1937): 7.

143. Quoted in "Old Digest ghost in stiches; science, ha! laughs ex-editor," *Washington Post* (November 4, 1948): 13.

3. 'THE DEFEAT OF THE POLLSTERS'

1. See, for example, Kathleen A. Frankovic, "AAPOR and the polls," in Paul B. Sheatsley and Warren J. Mitofsky, eds., *A Meeting Place: The History of the American Association for Public Opinion Research* (Ann Arbor, MI: AAPOR, 1992), 122. Frankovic wrote: "None of the 1948 polls continued surveying during the closing days of the campaign. Roper, in fact, ceased polling on the election in September, assuming a Dewey victory a foregone conclusion and not wishing to continue calling the 'horse

race.'" Haynes Johnson, a veteran political columnist for the *Washington Post*, declared in 1984 that, early in the 1948 campaign, Roper "had decided to discontinue polling because he believed Republican Thomas E. Dewey already had won the election." See Johnson, "Some fighting words for 'Poor Fritz' from 'Give 'em Hell' Harry," *Washington Post* (September 9, 1984): A2. See also Richard Harwood, "Conflicting campaign polls point to one certainty: Some are wrong," *Washington Post* (October 31, 1984): A6. Harwood wrote that "pollsters in 1948 decided early that Thomas E. Dewey would win and stopped polling in the final weeks."

2. Elmo Roper, *Where the People Stand*, script of CBS radio program (September 19, 1948): Box 38, folder 2388, Elmo Roper papers, Thomas J. Dodd Research Center, University of Connecticut, Storrs.

3. Roper's unpublished poll results were discussed in a post-election report by a committee of the Social Science Research Council. See "Processing, estimating, and adjustment of survey data," in Frederick Mosteller and others, *The Pre-election Polls of 1948: Report to the Committee on Analysis of Pre-election Polls and Forecasts* (New York: Social Science Research Council, 1949), 201–203. Roper's poll was conducted from October 25 to 28, 1948.

4. "This seems to be a hazardous way to arrive at accuracy," one analyst later wrote. See Charles W. Smith Jr., "Measurement of voter attitude," *Annals of the American Academy of Political and Social Science* 283 (September 1952): 150.

5. "These talks were largely rewritten versions" of Roper's columns in the *New York Herald Tribune*, a report by the Social Science Research Council pointed out. See Leonard W. Doob, "The public presentation of polling results," in Mosteller and others, *The Pre-election Polls of 1948*, 31.

6. Elmo Roper, *Where the People Stand*, script of CBS radio program (September 12, 1948), Roper papers. See also Doob, "The public presentation of polling results," 52.

7. Roper, *Where the People Stand*, script of CBS radio program (September 12, 1948), Roper papers.

8. Cited in "The Press: Back at the old stand," *Time* (October 6, 1952): 67.

9. Research in the 1940s tended to support the argument that the rhetoric of political campaigns had little effect on voters and decision-making. See, for example, Paul F. Lazarsfeld, "The election is over," *Public Opinion Quarterly* 8, 3 (Autumn 1944): 317–330. Lazarsfeld wrote (317), "In an important sense, modern Presidential campaigns are over before they begin." He likened (330) campaigns to "the chemical bath which develops a photograph. The chemical influence is necessary to bring out the picture, but only the picture pre-structured on the plate can come out."

10. Elmo Roper, "Poll unchanged by campaign, Roper still sees a Dewey sweep," *New York Herald Tribune* (November 1, 1948): 1, 2.

11. After the 1948 debacle, Crossley conceded: "We were perhaps lulled into believing that campaigns do not change or add votes. And yet looking back on some of our own figures, we see that is not entirely the case." Quoted in Gideon Seymour and others, "Should public opinion polls make election forecasts? A symposium," *Journalism Quarterly* 26, 2 (June 1949): 135–136.

12. "Final Crossley Poll summary" (October 29, 1948): Archibald M. Crossley papers, Thomas J. Dodd Research Center, University of Connecticut, Storrs.

13. See "Gallup defends polls," *New York Times* (October 28, 1948): 22.

14. George Gallup, "Final poll gives Dewey 49.5%, Truman 44.5% of popular vote," *Washington Post* (November 1, 1948): 1.

15. Gallup's combining the final two polls was described in Mosteller and others, *The Pre-Election Polls of 1948*, 217–218.

16. "For President," *Miami Herald* (November 1, 1948): 6A.

17. See David McCullough, *Truman* (New York: Simon & Schuster, 1992), 584.

18. See Zachary Karabell, *The Last Campaign: How Harry Truman Won the 1948 Election* (New York: Knopf, 2000), 200. Karabell quoted this advice offered by Bruce Barton, one of Dewey's image consultants: "I'd rather have ten marvelous speeches by a rested and confident candidate, all carefully planned for the radio and the newsreels, than a thousand back platform chats any one of which could produce an embarrassing slip."

19. George Van Slyke, "Dewey expected to win 32 states," *New York Sun* (November 1, 1948): 1.

20. "Will Truman ask Dewey to co-operate with him?" *Detroit Free Press* (November 2, 1948).

21. Fred Othman, "A fond farewell to Harry Truman," *Washington Daily News* (November 2, 1948): 21.

22. *Kiplinger Washington Letter* (October 30, 1948): Box 21, folder 1212, Crossley papers.

23. Drew Pearson, "Lineup of the Dewey 'team,'" *Washington Post* (November 3, 1948): B15. Six days after the election, Pearson seemed to grovel; he addressed Truman in his column, writing, "Although I was wrong in predicting your defeat, I am glad that I was wrong. And after that grand fight you put up, and regardless of any name you may have called me, I don't know anyone I would rather eat humble pie for than a good sport and a great battler like you." See Pearson, "A greater victory than FDR's," *Washington Post* (November 8, 1948): 15.

24. They included the *Louisville Courier Journal*, the *Altoona* [PA] *Tribune*, and the *Oneonta* [NY] *Star*. Other subscribing newspapers published the column with notes appended, explaining the column had been written and set in type before the election results were definitive. These newspapers included the *Portsmouth* [NH] *Herald*, the *McComb* [MS] *Enterprise-Journal*, the *Wilmington* [CA] *Press-Journal*, and the *Post-Register* of Idaho Falls, ID. The *Press-Journal* splashed Pearson's column on its front page, beneath a headline that read, "Just how wrong can they be . . .?" The *Post-Register* said in its note that "Pearson apparently took the word of the pollsters prior to the election in expecting a Dewey victory."

25. "Plays on politix," *Eugene* [OR] *Register-Guard* (November 5, 1948): 1. See also "The crow eaters," *Newsweek* (November 15, 1948): 56.

26. "Election forecast: 50 political experts predict a GOP sweep," *Newsweek* (October 11, 1948): 20.

27. Quoted in Morris L. Ernst and David Loth, *The People Know Best: The Ballots vs. the Polls* (Washington, DC: Public Affairs Press, 1949), 93.

28. Frank R. Kent, "Today a miracle could happen, but—," *Baltimore Sun* (November 2, 1948): A4.

29. Joseph and Stewart Alsop, "Flying dual control," *Washington Post* (November 3, 1948): 15.

30. Sam Stavisky, "'Persistence' is the dominating trait that carried Dewey to the presidency," *Washington Post* (November 3, 1948): 2.

31. Earl Wilson, "Oh, I'd rather be right than be Gallup or Roper," *New York Post* (November 4, 1948): 34.

32. Jennings Perry, "It's closer than you think," *New York Star* (October 26, 1948): 15.

33. Paul Gallico, "Thinking aloud: Thoughts on Election Day morning," *New York Journal-American* (November 2, 1948): 14. In his career, Gallico was a columnist, sportswriter, screenwriter, and novelist. Among his works was *The Poseidon Adventure*.

34. See, for example, Jay Richter, "Who'll win November elections? Here's crystal ball that works," *Wilmington* [OH] *News-Journal* (August 6, 1948): D2.

35. See Louis H. Bean, *How to Predict Elections* (New York: Knopf, 1948), 162. Bean wrote that "numerous signs at the end of 1947 point to another presidential term for the Democrats, the fifth in succession since 1928."

36. See "Expert's poll challenges Dewey cinch," *Mexico* [MO] *Ledger* (October 7, 1948): 3.

37. Fred Gutheim, "The 'Bean Poll' was right," *New York Herald Tribune* (November 7, 1948): A1.

38. Elmo Roper, letter to George Cornish (November 16, 1948): Box 5, folder 294, Roper papers.

39. "The seers: Up the Bean Poll," *Newsweek* (November 15, 1948): 39.

40. Quoted in Theodore Rosenof, "The legend of Louis Bean: Political prophesy and the 1948 election," *Historian* 62, 1 (October 2007): 72. "Thus in the end, however hesitatingly, Bean accepted the polls that consistently showed Dewey ahead nationally as they overrode his hopes and his own earlier analyses and projections," Rosenof wrote.

41. Eric Pace, "Louis H. Bean, 98, analyst best known for 1948 prediction," *New York Times* (August 8, 1994): B7.

42. J. Howard McGrath, telegram to Archibald M. Crossley (October 29, 1948): Box 21, folder 1205, Crossley papers. McGrath also argued that Crossley's estimates that Wallace and Thurmond would together get 4.9 percent of the popular vote were too generous and said that Truman was likely to win most of the "undecided" vote.

43. Archibald M. Crossley, telegram to J. Howard McGrath (November 1, 1948): Box 21, folder 1205, Crossley papers.

44. Quoted in "M'Grath calls on Gallup to adjust poll," *Salt Lake Tribune* (October 29, 1948): 2. The article was an Associated Press report.

45. Quoted in Anthony Leviero, "Truman accuses GOP of using polls to mislead public," *New York Times* (October 27, 1948): 1, 20. Truman also said that most people

weren't fooled by "sleeping polls." They know, he said, "that sleeping polls are bad for the system. They affect the mind. An overdose could be fatal."

46. Quoted in "Truman confident of a big victory," *New York Times* (October 30, 1948): 7.

47. See George McKee Elsey, *Unplanned Life: A Memoir* (Columbia: University of Missouri Press, 2005), 170. Elsey said Truman's prediction was made almost on the spur of the moment, while aboard the campaign train in Minnesota. "I was alone with Truman going over material for future whistle-stop talks," Elsey wrote. "He interrupted and told me to start writing. He began rattling off the names of the forty-eight states (Alaska and Hawaii were still territories). Knowing by heart the number of electoral votes for each state, he told me where to put them on the sheet I marked in columns for Truman, Dewey, Wallace, Thurmond, and Doubtful. When he'd finished, he asked, 'George, how many do I have?' Quickly adding, I answered, "340, Mr. President." For his part, Elsey conceded (171), "I thought Truman would lose" and receive only 219 electoral votes to Dewey's 270. John Franklin Carter, a journalist who joined the Truman campaign as a speechwriter and worked with Elsey, predicted the president would win twenty-seven states and 278 electoral votes. Carter did so in a newspaper article published three days before the election under the pseudonym "Jay Franklin." See Jay Franklin, "Truman election still forecast," *Decatur* [IL] *Herald* (October 30, 1948): 6.

48. See H. V. Kaltenborn, *Fifty Fabulous Years, 1900–1950: A Personal Review* (New York: Putman, 1950), 297. Kaltenborn noted that "while celebrating his election . . . at an Electoral College banquet, Harry S. Truman singled me out, and in a genial, laugh-provoking speech, gave an excellent imitation of my voice, diction, and comment" about Dewey's likely victory. "Such a rare distinction was hardly deserved," Kaltenborn added. "One might think I was the only one who had predicted Mr. Truman's defeat."

49. See "Election headlines," *Washington Post* (November 4, 1948): 17. One of the *Post*'s "extra" edition headlines read: "Presidential race is so close House may pick the winner; Democrats capture Congress."

50. See Marshall Andrews, "Truman declines invitation to be guest at 'crow banquet,'" *Washington Post* (November 5, 1948): 1.

51. Harold I. Gullan wrote in his book about the Truman-Dewey race: "Our collective memory of the 1948 presidential campaign as well as Harry Truman himself is captured by that photograph." See Gullan, *The Upset That Wasn't: Harry S. Truman and the Crucial Election of 1948* (Chicago: Ivan R. Dee, 1998), vii.

52. McCullough, *Truman*, 718.

53. Quoted in Ernest Leiser, "Blames pollsters for Dewey 'scoop,'" *New York Post* (November 4, 1948): 42. The publisher was further quoted as saying, "What do you suppose Dr. Gallup is going to do?"

54. Cited in Wilson, "Oh, I'd rather be right than be Gallup or Roper," *New York Post.*

55. See J. Y. Smith, "Post columnist Bill Gold dies," *Washington Post* (January 27, 1997): B1.

56. Bill Gold, "The District Line: Some second thoughts on the election," *Washington Post* (November 5, 1948): C8.

57. See Hal Boyle (Associated Press), "Pollster gags continuing at a dime a dozen," *Decatur* [IL] *Review* (November 6, 1948): 3. Boyle wrote that "horrible puns . . . are springing up like dandelions."

58. See H. I. Phillips, "The Sun Dial," *New York Sun* (November 5, 1948): 21.

59. "No more Gallup," *Chicago Daily News* (November 16, 1948): 14. The editorial also stated that the newspaper's editors had determined before the election that "polls had taken on an aura of scientific accuracy that they did not deserve. Their abysmal errors in election forecasting merely clinched the case."

60. Quoted in "Gallup tries again," *Akron Beacon Journal* (August 19, 1952): 6.

61. "Paper gives up the Gallup Poll," [Marshall, TX] *News Messenger* (November 14, 1948): 4.

62. "We've sworn off," *Pittsburgh Post-Gazette* (November 5, 1948): 10.

63. Net income data were contained in a memorandum to Elmo Roper dated August 3, 1951: Box 8, folder 454, Roper papers. A sum of $77,300 in 1948 was equivalent to $821,000 in 2019; a sum of $18,300 in 1949 was equivalent to $196,900 in 2019.

64. "Bad day for the pollsters," *Washington Evening Star* (November 4, 1948): A16.

65. "A lesson for all in fall-down of election polls," *Philadelphia Inquirer* (November 4, 1948): 20. The *Inquirer* editorial also said the polls were "so glaringly and spectacularly wrong as to raise fundamental questions about their value for any purpose."

66. "How did you forecast it?" *Bakersfield Californian* (November 3, 1948): 36.

67. "The defeated pollsters," *Newark Star-Ledger* (November 5, 1948): 18.

68. Marquis W. Childs, "The state of the nation by Marquis Childs," *New York Post* (November 4, 1948): 56.

69. Reprinted in E. B. White, *Writings from the New Yorker: 1925–1976* (New York: HarperCollins, 1990), 60.

70. Frederic C. Othman, "Gallup and Roper can help me eat my boiled crow," *Washington Daily News* (November 3, 1948): 35.

71. "An invitation to the President," *Washington Post* (November 4, 1948): 1. George Gallup joined in the banter, telling the publisher of the *Post*, Philip Graham, that he would bring his own crow to such a banquet. Gallup added in a telegram to Graham, "In our business we could undoubtedly use Mr. Truman's forecasting ability, but since he has another position for the next four years I would personally like to present a bouquet to him at your eat-crow dinner." See "Gallup offered to bring own crow to banquet," *Washington Post* (November 5, 1948): 3.

72. Edward T. Folliard, "Truman's defeat by wide margin seen; 51-million vote expected," *Washington Post* (November 2, 1948): 1.

73. "Let 'em eat turkey—HST," *Washington Post* (November 7, 1948): 1.

74. Cited in Edward T. Folliard, "President is greeted by crowd of 750,000," *Washington Post* (November 6, 1948): 1. The "dominant note" of the huge turnout, Folliard reported, "was affection—affection and admiration. It was a warm and happy salute to a gallant fighter who had everything against him but the people."

75. Elmo Roper, "Correcting the error," *New York Herald Tribune* (November 4, 1948): 29. See also "Election prophets ponder in dismay," *New York Times* (November 4, 1948): 8. Roper speculated, tentatively, that Truman's relentless campaign assaults on the Republican-controlled Eightieth Congress had been a factor in the surprise outcome.

76. Elmo Roper, *Where People Stand*, script of CBS radio program (November 7, 1948): 7: Roper papers.

77. Roper, *Where People Stand* script (November 7, 1948), Roper papers.

78. Archibald Crossley, letter to John R. Buckley (November 18, 1948): Box 21, folder 1209 Crossley papers.

79. Archibald Crossley, undated memorandum: Box 21, folder 1215, Crossley papers.

80. Archibald Crossley, letter to Roy S. Frothingham (January 7, 1949): Box 21, folder 1209, Crossley papers. Frothingham was president of Facts Consolidated, a market research firm in San Francisco.

81. Archibald Crossley, letter to Alfred M. Lee (January 4, 1949): Box 21, folder 1209, Crossley papers.

82. Archibald Crossley, "The public wants," unpublished manuscript, 1969: Box 29, Crossley papers.

83. Phyllis L. Gillis, typescript notes of interview with George Gallup (May 14, 1980): Series 2, box 1, Gallup Organization Papers, University of Iowa special collections, Iowa City.

84. Gillis, typescript notes of interview with Gallup (May 14, 1980), Gallup Organization Papers.

85. See George Gallup, "Why we won't be red-faced this time!" *Cosmopolitan* (November 1951): 99.

86. "The great fiasco," *Time* (November 15, 1948): 66. The *New York Herald Tribune* also called attention to Gallup's spinning, saying, "It is apparent . . . that the poll-takers have laid claim to a degree of accuracy they do not achieve."

87. See "The red-faced pollsters," *New York Herald Tribune* (November 5, 1948): 26.

88. George Gallup, "Answering the poll critics," text of speech delivered December 29, 1948, Cleveland, OH: bound volume, Gallup Organization Papers.

89. Gillis, typescript notes of interview with Gallup (May 14, 1980), Gallup Organization Papers.

90. George Gallup, remarks on NBC's *Meet the Press* program (November 14, 1948); recording retrieved from Moving Image Research Center, Library of Congress, Washington, DC.

91. Script of NBC radio program *Living 1948* (November 7, 1948): Gallup Organization Papers.

92. H. M. Beville Jr., letter to George Gallup (December 2, 1948): Series 13, box 6, Gallup Organization Papers. Beville was NBC's director of research.

93. Elmo Roper, letter to Paul Garrett (November 22, 1948): Box 5, Roper papers.

94. Archibald Crossley, "Notes on forecasting for Babson speech" (May 5, 1949): Box 21, folder 1209, Crossley papers.

95. "Situation wanted," *Time* (November 8, 1948): 25.

96. "What happened?" *Time* (November 15, 1948): 64.

97. Edward R. Murrow, script of *E. R. Murrow and the News*, CBS radio (November 5, 1948): scrapbook for 1948, Roper papers.

98. Quoted in "Editor lauds, blasts role of newspapers in election," *Bakersfield* [CA] *Californian* (November 12, 1948): 24. The article said Roberts was unable to attend the convention and his speech was read for him by the *Kansas City Star*'s news editor.

99. James Reston, "Why forecasts erred" (letters), *New York Times* (November 4, 1948): 28.

100. Reston, "Why forecasts erred," *New York Times*.

101. James Reston, *Deadline: A Memoir* (New York: Random House, 1991), 261.

102. Frank Conniff, "East Side, West Side: The professional forecasters," *New York Journal-American* (November 5, 1948): 25.

103. Richard H. Rovere, "Letter from a campaign train: En route with Dewey," *New Yorker* (October 16, 1948): 80–81.

104. Richard H. Rovere, "Letter from a campaign train: En route with Truman," *New Yorker* (October 9, 1948): 69.

105. Rovere, "Letter from a campaign train: En route with Truman," 71.

106. Rovere, "Letter from a campaign train: En route with Dewey," 79.

107. "What happened?" *Time*, 66. Nevertheless, the *Time* article stated, "the fact that the press had so misinterpreted events right under its nose raises the grave question of whether it was doing an equally bad job in interpreting news in other fields than politics."

108. See James Reston, "Why forecasts erred," *Editor and Publisher* (November 6, 1948): 5.

109. Don Hollenbeck, script of *CBS Views the Press* (November 13, 1948): Box 5, folder 269, Roper papers.

110. Peter Odegard, "Review of *The Pre-Election Polls of 1948* and *The Poll and Public Opinion*," *American Political Science Review* 44, 2 (June 1950): 462.

111. Mosteller and others, *The Pre-Election Polls of 1948*, viii.

112. Committee on the Analysis of Pre-election Polls and Forecasts of the Social Science Research Council, "Report on the analysis of pre-election polls and forecasts," *Public Opinion Quarterly* 12, 4 (Winter 1948–1949): 611.

113. The Princeton Election Consortium pegged Clinton's "win probability" at 98–99 percent. See Sam Wang, "All estimates point toward HRC >50% probability," Princeton Election Consortium, posted November 6, 2016, at: http://election.princeton.edu/2016/11/06/is-99-a-reasonable-probability/#more-18522. The *Huffington Post* pegged the probability of Clinton's election victory at 98 percent. See Natalie Jackson and Adam Hooper, "Forecast: President," *Huffington Post*, posted November 8, 2016, at: http://elections.huffingtonpost.com/2016/forecast/president

114. Committee on the Analysis of Pre-election Polls, "Report on the analysis of pre-election polls and forecasts," *Public Opinion Quarterly*, 609.

115. Committee on the Analysis of Pre-election Polls, "Report on the analysis of pre-election polls and forecasts," *Public Opinion Quarterly*, 609.

116. Courtney Kennedy and others, "An evaluation of 2016 election polls in the United States," American Association for Public Opinion Research (May 4, 2017), 2–3, 38; accessed May 5, 2017, at: https://www.aapor.org/Education-Resources /Reports/An-Evaluation-of-2016-Election-Polls-in-the-U-S.aspx

117. Committee on the Analysis of Pre-election Polls, "Report on the analysis of pre-election polls and forecasts," *Public Opinion Quarterly*, 610.

118. Committee on the Analysis of Pre-election Polls, "Report on the analysis of pre-election polls and forecasts," *Public Opinion Quarterly*, 601.

119. Committee on the Analysis of Pre-election Polls, "Report on the analysis of pre-election polls and forecasts," 602–603.

120. Quota sampling "is a method of representative random sampling," L. John Martin noted in 1984, "but it puts too much emphasis on 'representative' and not enough on 'random.'" See Martin, "The genealogy of public opinion polling," *Annals of the American Academy of Political and Social Science* 472 (March 1984): 21.

121. Archibald Crossley, letter to W. Edwards Deming (April 1, 1949): Crossley papers. He noted: "On some jobs we have very definite time limitations, and it is impossible for us within that limit to get a high percentage completion on individuals," making probability sampling considerably less appealing. "I really think that most of us in the research business are not normally getting any better than 85% [completion rates] with a large number of call-backs."

122. See, for example, Daniel Katz, "The polls and the 1944 election," *Public Opinion Quarterly* 8, 4 (Winter 1944): 472–473. In practice, Katz wrote, the quota-control method "suffers from one great source of error"—that "the selection of respondents is left in large part to the discretion of the interviewer," which often thwarted the selection of a random sample. In their 1949 book, Ernst and Loth offered this admittedly "extreme example" of an indifferent quota-control interviewer: "A young salesman employed as a poll interviewer on a part time basis (as most of them are) had to turn in his sample results before he got his pay. He would be told to get answers to a certain question from, say, a farmer, a housewife, a skilled workman in certain trades, a businessman in a certain income bracket, etc. But the pay, to his mind, hardly warranted looking up all these people. It was his common practice at the end of the month, when the questions were due, to ask fellow residents in his boarding house: 'If you were a farmer, what would be your answer?' 'If you were a working man making $4,000 a year, what would you say to this?'" See Ernst and Loth, *The People Know Best*, 117.

123. Committee on the Analysis of Pre-election Polls, "Report on the analysis of pre-election polls and forecasts," *Public Opinion Quarterly*, 609. The committee report also said of quota sampling (611–612): "These methods were known to have certain inherent weaknesses but were used again in 1948, in part because they were less costly

than the more high controlled methods that had been advocated by some sampling experts, and in part because tests of quota sampling methods had convinced the pollsters that they would work satisfactorily. . . . Past experience with quota sampling has demonstrated that it under-samples the groups having the very highest and the lowest incomes in the population."

124. See, for example, "Why pollsters erred: Asked wrong people," *New York Post* (December 27, 1948).

125. Archibald M. Crossley, "The disparity between the polls and the elections," paper prepared for conference on polling at University of Iowa, n.d.: Box 21, folder 1210, Crossley papers. Crossley also said, "Probability sampling may have been the answer" to the polling error in the 1948 election, "but unfortunately there is no proof."

126. Quoted in Norman C. Meier and Harold W. Saunders, eds., *The Polls and Public Opinion* (New York: Henry Holt, 1949), 203.

127. George Gallup, letter to Hadley Cantril (January 3, 1949): Gallup Organization Papers.

128. Quoted in Meier and Saunders, *The Polls and Public Opinion*, 288.

129. See Harold Brown, "Political pollsters turn wary," *New York Herald Tribune* (July 7, 1952): 14.

4. A TIE 'WOULD SUIT THEM FINE'

1. See "Wary pollsters put Eisenhower in lead, but find Stevenson and voters raise doubt," *New York Times* (October 31, 1952): 17.

2. Quoted in Erwin Knoll, "Polls won't be wrong; they just aren't saying," *Editor and Publisher* (November 1, 1952): 66.

3. George Gallup, "Vote results will test new poll procedures," *Los Angeles Times* (November 2, 1952): 1–20.

4. Henry McLemore, "The lighter side," *Los Angeles Times* (October 29, 1952): 28.

5. See William Henry Chamberlain, "Election retrospect," *Wall Street Journal* (November 7, 1952): 4.

6. Joe Williams, "Sports experts are bolder than political seers," *New York World-Telegram and Sun* (November 5, 1952): 38.

7. Arthur Krock, "In the nation: There are new faces among the prophets, too," *New York Times* (November 13, 1952): 30.

8. Frank Kent, "The pollsters again," *Baltimore Sun* (November 2, 1952): 14.

9. Kent, "The pollsters again," *Baltimore Sun.*

10. "The poll-takers," *Abilene [TX] Reporter-News* (October 29, 1952): 4-B.

11. McLemore, "The lighter side," *Los Angeles Times.*

12. "How pollsters plan to redeem themselves," *Business Week* (February 23, 1952): 22.

13. Quoted in "Back at the old stand," *Time* (October 6, 1952): 67. The article indirectly quoted Crossley as saying that "most of his 1948 clients are back."

14. See "Gallup tries again," *Akron Beacon Journal* (August 19, 1952): 6.

15. Archibald Crossley, "Eisenhower slightly ahead in final national poll," news release (October 31, 1952): Box 22, folder 1228, Archibald M. Crossley papers, Thomas J. Dodd Research Center, University of Connecticut, Storrs.

16. For example, Roper wrote to Stevenson following the Democratic convention in 1952, congratulating Stevenson and the Democratic party "on having secured the best available candidate for the Presidency." See Elmo Roper to Adlai Stevenson (July 30, 1952): Box 69, Adlai Stevenson papers, Seely G. Mudd Manuscript Library, Princeton University, Princeton, NJ.

17. Elmo Roper, note cards for NBC radio program (November 2, 1952): Box 39, folder 2440, Elmo Roper papers, Thomas J. Dodd Research Center, University of Connecticut, Storrs. See also script of NBC radio program (November 2, 1952): Box 39, folder 2439, Roper papers.

18. "3 pollsters cautious on vote but lean toward Eisenhower," *Baltimore Sun* (November 4, 1952): 4.

19. Elmo Roper, letter to Edward R. Murrow (January 27, 1953): Roper papers.

20. George Gallup, "Gallup finds race tight in poll's closing survey," *Los Angeles Times* (November 3, 1952): 1, 18. In a caveat that has been true for generations of pollsters, Gallup noted, "No scientific method is known today which can accurately predetermine the voting intentions of persons who are either undecided or unwilling to reveal their preference."

21. Gallup, "Gallup finds race tight," *Los Angeles Times*, 1. "In order to win," Gallup added (18), "Eisenhower must halt or reverse the present Stevenson trend and maintain his narrow margin in the crucial States."

22. See Chamberlain, "Election retrospect," *Wall Street Journal*, 4.

23. Walter Trohan, "Both parties worried; each sees victory," *Chicago Tribune* (November 2, 1952): 1.

24. Dewey L. Fleming, "Undecided voters hindering efforts to predict election," *Baltimore Sun* (November 2, 1952): 1. Whether undecided voters had not made up their minds or "are merely contemptuous of pollsters and are keeping their decisions to themselves is an interesting question," Fleming added.

25. James A. Hagerty, "Election outcome highly uncertain, survey indicates." *New York Times* (November 3, 1952): 1.

26. See Mervin D. Field, "Either-way electoral vote seen in final California Poll: Virtual tie found for top contenders," *Los Angeles Times* (November 3, 1952): 2. Field was the founder and director of the California Poll.

27. See "California vote of 91%—5,400,000—predicted," *Los Angeles Times* (October 29, 1952): 1. See also Ira Chinoy, "Battle of the Brains: Election-Night Forecasting at the Dawn of the Computer Age," PhD dissertation, University of Maryland (2010), 342–343; and Kyle Palmer, "Your guess is as good as mine," *Los Angeles Times* (November 2, 1952): B4.

28. See Field, "Either-way electoral vote seen in California," *Los Angeles Times*, 2.

29. See "3 pollsters cautious on vote but lean toward Eisenhower," *Baltimore Sun* (November 4, 1952): 4.

30. Arthur Krock, "In the nation: If it is as close as 'they' say," *New York Times* (November 4, 1952): 28.

31. Chinoy, "Battle of the Brains," 415.

32. Television was a small factor in the 1948 campaign. See Zachary Karabell, *The Last Campaign: How Harry Truman Won the 1948 Election* (New York: Knopf, 2000), 10. Karabell wrote (8) that television's emergence as a conspicuous force in the 1952 campaign "changed forever the way American politics are conducted."

33. Eisenhower's speech in Detroit on October 24, 1952, has been described as "one of the few orations in the history of presidential politics to be universally recognized not only as a key turning point in the campaign but as the rhetorical moment when the election was won." See Martin J. Medhurst, "Text and context in the 1952 Presidential campaign: Eisenhower's 'I Shall Go to Korea' speech," *Presidential Studies Quarterly* 30, 3 (September 2000): 482.

34. Chinoy, "Battle of the Brains," 379–380.

35. Eisenhower's victories in Florida, Texas, and Virginia were the first for a Republican presidential candidate in those states since the Reconstruction Era of the late nineteenth century. See John Robert Greene, *I Like Ike: The Presidential Election of 1952* (Lawrence: University Press of Kansas, 2017), 169–170.

36. In 1949, Gallup's polling anticipated the victory of Democrat Herbert H. Lehman in an election to fill a U.S. Senate seat from New York. Lehman's victory prompted Gallup to say, "I feel that now I can quit eating crow and try a little pheasant for a change." See "Happy George Gallup is eating pheasant after tiring of crow," [Blytheville, AR] *Courier News* (November 9, 1949): 1.

37. "Gallup Poll analysis of the election," advertisement in *Editor and Publisher* (November 8, 1952): 25.

38. "We're still human," *Iola* [KS] *Register* (November 11, 1952): 4.

39. See Harold Brown, "The pollsters redeem '48—a little," *New York Herald Tribune* (November 9, 1952): A5.

40. See "Newspaper election surveys beat professional pollsters," [Washington, DC] *Evening Star* (November 6, 1952): A-27. Truman in 1952 campaigned vigorously for Stevenson, who embraced most of the administration's policies.

41. Raymond Moley, "The crystal balls lie shattered," *Los Angeles Times* (November 19, 1952): A5.

42. Gladstone Williams, "Election results belie the pollsters," *Fresno* [CA] *Bee* (November 10, 1952): 22.

43. "Politics and polls," *Amsterdam* [NY] *Recorder* (November 11, 1952): in "Memory Book," box 40, David Lawrence papers, Mudd Manuscript Library, Princeton University.

44. "General Eisenhower wins," *Berkshire County* [MA] *Eagle* (November 5, 1952): 22.

45. Larry Wolters, "Television news and views," *Chicago Tribune* (November 6, 1952): part 5, p. 6.

46. "Polls prove absolutely worthless," [Huron, SD] *Huronite and Plainsman* (November 7, 1952): in "Memory Book," Lawrence papers.

47. "What happened to the pollsters?" *Troy* [NY] *Record* (November 6, 1952): 16.

48. Willis A. Overholser, "Worthless polls," *Chicago Tribune* (November 8, 1952): 11.

49. Frank J. Albus, letter to the editor, "Bridge for Gallup?" *Washington Post* (November 10, 1952): 8. The *Los Angeles Times* published a reader's letter that suggested dropping articles about polls "as meaningless nonsense" and instead "devote the space to something constructive," such as more of the work of Bruce Russell, the newspaper's political cartoonist. See John C. Robb, "Polls held useless," *Los Angeles Times* (November 7, 1952): A4.

50. See "Polls as election guides: Errors appear again," *U.S. News and World Report* (November 14, 1952): 32.

51. Script, *Edward R. Murrow with the News*, CBS News (November 5, 1952): 4, 5: Roper papers.

52. "The polls stumble," *Denton* [TX] *Record-Chronicle* (November 7, 1952): 4.

53. Chamberlain, "Election retrospect," *Wall Street Journal*.

54. Roper, letter to Murrow (January 27, 1953): Roper papers.

55. "At no time," he wrote a few weeks after the election, "did I say the race was close." See Elmo Roper, letter to Robert A. Baker (November 26, 1952): Roper papers. Roper made a similar claim in a post-election letter to Paul Lazarsfeld, a leading figure in social science research, stating, "The facts are that I never said flatly it was a close race or any other kind of race." See Roper, letter to Lazarsfeld (November 13, 1952): Roper papers. He also said in the letter to Lazarsfeld: "That we exhibited too much caution over our own figures is a charge to which I will readily plead guilty, and I now wish we had included a paragraph which was debated and left out [in Roper's final pre-election polling report]—a paragraph which read: 'If the Stevenson gains should accelerate sharply to the point where he takes all 14 percentage points of the 'in doubt' people, he could win with 51 percent of the popular vote; but if Eisenhower gets even as much as a third of them, it would bring him to 52 1/2 per cent—and that would mean an electoral landslide.' . . . I don't now believe such a statement would have been open to the charge of prediction, although it was left out deliberately because of a fear it might be."

56. Elmo Roper, letter to Floyd Albert Spencer (December 23, 1952): Roper papers. A sum of $20,000 in 1952 is the rough equivalent these days of more than $185,000.

57. A. M. Crossley, memorandum to Dave Wallace (November 17, 1952): Crossley papers. In the memorandum, Crossley characterized those details as being "For our own information only."

58. Roper, letter to Murrow (January 27, 1953), Roper papers.

59. Roper, letter to Baker (November 26, 1952), Roper papers.

60. Elmo Roper, letter to A. L. Zeitung (December 23, 1952): Roper papers.

61. Roper, letter to Lazarsfeld (November 13, 1952), Roper papers.

62. Quoted in Gideon Seymour and others, "Should public opinion polls make election forecasts? A symposium," *Journalism Quarterly* 26, 2 (June 1949): 142–143.

63. Quoted in "Pollsters poll selves on flop; see better day," *Chicago Tribune* (December 31, 1952): 5.

64. Quoted in "Proceedings of the American Association for Public Opinion Research," *Public Opinion Quarterly* 17, 4 (Winter 1953–1954): 531.

65. Quoted in "Proceedings," *Public Opinion Quarterly*, 532. Gallup reiterated that point in the run-up to the 1956 presidential election, stating, "What better way is there to learn and improve your research tools than to stick your neck out?" Quoted in "Polls point to an Ike victory but pollsters may hedge forecasts," *Wall Street Journal* (October 29, 1956): 18.

66. See "Proceedings," *Public Opinion Quarterly*, 533.

67. David Lawrence, "Pollsters should drop predictions," *Washington Evening Star* (November 11, 1952): A-9. Lawrence further wrote, "If the poll organizations . . . had made a study of the resentment attitudes of voters in cities and in farm districts, they doubtless would have furnished scientific information which would have been more valuable than the numerical totals to the political writers, political managers and others who can make their own inferences from the evidence."

68. Lawrence, "Pollsters should drop predictions," *Washington Evening Star*, A-9.

69. Lawrence's survey was scarcely the first of its kind. Surveys of editors by news organizations had been conducted at least since 1912, when, according to Claude E. Robinson, the *New York World* "asked newspaper correspondents in each state to predict the presidential pluralities for their state." Robinson reported that the "average plurality error for the 48 states (between the two leading candidates) was 9 percent." See Robinson, *Straw Votes: A Study of Political Prediction* (New York: Columbia University Press, 1932), 15.

70. David Lawrence, "Another poll names Eisenhower," *Washington Evening Star* (November 3, 1952): A-13. Lawrence's success in anticipating the landslide wasn't total: he estimated that Stevenson would win five states that he lost—Arizona, Missouri, Oklahoma, Tennessee, and Texas. And he offered no prediction about outcomes in Massachusetts and Washington, both of which Eisenhower won.

71. Krock, "In the nation: If it is close as 'they' say," *New York Times*.

72. Raymond Moley, "Newsmen are better prophets than pollsters," *Los Angeles Times* (November 22, 1952): A4.

73. Carl E. Brazier, "Thoughts while reading the Times," *Seattle Times* (November 7, 1952): in "Memory Book," Lawrence papers.

74. "The scared pollsters," *Tulsa* [OK] *Tribune* (November 6, 1952): in "Memory Book," Lawrence papers. The *Tribune* editorial also said, in reference to pollsters, that "their weakness seems to be that they make a guess, see how far they went wrong, and then on the next election juggle their figures to compensate for their error last time."

75. "Polls were running the wrong way," [Paterson, NJ] *Morning Call* (November 7, 1952): in "Memory Book," Lawrence papers.

76. See Alex Kingsbury, "David Lawrence: A profile," *U.S. News and World Report* (May 16, 2008); accessed July 10, 2018, at: https://www.usnews.com/news/national/articles/2008/05/16/david-lawrence-a-profile

77. Benjamin M. McKelway, former president of the Associated Press and former editor of the *Washington Evening Star*, quoted in "David Lawrence, the columnist, is dead," *New York Times* (February 12, 1973): 30.

78. See David Lawrence, "Dewey will be elected; House and Senate will be Republican," *Cumberland [MD] News* (November 2, 1948): 4.

79. Quoted in Charles Schneider, "Lubell rings bell with vote forecast," *New York World-Telegram and Sun* (November 6, 1952): 25.

80. Thomas B. Littlewood, *Calling Elections: The History of Horse-Race Journalism* (Notre Dame, IN: University of Notre Dame Press,1998), 124.

81. Samuel Lubell, *White and Black: Test of a Nation* (New York: Harper & Row, 1964), 175.

82. Quoted in Alexander P. Lamis and others, "Symposium on the work of Samuel Lubell," *PS: Politics and Science* 23, 2 (June 1990): 189. Meyer also said that "Lubell's skills were better suited to hypothesis building and concept construction than to empirical confirmation."

83. Winston Phelps, "Autopsy on the polls," *Providence [RI] Journal*, n.d.: in "Memory Book," Lawrence papers.

84. Committee on the Analysis of Pre-election Polls and Forecasts of the Social Science Research Council, "Report on the analysis of pre-election polls and forecasts," *Public Opinion Quarterly* 12, 4 (Winter 1948–1949): 600.

85. Crossley's remarks were made in a paper read for him at a meeting of the American Statistical Association in Chicago at the end of 1952. See "Pollsters poll selves on flop," *Chicago Tribune.*

86. See Greene, *I Like Ike*, 175. Greene wrote: "What must be said, in direct defiance of Stevenson's many apologists, was that he was a terrible candidate. He inspired very few people and energized even fewer."

87. Greene, *I Like Ike*, 173.

88. Greene, *I Like Ike*, 174.

89. Amy Fried, *Pathways to Polling: Crisis, Cooperation and the Making of Public Opinion Professions* (New York: Routledge, 2012), 128.

90. See "Summary of team reports," *New York Times* (November 4, 1956): 69.

91. Max Frankel, *The Times of My Life and My Life with The Times* (New York: Random House, 1999), 133.

92. See W. H. Lawrence, "Presidential race," *New York Times* (November 4, 1956): 1, 69. The article said that "it still seemed doubtful that General Eisenhower's margin would be as great as it was in 1952 when his popular-vote plurality reached 6,621,242."

93. Quoted in "Proceedings," *Public Opinion Quarterly*, 532.

94. In her history of survey research, Jean M. Converse wrote that Crossley never expanded beyond election polling of presidential campaigns because he "did not think the market would bear a third poll of public opinion" in addition to those of Gallup and Roper. See Converse, *Survey Research in the United States: Roots and Emergence, 1890–1960* (Berkeley: University of California Press, 1987), 112.

95. Archibald Crossley, "The public wants," unpublished manuscript, 1969: Crossley papers.

96. Converse, *Survey Research in the United States*, 112.

97. Peter B. Bart, "Poll-takers polled on '56 election say they're undecided," *Wall Street Journal* (November 9, 1955): 1.

98. Quoted in "Polls point to an Ike victory but pollsters may hedge forecasts," *Wall Street Journal* (October 29, 1956): 1, 18.

99. See "Record of Elmo Roper polls on presidential elections 1936–1956," n.d.: Box 15, folder 896, Roper papers.

100. Quoted in "Pollster calls campaign forecasting nightmare," *Los Angeles Times* (October 27, 1960): 11. Roper was quoted as saying, equivocally, "The only ringing forthright declaration that any pollster can make on the forthcoming Presidential vote is that it looks like a close election but either candidate could win in a landslide."

101. See Charles Grutzner, "3 of 4 major election polls give Kennedy the edge in close vote," *New York Times* (November 8, 1960): 18.

102. George Gallup, "Kennedy 49, Nixon 48 with 3 pct. undecided," *Washington Post* (November 7, 1960): A1.

103. See George Gallup, "'Dramatic shift' of voters seen with Kennedy receiving 53 pct.," *Washington Post* (November 4, 1960): 1.

104. Burns Roper, memorandum to staff (November 11, 1960): Box 15, folder 896, Roper papers.

105. Harris once prepared a memorandum to Roper claiming to log more hours than anyone in Roper's research department. Harris wrote that he went home four or five nights "with a brief-case loaded with work, and generally turn out the lights around 1 AM." He added, "I don't mean to blow my own horn on this, but you had a completely opposite impression [of Harris's work habits], and maybe, just maybe, this will put to rest that old canard that I generally waste my time on unimportant, extraneous telephone calls." Louis Harris, memorandum to Elmo Roper, n.d.: Box 84, Louis Harris papers, Wilson Library, University of North Carolina, Chapel Hill.

106. See David W. Moore, *The Superpollsters: How They Measure and Manipulate Public Opinion in America* (New York: Four Walls Eight Windows, 1992), 74. Moore quoted Harris as saying, "Roper was furious" about his departure. Moore further quoted Harris as saying, rather implausibly, that the clients "wanted me to do it. They persuaded me."

107. John F. Kraft, who left Elmo Roper's firm to join Harris's venture, said in a lengthy letter to Roper in 1961 that before quitting Roper's company, Harris had been "busy rounding up retainer clients on trips to the [West] Coast and Chicago, and obviously this was being done at your or your firm's expense." Kraft also claimed that Harris's "research standards are a whole story in themselves, from faked samples, faked tabulations, and not just where political research is concerned. There was some mess about a job done for the Stock Exchange. If the research people at the exchange were to ask for substantiation and verification of one of the surveys done for them, Lou couldn't produce the questionnaires." See John F. Kraft, letter to Elmo Roper

(October 3, 1961): Box 17, folder 1027, Roper papers. Kraft conducted polls for several U.S. senators, including Robert and Edward Kennedy, Frank Church, and Stuart Symington. Kraft also was an election analyst for ABC News. See "John F. Kraft, opinion analyst for political figures, 48, dies," *New York Times* (March 1, 1973): 44.

108. The study was published as a single-volume report. See Paul F. Lazarsfeld and Wagner Thielens Jr., *The Academic Mind: Social Scientists in a Time of Crisis* (Glencoe, IL: Free Press, 1958).

109. See Moore, *The Superpollsters*, 74.

110. Paul Lazarsfeld, letter to Louis Harris (January 10, 1957): Box 11, folder 638, Roper papers.

111. Harris also wrote, "Believe me, if you will, the scars have been mutual, and we have by now both purged ourselves of our grievances." Louis Harris, letter to Paul Lazarsfeld (January 11, 1957): Box 84, Harris papers.

112. "Private pollsters, politicians, and public opinion," *Newsweek* (October 1, 1962): 22.

113. Michael Wheeler, *Lies, Damn Lies, and Statistics: The Manipulation of Public Opinion in America* (New York: Liveright, 1976), 49, 51.

114. See Moore, *The Superpollsters*, 89.

115. Wheeler, *Lies, Damn Lies, and Statistics*, 56.

116. Quoted in Tom Wicker, "Nation will vote today; close presidential race predicted in late polls," *New York Times* (November 5, 1968): 1.

117. Quoted in Wheeler, *Lies, Damn Lies, and Statistics*, 27.

118. Quoted in Wheeler, *Lies, Damn Lies, and Statistics*, 56.

119. Cited in Thomas J. Foley, "Three top pollsters nearly hit bull's-eye," *Los Angeles Times* (November 8, 1968): 10.

120. Nixon won the election with 43.4 percent of the popular vote to Humphrey's 42.7 percent; Wallace received 13.5 percent of the vote. Gallup's final poll estimated that Nixon led by 43 percent to Humphrey's 42 percent and Wallace's 15 percent.

121. See "Pollsters, politicians, and journalists all came close in vote predictions," *New York Times* (November 7, 1968): 25.

122. Quoted in Foley, "Three top pollsters nearly hit bull's-eye," *Los Angeles Times*.

123. Quoted in Laurence M. Stern, "Most pollsters were accurate on the election," *Washington Post* (November 8, 1968): A2.

124. For references to Gallup's embrace of aspects of probability sampling, see Paul Perry, "Election survey procedures of the Gallup Poll," *Public Opinion Quarterly* 24, 3 (Autumn 1960): 531–542.

125. George Gallup, "The changing climate for public opinion research," *Public Opinion Quarterly* 21, 1 (Spring 1957): 25.

126. See Warren J. Mitofsky and Murray Edelman, "Election Night estimation," *Journal of Official Statistics* 18, 2 (June 2002): 169. CBS, they wrote, "tried to hire Morris Hansen as their first choice to run their new in-house election unit. Some years after we worked there we discovered a memo listing the names of prominent sampling statisticians that they contacted. All came from solid statistical backgrounds."

127. Quoted in Sean Alfano, "CBS exit poll pioneer dies," CBSNews.com (September 3, 2006); accessed July 21, 2019, at: https://www.cbsnews.com/news/cbs-exit-poll-pioneer-dies/2/

128. See Richard Morin, "The pioneer pollster whose credibility you could count on," *Washington Post* (September 6, 2006); accessed December 29, 2019, at: http://www.washingtonpost.com/wp-dyn/content/article/2006/09/05/AR2006090501477.html?noredirect=on

129. The network hired Mitofsky after its disastrous miscall of the 1966 gubernatorial election in Maryland, which pitted Republican Spiro T. Agnew against George Mahoney, a conservative Democrat and foe of opening housing. Mahoney's opponents in the Democratic primary election divided the liberal vote, effectively giving him the nomination. Agnew handily won election, carrying precincts dominated by minority and Democratic voters who found Mahoney repellant. The CBS election projection system in place at the time said Mahoney would win easily. See Dan Morganstein and David Marker, "A conversation with Joseph Waksberg," *Statistical Science* 15, 3 (2000): 304–305.

130. For a discussion about the emergence and soundness of random-digit dialing techniques, see J. Michael Brick and Clyde Tucker, "Mitofsky-Waksberg, learning from the past," *Public Opinion Quarterly* 71, 5 (January 2007): 706–709.

131. This point is made by Anthony Salvanto in *Where Did You Get This Number? A Pollster's Guide to Making Sense of the World* (New York: Simon & Schuster, 2018), 39.

132. See Robin Sproul, "Exit polls: Better or worse since the 2000 election?" Discussion paper, Joan Shorenstein Center on the Press, Politics and Public Policy (2008): 2.

133. Mitofsky and Edelman, "Election Night estimation," *Journal of Official Statistics*, 171. They wrote: "We interviewed voters at the polling place after they voted. We did it so we would have a better idea of what to expect. We were concerned that we would be misled by the results from the earliest sample precincts as they trickled in with their vote returns on Election Night."

134. A few years before Mitofsky's work in Kentucky, Lou Harris and others had experimented with techniques akin to prototypical exit polls. See Martin Plissner, *The Control Room: How Television Calls the Shots in Presidential Elections* (New York: Touchstone, 1999), 222 n.19.

135. See "CBS News will estimate winners in Kentucky races on 'CBS Evening News with Walter Cronkite' Nov. 7," CBS News press release (November 3, 1967): Box 8, Warren J. Mitofsky papers, Thomas J. Dodd Research Center, University of Connecticut, Storrs.

136. See Mitofsky and Edelman, "Election Night estimation," *Journal of Official Statistics*, 171.

137. See, among others, Plissner, *The Control Room*, 82–85.

138. "The economic efficiencies of the alliance were great," Martin Plissner wrote in his book about television and elections. "The *New York Times* circulation department

has a large telemarketing force, with long-distance phones at fixed monthly rates used mainly in the daytime. Public-opinion surveys are done mainly at night. The *Times* could make these facilities available for the joint operation at relatively little extra cost. CBS News supplied the technical expertise of Mitofsky and his election staff as well as the data-processing equipment and software, much of which was already in place for its election broadcasts." See Plissner, *The Control Room*, 105.

139. See Moore, *Superpollsters*, 276–277.

140. Moore, *Superpollsters*, 277–278. He noted (277), "When topics are polled in greater depth, CBS News often cannot use some of the material because of limited time" set aside for newscasts.

141. By the 1970s, Albert E. Gollin wrote in a fiftieth-anniversary issue of *Public Opinion Quarterly*, "a variety of influences flowed together to swell the demand for polling within the news media, 'pulled' by the demonstrated value of polls for political coverage in particular. The economics of polling encouraged a sharing of costs, giving rise to the joint polling operations of CBS News and *The New York Times*, *The Washington Post* and ABC News, and other media couples. Usually these involved a marriage of a print and a broadcast medium." See Gollin, "Polling and the news media," *Public Opinion Quarterly* 51, 4, part 2 (Winter 1987): S88.

142. Meyer was a professional journalist who studied social science research techniques during a year-long Nieman Fellowship at Harvard University. Afterward, he applied survey methodology in analyzing causes of Detroit's race riots in 1967, ruling out conventional explanations such as education and economic status. Frustrated aspirations emerged as a more likely explanation. The reports won a Pulitzer Prize for the *Detroit Free Press* in 1968. Meyer recalled years later, "If we had not gone into that project with specific theories to test, our stories might have been chaotic collections of just loosely related facts." See Philip Meyer, "Precision journalism and narrative journalism: Toward a unified field theory," *Nieman Reports* (October 18, 2012); accessed August 27, 2019, at: https://niemanreports.org/articles/precision-journalism-and-narrative-journalism-toward-a-unified-field-theory/

143. Philip Meyer, *Precision Journalism: A Reporter's Introduction to Social Science Methods* (Bloomington: Indiana University Press, 1973), 3. Meyer's argument encountered some skepticism inside the academy, which he later joined as a professor at the University of North Carolina at Chapel Hill. Elisabeth Noelle-Neumann, the internationally prominent German communications researcher, argued, for example, that Meyer had "seriously underestimate[d] the difficulties of bringing social research and journalists together." She noted that "the interview in journalism and the interview in social research have almost nothing in common," and added that journalists typically "are not used to thinking in terms of probabilities and acquiring knowledge from systematic comparison." She further wrote, "Unlike natural science, social research is essentially unable to command results that are entirely precise; it can only make observations with a higher or lower probability of accuracy. This is something journalists abhor." See Elisabeth Noelle-Neumann, "The public opinion research correspondent," *Public Opinion Quarterly* 44, 1 (January 1980): 589, 590, 593–594.

144. Meyer, *Precision Journalism*, 115–116.

145. Meyer, *Precision Journalism*, 14.

146. See Arnold H. Ismach, "Precision journalism: Coming of age," ANPA News Research Report 18 (March 9, 1979): 7. Ismach noted (8): "Many of the projects . . . are virtual carbon copies of syndicated opinion polls conducted by organizations such as Gallup and Harris. Newspapers thus obtain local comparisons to national sentiment or attempt to measure opinion on purely local issues."

147. Philip Meyer, "Presidential address: Polling as political science and polling as journalism," *Public Opinion Quarterly* 54, 3 (Fall 1990): 452.

148. See E.J. Dionne Jr., "1980 brings more pollsters than ever," *New York Times* (February 16, 1980): 10.

149. Dionne, "1980 brings more pollsters than ever," *New York Times*.

5. THE 'CLOSE RACE THAT NEVER HAPPENED'

1. "CBS News special report" (November 4, 1980): facsimile in Warren J. Mitofsky papers, Thomas J. Dodd Research Center, University of Connecticut, Storrs.

2. Script, *CBS Evening News with Walter Cronkite* (November 4, 1980): facsimile in Mitofsky papers.

3. See Fred Barnes, "Reagan surged to decisive win at end as Carter found no aces up his sleeve," *Baltimore Sun* (November 5, 1980): A1.

4. Bill Green, "The press, the polls, the vote," *Washington Post* (November 7, 1980): A18.

5. The *Washington Post*'s television critic, Tom Shales, wrote about Cronkite that night, "He was the grand old coach urging his team to one last victory and casting a disgruntled glance over his shoulder at his own replacement," who was CBS News correspondent Dan Rather. See Shales, "NBC's projections lead a dazzling TV data display," *Washington Post* (November 5, 1980): 1, 3.

6. The *Baltimore Sun*'s television critic wrote that "America witnessed two blowouts on TV" on Election Night 1980—"one by Ronald Reagan and the other by NBC." See Bill Carter, "NBC's speed left others gasping," *Baltimore Sun* (November 6, 1980): B1.

7. See, for example, "Scoop," *Wall Street Journal* (November 14, 1980): 30.

8. See Alvin P. Sanoff, "The perils of polling 1980," *Washington Journalism Review* (January/February 1981): 33.

9. See, for example, "Pollsters spat over why they erred so badly," *Los Angeles Times* (November 6, 1980): A15, A24. "Some of the pollsters, searching for explanations, were not kind to one another or to their critics and questioners," the article noted.

10. See, for example, Martin Plissner, *The Control Room: How Television Calls the Shots in Presidential Elections* (New York: Touchstone, 1999), 109.

11. Caddell told an interviewer a few years later, "I'm the one who told President Carter the night before the election that he was going to lose in a landslide. Talk about something difficult to do—how do you think that felt?" Quoted in Lois Romano, "Pollsters: The figures candidates count on," *Washington Post* (January 15, 1984): C1.

12. See Robert G. Kaiser, "Reading tea leaves: The brew never cooled for the pollsters," *Washington Post* (November 9, 1980): A1.

13. NBC News *Decision '80* Election Night coverage (November 4–5, 1980); accessed January 18, 2019, at: https://www.youtube.com/watch?v=CovNw-9fca4. Brinkley's colleague Tom Brokaw said in response that among other factors, the late-in-the-campaign debate showed Reagan "not to be an ogre, or a monster, or a guy eager to drop bombs across the landscape, in the eyes of the public."

14. Gartner later became president of NBC News. His tenure there ended in 1993, amid controversy about the network's *Dateline NBC* newsmagazine program, which had rigged vehicles to explode on impact, to demonstrate the supposed hazards of pickup trucks manufactured by General Motors Corporation.

15. Quoted in Green, "The press, the polls, the vote," *Washington Post.*

16. Michael Barone, "Reading between the polls," *Los Angeles Times* (November 7, 1980): D11.

17. Quoted in Green, "The press, the polls, the vote," *Washington Post.*

18. Green, "The press, the polls, the vote," *Washington Post.*

19. See "Pollsters search for error reasons," *Hartford [CT] Courant* (November 8, 1980): A13.

20. Kaiser, "Reading tea leaves," *Washington Post,* A1.

21. Plissner, *The Control Room,* 109. Plissner wrote that "no one" at CBS or the *Times* "doubted the poll's finding of a very close race."

22. See Barry Sussman and Robert G. Kaiser, "Volatile: With two days to go, polls find a narrow division," *Washington Post* (November 2, 1980): A1, A18.

23. Quoted in Clayton Jones, "Louis Harris: The pollster who was right and why," *Christian Science Monitor* (November 6, 1980): 9.

24. Louis Harris, "Harris methodology successful in predicting Reagan victory," ABC News–Harris Survey news release (November 6, 1980). See also Bill Hogan, "Behind the lines … in the 1980 polls," *Washington Journalism Review* (January–February 1981): 34.

25. Harris, "Harris methodology successful in predicting Reagan victory," ABC News–Harris Survey news release.

26. Michael Wheeler wrote in his book *Lies, Damn Lies, and Statistics* that "Harris is intensely disliked" by most of his professional colleagues. See Wheeler, *Lies, Damn Lies, and Statistics: The Manipulation of Public Opinion in America* (New York: Liveright, 1976), 48.

27. Quoted in Olivia Schieffelin Nordberg, "Polling 1980: Adrift in the ocean of possible truth," *American Demographics* (June 1981): 25.

28. Quoted in "Pollsters spat," *Los Angeles Times,* A24. Indeed, *The Atlantic* magazine engaged in a far-fetched scenario that the 1980 election would produce no Electoral College winner, throwing the selection of the president to the House of Representatives. "A deadlocked House election is not a sportive daydream; many consider it a nightmare," the *Atlantic* article declared. See Laurence H. Tribe and Thomas M. Rollins, "Deadlock," *The Atlantic* (October 1980); accessed August 18, 2019, at: https://

www.theatlantic.com/magazine/archive/1980/10/deadlock-what-happens-if-nobody-wins/494510/

29. Warren J. Mitofsky, notes of remarks to National Press Club (October 30, 1980): Box 22, "National Press Club speech, 1980" folder, Mitofsky papers.

30. Warren J. Mitofsky, untitled typescript of remarks to the American Association for Public Opinion Research, 1981 annual conference, Buck Hill Falls, PA: Box 10, Mitofsky papers.

31. George Gallup, "What happened to the polls?" *Washington Post* (November 12, 1980): A25.

32. Archibald Crossley, writing about the 1968 pre-election polls, recalled that in 1948, "reliance was placed on the theory that voting preferences changed very little in the later weeks of a campaign." See Archibald M. Crossley and Helen M. Crossley, "Polling in 1968," *Public Opinion Quarterly* 33, 1 (Spring 1969): 4.

33. Quoted in Nordberg, "Polling 1980," *American Demographics*, 25.

34. Warren J. Mitofsky, memorandum to Ernest Leiser (January 2, 1980): Box 2, Mitofsky papers.

35. Plissner, *The Control Room*, 108. The demands on Mitofsky as Election Day neared were described as enormous in an internal CBS News memorandum written in December 1980. "It is quite difficult for anyone not intimately connected with the [network's] election unit operation to comprehend the degree of strain, demands, drain on his intellect, energies and times to which Warren is subject," wrote Robert Chandler, a CBS News executive. "What I can tell you is that in the weeks before election, he tends to put in 14- to 16-hour days, including weekends, on a daily basis—he undergoes an endurance test which would tax most people. The demands range from computer programming and testing to statistical problems to polling tasks to setting up the logistics of exit polling and the computer program to deliver those results swiftly to editorial consultations on polls, election night and other questions. It is an extraordinary range of difficult and draining activity. He tends to be pulled in so many directions that he is quite literally unable to come into election night assured that everything is in place and ready to go." Chandler, memorandum to Ernest Leiser (December 3, 1980): Box 2, "Post 1980 review memos 1980–82" folder, Mitofsky papers.

36. John F. Stacks, "Where the polls went wrong," *Time* (December 1, 1980): 22. Forty years later, $22,500 would be the equivalent of more than $117,000.

37. Warren J. Mitofsky, "The 1980 pre-election polls: A review of disparate methods and results," *Proceedings of the American Statistical Association Survey Research Methods Section* (1981): 47.

38. Burns W. Roper, "Political polls: Some things that concern me," speech to the annual meeting of the American Association for the Advancement of Science, New York City (May 25, 1984): Box 11, Elmo Roper papers, Thomas J. Dodd Research Center, University of Connecticut, Storrs. Roper referred to gubernatorial elections in California, New York, and Texas, and the Senate race in Connecticut in 1982.

39. Roper, "Political polls," speech to the annual meeting of the American Association for the Advancement of Science.

40. Roper, "Political polls," speech to the annual meeting of the American Association for the Advancement of Science.

41. Quoted in "Pollsters spat," *Los Angeles Times*, A24.

42. Jimmy Carter, *Keeping Faith: Memoirs of a President* (Toronto: Bantam, 1982), 566.

43. Carter, *Keeping Faith*, 567.

44. See, for example, Jan Carroll, "Muskie assails Reagan as warmonger," Associated Press (October 11, 1980); retrieved from LexisNexis database. Edmund Muskie, Carter's secretary of state, insinuated that the United States during a Reagan presidency would be "endlessly at war all over the globe."

45. Roper, "Political polls," speech to the annual meeting of the American Association for the Advancement of Science. Exit polling by NBC News and the Associated Press on Election Day 1980 offered some support for Roper's assertion. By 89 percent to 72 percent, more self-identified Republicans chose Reagan than self-identified Democrats voted for Carter. In addition, John Anderson appealed more strongly to Democratic voters than he did to Republicans. See "General election poll results," NBC News, n.d.: Box 2, Mitofsky papers. See also Stanley Kelley, *Interpreting Elections* (Princeton, NJ: Princeton University Press, 1983). Kelley wrote (170) that "the commitment of voters to candidates in 1980 was unusually weak," noting that according to a post-election survey by Gallup, 27 percent of respondents said they had changed their minds during the 1980 campaign about which candidate to support.

46. Barnes, "Reagan surged to decisive win at end," *Baltimore Sun*, A16. Reagan biographer Lou Cannon had noted Reagan's victory in the Republican gubernatorial primary election in California in 1966 "provided the first clue that Reagan was a ballot box candidate who runs more strongly on election day than in the polls." See Cannon, *Reagan* (New York: Putnam, 1982), 112.

47. Barone, "Reading between the polls," *Los Angeles Times*.

48. "The story of Reagan's presidency should note that on election day [1980] he was a relatively unpopular victor," noted Stanley Kelley, a Princeton University political scientist. See Kelley, *Interpreting Elections*, 172.

49. Carter, *Keeping Faith*, 566.

50. See Adam Clymer, "Poll shows Iran and economy hurt Carter among late-shifting voters," *New York Times* (November 16, 1980): 1.

51. See Suzanne Garment, "Capital tremors: The morning after the night before," *Wall Street Journal* (November 7, 1980): 26.

52. See Richard E. Meyer and Roger Smith, "Media supplied clues to race's outcome," *Los Angeles Times* (November 6, 1980): B22. "Time and again," they wrote, "Carter appeared on the networks as an embattled President lashing out at his opponent and pleading with Democrats to 'come home.' Reagan appeared as an eager challenger, asking voters if they thought they were better off now than four years ago. Independent John B. Anderson appeared rarely."

53. Kaiser, "Reading tea leaves," *Washington Post*, A2.

54. "Transcript of the presidential debate between Carter and Reagan," *New York Times* (October 29, 1980): A26.

55. See E. J. Dionne Jr., "1980 brings more pollsters than ever," *New York Times* (February 16, 1980): 10.

56. See Nicholas Von Hoffman, "Public opinion polls: Newspapers making their own news?" *Public Opinion Quarterly* 44, 4 (Winter 1980): 573.

57. Quoted in C. David Rambo, "Newspapers join polling stampede," *Presstime* (March 1980): 25.

58. Another example, which emerged in the mid-1990s, was the so-called public journalism movement, which anticipated that news organizations would take engaged roles in identifying and pursuing measures to improve public life and the democratic process. A leading exponent of public journalism was Arthur Charity, author of *Doing Public Journalism* (New York: Guilford Press, 1995).

59. See Arnold H. Ismach, "Precision Journalism: Coming of age," ANPA News Research Report 18 (March 9, 1979): 8.

60. See Rambo, "Newspapers join polling stampede," *Presstime*, 24–26. "There will be a stampede of public-opinion surveys this year," Rambo wrote (24), "and newspapers will be kicking up their share of the dust." The article quoted Philip Meyer as saying (24), "There will be a lot of polls that are wrong" in 1980.

61. Albert E. Gollin, "Exploring the liaison between polling and the press," *Public Opinion Quarterly* 44, 4 (Winter 1980): 457. The press-polling relationship, Gollin also wrote (447), was "increasingly intimate."

62. Sanoff, "The perils of polling 1980," *Washington Journalism Review*, 33.

63. "Accuracy questions stop Illinois Poll series," *Rockford* [IL] *Register Star* (October 16, 1980): A1.

64. Jim George, "Poll: Reagan ahead; cutback issue to pass," [Rockford, IL] *Sunday Register Star* (October 12, 1980): 1.

65. See Pat Cunningham, "Reagan-Carter poll result questioned," *Rockford* [IL] *Register Star* (October 16, 1980): A4.

66. Quoted in "Accuracy questions stop Illinois Poll series," *Register Star*, A1.

67. See F. Richard Ciccone, "Carter-Reagan deadlock . . . now Iran steps in," *Chicago Tribune* (November 3, 1980): 1.

68. Barry G. Sussman and Robert G. Kaiser, "Volatile: With 2 days to go, polls find a narrow division," *Washington Post* (November 2, 1980): A1, A14.

69. David S. Broder, "Reagan is in the driver's seat," *Washington Post* (November 2, 1980): A1, A18.

70. See Green, "The press, the polls, the vote," *Washington Post*.

71. Haynes Johnson, "Election day had a few lessons to teach the out-of-touch set," *Washington Post* (November 16, 1980): A3. Johnson also wrote in his commentary: "Never has the criticism that Washington reporters are out of touch with the country been more justified than during the long 1980 presidential campaign period. And, to put it personally, never have I been struck so forcibly by the validity of that old public complaint."

72. Quoted in "Polls—snapshots of today," [Bloomington, IL] *Daily Pantagraph* (September 29, 1980): 2.

73. Quoted in "Washington Diarist: Errors," *The New Republic* (December 13, 1980): 43. In his final pre-election report for the *Washington Post*, Johnson wrote, "I have never found a president who attracted as little enthusiasm as Jimmy Carter. I am not saying that guarantees his defeat. I am saying that he has failed singularly to make himself felt as a force in people's lives." See Johnson, "American Portraits 1980: The summing up: One nation, troubled & divisible," *Washington Post* (November 3, 1980): D3.

74. Johnson, "Election day had a few lessons to teach the out-of-touch set," *Washington Post*.

75. Johnson, "Election day had a few lessons to teach the out-of-touch set," *Washington Post*.

76. Anne Keegan, "Election no surprise to ordinary folk," *Chicago Tribune* (November 6, 1980): 6.

77. Rick Kogan, "Anne Keegan: 1943–2011," *Chicago Tribune* (May 21, 2011); accessed March 10, 2020 at: https://www.chicagotribune.com/lifestyles/ct-xpm-2011–05–21-ct-met-keegan-obit-20110521-story.html.

78. Keegan, "Election no surprise to ordinary folk," *Chicago Tribune*.

79. Keegan, "Election no surprise to ordinary folk," *Chicago Tribune*.

80. Quoted in Tony Schwartz, "Pollsters denounce ABC's debate survey," *New York Times* (October 30, 1980): B19.

81. Quoted in Schwartz, "Pollsters denounce ABC's debate survey," *New York Times*.

82. See Philip F. Lawler, "Where the press went wrong," *Baltimore Sun* (November 12, 1980): A21.

83. See, for example, Plissner, *The Control Room*, 82–83.

84. Some viewers of the CBS election program learned about Reagan's projected victory when local CBS affiliates reported the NBC projections. Cited in Paul Wilson, "Election Night 1980 and the controversy over early projections," in William C. Adams, ed., *Television Coverage of the 1980 Presidential Election* (Norwood, NJ: Ablex Publishing, 1983), 148.

85. Bill Leonard, memorandum to Ernest Leiser (November 6, 1980): Box 2, "Post 1980 review memos 1980–82" folder, Mitofsky papers.

86. Ernest Leiser, memorandum to William Leonard (November 19, 1980): Box 2, "Post 1980 review memos 1980–82" folder, Mitofsky papers.

87. Warren J. Mitofsky, memorandum to Ernest Leiser (November 21, 1980): Box 2, "Post 1980 review memos 1980–82" folder, Mitofsky papers.

88. See "Scoop," *Wall Street Journal*, 30. Although it was extravagant in claims about the effects of the projections of Reagan's victory, the *Journal*'s editorial was largely a defense of the television networks' practices, stating: "What, after all, if they'd sat on their scoop? Would this have changed the outcome of the election? No. . . . It seems to us the more information a voter has, whether it be news of what his fellow voters are doing or news of the world in general, the stronger position a voter is in."

89. Ullman's defeat was more likely attributable to his having supported a form of a national sales tax, an issue that was unpopular in Oregon.

90. See "*PBS NewsHour* for November 20, 1980"; transcript retrieved from Lexis-Nexis database.

91. See Wilson, "Election Night 1980," 153–158.

92. Plissner, *The Control Room*, 84. He further wrote: "Newspaper reporters who wrote of such happenings were queried as to the time and place. Again, no luck. They had only heard from someone else, or read somewhere, that it had happened somewhere."

93. Plissner, *The Control Room*, 84.

94. William C. Adams, *Election Night News and Voter Turnout: Solving the Projection Problem* (Boulder, CO: Lynne Rienner Publishers, 2005), 128. Adams wrote (129), "If depressed turnout is the only issue to be addressed, the debate is over and there is no need to contemplate changes in public policy." See also John R. Carter, "Early projections and voter turnout in the 1980 presidential election," *Public Choice* 43, 2 (1984): 195–202.

95. See Michael Coakley, "Carter campaign in 11th-hour tour," *Chicago Tribune* (November 4, 1980): 1.

96. Quoted in Helen Thomas, "Tearful Carter tells Plains crowd 'I've tried,'" *Ukiah* [CA] *Daily Journal* (November 4, 1980): 2.

97. See Bernard Weinraub, "Democrat acts to keep backers solid, saying polls ignore shifts," *New York Times* (October 30, 1984): A1. "Mr. Mondale constantly evokes the name of Harry S. Truman," Weinraub wrote, adding, "The other day Mr. Mondale removed a cigar from his mouth before photographers began snapping. 'Truman didn't smoke cigars,' he said."

98. See ABC *World News Tonight* (October 26, 1984); transcript retrieved from LexisNexis database.

99. Bernard Weinraub, "Mondale, at Chicago rally, says 'tide is turning' in '84 election," *New York Times* (October 31, 1984): A20.

100. See Ray Kipp, "Mondale hopes for a Truman finish," *San Diego Union-Tribune* (October 31, 1984): A3. Kipp wrote that Mondale "looked to the ghost of Harry Truman to help him unlock the Democratic spirit that holds victory."

101. A political writer for the *Chicago Tribune* observed on Election Day 1984: "Mondale, who is a keen student of political history, probably has few illusions about his chances of pulling an upset and understands better than anyone that the chemistry of 1984 differs from that of 1948. For starters, Truman was the incumbent and Mondale is the challenger, and where Dewey was politically unappealing, Reagan is a masterful campaigner of the television age." See Steve Neal, "Mondale targets a big upset," *Chicago Tribune* (November 6, 1984): 4. See also Richard Cohen, "At the end of the trail," *Washington Post* (November 3, 1984): A19. Cohen wrote that results of the pre-election polls had "banished suspense and they've spoken so unambiguously only a fool could think they're wrong. Mondale is no fool."

102. Reagan also borrowed trappings of the 1948 campaign. In mid-October 1984, he took a two-hundred-mile railway tour of several Ohio towns, traveling aboard the

Pullman car that Truman had used in 1948. See Steven R. Weisman, "Reagan follows the tracks of Truman's 1948 train tour," *New York Times* (October 13, 1984): 9.

103. Quoted in Alex Brummer, "Dukakis finds second wind," [London] *Guardian* (October 21, 1988); retrieved from LexisNexis database.

104. See *Crier and Company*, CNN (September 8, 1992); transcript retrieved from LexisNexis database.

105. Quoted in Timothy J. McNulty, "Bush emphasizing 'I can' win attitude," *Chicago Tribune* (October 21, 1992): N13.

106. See "Bush's back to the wall, debate offers a chance," *Chicago Tribune* (October 19, 1992): NW5.

107. See Adam Nagourney, "Dole campaign ends with a misstep, conceding by mistake," *New York Times* (November 6, 1996): B4.

108. Quoted in Thomas Hardy, "In one last flurry, GOP hopeful says 'There's still time,'" *Chicago Tribune* (November 5, 1996): L1.

109. Quoted in Curt Anderson, "Still running behind, Dole hoping Truman upset a model for 1996," Associated Press (October 23, 1996); retrieved from LexisNexis database.

110. Quoted in Curt Anderson, "Dole visits Truman hometown, hopes for upset like '48," Associated Press (November 5, 1996); retrieved from LexisNexis database. Truman said in his 1948 speech: "The tide is rolling. All over the country I have seen it in the people's faces. The people are going to win this election." Cited in Robert E. Kelly, *Neck and Neck to the White House: The Closest Presidential Elections, 1796–2000* (Jefferson, NC: McFarland, 2011), 141.

111. Quoted in Richard Morin, "Dole win would cast pall on poll-bearers," *Washington Post* (November 5, 1996): 10.

112. See Warren J. Mitofsky, "Was 1996 a worse year for polls than 1948?" *Public Opinion Quarterly* 62, 2 (Summer 1998): 238, table 1.

113. Richard Morin, "Poll-axed: The maverick predictor who beat us all," *Washington Post* (November 10, 1996): C5. Italics in the original. Zogby's unorthodox techniques, Morin wrote, included selecting samples from listed telephone numbers, rather than using random-digit dialing to reach households with unlisted numbers. Also, Zogby's interviewers placed their calls from 9 a.m. to 9 p.m.; most pollsters worked in the evenings, to avoid samples that included large numbers of retirees or homebound persons.

114. Everett Carll Ladd, "The election polls: An American Waterloo," *Chronicle of Higher Education* (November 22, 1996); accessed March 10, 2020 at: https://www-chronicle-com.proxyau.wrlc.org/article/The-Election-Polls-An/75572

115. Ladd, "The election polls," *Chronicle of Higher Education*.

116. Mitofsky, "Was 1996 a worse year for polls than 1948?" *Public Opinion Quarterly*, 230.

117. Mitofsky, "Was 1996 a worse year for polls than 1948?" *Public Opinion Quarterly*.

118. Mitofsky, "Was 1996 a worse year for polls than 1948?" *Public Opinion Quarterly*, 242.

119. Mitofsky, "Was 1996 a worse year for polls than 1948?" *Public Opinion Quarterly*, 248.

120. See Lynn Mason, Kathleen Frankovic, and Kathleen Hall Jamieson, "CBS News coverage of Election Night 2000: Investigation, analysis, recommendations," Report for CBS News (January 2001): 51.

6. 'TELEVISION'S VERSION OF "DEWEY DEFEATS TRUMAN"'

1. William Saletan, "Why Bush is toast," Slate.com (September 14, 2000); accessed March 10, 2020, at: https://slate.com/news-and-politics/2000/09/why-bush-is-toast.html

2. Saletan, "Why Bush is toast," Slate.com.

3. Saletan, "Why Bush is toast," Slate.com.

4. Thomas E. Mann of the Brookings Institution noted that "Gore never felt comfortable running on the Clinton-Gore record. His obsession with separating himself from Clinton and running on the future, not the past, kept him from sharply framing the election as a referendum on good times. And Clinton himself, one of the most effective politicians in U.S. history, was perforce relegated to fundraising and selective forays into Democratic strongholds." Mann, "Why a presidential dead heat in 2000? A considered opinion" Brookings Institution (December 1, 2001); accessed May 22, 2019, at: https://www.brookings.edu/articles/why-a-presidential-dead-heat-in-2000-a-considered-opinion/

5. Howard Fineman and Bill Turque, "How Al will fight back," *Newsweek* (14 August 2000); retrieved from LexisNexis database.

6. Joan Konner, James Risser, and Ben Wattenberg, "Television's performance on Election Night 2000: A report for CNN," CNN (January 29, 2001): 32; accessed May 24, 2019, at: http://edition.cnn.com/2001/ALLPOLITICS/stories/02/02/cnn.report/cnn.pdf

7. See Linda Mason, Kathleen Frankovic, and Kathleen Hall Jamieson, "CBS News coverage of Election Night 2000: Investigation, analysis, recommendations." CBS News (January 2001): 51.

8. David Von Drehle, "The night that would not end," *Washington Post* (November 9, 2000): A1.

9. Lori Robertson, "Polled enough for ya?" *American Journalism Review* (January/February 2001): 29.

10. Robert S. Erikson, "The 2000 presidential election in historical perspective," *Political Science Quarterly* 116, 1 (Spring 2001): 39.

11. See Michael W. Traugott, "Assessing poll performance in the 2000 campaign," *Public Opinion Quarterly* 65, 3 (Autumn 2001): 390.

12. Alison Mitchell, "A modest poll proposal," *New York Times* (October 8, 2000): sect. 4, p. 5.

13. Mitchell, "A modest poll proposal," *New York Times*, 5. Richard Morin, polling director of the *Washington Post*, dismissed Mitchell's suggestion as "naïve" and quoted

Robert Worcester of the British research firm MORI as saying a ban on polling would create a situation as in France, "where the publication of polls are banned for the seven days before elections, to give the politicians the opportunity to lie to the voters about their private polls." See Morin and Claudia Deane, "What's behind Gallup's volatile poll numbers?" *Washington Post* (October 11, 2000); retrieved from LexisNexis database.

14. See Andrew Kohut, "Low marks for polls, media," *Columbia Journalism Review* (January/February 2001): 25.

15. "Despite uncertain outcome, Campaign 2000 highly rated," Pew Research Center report (November 16, 2000): 15. Also, 29 percent of respondents to the Pew survey assigned pollsters grades of "A" or "B."

16. "Despite uncertain outcome, Campaign 2000 highly rated," Pew Research Center report. Andrew Kohut, director of Pew Research, said pollsters in 2000 merited an overall grade of A-minus. Pew's final pre-election poll placed Bush ahead of Gore by 49 percent to 47 percent. See B. Drummond Ayres Jr., "In hindsight, fair showing for foresight," *New York Times* (November 9, 2000): B2.

17. Kohut, "Low marks for polls, media," *Columbia Journalism Review*, 25.

18. Other tracking polls reported throughout the fall campaign included those conducted by the Rasmussen Group, Zogby International, and voter.com. See Traugott, "Assessing poll performance in the 2000 campaign," *Public Opinion Quarterly*, 399.

19. Michael Traugott, a perceptive analyst of the campaign's polling, noted that the brunt of criticism about tracking polls in 2000 "was directed at the Gallup/CNN /USA Today tracking poll results." See Traugott, "Assessing poll performance in the 2000 campaign," *Public Opinion Quarterly*, 399. Traugott further noted (400) that the standard deviation in Gallup's tracking polls was greater than in the others conducted during the campaign.

20. Kohut, "Low marks for polls, media," *Columbia Journalism Review*.

21. See Pippa Norris, "Too close to call: Opinion polls in Campaign 2000," *Harvard Journal of Press/Politics* 6, 1 (February 2001): 4.

22. Kohut, "Low marks for polls, media," *Columbia Journalism Review*.

23. Richard Morin, "Gallup's October surprise," *Washington Post* (October 15, 2000): B5.

24. William Saletan, "Pollish sausage," Slate.com (October 27, 2000); accessed June 18, 2018, at: https://slate.com/news-and-politics/2000/10/pollish-sausage.html

25. Alan Abramowitz, "Remembering Gallup's wacky 2000 tracking poll," *Huffington Post* (September 7, 2008); accessed May 22, 2019, at: https://www.huffpost.com /entry/remembering-gallups-wacky_b_117594

26. Frank Newport, interview, "Gore fights two-front war," CNN *Inside Politics* (October 27, 2000); retrieved from LexisNexis database.

27. Richard Morin, interview, "Gore fights two-front war," CNN *Inside Politics* (October 27, 2000); retrieved from LexisNexis database.

28. For example, Ed Goeas, who conducted the Battleground 2000 poll, said after the election, "If you look at the vast majority of the polling organizations out there, the

volatility really has not been there." Quoted in Allison Stevens, "Pundits and pollsters saw photo finish in the making," *The Hill* [Washington, DC] (9 November 2000); retrieved from LexisNexis database.

29. Andrew Kohut, "Polls speed down slippery slope, but they don't have to," *Columbia Journalism Review* (November/December 2000): 66.

30. Morin, "Gallup's October surprise," *Washington Post*.

31. Saletan, "Pollish sausage," Slate.com.

32. Robert S. Erikson, Costas Panagopoulos, and Christopher Wlezien, "Likely (and unlikely) voters and the assessment of campaign dynamics," *Public Opinion Quarterly* 68, 4 (Winter 2004): 600.

33. As the authors of the journal article wrote, "Likely voters early in the campaign do not necessarily represent likely voters on Election Day." See Erikson, Panagopoulos, and Wlezien, "Likely (and unlikely) voters," *Public Opinion Quarterly*, 591.

34. See Erikson, Panagopoulos, and Wlezien, "Likely (and unlikely) voters," *Public Opinion Quarterly*, 599–600. Michael Traugott wrote, "The differences in the tracking polls, especially the difference between Gallup data and the others, suggest that there should be more public scrutiny of their methodologies." See Traugott, "Assessing poll performance in the 2000 campaign," *Public Opinion Quarterly*, 402.

35. Traugott, "Assessing poll performance in the 2000 campaign," *Public Opinion Quarterly*, 391.

36. Quoted in "Zogby sees sampling and turnout model as keys to his polls' accuracy," *White House Bulletin* (Alexandria, VA: Bulletin Broadfaxing Network) (November 9, 2000); retrieved from LexisNexis database.

37. Quoted in Larissa MacFarquhar, "The Pollster: Does John Zogby know who will win the election?" *New Yorker* (October 18, 2004): accessed November 17, 2017, at: https://www.newyorker.com/magazine/2004/10/18/the-pollster

38. Quoted in Kathleen Hall Jamieson and Paul Waldman, eds., *Electing the President, 2000: The Insiders' View* (Philadelphia: University of Pennsylvania Press, 2001), 119.

39. See Chris Suellentrop, "Why online polls are bunk," Slate.com (January 12, 2000); accessed May 23, 2019, at: https://slate.com/news-and-politics/2000/01/why-online-polls-are-bunk.html

40. Quoted in John Simons, "Are political polls via Internet reliable? Yes? No? Maybe?" *Wall Street Journal* (April 13, 1999); accessed May 23, 2019, at: https://www.wsj.com/articles/SB923957499521692

41. The Marist College sample was fairly small for a final pre-election poll. It included 623 likely voters who were interviewed on Wednesday and Thursday before the election. See "Bush ahead of Gore in nationwide poll," Associated Press (November 3, 2000); retrieved from LexisNexis database.

42. Traugott, "Assessing poll performance in the 2000 campaign," *Public Opinion Quarterly*, 391.

43. Traugott, "Assessing poll performance in the 2000 campaign," *Public Opinion Quarterly*, 417.

44. Traugott, "Assessing poll performance in the 2000 campaign," 390. Traugott was referring to Everett Carll Ladd's disputed assessment that polls in the 1996 presidential campaign were worse than those in 1948 and as such merited review by "a blue-ribbon panel of experts—from academia, commercial polling firms and the news media—who should recommend ways to improve the accuracy of polling and of news reports about the surveys' findings." See Ladd, "The pollsters' Waterloo," *Wall Street Journal* (November 19, 1996): A22.

45. See "Reaction to Governor George W. Bush's DUI arrest 24 years ago and its impact on the election," ABC News *Nightline* (November 2, 2000); transcript retrieved from LexisNexis database.

46. Quoted in "Reaction to Governor George W. Bush's DUI arrest 24 years ago," ABC News *Nightline*. Soon after Erin Fehlau's scoop, it emerged that a veteran reporter for the *Portland Press Herald* newspaper in Maine had learned three months earlier about Bush's arrest but, after consulting his editor, did not pursue the matter. See Alicia C. Shepard, "Free Press," *American Journalism Review* (January/February 2001): 12. "Instead of the story breaking in July," Shepard noted, "it broke five days before the election, obscuring the issue of responsibility and drunk driving. The focus became criticism of the media for publicizing the arrest so close to Election Day." The reporter, Ted Cohen, said of missing the scoop: "I failed to follow my heart, which told me I had a big story, the biggest of my career, a national story, perhaps the biggest locally generated story the Press Herald has ever had. Make that, the biggest story the Press Herald has never had." See Cohen, "The greatest scoop I never had," *American Journalism Review* (December 2000): 19.

47. See "Voters indifferent to DUI arrest news," *St. Petersburg [FL] Times* (November 5, 2000): 6A.

48. For example, Michael Barone, a veteran political analyst for *U.S. News and World Report*, said, "It will be an unambiguous win" for Bush, by 50 percent to 44 percent. Robert Novak of CNN predicted Bush would win 320 electoral votes to Gore's 230 votes. Peggy Noonan of the *Wall Street Journal* said Bush would defeat Gore by nine percentage points and win 411 electoral votes. See "Predictions: Potpourri of picks from pundits to professors," *National Journal* Hotline (November 6, 2000); retrieved from LexisNexis database.

49. As political analyst James E. Campbell observed, "In a close election like 2000, anything can make the difference between winning and losing" and "even marginal effects can prove decisive." See Campbell, "The Curious and Close Campaign of 2000," in William Crotty, ed., *America's Choice 2000* (New York: Westview Press, 2001), 118.

50. By way of explanation, Bush said he had wanted to shield his daughters from embarrassing news about his drunk-driving record. "I didn't want to talk about this in front of my daughters," he said after the news had broken. "I told my daughters they shouldn't be drinking and driving." See "Reaction to Governor George W. Bush's DUI arrest," ABC News *Nightline*.

51. Adam Cohen, "Fallout from a midnight ride," *Time* (November 4, 2000); accessed January 15, 2019, at: http://content.time.com/time/nation/article/0,8599,59739,00.html

52. George W. Bush, *Decision Points* (New York: Crown Publishers, 2010), 76. Karl Rove in his memoir said the DUI harmed Bush's candidacy "a lot," knocking the campaign "off message at a critical time" and presenting it with a credibility problem. Moreover, Rove wrote, "Many Americans had been drawn by [Bush's] pledge to restore integrity to the Oval Office and now he had surprised them with a DUI." See Rove, *Courage and Consequence: My Life as a Conservative* (New York: Threshold Editions, 2010), 192–193.

53. See, for example, Erikson, "The 2000 presidential election in historical perspective," *Political Science Quarterly*, 41–42, 52.

54. Some analysts dismissed the prospect of a split decision. Stephen Hess of the Brookings Institution said, for example, that the scenario was "one of the more unlikely things that can happen in politics." Quoted in Steven Thomma, "Scenario arises of winning popular vote, losing race," [San Jose, CA] *Mercury News* (October 31, 2000): 14A.

55. See Erikson, "The 2000 presidential election in historical perspective," *Political Science Quarterly*, 42. Erikson wrote: "Based on the polls, one could foresee a narrow Bush win in the popular vote with a less certain outcome in the Electoral College. Thus, observers saw that conceivably Gore would win the Electoral College but without a popular vote mandate."

56. See Richard A. Ryan, Gebe Martinez, and Darci McConnell, "Close race keeps drama at fever pitch; experts speculate Bush could win popular vote but lose the presidency," *Detroit News* (November 5, 2000): 13A. The article quoted pollster John Zogby as saying, "There is a real possibility of a split decision on election day." Other journalists recognized that a split decision could go either way. Michael Powell of the *Washington Post* wrote on the eve of the election: "Welcome to electoral college poker, in which Al Gore might lose the popular vote but win a majority of electoral votes, and so be crowned our president-elect. Or the reverse." But, Powell asked, "are Americans prepared for the triumphant loser? The World Series champion that wins the final game by a score of 5–6? The Olympic sprinter who finishes three-tenths of a second off the pace and raises his arms in victory?" See Powell, "The Electoral College's quirky pass-fail policy," *Washington Post* (November 7, 2000): C1.

57. Mark Siegel on "George W. Bush arrested for drunk driving 24 years ago; could a candidate win electoral college and lose popular vote this year?" MSNBC *The News with Brian Williams* program (November 2, 2000); transcript retrieved from LexisNexis database.

58. See Rachel Smolkin, "In a race like this, the winner might lose," *Pittsburgh Post-Gazette* (November 5, 2000); retrieved from LexisNexis database. Smolkin wrote that a split verdict was unlikely but the prospect was "intriguing." She added that such an outcome "would cause a hullabaloo."

59. Cokie Roberts on "Reviewing some possible outcomes of the presidential election," NPR *Morning Edition* program (November 6, 2000); transcript retrieved from LexisNexis database.

60. Konner, Risser, and Wattenberg, "Television's performance on Election Night 2000," 1.

61. Konner, Risser, and Wattenberg, "Television's performance on Election Night 2000," 3.

62. A report prepared by ABC News said exit-poll data were among the "principal causes of the flawed projection for Mr. Gore in Florida." The report noted that exit-poll results had overstated Gore's lead. See "Statement of ABC News concerning the 2000 election projections," ABC News (February 8, 2000). See also Warren J. Mitofsky, "Voter News Service after the fall," *Public Opinion Quarterly* 67, 1 (Spring 2003): 47.

63. The report for CBS about the miscalls on Election Night included this discussion by Kathleen Frankovic about how exit-polls figure in network projections: "Races are called based on several sources of data. The first is the exit poll, conducted throughout the day in a sample of precincts throughout a state. . . . If the exit-poll data, processed through a series of calculations and decision models, indicate an expected clear lead for a candidate, the state can be called at poll-closing time. In many elections, the exit polls do not provide the information necessary to call a race. Therefore, actual vote results are collected from a larger sample that includes the exit-poll precincts. This process begins after the polls close, and the calculations from these sample precincts are used to call races in which the leads are smaller or the results are a surprise. In very close races, a call must await until the tabulation of a significant number of actual votes from every section of a state." See Mason, Frankovic, and Jamieson, "CBS News coverage of Election Night 2000," 56.

64. Richard A Posner, a federal appellate judge, said in his book about the 2000 election that exit polls "reflect what voters thought they did in the voting booth." See Posner, *Breaking the Deadlock: The 2000 Election, the Constitution, and the Courts* (Princeton, NJ: Princeton University Press, 2001), 61.

65. This point was made by Claire Wardle and others in "The Voter News Service and the 2000 Election Night calls," *American Behavioral Science* 44, 12 (August 2001): 2307.

66. See Wardle and others, "The Voter News Service and the 2000 Election Night calls," *American Behavioral Science*, 2307. "Until a problem occurred," the article noted, "there was no allusion to VNS at all on CBS."

67. Jeff Greenfield, *Oh, Waiter! One Order of Crow!* (New York: Putman, 2001), 4.

68. Bush's senior adviser, Karl Rove, complained the exit polls were "screwed up beyond historic standards" and "almost beyond belief. Actually, they were beyond belief." See Rove, *Courage and Consequence*, 194.

69. Joe Lenski, memorandum to Tom Hannon, appendix 3 in Konner, Risser, and Wattenberg, "Television's performance on Election Night 2000," i. Lenski and Warren Mitofsky made election projections in 2000 for CNN and CBS News.

70. These erroneous exit-poll estimates were presented in Lenski's memorandum to Hannon, appendix 3 in Konner, Risser, and Wattenberg, "Television's performance on Election Night 2000."

71. Cited in appendix 4 in Konner, Risser, and Wattenberg, "Television's performance on Election Night 2000," i.

72. See Joan Konner, "The case for caution: This system is dangerously flawed," *Public Opinion Quarterly* 67, 1 (Spring 2003): 11.

73. Cited in Konner, "The case for caution," *Public Opinion Quarterly*, 11.

74. See Mitofsky, "Voter News Service after the fall," *Public Opinion Quarterly*, 51. Mitofsky wrote that "Voter News Service used a high percentage of first-time interviewers for conducting the exit polls" but did not specify how extensively those interviewers had been used.

75. See Konner, "The case for caution," *Public Opinion Quarterly*, 14. Voter News Service estimated that absentee voting would represent 7.5 percent of all voting in Florida. In fact, 12 percent of the vote there was cast by absentee ballot.

76. Konner, Risser, and Wattenberg, "Television's performance on Election Night 2000," 3, 19

77. Dan Rather, "CBS News election night," CBS News (November 7, 2000); transcript retrieved from LexisNexis database.

78. Reg Henry, a writer for the *Pittsburgh Post-Gazette*, stated in panning the anchor's "goofy remarks" that Rather was "as annoying as a tick behind a mule's ear." See Henry, "Dan Rather's silly sayings sally forth," *Pittsburgh Post-Gazette* (November 14, 2000); retrieved from LexisNexis database.

79. Steve Johnson of the *Chicago Tribune* sought to explain Rather's aphorisms in an article a week after the election. The "frog had side pockets" comment, Johnson wrote, was meant to address "the pointlessness of 'if formulations.'" See Johnson, "Dan Rather's metaphors anchored in folksy truisms," *Los Angeles Times* (November 14, 2000); accessed May 21, 2019, at: https://www.latimes.com/archives/la-xpm-2000-nov-14-ca-51302-story.html

80. Quoted in Howard Kurtz, "Exit wounds: Polls led networks astray," *Washington Post* (November 9, 2000): A31.

81. Greenfield, *Oh, Waiter! One Order of Crow!* 83. Greenfield noted that moments before the retraction, CNN's polling expert, Bill Schneider, said the network's analysts had "a pretty high degree of assurance" about Gore's having won Florida.

82. Quoted in Louis Menand, "Anchors astray," *New Yorker* (November 20, 2000): 40.

83. "ABC 2000: The vote," ABC News special report (November 8, 2000); transcript retrieved from LexisNexis database.

84. Howard Kurtz, the media writer for the *Washington Post* observed: "The two botched calls . . . were more than a black eye for some of the country's most elite news organizations. They were a reminder that television creates and sometimes distorts reality, to the point that Gore called Bush to concede (before calling back to un-concede) based on what he'd seen on the tube." See Kurtz, "Exit wounds," *Washington Post*.

85. Quoted in Kevin Sack and Frank Bruni, "How Gore stopped short on his way to concede," *New York Times* (November 9, 2000): A1, B9.

86. See Von Drehle, "The night that would not end," *Washington Post*, A1. Bush wrote in his memoir, "I don't know about snippy, but I was hot. Just when I thought

this wild race had ended, we were back at the starting gate." Bush said he contemplated declaring victory despite Gore's retraction, but decided against doing so. See Bush, *Decision Points*, 78.

87. Quoted in Charlie McCollum, "The media stumble," [San Jose, CA] *Mercury News* (November 9, 2000): 18A.

88. Quoted in Henry, "Dan Rather's silly sayings," *Pittsburgh Post-Gazette*. Henry observed that "old Dan seems to have gotten a bit carried away on election night, and even if you were a real down-home person, this babble would have left you scratching your head with the coal tongs."

89. Mitofsky, "Voter News Service after the fall," *Public Opinion Quarterly*, 54.

90. William Saletan, "Burnt toast," Slate.com (November 9, 2000); accessed February 22, 2018, at: https://slate.com/news-and-politics/2000/11/burnt-toast.html. Saletan's final prediction was that Gore would win the election with 284 electoral votes to Bush's 254 votes. See "U.S. elections—the pundits' predictions," [London] *Independent* (November 7, 2000); retrieved from Factiva database.

91. Leon Neyfakh, "Stop trying to make 'flytrap' happen: Slate's greatest failures," Slate.com (September 27, 2016); accessed May 25, 2019, at: https://slate.com/news-and-politics/2016/09/the-paywall-bush-is-toast-monkeyfishing-and-other-slate-failures.html

92. William Saletan, "Warm bread," Slate.com (August 3, 2004); accessed May 25, 2019, at: https://slate.com/news-and-politics/2004/08/bush-s-grim-poll-numbers.html

7. 'PRESIDENT KERRY'

1. Dan Berry, "Jimmy Breslin, whose pen rattled the mighty in New York, dies at 88," *New York Times* (March 19, 2017): A1.

2. Jack Newfield and Wayne Barrett, *City for Sale* (New York: Harper & Row, 1988), 63.

3. Jimmy Breslin, "I'm right—again. So I quit. Beautiful," *Newsday* (November 2, 2004): A2. An appended editor's note said, "This is Jimmy Breslin's last regular column for *Newsday*. He will write from time to time."

4. Cell phone–only voters made up only about 7 percent of the electorate on Election Day 2004, according to exit-poll data examined by Scott Keeter, director of surveys for the Pew Research Center. See Keeter, "The impact of cell phone noncoverage bias on polling in the 2004 presidential election," *Public Opinion Quarterly* 70, 1 (Spring 2006): 90.

5. Breslin, "I'm right—again," *Newsday*.

6. Breslin, "I'm right—again," *Newsday*.

7. "What George Gallup was to public opinion polls, Mitofsky was to election exit polling," CBS News said in its obituary about Mitofsky. His death, the network said, "leaves a large void in an area of expertise few understand well." See Vaughn Ververs, "Exit the exit poll master," CBS News (September 7, 2006); accessed December 31, 2018, at: https://www.cbsnews.com/news/exit-the-exit-poll-master/

8. See Brooke Gladstone and Bob Edwards, "Media elites vs. public opinion," NPR *Morning Edition* program (November 3, 1998); transcript retrieved from LexisNexis database.

9. See Richard Morin, "Surveying the damage," *Washington Post* (November 21, 2004): B1. "A few more presidential elections like this one," Morin wrote in the aftermath of the exit poll failure, "and the public will learn to do the right thing and simply ignore news of early exit poll data."

10. George W. Bush, *Decision Points* (New York: Crown, 2010), 294.

11. Bush, *Decision Points*, 294.

12. See Morin, "Surveying the damage," *Washington Post.*

13. Polling analyst Mark Blumenthal, author of the *Mystery Pollster* blog, expressed befuddlement about why the networks and the National Election Pool "gave no consideration to the virtual certainty that these numbers would make their way into the public domain. It ought to be obvious . . . that giving exit polls to 500 or so reporters, editors and producers—all of whom have phones and computers—is essentially the same as putting them in the public domain. It was not exactly a surprise that the leaked exit polls would be all over the Internet, yet they had no strategy to help the consumers of leaked numbers understand what they were looking at." See Blumenthal, "Exit polls: What we know," *Mystery Pollster* blog (November 4, 2004); accessed December 29, 2018, at: https://www.mysterypollster.com/main/2004/11/exit_polls_what_1.html

14. Matthew Dowd, quoted in Kathleen Hall Jamieson, ed., *Electing the President 2004: The Insiders' View* (Philadelphia: University of Pennsylvania Press, 2006), 88.

15. Jim Rutenberg, "Early night for viewers becomes a cliffhanger," *New York Times* (November 3, 2004): A1.

16. See Robert Shrum, *No Excuses: Concessions of a Serial Campaigner* (New York: Simon & Schuster, 2007), xiii.

17. See Joan Vennochi, "An election day secret," *Boston Globe* (December 7, 2004); accessed May 20, 2019, at: http://archive.boston.com/news/globe/editorial_opinion /oped/articles/2004/12/07/an_election_day_secret/. Vennochi, a columnist for the *Globe*, wrote that Shrum was "flush with exit poll excitement and reportedly turned to Kerry early on election night to ask: 'Can I be the first to call you Mr. President?'" Another version quoted Mike McCurry, an adviser to Kerry who was a White House press secretary during the Bill Clinton presidency, as saying that Shrum took Kerry aside on Election Night and said, "Let me be the first to call you Mr. President." Quoted in E. J. Kessler, "Campaign confidential," *The Forward* [New York] (December 10, 2004): 7. The *New York Times* repeated the dramatized version in late September 2008, shortly after Shrum had publicly predicted that Barack Obama would win the presidency. "This could normally be taken as a good sign, but Mr. Shrum . . . has a troubling record of uttering famous last words that declare Democratic victories," the *Times* noted. "It was Mr. Shrum who planted this memorable election night kiss of death onto John Kerry in 2004: 'Can I be the first to call you Mr. President?' Shrum asked Kerry after exit polls showed him defeating President Bush. Four years earlier, after television networks called Florida for Al Gore, Mr. Shrum said to a group of

Mr. Gore's aides in Nashville, 'We've finally pushed the boulder up the hill,' according to two people who were with him that night." See Mark Leibovich, "More famous last words?" *New York Times* (September 30, 2008): 25.

18. John Kerry, *Every Day Is Extra* (New York: Simon & Schuster, 2018), 324. Kerry said he so replied "not just because I was superstitious, but because I knew too much could happen between the exit polls and the counting. I refused myself any premature celebration, though the polls did raise my hopes."

19. Shrum did not respond to email messages, seeking to clarify what he had said to Kerry.

20. Shrum, *No Excuses*, xiii.

21. Kerry, *Every Day Is Extra*, 324.

22. See Jim Geraghty, *Voting to Kill: How 9/11 Launched the Era of Republican Leadership* (New York: Touchstone, 2006), 286.

23. See John Tierney, "Political points: Now that the dust has settled," *New York Times* (November 7, 2004): 34.

24. "I thought we captured a trend," Zogby said the day after the election, "but apparently that result didn't materialize." Quoted in Nick Anderson and Faye Fiore, "Exit polls: Early data for Kerry proved misleading," *Los Angeles Times* (November 4, 2004): A17.

25. Calculations by Randall J. Jones Jr. in "The state of presidential election forecasting: The 2004 experience," *International Journal of Forecasting* 24 (2008): 316.

26. Quoted in Louis Menand, "Permanent fatal errors: Did the voters send a message?" *New Yorker* (November 29, 2004); accessed June 24, 2014, at: http://www.newyorker.com/archive/2004/12/06/041206fa_fact_menand?currentPage=all. Mellman said in an oral history interview years later that "there was one time I thought we were going to win. It was election night, when the exit poll people called me and told me that we were winning Ohio and Florida and sundry other places. And they said, 'There's really little doubt about it.' So, once they told me that, that's the first time I believe[d] we were going to win." See Mark Mellman, interview with Center for Presidential History, "The Election of 2004 Collective Memory Project," Southern Methodist University (October 15, 2013); accessed December 31, 2018, at: http://cphcmp.smu.edu/2004election/mark-mellman-2/

27. See Rutenberg, "Early night for viewers," *New York Times*.

28. Cited in Rutenberg, "Early night for viewers," *New York Times*.

29. Menand, "Permanent fatal errors," *New Yorker*.

30. Cal Thomas, "Election 2004—Democrats lose more than vote," [Greenwood, SC] *Index-Journal* (November 7, 2004): 10.

31. Conor O'Clery, "False dawn for Kerry as exit polls weaved a tangled web," *Irish Times* (November 6, 2004): 10.

32. Cited in "The 7 hour presidency of JFK2 (political pros react to network exit polling debacle)," FreeRepublic.com (November 4, 2004); accessed March 2, 2018, at: http://www.freerepublic.com/focus/f-news/1269011/posts. See also Anderson and Fiore, "Early data for Kerry proved misleading," *Los Angeles Times*. The article men-

tioned the "7 hour presidency" headline, noting it referred "to the period of time . . . when raw exit poll numbers were flying through newsrooms and around the Internet. Such data caused Sen. Susan Collins (R-Maine) to become so despondent at one point . . . that she e-mailed her mother: 'All is lost.'"

33. Quoted in Anderson and Fiore, "Early data for Kerry proved misleading," *Los Angeles Times.* In addition, polling analyst Blumenthal pointed out that bloggers weren't alone in their mistaken belief that Kerry was heading to victory. "Very serious reporters from very serious media outlets jumped to the conclusion that Kerry was running the table, just like all those 'unsophisticated' bloggers," he wrote. See Blumenthal, "Exit polls: What we know," *Mystery Pollster* blog.

34. Jack Shafer, "Press box: Exit zone," Slate.com (November 6, 2004); retrieved from LexisNexis database.

35. Steve Coll, "Managing Editor Steve Coll," *Washington Post* online conversation (November 3, 2004); accessed December 31, 2018, at: http://www.washingtonpost .com/wp-dyn/articles/A13590–2004Oct31.html?noredirect=on

36. See "Evaluation of Edison/Mitofsky Election System 2004, prepared by Edison Media Research and Mitofsky International for the National Election Pool" (January 19, 2005): 31–33.

37. "Evaluation of Edison/Mitofsky Election System 2004," 3.

38. "Evaluation of Edison/Mitofsky Election System 2004," 4.

39. Details from "Evaluation of Edison/Mitofsky Election System 2004," 49.

40. See "Evaluation of Edison/Mitofsky Election System 2004," 52.

41. See "Evaluation of Edison/Mitofsky Election System 2004," 46.

42. Edison/Mitofsky memorandum to NEP [National Election Pool] Steering Committee (December 8, 2004): Box 5, Warren J. Mitofsky papers, Thomas J. Dodd Research Center, University of Connecticut, Storrs.

43. Warren J. Mitofsky, plenary speech, AAPOR national conference (May 14, 2005), Miami Beach, FL.

44. Walter Shapiro, "A funny thing happened on the way out of the polls," *USA Today* (November 3, 2004); retrieved from NexisUni database.

45. Mitofsky said he suspected that "the logos of six news organizations on the top of the [questionnaire] are not improving the response rate, as we had hoped they might. We don't know this for a fact." Mitofsky, plenary speech, AAPOR national conference (May 14, 2005).

46. Quoted in John Cook, "Early exit polls overstated Kerry results, media group says," *Chicago Tribune* (January 20, 2005); accessed June 7, 2018, at: https://www .chicagotribune.com/news/ct-xpm-2005–01–20–0501200297-story.html

47. Nate Cohn, "Debunking idea that win was stolen from Bernie Sanders," *New York Times* (June 28, 2016): A3.

48. See Jim Rutenberg, "Once-bitten networks vow not to make hasty calls," *New York Times* (November 2, 2004): A24. Rutenberg reported, "Officials at every major news network said they were instructing their anchors and analysts to avoid declaring a result in any state where they are uncertain about the outcome, no matter what

others have reported—essentially asking competitive network news reporters to quash an instinct as natural as drinking water."

49. Mitofsky, plenary speech, AAPOR national conference (May 14, 2005).

50. See Blumenthal, "Exit polls: What we know," *Mystery Pollster* blog.

51. Quoted in Jim Rutenberg, "Reports says problems led to skewed surveying data," *New York Times* (November 5. 2004): A23.

52. See Richard Morin, "The pioneer pollster whose credibility you could count on," *Washington Post* (September 6, 2006): C1.

53. Quoted in Morin, "The pioneer pollster whose credibility you could count on," *Washington Post*. Mitofsky was seventy-one years old when he died in September 2006.

54. Coll, "Managing Editor Steve Coll," *Washington Post* online conversation.

55. Robert F. Kennedy Jr., "Was the 2004 election stolen?" *Rolling Stone* (June 15, 2006); article retrieved from ProQuest database.

56. Quoted in Kennedy, "Was the 2004 election stolen?" *Rolling Stone*. Morris made the claim in a commentary for *The Hill* newspaper in Washington, DC. He also wrote: "Exit polls cannot be as wrong across the board as they were on election night. I suspect foul play." See Dick Morris, "Those faulty exit polls were sabotage," *The Hill* (November 4, 2004); accessed January 5, 2019, at: https://thehill.com/opinion/columnists/dick-morris/4723-those-faulty-exit-polls-were-sabotage

57. "Dick Morris is entitled to his opinion, but many others with more relevant exit poll experience disagree," polling analyst Mark Blumenthal wrote in assessing Kennedy's *Rolling Stone* article. See Blumenthal, "Is RFK, Jr. right about exit polls? Part 1," *Mystery Pollster* blog (June 5, 2006); accessed March 10, 2020, at: https://mysterypollster.com/2006/06/is_rfk_jr_right-2/

58. Morin, "Surveying the damage," *Washington Post*.

59. Mitofsky markup of Kennedy, "Was the 2004 election stolen?" *Rolling Stone*: Box 17, Mitofsky papers.

60. Mitofsky markup of Kennedy, "Was the 2004 election stolen?" *Rolling Stone*, Mitofsky papers.

61. Mark Blumenthal, "Is RFK Jr., right about exit polls? Part IV," *Mystery Pollster* blog (July 6, 2006); accessed March 10, 2020 at: https://mysterypollster.com/2006/07/is_rfk_jr_right/. Blumenthal deplored "the way Robert Kennedy has chosen to take such liberties with the truth in his discussion of the exit polls."

62. See Mark Crispin Miller, "None dare call it stolen," *Harper's Magazine* (August 2005): 39–46. "The press," Miller wrote (40), "has had little to say about most of the strange details of the election—except, that is, to ridicule all efforts to discuss them." The article drew heavily on "Preserving democracy: What went wrong in Ohio," a report prepared by Democrats on the Judiciary Committee of the U.S. House of Representatives, the most senior of whom was John Conyers Jr. of Michigan, who spearheaded the study.

63. See Mark Hertsgaard, "Recounting Ohio: Was Ohio stolen? You may not like the answer," *Mother Jones* (November 2005); accessed January 5, 2019, at: https://www.motherjones.com/media/2005/11/recounting-ohio/. Hertsgaard also wrote: "In the

end, reasonable people may differ about the strength of the skeptics' case. Personally I came away persuaded there was indeed something rotten in the state of Ohio in 2004. Whether by intent or negligence, authorities took actions that prevented many thousands of citizens from casting votes and having them counted."

64. Michael P. O'Grady, quoted in Hertsgaard, "Recounting Ohio," *Mother Jones*.

65. Hertsgaard, "Recounting Ohio," *Mother Jones*. He also wrote, "And is it really so strange to imagine that Bush supporters—who tend to distrust the supposedly liberal news media—might not answer questions from pollsters bearing the logos of CBS, CNN, and the other news organizations financing the polling operation?"

66. See Sheryl Gay Stolberg and James Dao, "Congress ratifies Bush victory after a rare challenge," *New York Times* (January 7, 2005): A19.

67. Quoted in Frank Cerabino, "Left-wing pollster Zogby praised on the right," *Palm Beach* [FL] *Post* (October 29, 2004): 9A.

68. Tierney, "Political points," *New York Times*.

69. Michael W. Traugott, "Abstract: The accuracy of the national preelection polls in the 2004 presidential election," *Public Opinion Quarterly* 69, 5 (2005): 642.

70. Jim Rutenberg, "Bush leads. Make that Kerry. Why can't the pollsters agree?" *New York Times* (October 19, 2004): A1.

71. David W. Moore, *The Opinion Makers: An Inside Exposes the Truth behind the Polls* (Boston: Beacon Press, 2008), xii–xiii.

72. Criticism of polls, Kathleen A. Frankovic observed, "reached a new intensity in 2004." See Frankovic, "Reporting 'the polls' in 2004," *Public Opinion Quarterly* 69, 5 (2005): 683. Frankovic then was director of surveys for CBS News.

73. The advertisement's estimated cost was noted by Frank Newport, Gallup's editor-in-chief, in a scholarly journal article about the MoveOn-Gallup controversy. See Robert P. Daves and Frank Newport, "Pollsters under attack: 2004 election incivility and its consequences," *Public Opinion Quarterly* 69, 5 (2005): 675.

74. The ad began this way: "If John Kerry believed in the Gallup poll, he might as well give up. A couple of weeks ago, a highly publicized Gallup poll of 'likely voters' showed President Bush with a staggering 14-point lead. But wait a minute. Seven other polls of likely voters were released that same week. On average, they showed Bush with just a three-point lead. No one else came close to Gallup's figures. And this isn't the first time the prestigious Gallup survey has been out on a limb with pro-Bush findings. What's going on here? It's not exactly that Gallup's cooking the books. Rather, they are refusing to fix a longstanding problem with their likely voter methodology." About Gallup Jr., the ad said: "Why hasn't he pushed for an update of the company's likely voter modeling, which his own father pioneered in the 1950s? Gallup, who is a devout evangelical Christian, has been quoted as calling his polling 'a kind of ministry.' And a few months ago, he said 'the most profound purpose of polls is to see how people are responding to God.' We thought the purpose is to faithfully and factually report public opinion."

75. Polling analyst Mark Blumenthal wrote in his *Mystery Pollster* blog that "it is appropriate to question Gallup's likely voter model, and likely voter models generally,

but the tone and substance of the MoveOn advertisement just goes too far. . . . Whatever doubts I have about Gallup's model, I don't believe for a minute that they are intentionally 'Gallup-ing to the Right,' as MoveOn loudly charges." See Blumenthal, "MoveOn vs. Gallup," *Mystery Pollster* blog (September 29, 2004); accessed March 10, 2020, at: https://mysterypollster.com/2004/09/moveon_vs_gallu.html

76. Quoted in Richard Morin, "Don't ask me: As fewer cooperate on polls, criticism and questions mount," *Washington Post* (October 28, 2004): C1.

77. Daves and Newport, "Pollsters under attack," *Public Opinion Quarterly*, 675. The article also said (674), "The specific allegations in the ad relating to George Gallup Jr. were based on the technique of guilt by innuendo and implied causal association."

78. Rochelle Olson, "40 Republicans protest newspaper's polls," [Minneapolis] *Star Tribune* (September 21, 2004): 3B.

79. Morin, "Don't ask me," *Washington Post.*

80. Olson, "40 Republicans protest newspaper's polls," *Star Tribune.*

81. Daves and Newport, "Pollsters under attack," *Public Opinion Quarterly*, 674.

82. Morin, "Don't ask me," *Washington Post.*

83. Jimmy Breslin, "Making call on sham of political polling," *Newsday* (September 16, 2004): A2.

84. Breslin, "Making call on sham of political polling," *Newsday.*

85. Breslin, "Making call on sham of political polling," *Newsday.*

86. Quoted in Morin, "Don't ask me," *Washington Post.*

87. See Keeter, "The impact of cell phone noncoverage bias on polling in the 2004 presidential election," *Public Opinion Quarterly*, 88, 94. Keeter also wrote (98), "In the 2004 election the telephone polls were helped by the fact that CPO [cell phone–only] voters were still a relatively small segment of the electorate and were similar politically to others in their age groups." In 2004, more than 90 percent of American adults had landline telephones. See Mark Blumenthal, "Polling has changed. The way we read (and sometimes misread) it has not," *Mystery Pollster* blog (January 10, 2020); accessed March 10, 2020, at: https://mysterypollster.com/2020/01/polling-has-changed-the-way-we-read-and-sometimes-misread-it-has-not/

88. Quoted in Morin, "Don't ask me," *Washington Post.*

89. Quoted in Eric Burns, "Quick takes on the media," *FoxNews Watch* program (October 30, 2004); transcript retrieved from LexisNexis database.

90. Arianna Huffington, interview on NPR *On the Media* program (October 22, 2004); transcript accessed June 10, 2019, at: https://www.wnycstudios.org/story/130106-polls-be-gone

91. See Michael Traugott, "Presidential address: Polling in the public's interest," *Public Opinion Quarterly* 64, 3 (Autumn 2000): 383.

8. 'GALLUP VS. THE WORLD'

1. Frank Newport, and others, "Romney 49%, Obama 48% in Gallup's final election survey," Gallup Organization news release (November 5, 2012); accessed June 13, 2017,

at: https://news.gallup.com/poll/158519/romney-obama-gallup-final-election-survey .aspx?g_source=ELECTION_2012&g_medium=topic&g_campaign=tiles. See also Ezra Klein, "Gallup poll presents an interesting possibility," *Washington Post* (October 20, 2012): A2. Klein took a close look at a Gallup tracking poll that showed Romney leading by seven percentage points and noted that Gallup's accompanying data showed Obama leading in all sections of the country but the South. That, Klein suggested, could mean "we're headed for an electoral college / popular vote split." He wrote that he spoke with Gallup's editor-in-chief Frank Newport about that prospect and quoted him as saying, "That's certainly what it looks like."

2. Paul Starr, a Princeton University professor of sociology and public affairs, wrote in a review of Nate Silver's *The Signal and the Noise: Why So Many Predictions Fail— But Some Don't*, "In the history of election forecasting, 2012 was 1936 all over again, with the roles updated." See Starr, "Tomorrow Today," *New Republic* (December 31, 2012): 39.

3. Cited in Alan Abramowitz, "Is Gallup heading for another big miss?" *Huffington Post* (October 20, 2012); accessed March 11, 2018, at: https://www.huffpost.com/entry /election-polls-gallup_b_1989865

4. Cited in Andy Sullivan, "As other polls show tight race, Gallup stands apart," Reuters (October 19, 2012); accessed June 1, 2019, at: https://www.reuters.com/article /us-usa-campaign-gallup/as-other-polls-show-tight-race-gallup-stands-apart-idUS-BRE89J02720121020

5. Karl Rove, "Sifting the numbers for a winner," *Wall Street Journal* (November 1, 2012): A15.

6. Michael Barone, "Barone: Going out on a limb, Romney beats Obama, handily," *Washington Examiner* (November 2, 2012); accessed June 1, 2019, at: https://www .washingtonexaminer.com/barone-going-out-on-a-limb-romney-beats-obama-hand-ily#.UJVZtIZj74Z

7. "Peggy Noonan's blog: Monday Morning," *Wall Street Journal* (November 5, 2012); posted at: https://blogs.wsj.com/peggynoonan/2012/11/05/monday-morning/

8. "Peggy Noonan's blog: Monday Morning," *Wall Street Journal*.

9. "Peggy Noonan's blog: Monday Morning," *Wall Street Journal*.

10. See Harry J. Enten, "How the 2012 election polling really was skewed—for Mitt Romney," [London] *Guardian* (November 21, 2012); accessed March 4, 2018, at: https://www.theguardian.com/commentisfree/2012/nov/21/2012-election-polling-skewed-for-mitt-romney. "Overall," Enten wrote, "it's fairly clear that the national polls missed the mark, big time." He further wrote, "Few will talk about the national miss because Obama won."

11. John Cassidy, writing in the *New Yorker*, said: "There's no getting away from the fact that the President's adroit response to the storm has had a significant effect on public opinion. After being behind in the national polls for most of October, he has now reestablished a narrow lead." See Cassidy, "How much did Hurricane Sandy help Obama?" *New Yorker* (November 4, 2012); accessed June 4, 2019, at: https://www .newyorker.com/news/john-cassidy/how-much-did-hurricane-sandy-help-obama

12. "Obama gains edge in campaign's final days," Pew Research Center (November 4, 2012); accessed June 4, 2019, at: https://www.people-press.org/2012/11/04/obama-gains-edge-in-campaigns-final-days/. Pew said Obama had improved his lead over Romney by twelve percentage points in Northeastern states, where the storm's effects were most pronounced.

13. See Mitchell Landsberg, "Rand tries something different, gets same results: Obama leading," *Los Angeles Times* (September 29, 2012); accessed June 4, 2019, at: https://www.latimes.com/politics/la-xpm-2012-sep-29-la-pn-rand-poll-obama-leads-20120929-story.html

14. See Tom Chivers, "Nerds 1, pundits 0," [London] *Telegraph* (November 7, 2012); retrieved from LexisNexis database. Chivers said the election outcome was "an emphatic vindication for the Nerdstrodamus, Nate Silver."

15. Nate Silver, "Uncertainty clouds polling, but Obama remains Electoral College favorite," *New York Times* FiveThirtyEight blog (October 22, 2012); retrieved from LexisNexis database.

16. Erick Wemple, "The New York Times's failure to keep Nate Silver: What it means," *Washington Post* (July 22, 2013); accessed March 11, 2020, at: https://www.washingtonpost.com/blogs/erik-wemple/wp/2013/07/22/the-new-york-timess-failure-to-keep-nate-silver-what-it-means/. Wemple noted that journalism was a "quantitatively challenged profession" that had not "spawned a population of little Nate Silvers."

17. Quoted on David Folkenflik, "Statistician Nate Silver scores big on election night," NPR *All Things Considered* program (November 7, 2012); transcript retrieved from LexisNexis database.

18. Nate Silver, "The media has a probability problem," *FiveThirtyEight* (September 21, 2017); accessed September 27, 2017, at: https://fivethirtyeight.com/features/the-media-has-a-probability-problem/. He said his predictions about the 2012 outcome "may have given people a false impression about how easy it is to forecast elections."

19. Nate Silver, "What the fox knows," *FiveThirtyEight* (March 17, 2014); accessed March 7, 2018, at: https://fivethirtyeight.com/features/what-the-fox-knows/

20. Nate Silver, interview with David Folkenflik, NPR *All Things Considered* program (November 7, 2012); transcript retrieved from LexisNexis database.

21. Silver, "Uncertainty clouds polling," *New York Times* FiveThirtyEight blog.

22. Nate Silver, "New audit allegations show flawed statistical thinking," *New York Times* FiveThirtyEight blog (May 17, 2013); posted at: https://fivethirtyeight.blogs.nytimes.com/2013/05/17/new-audit-allegations-show-flawed-statistical-thinking/?smid=tw-fivethirtyeight&seid=auto

23. Quoted in Mark Landler, "Obama promises speedy aid as storm takes on added political weight," *New York Times* (October 30, 2012): A10.

24. Nate Silver, "Obama's Electoral College 'firewall' holding in polls," *New York Times* FiveThirtyEight blog (November 1, 2012); accessed March 8, 2018, at: https://fivethirtyeight.blogs.nytimes.com/2012/11/01/oct-31-obamas-electoral-college-firewall-holding-in-polls/

25. Silver, "Obama's Electoral College 'firewall' holding in polls," *New York Times* FiveThirtyEight blog.

26. Tina Daunt, "Nate Silver: How the New York Times' election blogger became Hollywood's Xanax," Hollywoodreporter.com (November 1, 2012); accessed March 6, 2018, at: https://www.hollywoodreporter.com/news/nate-silver-how-new-york-385114. Daunt wrote that "the only calming agent more popular than Xanax is Nate Silver's FiveThirtyEight blog on *The New York Times* website."

27. See Rosie Gray, "Why liberals cling to Nate Silver," BuzzFeed News (October 29, 2012); accessed March 5, 2018, at: https://www.buzzfeednews.com/article/rosiegray/why-liberals-cling-to-nate-silver. "Here in New York," Gray wrote, "Silver is very much on the tongue of the media and the left-leaning professional elite: Everyone from photographers to the managing partner of a major law firm cops to hitting refresh every hour to stay sane. And out in the Democratic hinterlands, the reaction is much the same."

28. For example, Silver wrote during the closing days of the 2012 campaign that "describing the race as a 'toss-up' reflects an uninformed interpretation of the evidence." See Silver, "Obama's Electoral College 'firewall' holding in polls," *New York Times* FiveThirtyEight blog. On another occasion, following the 2012 election, Silver said "punditry" was "fundamentally useless." Quoted in Dylan Byers, "Nate Silver: 'Punditry is fundamentally useless,'" *Politico* (December 13, 2012); accessed June 4, 2019, at: https://www.politico.com/blogs/media/2012/12/nate-silver-punditry-is-fundamentally-useless-151881

29. Nate Silver, "Gallup vs. the World," *New York Times* FiveThirtyEight blog (October 18, 2012); accessed March 11, 2020, at: https://fivethirtyeight.com/features/gallup-vs-the-world/

30. Silver, "Gallup vs. the World," *New York Times* FiveThirtyEight blog.

31. Silver, "Gallup vs. the World," *New York Times* FiveThirtyEight blog.

32. Silver, "Uncertainty clouds polling," *New York Times* FiveThirtyEight blog.

33. See Harry Enten, "Are bad pollsters copying good pollsters?" *FiveThirtyEight* (August 11, 2014); accessed February 11, 2018, at: https://fivethirtyeight.com/features/are-bad-pollsters-copying-good-pollsters/

34. Dylan Byers, "Nate Silver: One-term celebrity?" *Politico* (October 29, 2012); accessed March 5, 2018, at: https://www.politico.com/blogs/media/2012/10/nate-silver-one-term-celebrity-147618

35. Dylan Byers, "Top 10 media stories of 2012," *Politico* (December 24, 2012); retrieved from LexisNexis database.

36. Quoted in Evan Puschak, "Campaign calculus: Nate Silver's predictions from the conventions to the election," MSNBC.com (November 9, 2012); accessed March 11, 2020, at: http://www.msnbc.com/the-last-word/campaign-calculus-nate-silvers-predictions

37. See "[Unskewed Polls] Final projection: Romney 275 electoral votes to Obama 263 electoral votes," FreeRepublic.com (November 6, 2012); accessed March 11, 2020, at: http://www.freerepublic.com/focus/news/2955525/posts?page=9

38. Quoted in Byers, "Nate Silver: One-term celebrity?" *Politico*.

39. Quoted in Byers, "Nate Silver: One-term celebrity?" *Politico*. Silver also said on a CNN program, "I think some of the critics that I've had are not very good at doing math and probability." See Piers Morgan, CNN *Piers Morgan Tonight* (October 30, 2012); transcript retrieved at LexisNexis.

40. Margaret Sullivan, "Under attack, Nate Silver picks the wrong defense," *New York Times* Public Editor's Journal (November 1, 2012); retrieved from LexisNexis database.

41. Sullivan, "Under attack, Nate Silver picks the wrong defense," *New York Times*.

42. Sullivan, "Under attack, Nate Silver picks the wrong defense," *New York Times*.

43. Margaret Sullivan, "The Times's Washington bureau chief, and legions of others, in defense of Nate Silver," *New York Times* Public Editor's Journal (November 2, 2012); retrieved from LexisNexis database.

44. Margaret Sullivan, "A year in the life of a watchdog," *New York Times* (September 1, 2013): SR12.

45. Quoted in Alexander C. Kaufman, "For Nate Silver, the apologies are trickling in," *The Wrap* (November 21, 2012); retrieved from LexisNexis database.

46. Nate Silver, "Which polls fared best (and worst) in the 2012 presidential race," *New York Times* FiveThirtyEight blog (November 10, 2012); retrieved from LexisNexis database. During the campaign, Silver pointed to the Gallup poll's showing a substantial lead for Romney, saying, "No other survey indicates a result at all like that, but that poll gets a disproportionate amount of attention." See Flora Lichtman, "Making sense of presidential polls," NPR *Science Friday* program (October 19, 2012); transcript retrieved from LexisNexis database.

47. Frank Newport, "Polling, likely voters, and the Law of the Commons," Gallup Organization statement (November 9, 2012); accessed June 1, 2019, at: https://news.gallup.com/opinion/polling-matters/169877/polling-likely-voters-law-commons.aspx

48. Tom Keene and Ken Prewitt, "Gallup Poll EIC Frank Newport talks politics on Bloomberg Radio," *Bloomberg Surveillance* radio program (September 21, 2012); retrieved from LexisNexis database. Newport also said: "Our opinion at Gallup is if we didn't poll, he would have nothing to analyze. So it is kind of a law of the commons. Everybody makes a decision to stop polling because they can just aggregate other people's polls, after a while there will be no polls to aggregate."

49. Newport, "Polling, likely voters, and the Law of the Commons," Gallup Organization statement.

50. Andrew Leonard, "Gallup is very upset at Nate Silver," Salon.com (November 12, 2012); accessed August 21, 2017, at: https://www.salon.com/2012/11/13/gallup_is_very_upset_at_nate_silver/

51. "Without Gallup's crappy polls, Nate Silver is nothing, says Gallup," *Wonkette* blog (November 14, 2012); retrieved from LexisNexis database.

52. John Reinan, "Why Gallup hates Nate Silver," MinnPost [Minneapolis] (November 19, 2012); accessed June 3, 2019, at: https://www.minnpost.com/business/2012/11/why-gallup-hates-nate-silver. Reinan also wrote, "It's the same *cri de coeur* that has come from the traditional media in recent years: If we do the work,

and others piggyback on it, eventually there won't be anyone left to do the work in the first place."

53. Walter Shapiro, "What if there are fewer polls in 2016?" *Columbia Journalism Review* (November 27, 2012); accessed May 31, 2019, at: https://archives.cjr.org/united_states_project/fewer_polls_in_2016.php

54. Harry Enten, "USA Today drops Gallup as its pollster: What took so long?" [London] *Guardian* (January 19, 2013); retrieved from LexisNexis database.

55. Nate Cohn, "USA Today's divorce from Gallup is good news for everyone but Gallup," *New Republic* (January 23, 2013); accessed June 1, 2019, at: https://newrepublic.com/article/112112/usa-todaygallup-break-good-news-election-watchers

56. "Gallup, don't let the door hit you on the way out," *National Journal* Hotline newsletter (March 22, 2006); retrieved from LexisNexis database.

57. See "Gallup polling drops CNN after 'low rating'; full memo revealed," *Drudge Report* (March 21, 2006); accessed June 3, 2019, at: http://www.freerepublic.com/focus/f-news/1600631/posts

58. "Gallup, don't let the door hit you," *National Journal* Hotline.

59. David W. Moore, *The Opinion Makers: An Insider Exposes the Truth behind the Polls* (Boston: Beacon Press, 2008), 20.

60. Moore, *The Opinion Makers*, 21.

61. Scott Clement, "Gallup explains what went wrong in 2012," *Washington Post* (June 4, 2013); retrieved from LexisNexis database.

62. Clement, "Gallup explains what went wrong," *Washington Post*.

63. "Gallup 2012 presidential election polling review," Gallup Organization report (June 4, 2013); retrieved August 21, 2017, at: https://news.gallup.com/poll/162887/gallup-2012-presidential-election-polling-review.aspx

64. "Gallup 2012 presidential election polling review," Gallup Organization report.

65. Quoted in Jonathan Easley, "Gallup overhauls polls after 2012 failure," *The Hill* (June 4, 2013); accessed June 3, 2019, at: http://thehill.com/blogs/ballot-box/polls/303339-gallup-overhauling-polling-methods-after-failure-in-2012-election

66. Quoted in Megan Thee-Brenan, "Gallup ends 'horse race' polling of 2016 presidential race to focus on issues," *New York Times* First Draft blog (October 7, 2015); accessed November 11, 2019, at: https://www.nytimes.com/politics/first-draft/2015/10/07/poll-watch-gallup-ends-horse-race-polling-of-2016-presidential-race-to-focus-on-issues/

67. See "Proceedings of the American Association for Public Opinion Research," *Public Opinion Quarterly* 17, 4 (Winter 1953–1954): 531.

68. Harry Enten, "Gallup gave up. Here's why that sucks," *FiveThirtyEight* (October 7, 2015); accessed January 12, 2018, at: https://fivethirtyeight.com/features/gallup-gave-up-heres-why-that-sucks/

69. Peter D. Hart, "Gallup's 2016 decision—and our loss," *Wall Street Journal* (October 14, 2015); accessed November 11, 2019, at: https://blogs.wsj.com/washwire/2015/10/14/gallups-2016-decision-and-our-loss/

70. See Moore, *The Opinion Makers*, 20–21.

71. U.S. government amended complaint against the Gallup Organization (November 27, 2012); accessed October 25, 2019, at: https://vsg-law.com/wp-content /uploads/2012/11/b-relators_first_amended_complaint_lindley_gallup.pdf

72. See Barbara Soderlin, "Gallup plans changes, will pay $10.5 million in deal to settle case," [Omaha] *World-Herald* (July 15, 2013); accessed June 1, 2019, at: https:// www.omaha.com/money/gallup-plans-changes-will-pay-million-in-deal-to-settle /article_2a4e64b4-bb09–564c-9a65-a1fc49b73356.html

73. See Carrie Johnson, "DOJ sues Gallup for overcharging on contracts," NPR *All Things Considered* program (November 30, 2012); accessed October 25, 2019, at: https:// www.npr.org/2012/11/30/166260531/doj-sues-gallup-for-overcharging-on-contracts

74. Margaret Sullivan, "Nate Silver went against the grain for some at the Times," *New York Times* (July 22, 2013); accessed November 11, 2019, at: https://publiceditor.blogs .nytimes.com/2013/07/22/nate-silver-went-against-the-grain-for-some-at-the-times/

75. Sullivan, "Nate Silver went against the grain," *New York Times*.

76. See "Nate Silver makes move to ESPN," ESPN.com (22 July 2013); accessed March 11, 2020, at: https://www.espn.com/espn/story/_/id/9499752/nate-silver-joins-espn-multifaceted-roleGators%20LB%20arrested%20for%20barking%20at%20 police%20dog

77. Quoted in Walt Hickey, "Nate Silver: As tempting as it would be to 'drop the mic' and leave a winner, I'll be back in 2014 and 2016," BusinessInsider.com (November 14, 2012); accessed March 11, 2020, at: https://www.businessinsider.com/nate-silver-deadspin-polls-election-obama-romney-2012–11

9. 'THE NIGHT THAT WASN'T SUPPOSED TO HAPPEN'

1. Nate Silver, "Donald Trump is winning the polls—and losing the nomination," *FiveThirtyEight* (August 11, 2015); accessed May 26, 2019, at: https://fivethirtyeight .com/features/donald-trump-is-winning-the-polls-and-losing-the-nomination/

2. Nate Silver, "How I acted like a pundit and screwed up on Donald Trump," *FiveThirtyEight* (May 18, 2016); accessed March 7, 2018, at: https://fivethirtyeight.com /features/how-i-acted-like-a-pundit-and-screwed-up-on-donald-trump/

3. Liz Spayd, "Want to know what America's thinking? Try asking," *New York Times* (November 9, 2016); accessed June 3, 2017, at: https://www.nytimes.com/2016/11/10 /public-editor/want-to-know-what-americas-thinking-try-asking.html

4. See David Chalian, "Road to 270: CNN's latest Electoral College map," CNN (November 8, 2016); accessed May 27, 2019, at: https://www.cnn.com/2016/11/04 /politics/road-to-270-electoral-college-map-november-4-duplicate/index.html

5. Steven Shepard, "Trump hangs tough in battleground states," *Politico* (November 7, 2016); accessed May 23, 2018, at: https://www.politico.com/story/2016/11/trump-battleground-states-230875

6. See "Clinton leads by 6 points," Monmouth University Polling Institute news release (November 7, 2016); accessed May 27, 2019, at: https://www.monmouth.edu /polling-institute/reports/MonmouthPoll_US_110716/. See also Josh Clinton and

others, "Poll: On eve of Election Day, Clinton maintains her edge over Trump," NBC-News.com (November 7, 2016); accessed July 11, 2019, at: https://www.nbcnews.com/storyline/data-points/poll-eve-election-day-clinton-maintains-her-edge-over-trump-n678816

7. See John Merline, "Trump holds 2-point lead over Clinton as Election Day arrives," *Investor's Business Daily* (November 8, 2016); accessed May 27, 2019, at: https://www.investors.com/politics/trump-holds-2-point-lead-over-clinton-as-election-day-arrives-final-ibd-tipp-poll-results/. *Investor's Business Daily* conducted the poll with the TechnoMetrica Institute of Policy and Politics.

8. See Adam Goldman and Alan Rappeport, "New emails jolt Clinton campaign in race's last days," *New York Times* (October 29, 2016): A1.

9. Matthew Yglesias, "Why I think Nate Silver's model underrates Clinton's odds," *Vox* (November 7, 2016); accessed April 14, 2018, at: https://www.vox.com/policy-and-politics/2016/11/7/13550068/nate-silver-forecast-wrong

10. Silver said in the days before the November election. "We've learned that we have to be careful about how we convey uncertainty." Quoted in Margaret Sullivan, "Nate Silver blew it when he missed Trump. Now he really needs to get it right," *Washington Post* (October 30, 2016); retrieved from LexisNexis database.

11. The polls-based forecast models "helped crystalize the erroneous belief that Clinton was a shoo-in for president," the American Association for Public Opinion Research said in a report about polling in the 2016 election. See Courtney Kennedy and others, "An evaluation of 2016 election polls in the United States," American Association for Public Opinion Research (May 4, 2017), accessed May 5, 2017, at: https://www.aapor.org/Education-Resources/Reports/An-Evaluation-of-2016-Election-Polls-in-the-U-S.aspx

12. Cited in Paulina Firozi, "Pollster eats bug on live TV after being wrong about election," *The Hill* (November 12, 2016); accessed May 28, 2019, at: https://thehill.com/blogs/blog-briefing-room/news/305707-pollster-eats-bug-on-live-tv-after-being-wrong-about-election

13. "I figure we're going to lose but, you know, hey, this [campaigning] is sort of cool. I'd never did this stuff before," Trump said at what was called a "thank you rally" in suburban Milwaukee. See "Trump picks Tillerson for State," Fox News *Lou Dobbs Tonight* program (December 13, 2016); transcript retrieved from LexisNexis database.

14. Quoted in Gregory Krieg, "The day that changed everything: Election 2016, as it happened," CNN.com (November 8, 2017); retrieved from LexisNexis database. Amy Chozick, a *New York Times* reporter who covered Clinton's campaign, was aboard the plane, too, and wrote in a book of reminiscences: "I could hear Hillary's belly laugh. She wore an ample open-mouthed smile. In ten years of covering Hillary, the formative years of my adult life, really, I had never seen her so happy." See Chozick, *Chasing Hillary: Ten Years, Two Presidential Campaigns, and One Intact Glass Ceiling* (New York: HarperCollins, 2018), 4.

15. The *New York Times* described the Javits Center as "the unglamorous glass fortress on Manhattan's West Side." See Matt Flegenheimer, "Clinton to ring in election under a real 'glass ceiling': Manhattan's Javits Center," *New York Times* (October

27, 2016); retrieved from LexisNexis database. See also Jonathan Allen and Amie Parnes, *Shattered: Inside Hillary Clinton's Doomed Campaign* (New York: Crown, 2017), 373. The Javits Center, they wrote, "was chosen in large part because of its distinctive feature: a glass ceiling."

16. "Everything Hillary was hearing and seeing pointed to a victory," Jonathan Allen and Amie Parnes wrote in their account of Clinton's campaign. See Allen and Parnes, *Shattered,* 370.

17. See Julia Turner and Josh Voorhees, "Where VoteCastr went wrong: Assessing our Election Day experiment," Slate.com (November 11, 2016); accessed July 9, 2019, at: https://slate.com/news-and-politics/2016/11/where-slates-election-day-partner-ship-with-votecastr-went-wrong.html. See also Alexandra Alter, "Rocky start for VoteCastr, a tech start-up promising real-time data," *New York Times* (November 9, 2016); retrieved from LexisNexis database. The *Times* reported: "VoteCastr got off to a rocky start. First, there was an unexpected delay when its data team faced technical glitches and was unable to update the site early in the day as promised. It got worse as the day went on. At 11:57 a.m., VoteCastr posted on Twitter that its Nevada projections were off because they had erroneously included the Green Party candidate Jill Stein— who was not on the state ballot—in its survey. Then, shortly after 3 p.m., Slate posted an update saying that the state maps were inaccurate, because they represented only Election Day turnout data, and not early vote estimates. The maps were removed and later updated." The television writer for the *New York Daily News* dismissed VoteCastr as "nothing more than math porn for people starved for data" that "ultimately contrib-uted nothing." See Don Kaplan, "Channeling their inner statistics," *New York Daily News* (November 9, 2016): 20.

18. See Paul Vigna, "Traders jump on 'live' polling data, send stocks higher," *Wall Street Journal* (November 8, 2016); accessed July 9, 2016, at: https://blogs.wsj.com /moneybeat/2016/11/08/traders-jump-on-live-polling-data-send-stocks-higher/

19. Quoted in Brian Stetler, "In their own words: The story of covering Election Night 2016," CNN Business (January 5, 2017); accessed May 23, 2017, at: https:// money.cnn.com/2017/01/05/media/election-night-news-coverage-oral-history/

20. Kristen Soltis Anderson, interview with BBC, n.d.; accessed August 21, 2019, at: https://www.bbc.com/news/world-us-canada-41861675

21. Quoted in "The untold story of Election Day 2016," *Esquire* (November 6, 2017); accessed November 6, 2017, at: https://www.esquire.com/news-politics/a13266971 /election-2016-behind-the-scenes/

22. Quoted in "The untold story of Election Day 2016," *Esquire.*

23. In a note published after the election, the editors of *New York* said that "seeing the cover on the newsstand after Election Day makes us cringe" and added that the outcome "turned an image meant to be provocative into one that perhaps feels hubris-tic instead." They also said the cover was intended to be "more complex" than the infamous *Chicago Tribune* front page announcing, "Dewey defeats Truman." See "From the editors: About that Trump cover," *New York* (November 14, 2016); retrieved from ProQuest database.

24. See Sam Stein, "America has done what seemed unthinkable. Donald Trump is the next president," *Huffington Post* (November 9, 2016); retrieved from LexisNexis database.

25. Faithless electors reduced Trump's electoral vote to 304 and Clinton's to 227.

26. Phillip Reese, "How California votes may hand Clinton the popular vote—even if she loses the election," *Sacramento Bee* (November 3, 2016); accessed May 24, 2018, at: https://www.sacbee.com/news/databases/article112162287.html. Asked whether he received many kudos for his discerning pre-election assessment, Reese said: "My editor was quite impressed, if I recall. But other than that, not really. I think the majority of my readers—this being California—voted Hillary. To them, I might have seemed a little like a prophet bearing bad news!" Reese, email statement to author (June 4, 2019).

27. Quoted in Anthony Zurcher, "Remembering the night that changed America," BBC News (November 7, 2017); accessed August 21, 2019, at: https://www.bbc.com/news/world-us-canada-41861675

28. See Trevor Noah, "Live on Election Night," *The Daily Show with Trevor Noah* (November 8, 2016); video accessed October 8, 2017, at: http://www.cc.com/video-clips/juzdrn/the-daily-show-with-trevor-noah-live-on-election-night

29. Quoted in Paul Farhi, "Pollsters wonder: How did calculations go so wrong?" *Washington Post* (November 10, 2016): A43.

30. See David Remnick, "An American tragedy," *New Yorker* (November 9, 2016); accessed May 28, 2019, at: https://www.newyorker.com/news/news-desk/an-american-tragedy-2

31. "How did the polls get it wrong?" *Economist* (November 9, 2016); accessed March 19, 2018, at: https://www.economist.com/the-economist-explains/2016/11/09/how-did-the-polls-get-it-wrong?fsrc=scn/fb/te/bl/ed/howdidthepollsgetitwrong

32. Joshua Norman, "Why did many polls seem to miss a Trump victory?" CBS News (November 9, 2016); accessed May 27, 2019, at: https://www.cbsnews.com/news/why-did-many-polls-seem-to-miss-a-trump-victory/

33. See "AAPOR to examine 2016 Presidential election polling," American Association for Public Opinion Research news release (November 9, 2016); accessed May 25, 2018, at: https://www.aapor.org/Publications-Media/Press-Releases/AAPOR-to-Examine-2016-Presidential-Election-Pollin.aspx

34. Andrew Mercer, Claudia Deane, and Kyley McGeeney, "Why 2016 election polls missed their mark," Pew Research Center (November 9, 2016); accessed May 24, 2018, at: https://www.pewresearch.org/fact-tank/2016/11/09/why-2016-election-polls-missed-their-mark/

35. Jim Rutenberg, "News media again misreads complex pulse of the nation," *New York Times* (November 9, 2016): P15. Election Day, Rutenberg noted, "had been preceded by more than a month of declarations that the race was close but essentially over."

36. Natalie Jackson, "Don't swear off polls, help fix the problems," *Huffington Post* (January 6, 2017); retrieved from LexisNexis database.

37. Natalie Jackson, remarks in online seminar, "Polling and forecasting in the 2016 election," International Methods Colloquium (January 27, 2017); accessed October 1, 2019, at: https://www.youtube.com/watch?v=ZVuWI4UvCPc

38. Gregory Holyk, remarks at panel, "Tracking the election to understand Trump's win," (May 21, 2017); annual conference of the American Association for Public Opinion Research, New Orleans.

39. See Kennedy and others, "An evaluation of 2016 election polls," American Association for Public Opinion Research.

40. Sean Trende, "It wasn't the polls that missed, it was the pundits," *RealClear-Politics* (November 12, 2016); accessed March 14, 2018, at: https://www.realclearpolitics.com/articles/2016/11/12/it_wasnt_the_polls_that_missed_it_was_the_pundits_132333.html

41. The *Los Angeles Times* forecast Clinton to win 352 electoral votes. See David Lauter and Mark Z. Barabak, "Our final map has Clinton winning with 352 electoral votes," *Los Angeles Times* (November 6, 2016); accessed February 11, 2018, at: https://www.latimes.com/nation/politics/trailguide/la-na-trailguide-updates-here-s-our-final-electoral-map-of-the-1478473458-htmlstory.html

42. Nate Silver, "Election update: Why our model is more bullish than others on Trump," *FiveThirtyEight* (October 24, 2016); accessed May 31, 2019, at: https://fivethirtyeight.com/features/election-update-why-our-model-is-more-bullish-than-others-on-trump/

43. Nate Silver, "The real story of 2016," *FiveThirtyEight* (January 19, 2017); accessed May 25, 2017, at: https://fivethirtyeight.com/features/the-real-story-of-2016/. Silver noted, "We even got into a couple of very public screaming matches with people who we thought were unjustly overconfident in Trump's chances," a reference to his sharp exchanges on Twitter with Ryan Grim, an editor of the *Huffington Post* who had accused Silver of adjusting polling data so that they "fit where he thinks the polls truly are"—showing the race was tighter than most analysts recognized. See Grim, "Nate Silver is unskewing polls—all of them—in Trump's direction," *Huffington Post* (November 5, 2016); accessed May 30, 2019, at: https://www.huffpost.com/entry/nate-silver-election-forecast_n_581e1c33e4b0d9ce6fbc6f7f?ncid=engmodushpmg00000004

44. Had Clinton carried California by Barack Obama's margin over Mitt Romney in 2012—a little more than three million votes—her plurality nationally would have been trimmed to 1.615 million votes. See also John Merline, "It's official: Clinton's popular vote win came entirely from California," *Investor's Business Daily* (December 16, 2016); accessed May 24, 2018, at: https://www.investors.com/politics/commentary/its-official-clintons-popular-vote-win-came-entirely-from-california/

45. Philip Meyer, whose book *Precision Journalism* was instrumental in bringing the techniques of survey research into the American newsroom, observed in 1987, "The main source of news value in a pre-election poll is its clue to how the election will turn out." See Meyer, "Commentary: Polls are predictions (so let's stop kidding ourselves)," *Newspaper Research Journal* 8, 3 (Spring 1987): 83.

46. Patrick Murray, director of the Monmouth University Polling Institute, posed a similar question at the AAPOR conference in 2018. See Murray, "The hits and misses: Election poll accuracy in the U.S. and around the world," AAPOR panel presentation (May 18, 2018); AAPOR annual conference, Denver.

47. See Nate Silver, "The polls are all right," *FiveThirtyEight* (May 30, 2018); accessed June 11, 2018, at: https://fivethirtyeight.com/features/the-polls-are-all-right/. By Silver's calculations, the average polling error was 4.4 percentage points in 2000; 3.2 points in 2004; 3.6 points in 2008; 3.6 points in 2012, and 4.8 points in 2016.

48. Sixty-one percent of voters thought the Democrats most likely would win the 2016 presidential election, compared to 33 percent who thought the Republicans would win, according to survey data compiled by the American National Election Studies, a collaborative project of Stanford University and the University of Michigan. Cited in Nate Silver, "The media has a probability problem," *FiveThirtyEight* (September 21, 2017); accessed September 27, 2017, at: https://fivethirtyeight.com/features/the-media-has-a-probability-problem/

49. John Cassidy, "Media culpa? The press and the election result," *New Yorker* (November 11, 2016); accessed March 30, 2018, at: https://www.newyorker.com/news/john-cassidy/media-culpa-the-press-and-the-election-result

50. Alan Murray, "Polling and the Trump big fail," *Fortune* (November 14, 2016); accessed March 3, 2018, at: http://fortune.com/2016/11/14/polling-donald-trump-pew-fail/. Mark Blumenthal, a polling analyst in Washington, DC, who collaborated on AAPOR's post-election report, said at a news conference when the document was released that in 2016 "the polling was just wrong enough, nationally and at the state level, [so that] everybody got the wrong impression about what was going to happen." See Blumenthal, remarks at AAPOR news conference (May 4, 2017); video recording accessed August 24, 2019, at: https://www.facebook.com/AAPOROnline/videos/10155341923092174/

51. See Andrew Gelman and Julia Azari, "19 things we learned from the 2016 election," *Statistics and Public Policy* 4, 1 (2017): 4.

52. Spayd, "Want to know what America's thinking? Try asking," *New York Times*.

53. The American Association for Public Opinion Research, AAPOR, said in its report that state-level polls in 2016 "did have a historically bad year, at least within the recent history of the past four elections." See Kennedy and others, "An evaluation of 2016 election polls," American Association for Public Opinion Research, 12. AAPOR said its evaluation of 423 state polls completed within the closing thirteen days of the campaign showed an average absolute error of 5.1 percentage points. The "average absolute error" was determined by subtracting the average margin of the polls from the difference in the popular vote. Essentially, the lower the absolute error, the more accurate the polling. The average absolute error in the national polls in 2016 was 2.2 percentage points, AAPOR's report said. That was nearly as close as the average absolute error in the 2008 election, which was 1.8 percentage points. See Kennedy and others, "An evaluation of 2016 election polls," American Association for Public Opinion Research, 10.

54. Nate Cohn, "After a tough 2016, many pollsters haven't made adjustments," *New York Times* (November 7, 2017): A17.

55. Trump would have boosted his electoral vote advantage had he received a total of 77,700 more votes, distributed to his advantage, in Minnesota, New Hampshire, and Nevada. Winning those states would have expanded Trump's total by twenty electoral votes.

56. See Todd Spangler, "Trump gains in Michigan," *Detroit Free Press* (November 5, 2016): 1A. The *Free Press* reported the next day that voters in Michigan and elsewhere "are facing a far more uncertain outcome than it appeared just four or five weeks ago." See Todd Spangler, "Analysis: State and nation up for grabs as momentum shifts," *Detroit Free Press* (November 6, 2016): 1A.

57. Quoted in David Weigel, "State pollsters, pummeled by 2016, analyze what went wrong," *Washington Post* (December 30, 2016); retrieved from LexisNexis database.

58. Quoted in Weigel, "State pollsters, pummeled by 2016," *Washington Post.*

59. Charles Franklin, telephone interview with author (February 27, 2018).

60. Kennedy and others, "An evaluation of 2016 election polls," American Association for Public Opinion Research, 36. The report also said (37) that "highly educated voters were terrible proxies for the voters at the lowest education level. At least that was the case nationally and in the pivotal states in the Upper Midwest."

61. Nate Silver, "Why FiveThirtyEight gave Trump a better chance than almost anyone else," *FiveThirtyEight* (November 11, 2016); accessed May 31, 2019, at: https://fivethirtyeight.com/features/why-fivethirtyeight-gave-trump-a-better-chance-than-almost-anyone-else/

62. Darrel Rowland, "Dispatch poll virtually tied," *Columbus Dispatch* (November 6, 2016): 1A. The Dispatch Poll was based on returns from 1,151 registered voters in Ohio.

63. Jeff Nesbit, "2016's election data hero isn't Nate Silver. It's Sam Wang," *Wired* (November 7, 2016); accessed March 27, 2018, at: https://www.wired.com/2016/11/2016s-election-data-hero-isnt-nate-silver-sam-wang/

64. Sam Wang, "Looking ahead," Princeton Election Consortium (November 9, 2016); accessed September 27, 2017, at: http://election.princeton.edu/2016/11/09/aftermath/

65. Alexandra King, "Poll expert eats bug after being wrong about Trump," CNN.com (November 12, 2016); accessed July 12, 2018, at: https://www.cnn.com/2016/11/12/politics/pollster-eats-bug-after-donald-trump-win/index.html

66. See Daniel Katz, "The public opinion polls and the 1940 election," *Public Opinion Quarterly* 5, 1 (March 1941): 52.

67. Hugh S. Johnson, "General Johnson says: He'll eat that column if necessary," *Knoxville News-Sentinel* (November 7, 1940): 23. Johnson further wrote about eating his column: "Dr. Gallup ate it before I did. He got so jittery that he covered himself on every side and finally said that the election was so close that a breath could swing it either way. Some breath!" Gallup's final pre-election estimate showed Roosevelt ahead by 52 percent to 48 percent. Roosevelt won the election by nearly ten percentage points.

Although Gallup had estimated a closer margin for Roosevelt, he declared that "the established scientific sampling polls came through the election with flying colors." Quoted in "Dr. Gallup cites surveys' success," *New York Times* (7 November 1940): 15.

68. Samuel Wang, interview with author (June 19, 2018).

69. See Kyle Pope, "Here's to the return of the journalist as malcontent," *Columbia Journalism Review* (November 9, 2016); accessed May 28, 2019, at: https://www.cjr .org/criticism/journalist_election_trump_failure.php

70. Pope, "Here's to the return of the journalist as malcontent," *Columbia Journalism Review*. Pope returned to the topic in early 2020, writing: "It is now obvious that we as an industry have learned nothing from the fundamental failures that led to the election of 2016. . . . A journalistic reckoning I hoped would materialize never did; Twitter, outrage, and a million arbitrarily urgent news cycles got in the way." See Kyle Pope, "The one way Sanders is the new Trump," *Columbia Journalism Review* (February 27, 2020); accessed March 1, 2020, at: https://www.cjr.org/first_person/one-way-sanders-is-the-new-trump.php

71. Or as *The Atlantic*'s Peter Beinart wrote about Trump and journalists: "The more audaciously he lies, the more audaciously they must tell the truth. The risks of doing so are tremendous. The rewards are being able to say that when Donald Trump threatened American liberal democracy like no candidate in modern history, you met his challenge square on." See Beinart, "The death of he-said, she-said journalism," *The Atlantic* (September 19, 2016); accessed July 12, 2019, at: https://www .theatlantic.com/politics/archive/2016/09/the-death-of-he-said-she-said-journalism /500519/

72. David Mindich, "For journalists covering Trump, a Murrow moment," *Columbia Journalism Review* (July 15, 2016); accessed March 24, 2019, at: https://www.cjr .org/analysis/trump_inspires_murrow_moment_for_journalism.php

73. For a discussion of the media-driven myths attached to the Murrow broadcast about McCarthy, see W. Joseph Campbell, *Getting It Wrong: Debunking the Greatest Myths in American Journalism*, 2nd ed. (Oakland: University of California Press, 2017), 44–66.

74. David Zurawik, "Biggest loser of the 2016 presidential election? The media," *Baltimore Sun* (November 4, 2016); accessed March 27, 2018, at: https://www.baltimoresun .com/opinion/columnists/zurawik/bs-ae-zontv-election-press-fail-20161104-story.html

75. See Michael Barbaro, "Trump gives up a lie but refuses to repent," *New York Times* (September 17, 2016): A1. At issue was Trump's persistent claim, finally retracted in September 2016, that President Barack Obama had been born outside the United States. Barbaro's article, labeled a news analysis, said Trump had for years "nurtured" the bogus claim, "like a poisonous flower, watering and feeding it with an ardor that still baffles and embarrasses many around him."

76. Quoted in Zurawik, "Biggest loser of the 2016 presidential election?" *Baltimore Sun*. The *Vox* editor, Emmett Rensin, also wrote, "It's never a shame to storm the barricades set up around a fascist." He was suspended from *Vox* the next day.

77. Art Swift, "Americans' trust in mass media sinks to new low," *Gallup News* (September 14, 2016); accessed July 12, 2019, at: https://news-gallup-com.proxyau.wrlc.org/poll/195542/americans-trust-mass-media-sinks-new-low.aspx. Just 32 percent of Americans had "a great deal" or "a fair amount" of trust and confidence in the media to cover the news fairly and accurately, Gallup reported. That represented the lowest level of confidence in the news media since Gallup began asking the question in 1972.

78. See Susan Page and Karina Shedrofsky, "Poll: 51% fear Election Day violence," *USA Today* (October 27, 2016): 1A. "Few in either camp believe the news media is objective in this election," they wrote.

79. Jack Shafer and Tucker Doherty, "The media bubble is worse than you think," *Politico Magazine* (May/June 2017); accessed March 3, 2019, at: https://www.politico.com/magazine/story/2017/04/25/media-bubble-real-journalism-jobs-east-coast-215048

80. "Unthinkability bias" was invoked by Sean Trende in "Trump, Brexit, and the state of the race," *RealClearPolitics* (June 28, 2016); accessed July 1, 2019, at: https://www.realclearpolitics.com/articles/2016/06/28/trump_brexit_and_the_state_of_the_race_131036.html

81. Margaret Sullivan, interview on *PBS NewsHour* (November 9, 2016); video accessed July 10, 2019, at: https://www.youtube.com/watch?v=wW5tkhJZ_T8

82. "The Trump revolt," *New York Times* (November 9, 2016): A26.

83. Patrick Healy and Jeremy W. Peters, "Democrats, students, and foreign allies face the reality of a Trump presidency," *New York Times* (November 10, 2016): A1.

84. Philip Rucker and Robert Costa, "GOP braces for Trump loss, roiled by refusal to accept election results," *Washington Post* (October 20, 2016); accessed February 11, 2018, at: https://t.co/dRqciB4Gpu

85. Jonathan Martin and Alexander Burns, "Confidence even as Clinton's momentum slows," *New York Times* (November 1, 2016): A1.

86. Martin and Burns, "Confidence even as Clinton's momentum slows," *New York Times.*

87. Jim Rutenberg, interview on *PBS NewsHour* (November 9, 2016); video accessed July 10, 2019, at: https://www.youtube.com/watch?v=wW5tkhJZ_T8

88. "Everybody denounces pack journalism, including the men who form the pack," Crouse wrote. "Any self-respecting journalist would sooner endorse incest than come out in favor of pack journalism. It is the classic villain of every campaign year. Many reporters and journalism professors blame it for everything that is shallow, obvious, meretricious, misleading, or dull in American campaign coverage." Timothy Crouse, *The Boys on the Bus* (New York: Random House, 1973), 8. More recently, the media critic for the *Washington Post*, Margaret Sullivan, picked up that theme, writing that "virtually every newsroom has at least some political reporters. And they often run in packs, producing scoop-oriented coverage that's not much different from their peers at other networks or newspapers." See Sullivan, "The election story being overlooked: Voting itself," *Washington Post* (March 9, 2020): C1.

89. Nate Silver, "There really was a media bubble," *FiveThirtyEight* (March 10, 2017); accessed September 27, 2017, at: https://fivethirtyeight.com/features/there-really-was-a-liberal-media-bubble/

90. Quoted in "Senator sees danger in control of news," *Minneapolis Star* (February 22, 1963): 3.

91. Michael Kelly, "The know-nothing media," *Washington Post* (November 10, 1999): A39.

92. Deborah Howell, "Remedying the bias perception," *Washington Post* (November 16, 2008): B6.

93. Kyle Pope, "Do this, not that: 8 tips for covering the 2020 presidential race," *Columbia Journalism Review* (January 8, 2019); accessed August 20, 2019 at: https://www.cjr.org/analysis/media-2020-election.php. Pope offered this advice: "Reporters and their news organizations were massively wrong in assuming the results of 2016, and the people they respected, and quoted, helped them get there. Do away with this kind of reporting entirely, and follow the rules of basic journalism: write what you *know*."

94. Silver, "The media has a probability problem," *FiveThirtyEight*.

95. See Larissa MacFarquhar, "Trumptown," *New Yorker* (October 10, 2016); retrieved from ProQuest database.

96. Will Rahn, "Commentary: The unbearable smugness of the press," CBSNews.com (November 10, 2016); accessed March 27, 2018, at: https://www.cbsnews.com/news/commentary-the-unbearable-smugness-of-the-press-presidential-election-2016/

97. Quoted in Joe Pompeo and others, "What went wrong? Eleven takes from media veterans," *Politico* (November 10, 2016); accessed March 27, 2018, at: https://www.politico.com/blogs/on-media/2016/11/what-the-media-missed-editors-executives-and-journalists-weigh-in-231167

98. Quoted in Pompeo and others, "What went wrong?" *Politico*.

99. See Amy Chozick, "Republicans pounce as Clinton denigrates many of Trump's backers," *New York Times* (September 11, 2016): A18. Clinton said to laughter and applause at a fundraising event in Manhattan: "You know, to just be grossly generalistic, you could put half of Trump's supporters into what I call the basket of deplorables. Right? The racist, sexist, homophobic, xenophobic, Islamaphobic—you name it. And unfortunately there are people like that. And he has lifted them up."

100. Shafer and Doherty, "The media bubble is worse than you think," *Politico Magazine*.

101. Pope, "Here's to the return of the journalist as malcontent," *Columbia Journalism Review*. He further wrote: "Now a new era needs to begin, a period in which reporting takes precedent over opinion, when journalists are willing to seek out and understand people with whom they may have profound personal and philosophical differences. For decades, centuries even, that has been the definition of journalism."

102. Nate Silver, "Why you shouldn't always trust the inside scoop," *FiveThirtyEight* (February 27, 2017); accessed November 11, 2019, at: https://fivethirtyeight.com/features/why-you-shouldnt-always-trust-the-inside-scoop/

103. "In the end," wrote Aaron Maté of *The Nation*, the report of special counsel Robert Mueller showed "the Trump-Russian collusion narrative embraced and evangelized by the U.S. political and media establishments to be a piece of fiction." See Maté, "The Mueller Report indicts that Trump-Russia conspiracy theory," *The Nation* (April 26, 2019); accessed April 28, 2019, at: https://www.thenation.com/article/russiagate-trump-mueller-report-no-collusion/

104. Jack Shafer, "Previously thought to be true," Slate.com (June 4, 2004); accessed April 26, 2014, at: https://slate.com/id/2101754/. Shafer wrote that newspapers' "credibility would soar if they established a conspicuous place where they could routinely steer seriously defective coverage into editorial dry dock for refitting."

105. Matt Taibbi, "Taibbi: On Russiagate and our refusal to face why Trump won," *Rolling Stone* (March 29, 2019); accessed March 31, 2019, at: https://www.rollingstone.com/politics/politics-features/taibbi-trump-russia-mueller-investigation-815060/

106. See Peter J. Boyer, "The paper of 'gotcha!'" *Esquire* (April 2019); retrieved from ProQuest database.

107. Quoted in Stanley Ember, "The Times names longtime journalist public editor," *New York Times* (May 19, 2016): B5.

108. Spayd, "Want to know what America's thinking?" *New York Times*.

109. Spayd, "Want to know what America's thinking?" *New York Times*.

110. Liz Spayd, "One thing voters agree on: Better campaign coverage was needed," *New York Times* (November 20, 2016): SR9. Spayd also wrote: "I found myself wishing someone from the newsroom was on the line with me, especially to hear how many of the more liberal voters wanted more balanced coverage. Not an echo chamber of liberal intellectualism, but an honest reflection of reality."

111. Spayd, "One thing voters agree on," *New York Times*.

112. Liz Spayd, "Bret Stephens takes on climate change. Readers unleash their fury," *New York Times* (May 3, 2017); accessed July 12, 2019, at: https://www.nytimes.com/2017/05/03/public-editor/bret-stephens-climate-change-liz-spayd-public-editor.html

113. "We built our newsroom to cover one story," Dean Baquet, the *New York Times*'s executive editor, told his staff in 2019, a reference to suspected election-collusion between Trump and the Kremlin. Quoted in Ashley Feinberg, "The New York Times unites vs. Twitter," Slate.com (August 15, 2019); accessed August 16, 2019, at: https://slate.com/news-and-politics/2019/08/new-york-times-meeting-transcript.html. Jill Abramson, a former executive editor of the *Times*, said the news pages "were unmistakably anti-Trump." See Abramson, *Merchants of Truth: The Business of News and the Fight for Facts* (New York: Simon & Schuster, 2019), 390.

114. "There was surprise and some outrage" at the *Times* when the public editor's position was eliminated, Jill Abramson wrote in her book. See Abramson, *Merchants of Truth*, 385.

115. Liz Spayd, "The public editor signs off," *New York Times* (June 2, 2017); accessed March 25, 2018, at: https://www.nytimes.com/2017/06/02/public-editor/liz-spayd-

final-public-editor-column.html. Spayd wrote in closing, "Time to rip off the Kevlar and turn out the lights."

116. Spayd, "The public editor signs off," *New York Times*. Spayd faded from public view. She became a consultant to Facebook, advising the social media giant on becoming more transparent about its privacy policies.

CONCLUSION

1. Quoted in Gideon Seymour and others, "Should public opinion polls make election forecasts? A symposium," *Journalism Quarterly* 26, 2 (June 1949): 141.

2. Courtney Kennedy, remarks at panel, "AAPOR election panel review" (May 19, 2017); annual conference of the American Association for Public Opinion Research, New Orleans.

3. Courtney Kennedy and others, "An evaluation of 2016 election polls in the United States," American Association for Public Opinion Research (May 4, 2017); accessed May 5, 2017, at: https://www.aapor.org/Education-Resources/Reports/An-Evaluation-of-2016-Election-Polls-in-the-U-S.aspx. The report noted, "It is a persistent frustration within polling and the larger survey research community that the profession is judged based on how these often under-budgeted state polls perform relative to the election outcome."

4. See Jim Clifton, "Gallup poll: New editor, new direction," Gallup Organization news release (December 21, 2018); retrieved from LexisNexis database. Clifton's statement said Gallup "will reduce much of our coverage of the electorate, as it is well covered now by a plethora of polling organizations." See also Steven Shepard, "Gallup retreats from political polling again under new leadership," *Politico* (December 21, 2018); accessed March 17, 2020, at: https://www.politico.com/story/2018/12/21/gallup-political-polling-leadership-1072151

5. John Myers, "Field Poll shuts down," *Los Angeles Times* (December 12, 2016): B3. The poll was originally called the California Poll but renamed to recognize its founder, Mervin Field, who died in 2015. He was ninety-four years old.

6. See Steven Shepard, "Behind America's exit poll schism," *Politico* (May 18, 2019); accessed May 19, 2019, at: https://www.politico.com/story/2019/05/18/election-exit-polls-2020–1331755

7. Nate Cohn, "Live from the battleground districts: Polls of the key races for House control," *New York Times* (September 6, 2018); accessed June 6, 2019, at: https://www.nytimes.com/2018/09/06/upshot/midterms-2018-polls-live.html. Cohn wrote that "we think you'll come away impressed by how often the polls still seem to end up near the truth."

8. Nate Silver, "The state of the polls, 2019," *FiveThirtyEight* (November 5, 2019); accessed November 8, 2019, at: https://fivethirtyeight.com/features/the-state-of-the-polls-2019/

9. Stephanie Slade, "Why polls don't work," *Reason* (February 2016); accessed 18 August 2017, at: https://reason.com/archives/2016/01/14/why-polls-dont-work/print

10. This point was made by Andrew Smith of the University of New Hampshire at the AAPOR conference in 2017. Smith, remarks at panel, "2016 pre-election polling: Methods and accuracy in context" (May 20, 2017); annual conference of the American Association for Public Opinion Research, New Orleans. See also Cliff Zukin, "What's the matter with polling?" *New York Times* (June 20, 2015); accessed October 9, 2017, at: https://www.nytimes.com/2015/06/21/opinion/sunday/whats-the-matter-with-polling.html. Zukin wrote: "We'll have to go through a period of experimentation to see what works, and how to better hit a moving target."

11. See Silver, "The state of the polls, 2019," *FiveThirtyEight*.

12. For a critique along these lines, see David W. Moore, *The Opinion Makers: An Insider Exposes the Truth behind the Polls* (Boston: Beacon Press, 2008).

13. Rensis Likert, "Public opinion polls," *Scientific American* 179, 6 (December 1948): 11. Likert wrote, "The polls must use methods which will assure that their results are reasonably accurate on all issues and at all times."

14. Sarah E. Igo, *The Averaged American: Surveys, Citizens, and the Making of a Mass Public* (Cambridge, MA: Harvard University Press, 2009), 186, 187.

15. Stuart Chase, "Are the polls finished?" *The Nation* (December 4, 1948): 629.

16. A history of AAPOR makes no mention of Stuart Chase's suggestion but notes he attended the organization's meeting in 1947 and criticized pre-election polls as "exciting and entertaining dope" but "completely meaningless." See Kathleen A. Frankovic, "AAPOR and the polls," in Paul B. Sheatsley and Warren J. Mitofsky, eds., *A Meeting Place: The History of the American Association for Public Opinion Research* (Ann Arbor, MI: AAPOR, 1992), 120.

17. Nate Silver, "The media has a probability problem," *FiveThirtyEight* (September 21, 2017); accessed September 27, 2017, at: https://fivethirtyeight.com/features/the-media-has-a-probability-problem/

18. See MSNBC *Hardball with Chris Matthews* (January 9, 2008); program transcript retrieved June 6, 2019, at: http://www.nbcnews.com/id/22598268/ns/msnbc-hardball_with_chris_matthews/t/hardball-chris-matthews-jan-pm-et/. "And I think they're getting better all the time," Matthews added.

19. Timothy P. Johnson, "Legitimacy, wicked problems, and public opinion research," 2018 presidential address, American Association for Public Opinion Research (May 17, 2018); transcript accessed May 21, 2018, at: https://www.aapor.org/About-Us/History/Presidential-Addresses/2018-Presidential-Address.aspx

20. Johnson, "Legitimacy, wicked problems, and public opinion research."

21. See "AAPOR to examine 2016 Presidential election polling," American Association for Public Opinion Research news release (November 9, 2016); accessed May 25, 2018, at: https://www.aapor.org/Publications-Media/Press-Releases/AAPOR-to-Examine-2016-Presidential-Election-Pollin.aspx

22. Zukin, "What's the matter with polling?" *New York Times*.

23. Will Jennings and Christopher Wlezien, "Election polling errors across time and space," *Nature Human Behavior* 2, 4 (April 2018): 276, 282.

24. Jennings and Wlezien, "Election polling errors across time and space," 282. In presenting the research at AAPOR's annual conference in 2018, Wlezien noted, "This is not the final word" on the subject. See Wlezien, "The hits and misses: Election poll accuracy in the U.S. and around the world," AAPOR panel presentation (May 18, 2018); AAPOR annual conference, Denver.

25. Quoted in Melina Delkic, "How we cover elections: Live polling," *New York Times* (November 2, 2018); accessed June 6, 2019, at: https://www.nytimes .com/2018/11/02/reader-center/how-we-cover-elections-live-polling.html?searchResult Position=1

SELECT BIBLIOGRAPHY

COLLECTIONS CONSULTED

Bell, Edward Price, papers, Newberry Library, Chicago.

Crossley, Archibald M., papers, Thomas J. Dodd Research Center, University of Connecticut, Storrs.

Eisenhower, Dwight D., papers, Eisenhower Presidential Library and Museum, Abilene, Kansas.

Gallup Organization Papers, University of Iowa special collections, Iowa City.

Hamilton, John D. M. papers, Manuscript Division, Library of Congress, Washington, DC.

Harris, Louis, papers, Wilson Library, University of North Carolina, Chapel Hill.

Landon, Alfred, papers, Kansas State Historical Society, Topeka.

Lawrence, David, papers, Seeley G. Mudd Manuscript Library, Princeton University, Princeton, NJ.

Mitofsky, Warren J., papers, Dodd Research Center, University of Connecticut.

National Committee of the Democratic Party, papers, Franklin D. Roosevelt Presidential Library and Museum, Hyde Park, NY.

Roosevelt, Franklin D., papers, Roosevelt Presidential Library and Museum, Hyde Park, NY.

Roper, Elmo, papers, Dodd Research Center, University of Connecticut.

Stevenson, Adlai E., papers, Seely G. Mudd Manuscript Library, Princeton University, Princeton, NJ.

Truman, Harry S., papers, Truman Presidential Library and Museum, Independence, MO.

BOOKS AND ARTICLES

Abramson, Jill. *Merchants of Truth: The Business of News and the Fight for Facts.* New York: Simon & Schuster, 2019.

Adams, William C. *Election Night News and Voter Turnout: Solving the Projection Puzzle.* London: Lynne Rienner, 2005.

———, ed. *Television Coverage of the 1980 Presidential Campaign.* Norwood, NJ: Ablex Publishing, 1983.

Allen, Jonathan, and Amie Parnes. *Shattered: Inside Hillary Clinton's Doomed Campaign.* New York: Crown, 2017.

Asher, Herbert. *Polling and the Public: What Every Citizen Should Know,* 8th ed. Washington, DC: CQ Press, 2012.

Barber, James David. *The Pulse of Politics: Electing Presidents in the Media Age.* New York: W. W. Norton & Company, 1980.

Bean, Louis H. *How to Predict Elections.* New York: Knopf, 1948.

Berinsky, Adam J. *New Directions in Public Opinion.* New York: Routledge, 2016.

Berinsky, Adam J., and others. "Revisiting public opinion in the 1930s and 1940s," *PS: Political Science and Politics* 44, 3 (July 2011): 515–520.

Brick, J. Michael. "The future of survey sampling," *Public Opinion Quarterly* 75, 5 (2011): 872–888.

Brick, J. Michael, and Clyde Tucker. "Mitofsky-Waksberg: Learning from the past," *Public Opinion Quarterly* 71, 5 (January 2007): 703–716.

Broh, C. Anthony. "Horse-race journalism: Reporting the polls in the 1976 presidential election," *Public Opinion Quarterly* 44, 4 (Winter 1980): 514–529.

Bryson, Maurice C. "The *Literary Digest* poll: Making of a statistical myth," *American Statistician* 30, 4 (November 1976): 184–185.

Bush, George W. *Decision Points.* New York: Crown Publishers, 2010.

Campbell, W. Joseph. *Getting It Wrong: Debunking the Greatest Myths in American Journalism.* Oakland: University of California Press, 2017.

Carter, Jimmy. *Keeping Faith: Memoirs of a President.* Toronto: Bantam, 1982.

Carter, John R. "Early projections and voter turnout in the 1980 presidential election," *Public Choice* 43, 2 (1984): 195–202.

Chozick, Amy. *Chasing Hillary: Ten Years, Two Presidential Campaigns, and One Intact Glass Ceiling.* New York: HarperCollins, 2018.

Committee on Analysis of Pre-Election Polls and Forecasts of the Social Science Research Council. "Report on the Analysis of Pre-Elections and Forecasts." *Public Opinion Quarterly* 12, 4 (Winter 1948–49): 599–622.

Converse, Jean M. *Survey Research in the United States: Roots and Emergence, 1890–1960.* Berkeley: University of California Press, 1987.

Crespi, Irving. *Pre-Election Polling: Sources of Accuracy and Error.* New York: Russell Sage Foundation, 1988.

Crossen, Cynthia. *Tainted Truth: The Manipulation of Fact in America.* New York: Simon & Schuster, 1994.

Crossley, Archibald M. "Straw polls in 1936," *Public Opinion Quarterly* 1, 1 (January 1937): 24–35.

Crotty, William, ed. *America's Choice 2000*. New York: Westview Press, 2001.

Daves, Robert P., and Frank Newport. "Pollsters under attack: 2004 election incivility and its consequences," *Public Opinion Quarterly* 69, 5 (2005): 670–681.

Donaldson, Gary A. *Truman Defeats Dewey*. Lexington: University of Kentucky Press, 1998.

Erikson, Robert S. "The 2000 presidential election in historical perspective," *Political Science Quarterly* 116, 1 (Spring 2001): 29–52.

Erikson, Robert S., Costas Panagopoulos, and Christopher Wlezien. "Likely (and unlikely) voters and the assessment of campaign dynamics," *Public Opinion Quarterly* 68, 4 (Winter 2004): 588–601.

Erikson, Robert S., and Christopher Wlezien. *The Timeline of Presidential Elections: How Campaigns Do (and Do Not) Matter*. Chicago: University of Chicago Press, 2012.

Ernst, Morris L., and David Loth. *The People Know Best: The Ballots vs. the Polls*. Washington, DC: Public Affairs Press, 1949.

Farley, James A. *Behind the Ballots: The Personal History of a Politician*. New York: Harcourt, Brace, 1938.

Frankovic, Kathleen A. "Reporting 'the polls' in 2004," *Public Opinion Quarterly* 69, 5 (2005): 682–697.

Freeman, Steven F., and Joel Bleifuss. *Was the 2004 Presidential Election Stolen? Exit Polls, Election Fraud, and the Official Count*. New York: Seven Stories Press, 2006.

Fried, Amy. *Pathways to Polling: Crisis, Cooperation and the Making of Public Opinion Professions*. New York: Routledge, 2012.

Gallup, George. "A reply to 'The Pollsters,'" *Public Opinion Quarterly* 13, 1 (Spring 1949): 179–180.

———. "The changing climate for public opinion research," *Public Opinion Quarterly* 21, 1 (Spring 1957): 23–27.

———. *The Sophisticated Poll Watcher's Guide*. Princeton, NJ: Princeton Opinion Press, 1976.

Gallup, George, and Saul Forbes Rae. *The Pulse of Democracy: The Public-Opinion Poll and How It Works*. New York: Simon & Schuster, 1940.

Gelman, Andrew, and Julia Azari. "19 things we learned from the 2016 election," *Statistics and Public Policy* 4, 1 (2017): 1–10.

Gollin, Albert E. "Exploring the liaison between polling and the press," *Public Opinion Quarterly* 44, 4 (Winter 1980): 445–461.

Goulden, Joseph C., ed. *Mencken's Last Campaign: H. L. Mencken on the 1948 Election*. Washington, DC: New Republic Book Company, 1976.

Greene, John Robert. *I Like Ike: The Presidential Election of 1952*. Lawrence: University Press of Kansas, 2017.

Greenfield, Jeff. *"Oh, Waiter! One Order of Crow!" Inside the Strangest Presidential Election Finish in American History*. New York: G. P. Putnam's Sons, 2001.

Gullan, Harold I. *The Upset That Wasn't: Harry S. Truman and the Crucial Election of 1948*. Chicago: Ivan R. Dee, 1998.

Hillygus, D. Sunshine. "The evolution of election polling in the United States," *Public Opinion Quarterly* 75, 5 (2011): 962–981.

Hitchens, Christopher. "Voting in the passive voice: What polling has done to American democracy," *Harper's Magazine* (April 1992): 45–52.

Igo, Sarah E. *The Averaged American: Surveys, Citizens, and the Making of a Mass Public*. Cambridge, MA: Harvard University Press, 2009.

Ismach, Arnold H. "Polling as a news-gathering tool," *Annals of the American Academy of Political and Social Science* 472 (March 1984): 106–118.

Jamieson, Kathleen Hall, ed. *Electing the President, 2004: The Insiders' View*. Philadelphia: University of Pennsylvania Press, 2006.

Jamieson, Kathleen Hall, and Paul Waldman, eds. *Electing the President, 2000: The Insiders' View*. Philadelphia: University of Pennsylvania Press, 2001.

Jennings, Will, and Christopher Wlezien. "Election polling errors across time and space," *Nature Human Behavior* 2, 4 (April 2018): 276–283.

Karabell, Zachary. *The Last Campaign: How Harry Truman Won the 1948 Election*. New York: Knopf, 2000.

Katz, Daniel. "The polls and the 1944 election," *Public Opinion Quarterly* 8, 4 (Winter 1944): 468–482.

———. "The public opinion polls and the 1940 election," *Public Opinion Quarterly* 5, 1 (March 1941): 52–78.

Keeter, Scott. "The impact of cell phone noncoverage bias on polling in the 2004 presidential election," *Public Opinion Quarterly* 70, 1 (Spring 2006): 88–98.

Kelley, Stanley. *Interpreting Elections*. Princeton, NJ: Princeton University Press, 1983.

Kennedy, Courtney, and others. "An evaluation of 2016 election polls in the United States," American Association for Public Opinion Research (May 4, 2017): https://www.aapor.org/Education-Resources/Reports/An-Evaluation-of-2016-Election-Polls-in-the-U-S.aspx

Kerry, John. *Every Day Is Extra*. New York: Simon & Schuster, 2018.

Kohut, Andrew. "Low marks for polls, media," *Columbia Journalism Review* (January/February 2001): 25.

———. "Polls speed down slippery slope, but they don't have to," *Columbia Journalism Review* (November/December 2000): 66–67.

Konner, Joan. "The case for caution: This system is dangerously flawed," *Public Opinion Quarterly* 67, 1 (Spring 2003): 5–18.

Lamis, Alexander P., and others. "Symposium on the work of Samuel Lubell," *PS: Politics and Science* 23, 2 (June 1990): 184–191.

Lavrakas, Paul J., and Jack K. Holley. *Polling and Presidential Election Coverage*. Newbury Park, CA: Sage, 1991.

Lavrakas, Paul J., Michael W. Traugott, and Peter V. Miller, eds. *Presidential Polls and the News Media*. Boulder, CO: Westview Press, 1995.

Lazarsfeld, Paul F. "The election is over," *Public Opinion Quarterly* 8, 3 (Autumn 1944): 317–330.

Likert, Rensis. "Public opinion polls," *Scientific American* 179, 6 (December 1948): 7–11.

Littlewood, Thomas B. *Calling Elections: The History of Horse-Race Journalism.* Notre Dame, IN: University of Notre Dame Press, 1998.

Lohr, Sharon L., and J. Michael Brick. "Roosevelt predicted to win: Revisiting the 1936 *Literary Digest* poll," *Statistics, Politics and Policy* 8, 1 (2017): 65–84.

Lusinchi, Dominic. "'President' Landon and the 1936 *Literary Digest* poll," *Social Science History* 36, 1 (Spring 2012): 23–54.

———. "Straw poll journalism and quantitative data," *Journalism Studies* 16, 3 (2015): 417–432.

Martin, Elizabeth, Michael W. Traugott, and Courtney Kennedy. "A review and proposal for a new measure of poll accuracy," *Public Opinion Quarterly* 69, 3 (Fall 2005): 342–369.

Martin, L. John. "The genealogy of public opinion polling," *Annals of the American Academy of Political and Social Science* 472 (March 1984): 12–23.

McCoy, Donald R. *Landon of Kansas.* Lincoln: University of Nebraska Press, 1966.

McCullough, David. *Truman.* New York: Simon & Schuster, 1992.

Meier, Norman C., and Harold W. Saunders, eds. *The Polls and Public Opinion.* New York: Henry Holt, 1949.

Meyer, Philip. "Commentary: Polls are predictions (so let's stop kidding ourselves)," *Newspaper Research Journal* 8, 3 (Spring 1987): 83–88.

———. *Precision Journalism: A Reporter's Introduction to Social Science Methods.* Bloomington: Indiana University Press, 1973.

———. "Presidential address: Polling as political science and polling as journalism." *Public Opinion Quarterly* 54, 3 (Fall 1990): 451–459.

———. "Stop pulling punches with polls," *Columbia Journalism Review* (November/December 1991): 64–67.

Miller, Mark Crispin. "None dare call it stolen," *Harper's Magazine* (August 2005): 39–46.

Mitofsky, Warren J. "The 1980 pre-election polls: A review of disparate methods and results," *Proceedings of the American Statistical Association Survey Research Methods Section* (1981): 47–52.

———. "Review: Was 1996 a worse year for polls than 1948?" *Public Opinion Quarterly* 62, 2 (Summer 1998): 230–249.

———. "Voter News Service after the fall." *Public Opinion Quarterly* 67, 1 (Spring 2003): 45–58.

Mitofsky, Warren J., and Murray Edelman. "Election Night estimation," *Journal of Official Statistics* 18, 2 (June 2002): 165–179.

Moore, David W. *The Opinion Makers: An Insider Exposes the Truth behind the Polls.* Boston: Beacon Press, 2008.

———. *The Superpollsters: How They Measure and Manipulate Public Opinion in America.* New York: Four Walls Eight Windows, 1992.

Morganstein, Dan, and David Marker. "A conversation with Joseph Waksberg," *Statistical Science* 15, 3 (2000): 299–312.

Mosteller, Frederick, and others. *The Pre-Election Polls of 1948*. New York: Social Science Research Council, 1949.

Noelle-Neumann, Elisabeth. "The public opinion research correspondent," *Public Opinion Quarterly* 44, 1 (January 1980): 585–597.

Norris, Pippa. "Too close to call: Opinion polls in Campaign 2000," *Harvard Journal of Press/Politics* 6, 1 (February 2001): 3–10.

Ogilvy, David. *An Autobiography*. New York: Wiley, 1997.

Ohmer, Susan. *George Gallup in Hollywood*. New York: Columbia University Press, 2006.

Owen, Diana. *Media Messages in American Presidential Elections*. Westport, CT: Greenwood, 1991.

Perry, Paul. "Election survey procedures of the Gallup Poll," *Public Opinion Quarterly* 24, 3 (Autumn 1960): 531–542.

Pietrusza, David. *1948: Truman's Improbable Victory and the Year That Transformed America's Role in the World*. New York: Union Square Press, 2011.

Plissner, Martin. *The Control Room: How Television Calls the Shots in Presidential Elections*. New York: Touchstone, 2000.

Posner, Richard. *Breaking the Deadlock: The 2000 Election, the Constitution, and the Courts*. Princeton, NJ: Princeton University Press, 2001.

Reston, James. *Deadline: A Memoir*. New York: Random House, 1991.

Robertson, Lori. "Polled enough for ya?" *American Journalism Review* (January/February 2001): 29–33.

Robinson, Claude E. *Straw Votes: A Study of Political Prediction*. New York: Columbia University Press, 1932.

Robinson, Michael J., and Margaret A. Sheehan. *Over the Wire and on TV: CBS and UPI in Campaign '80*. New York: Russell Sage Foundation, 1983.

Rogers, Lindsay. *The Pollsters: Public Opinion, Politics, and Democratic Leadership*. New York: Knopf, 1949.

Roper, Elmo. "Sampling public opinion," *Journal of American Statistical Association* 35, 210 (June 1940): 325–334.

Rosenof, Theodore. "The legend of Louis Bean: Political prophesy and the 1948 election," *Historian* 62, 1 (October 2007): 63–78.

Salvanto, Anthony. *Where Did You Get This Number? A Pollster's Guide to Making Sense of the World*. New York: Simon & Schuster, 2018.

Schram, Martin. *The Great American Video Game: Presidential Politics in the Television Age*. New York: Morrow and Company, 1987.

Seymour, Gideon, and others. "Should public opinion polls make election forecasts? A symposium," *Journalism Quarterly* 26, 2 (June 1949): 131–144.

Shelley, Mack C., II, and Hwarng-Du Hwang, "The mass media and public opinion polls in the 1988 presidential election: Trends, accuracy, consistency, and events," *American Politics Quarterly* 19, 1 (January 1991): 59–79.

Sheppard, Si. *The Buying of the Presidency? Franklin D. Roosevelt, the New Deal, and the Election of 1936*. Santa Barbara, CA: Praeger, 2014.

Shrum, Robert. *No Excuses: Concessions of a Serial Campaigner*. New York: Simon & Schuster, 2007.

Smith, Charles W., Jr. "Measurement of voter attitude," *Annals of the American Academy of Political and Social Science* 283 (September 1952): 148–155.

Smith, Richard Norton. *Thomas E. Dewey and His Times*. New York: Simon & Schuster, 1982.

Smith, Tom W. "The first straw? A study of the origins of election polls," *Public Opinion Quarterly* 54, 1 (Spring 1990): 21–36.

Squire, Peverill, "Why the 1936 *Literary Digest* poll failed," *Public Opinion Quarterly* 52, 1 (Spring 1988): 125–133.

Stuckey, Mary E. *Voting Deliberatively: FDR and the 1936 Presidential Campaign*. University Park: Pennsylvania State University Press, 2015.

Thomas, Evan. *Election 2004: How Bush Won and What You Can Expect in the Future*. New York: Public Affairs, 2004.

Traugott, Michael W. "Assessing poll performance in the 2000 campaign," *Public Opinion Quarterly* 65, 3 (Autumn 2001): 389–419.

———. "Can we trust the polls? It all depends," *Brookings Review* 21, 3 (Summer 2003): 8–11.

———. "The accuracy of the national preelection polls in the 2004 presidential election," *Public Opinion Quarterly* 69, 5 (2005): 642–654.

Trescott, Paul. "How polls can help newspapers," *Public Opinion Quarterly* 13, 1 (Spring 1949): 17–22.

Von Hoffman, Nicholas. "Public opinion polls: Newspapers making their own news?" *Public Opinion Quarterly* 44, 4 (Winter 1980): 572–573.

Wardle, Claire, and others. "The Voter News Service and the 2000 Election Night calls," *American Behavioral Science* 44, 12 (August 2001): 2606–2613.

Wheeler, Michael. *Lies, Damn Lies, and Statistics: The Manipulation of Public Opinion in America*. New York: Liveright, 1976.

INDEX

NOTE: Page numbers in *italics* refer to photos.

Founded in 1893,
UNIVERSITY OF CALIFORNIA PRESS
publishes bold, progressive books and journals
on topics in the arts, humanities, social sciences,
and natural sciences—with a focus on social
justice issues—that inspire thought and action
among readers worldwide.

The UC PRESS FOUNDATION
raises funds to uphold the press's vital role
as an independent, nonprofit publisher, and
receives philanthropic support from a wide
range of individuals and institutions—and from
committed readers like you. To learn more, visit
ucpress.edu/supportus.